Literary South Carolina

Literary South Carolina

by Edwin C. Epps

foreword by Thomas L. Johnson

2004

First printing, January 2004

Front cover, title page, and back cover photographs of Caroliniana Library,
    Columbia, South Carolina by Mark Olencki. The Caroliniana, located on
    the USC campus, is the respository of much of South Carolina's literary history.
Family support—Diana, Weston, Patches, Sweety, Sammy, and Target
Printed by McNaughton & Gunn, Inc., Michigan

Library of Congress Cataloging-in-Publication Data

Epps, Edwin C., 1948-
    Literary South Carolina / by Edwin C. Epps.
    p. cm.

ISBN 1-891885-35-9 (alk. paper) — ISBN 1-891885-32-4 (soft cover: alk. paper)

1. American literature—South Carolina—History and criticism.
2. Authors, American—Homes and haunts—South Carolina. 3. Literary
landmarks—South Carolina. 4. South Carolina—Intellectual life.
5. South Carolina—In literature. 6. South Carolina—Biography. I. Title.

    PS266.S6E67 2004
    810.9'9757—dc22

                                     2003023128

Hub City Writers Project
Post Office Box 8421
Spartanburg, South Carolina 29305
(864) 577-9349 · fax (864) 577-0188 · www.hubcity.org

Table of Contents

The Hub City Writers Project gratefully acknowledges the financial support of the following sponsors who helped make this publication possible:

Bea and Dennis Bruce
The Phifer/Johnson Foundation
The South Carolina Arts Commission
The South Carolina Humanities Council
The South Carolina Library System
Catherine E. Woodard

We also thank the following people who contributed their expertise or labor toward the creation of *Literary South Carolina*:

Robin Copp, South Caroliniana Library
Beth Ely, Hub City assistant, fact checker, and proofreader
Sara June Goldstein, literary arts coordinator at the
South Carolina Arts Commission
Harlan Greene, Charleston County Library
Jim Harrison, Converse College Library
Herb Hartsook, South Caroliniana Library
Pamela Ivey Huggins, Hub City assistant
Tom Johnson, content editor and proofreader
Patti Just, SCETV's "Writers' Circle of South Carolina"
John Lane, content editorial assistant
Jill McBurney, proofreader
Mark Olencki, book designer and photographer
Gibson Smith, proofreader
Tina Smith, photo scanning and retrieval
Philip Stone, Wofford College Library
Betsy Teter, Hub City executive editor
Susan Thoms, indexer and proofreader

For Catherine and William,
the hearts of my heart

Foreword

by Thomas L. Johnson

Edwin Epps's remarkable panoramic history of literary South Carolina is a timely new reading and reminder of the state's rich written and storytelling tradition—what an earlier historian, University of South Carolina English professor George Armstrong Wauchope referred to in his landmark 1910 anthology, *The Writers of South Carolina*, as "our splendid literary heritage." Later, journalist Stanhope Sams, in his introduction to Hartsville educator John C Hungerpiller's 1931 book, *South Carolina Literature*, would claim that what the state's writers created was something vital and spirited—"a shining achievement"—and would assert that there was "no better or pleasanter way to learn the history, character and quality of a people than through its literature."

Epps's formal antecedents lie chiefly in two other early twentieth-century works. The first was written a century ago by a young and perceptive Ludwig Lewisohn under the title "The Books We Have Made" and published serially in the Sunday edition of the Charleston *News and Courier* (July 5 though September 20, 1903). It is a brief but astute account of South Carolina's literary history from the colonial period to the dawn of the twentieth century, in which Lewisohn—a German immigrant who grew up in St. Matthews and Charleston and who himself would go on to become a prolific author with an international reputation—claimed that "more people cared for pure literature here, and cared for it more sincerely, than in any other province."

The other precedent is a later work by Wauchope, his *Literary South Carolina*, published in December 1923 as Bulletin No. 133 in a semimonthly series issued by the University of South Carolina. Subtitled "A Short Account of the Progress of Literature and the

Principal Writers and Books from 1700 to 1923," this monograph places South Carolina's early literary history squarely in the English tradition and characterizes it as conservative and orthodox in style and choice of theme. In writing of the later diversity in America's linear heritage and South Carolina's place in it, Wauchope states that "literature may indeed be regarded as merely one of the crops of the country" and that "each crop varies greatly according to the section which produces it." "The literary crop especially bears a closer relation than is generally supposed to the locality in which it is found," he concludes. In his 1910 book, Wauchope had also insisted that literary appreciation must begin at home and that a manual which included reference material on various writers could "suggest starting points for special investigation, reports, and discussions."

It is none too soon—in fact, at the dawn of the twenty-first century it is needful and useful—to have a new appraisal and to take stock of both the past and the present literary scenes in the Palmetto State. And because South Carolina's literary achievement is no longer exclusively limited to or focused upon Charleston and the Lowcountry, as was once the case, it is fitting that the latest effort should be undertaken by an Upcountry schoolman in conjunction with Spartanburg's award-winning Hub City Writers Project, itself a good example of the dynamic state of literary affairs in our region of the South.

Epps's comprehensive work is intrinsically valuable for its reconsideration and evaluation of 335 years of literary trend and tradition in South Carolina, with special emphasis upon the contributions made by the state's principal authors. It will also prove invaluable as a handy reference work, particularly for its up-to-date bibliography and its thumbnail sketches of outstanding current and emerging writers.

Of primary interest here is how Epps's work functions as both beneficiary and indicator of the flurry of literary activity that has been going on in South Carolina for almost forty years. Many factors have contributed to the state's emergence as an important player in the new Southern literary renaissance that occurred during the last third of the twentieth century. One of the principal ones was the establishment of the writer-in-residence program at the University of South Carolina in the 1960s and the arrival in Columbia of poet and novelist James Dickey, whose presence and instruction had untold impact upon a generation of young writers. That influence has been further manifested through the work there of such writers as Ennis Rees, William Price Fox, Janette Turner Hospital, and Kwame Dawes—as well as through the university's intermittent program of bringing other writers of national or international prominence to campus as readers or lecturers for brief periods of time. Other universities and colleges in the state— Clemson, Furman, Winthrop, Wofford, Converse, and the College of Charleston come to mind—have also created excellent writing programs and engaged outstanding authors for their students.

Additional developments contributing to or reflecting a rising literary consciousness and productivity in the state during the last third of the twentieth century include the publication in 1971 of *A Tricentennial Anthology of South Carolina Literature 1670-1970*, in which the editors in their introduction reiterated William Gilmore Simms's philosophy that "each state, each region, must develop its own literary sources if there is ever to be a distinctive national literature"; the founding in the Upcountry of *The South Carolina Review*, which for many years has been associated with Clemson University and which has published outstanding work not only by South Carolinians but by nationally recognized writers as well; the work of the literary arts division of the South Carolina Arts Commission (especially under the leadership of directors Steve Lewis and Sara June Goldstein), with its multiple programs utilizing the talents of both in-state and out-of-state authors; and the establishment in 1986 of the South Carolina Academy of Authors, with its dual agenda of identifying and celebrating the state's outstanding writers, and of granting fellowships to emerging ones.

There also has been the proliferation of local and regional writers' workshops and conferences over the past quarter century, as well as the establishment or continuation of literary awards programs—notably those offered in poetry by the venerable Poetry Society of South Carolina, which has been publishing its winners in an annual yearbook since its founding in Charleston in 1920; and those offered in the short story through the South Carolina Fiction Project, sponsored since 1984 by the South Carolina Arts Commission in partnership with *The State* newspaper in Columbia and, since 1993, with Charleston's *Post and Courier*.

Among other important factors in the state's literary scene over the past generation has been the work of William W. (Bill) Starr, who as cultural affairs editor of *The State* focused much of his attention as literary critic upon South Carolina writers. Key bookstores around the state have also played an important role in raising local literary consciousness—none more so than The Happy Bookseller in Columbia, whose longtime owner, Rhett Jackson, not only promoted the work of writers in the state but also brought national attention to South Carolina through his active leadership in the American Booksellers Association.

Then there have been the publishers across the state, whose book lists—in addition to including many works by state and local authors—have indicated a wider engagement with the American literary scene, bringing forth from South Carolina books of national importance by and about writers of international renown. Among these have been the University of South Carolina Press and Bruccoli Clark Layman in Columbia, Sandlapper Publishing in Orangeburg, Wyrick and Company in Charleston, the Reprint Company in Spartanburg—and of course the latter city's Hub City Writers Project.

Interest in literary matters has been further generated by the appointment of the state's poets laureate, five of whom have been named sequentially to the office since the death of the legendary Archibald Rutledge in 1973: i.e., Helen von Kolnitz Hyer (1974-1983); Ennis Rees (1984-1985); Grace Beacham Freeman (1985-1986); Bennie Lee Sinclair (1986-2000); and Marjory Wentworth, appointed in 2003 by Governor Mark Sanford as South Carolina's sixth poet laureate.

The appearance of this work coincides closely with the publication in 2003 of a new literary map of South Carolina, the most extensive and inclusive such item ever produced in the state. Published under the leadership of the Palmetto Book Alliance and the sponsorship of the South Carolina State Library, the map acts both as a guide to the state's literary treasures for the general public and as an educational tool for students. Writers from every county are represented on the map, and it includes, among other informational units, the most extensive listing ever assembled of the state's African-American writers. This book and the map can be used hand in hand in studying the state's literary history.

None of these influences, factors, or elements that have been so important through the years in shaping South Carolina's literary scene and sensibility, however, can ultimately create or replace the basic phenomenon of the solitary writer sitting with pen or pencil in hand before a blank yellow legal pad, or at a typewriter, or—more likely now—a computer keyboard, setting down according to whatever lights or promptings or impulses, ideas or feelings he or she may have, the words that in some way become that worthy work or masterpiece—poem, short story, novel, drama, screenplay, essay, or feature article. Somehow, with great assistance and under many influences—or with almost none—distinctive voices have emerged and continue to emerge from all corners of the Palmetto State.

But readers must also emerge, in whatever way they too are created and encouraged. The literary craft is an empty one if there is no one to read and to appreciate what has been written.

From time to time it doesn't hurt to tell the "story of the stories" and of the tellers who have made them in our midst—and perhaps on our behalf. The time for Mr. Epps's history is now—an appropriate one, not far from the turn of centuries.

Read on. Discover. Enjoy. And take to heart the words of Ludwig Lewisohn, who remarked in that work of his a hundred years ago:

> Civilizations flourish and decay, wars are fought and forgotten, but the voice of the muse is enduring as the stars, its appeal can only cease when the great essential elements of our nature fail us, and these cannot die.

—Spartanburg
November 17, 2003

Preface

The first Southern books I can remember from my childhood were two histories of the Civil War and the government of the Confederate States of America written by Jefferson Davis and Alexander H. Stephens, the president and vice-president of the Confederacy. These *apologiae*, which sought to justify the existence of the Confederate States of America to a postwar nation still in the grips of Reconstruction—each two-volume set printed on cheap pulp paper and bound in shabby suede drying to powder beneath my touch—rested in the bottom of a five-section glass-front oak bookcase in the entrance hall of my grandparents' house at 300 Jones Avenue in Marion, South Carolina. They had originally belonged to my great-grandfather J.W.G. Smithy, whose name was proudly inscribed in faded ink on each front flyleaf.

As I first thumbed through these books in eight- or nine-year-old awe in the mid-fifties, I was struck mainly by the antique mustiness of the volumes. Not only was the leather easily smudged off the fronts, but the paper itself was so brittle that it cracked in my fingers if I wasn't careful handling the pages. The smell too testified to the ancient origin of these tomes, suggesting at once the remoter recesses of high-ceilinged libraries and the despair of a dream long since betrayed. Still, in these old books treasured by my great-grandfather as valuable documents recording the history of his own early days, I discovered the first stirrings of my own fifty-years-long love affair with Southern books.

Other shelves in the house on Jones Avenue contained an 1843 collection of John C. Calhoun's *Speeches*; an early edition of DuBose

1

Heyward's *Porgy*; a volume testifying to the valor of the Southern women who tended not only the wounds of their men in "the War of Northern Aggression" but also their land, their businesses, and their children; and a short collection of stories embodying the folklore of those South Carolinians who still in my youth were called "nigras" or "darkies" by members of my own family. I eventually grew out of this early fixation upon a time and place inaccurately and incompletely rendered, but I never outgrew my love for the literature of the South in general and of South Carolina in particular.

In school I became acquainted with Southern poetry. The lyrics of the State Song "Carolina" were a poem by Henry Timrod, and we learned it by heart in Miss Swearingen's music class. Later, while in high school, I began to read seriously historians' accounts of the Civil War, beginning with the works of Bruce Catton. I also began collecting stamps of the Confederacy and exchanged my first letters with an author, the elderly Munro d'Antignac, who lived in the small town of Griffin, Georgia, and who had written a book with the romantic (to me, at least) title *Confederate Stamps, Old Letters and History*.

My acquaintance with the world of Sandlapper letters and culture was leisurely, occasional, and haphazard during this stage of my literary education. It lapsed into nearly total neglect when I went away to college in 1967, swept aside by the more urgent concerns of Vietnam, civil rights, and the tragic assassinations of the leaders in whom so much hope was placed by so many. I forsook Timrod and William Gilmore Simms and DuBose Heyward for Norman Mailer, James Baldwin, and Eldridge Cleaver.

When I returned for graduate school at the University of South Carolina in 1971, however, I deliberately took time out of a schedule heavy in its emphasis on eighteenth- and nineteenth-century English literature to sign up for a seminar on the literature of the South taught by the legendary Milledge Siegler, a cantankerous, opinionated ex-military man of a professor whose first act upon entering our seminar room on the first day of class was to toss an ashtray across the room into the trash can.

As difficult as Siegler may have been, he was also deeply and broadly grounded in Southern literature, and in his seminar I began to learn who the real writers of the South were and what the concerns were that they wrote about. We read Faulkner, of course, but we also read Sidney Lanier's *Tiger-Lilies*, Heyward's *Porgy*, the short stories of Flannery O'Connor, and the elegant prose of Eudora Welty. We listened to Siegler's rich baritone rendition of Lanier's "Thar's More in the Man Than Thar is in the Land," and then we discussed the Southern Agrarians. We read Thomas Wolfe and Red Warren, and even the yarns of Davy Crockett, a Tennessean, and Johnson Jones Hooper's Simon Suggs, "Late of the Tallapoosa Volunteers." It was as if a key had turned the tumblers of a rusty, neglected lock and opened the way to the highways and byways of a world I should have traveled more leisurely many years before.

Another event of my early graduate education also led me into the literature of my native state, though via another portal. Professor John Kimmey, under whose caring and careful supervision all graduate teaching assistants at the University of South Carolina valiantly toiled in those days in order to establish community among a group of young scholars otherwise harried almost beyond belief by the joint demands of their own studies and their teaching obligations, required that we read and then discuss current texts about the real world of teaching. One that I chose was Pat Conroy's *The Water Is Wide*, the fictionalized account of Conroy's year of teaching on then-isolated Daufuskie Island. I was so mesmerized by Conroy's tale and his skill in telling it that I have eagerly read everything he has written since, and wrote my own doctoral dissertation on Conroy's year on Daufuskie.

Other influences led me farther down the path of Palmetto State literature. Professor Bernie Dunlap's seminar in late Victorian literature and culture included occasional irresistible detours into Dunlap's own studies at the University of the South and cogent remarks about his own favorite authors, among whom were Southerners. Later, while teaching English at Spring Valley High School in Columbia in the mid-seventies, I heard Tommy Scott Young perform his jazz poems on several occasions. A number of times I listened as James Dickey read from his work, the continuation of a tradition that began when I was a student at Emory and heard a buckskin-clad, leather-capped poet drunkenly read to a patiently indulgent audience in downtown Atlanta.

In the seventies I also became a full-time antiquarian bookseller for two years in Staunton, Virginia, and among other areas of concentration, I specialized in Southern authors. One of my most fondly remembered catalogue items was a first-printing copy of *Gone With the Wind*, and I'm still hoping to turn up one of the rare, privately-printed copies of the first edition of Conroy's *The Boo*. Later, as I settled more comfortably back into the profession of teaching in Spartanburg in the early eighties, I was able to meet many South Carolina authors through my involvement with the South Carolina Writing Improvement Network and the South Carolina Council of Teachers of English. Also, my eighth-grade students, who were studying South Carolina history in their social studies classes, researched and presented projects on the state's authors. Many of these authors graciously consented to being interviewed by my students, and together we raptly read the answers to our questions from Mark Steadman, Dori Sanders, Josephine Humphreys, and others.

The sum total of my nearly fifty years' acquaintance with South Carolina literature has been many hours of absolutely delightful late-night, squinty-eyed perusal of a surprisingly wide variety of fiction, nonfiction, poetry, journalistic reportage, confession, and historical reflection. The scope and the nature of this variety are but hinted at in the University of South Carolina Press's *Tricentennial*

Anthology of South Carolina Literature, published in conjunction with the state's tricentennial celebration in 1971, now sadly long out of print and woefully in need of updating. The field is a broad one indeed, and the current batch of Palmetto State writers is as good as any, ranging from the excellence of truly original and substantive poets like Susan Ludvigson and Ron Rash to serious novelists' novelists like Josephine Humphreys and Pat Conroy, the sublimely witty humorist William Price Fox, and—man for all literary seasons—the now deceased Jim Dickey.

What I have tried to do in the pages that follow is to suggest something of the broad base that forms the foundation on which the current edifice of literary South Carolina is constructed—the authors traditionally regarded as essential or classic or seminal—as well as to briefly paint in broad strokes a picture of the contemporary legion of writers from the Palmetto State who are important or popular or otherwise noteworthy, some of whom will undoubtedly themselves one day become regarded as classics. There is even the important question of what qualifies as *literature*. Should we include history? If not, we exclude not only David Ramsay, David Duncan Wallace, and Asa H. Gordon but also more contemporaneous figures like Lewis P. Jones, Walter Edgar, and George Rogers, each of whom has written for a general audience and each of whom has already helped to reshape the ways we view our state's history. Besides, there is before us the example of Macaulay and Churchill in English literature. And what of the relatively new genres of young adult and children's literature? Do Betsy Byars and Peggy Parish deserve spots alongside Josephine Humphreys and Bret Lott? Is so-called *popular* writing—the works, say, of Elizabeth Boatwright Coker or John Jakes—to be compared to more consciously "literary" work, say, the novels of Percival Everett or Padgett Powell?

And since I have now mentioned an African-American South Carolina writer in Percival Everett, it is also worth mentioning that there are a number of such writers who deserve much greater attention than they have yet received. Benjamin Brawley, Alice Childress, Benjamin Mays, Kelly Miller, Dori Sanders and Eleanora Tate all come readily to mind besides Everett, but their presence has often been overlooked. The widely and otherwise justly praised *Tricentennial Anthology of South Carolina Literature* in fact contained no African-American writers among the thirty-nine authors chosen for inclusion.

In spite of—in fact often *because of*—the difficulties and vicissitudes inherent in making such choices, in what follows I have deliberately set myself several conscious tasks: first, to recognize those authors who have traditionally been regarded as the benchmarks of the state's literary heritage; second, to add to that number a group of equally worthy writers who have been unjustly neglected or forgotten; and third, to suggest another group of relatively recent authors who look likely to survive and to be judged significant in the future. In making my choices, I have of course relied upon the opinions, sometimes quite vocally expressed, of many experts both older and wiser than myself. In every instance, however, the final decisions on whom to include and how to rank or value them have been mine alone. I can only plead my best intentions and sincerest hard labor in justification of my actions.

What follows is, first, a narrative overview of literary South Carolina in all of its variety from the very beginning through roughly the middle of the twentieth century; and second, a more concise presentation of contemporary and emerging writers active for the most part in the past two generations and, also for the most part, still productive today. Within this overview, I have provided extended commentary and fuller bibliographies of the major figures; in the directory of contemporary figures I have commented on the work of each author included, but that I have been unable to read all of the works of all of them should be understood as inevitable. Finally, I have also sketched a brief portrait of the in-state publishing houses and other organizations that support literary South Carolina.

What next? The citizens of South Carolina have long needed an updated, more inclusive anthology of their writers. The sheer number of writers included herein and both the breadth and depth of their work should be proof enough of this assertion. Perhaps a consortium of presses and/or a small committee of editors may tackle this job before too long. Twenty-first century readers sorely need a comprehensive and truly representative collection of the state's best writing from the past.

The opinions expressed in these pages are strictly mine, of course, as are all errors both of omission and commission. Whatever examples of elucidation and excellence there may be here have been inspired by a muse who usually sits upon other shoulders than mine.

1 CHAPTER

Prelude and Beginnings

The classic mispronouncement on the culture of the South, issued over eighty years ago but still quoted with some regularity, is H.L. Mencken's famous characterization of the region as the "Sahara of the Bozart." "Down there," he wrote, "a poet is now almost as rare as an oboe-player, a dry-point etcher or a metaphysician" (*Prejudices*, Second Series [New York: Alfred A. Knopf, 1920], 136). The region's own writers have often contributed, if unwittingly at times, to this perception among those living in other parts of the country. The work of the naif South Carolina versifier J. Gordon Coogler, for example, lives on in uncomfortable literary infamy because he penned the lines "Alas! For the South, her books have grown fewer—/She never was much given to literature." This couplet became grist for Mencken's mill, and he took great relish in quoting it.

The truth, of course, is both more complex and more readily apparent than either Mencken's or Coogler's words suggest. In the "Prologue" to Pat Conroy's *The Prince of Tides*, Conroy's narrator writes, "My wound is geography. It is also my anchorage, my port of call." These words come closer to the mark, especially for many contemporary writers from South Carolina. Proud to be of the state as natives or adoptive sons or daughters, some are also cursed by the association. Parochial as often from choice as from necessity, however, they draw strength from their native soil only to find limitation in what some consider its inadequate nurture. So some flee to relocate elsewhere; others, though, continue to embrace its

J. Gordon Coogler

rich pluff mud, sandy loam, and red clay to fashion distinctive voices out of these hybrid nutrients. In the process, those who are most successful find themselves walking a broader stage and addressing a wider audience.

Beginnings: The Colonial and Early National Periods

It was not always so of course. In broad outline, the history of the literature of the Palmetto State rather neatly parallels that of the nation as a whole. The first period encompasses the state's birth and maturation as one of the original thirteen colonies and coincides with the prominence of Charleston as one of the centers of colonial and, later, early national culture. The earliest titles from this period can be construed as "literature" only loosely. They include travel narratives such as English sea captain **William Hilton**'s *Relation of a Discovery Lately Made on the Coast of Florida* (1664), **John Lawson**'s *New Voyage to Carolina* (1709), Commission of the Indian Trade agent **Thomas Nairne**'s *A Letter from South Carolina, Giving an Account of Its Soil, Air, Products, Trade, Government, Laws, Religion, People, Military Strength, Etc. of That Province* (1710), and Philadelphia naturalist **William Bartram**'s *Travels* (1791). These were closely followed, as in the literature of other former colonies—notably Virginia—by the appearance of histories like **David Ramsay**'s *History of South-Carolina, from Its Settlement in 1670, to the year 1808 and his two-volume History of the Revolution in South Carolina* (1785); the papers of prominent political figures such as **Henry Laurens (1724-1792)**; and journals and letterbooks, most often essentially economic and agrarian in nature, such as those of eighteenth-century South Carolinians **Eliza Lucas Pinckney (1723-1793)** and **Robert D. Pringle (d. 1776)**, both published in accessible formats in the mid-twentieth century. As valuable and as entertaining as they are, however, many of the early histories and travelers' accounts of South Carolina were neither written by South Carolinians nor published in the colony—not even in most cases in America at all—so it is hard to qualify many of them as "South Carolina literature."

Henry Laurens
Courtesy, National Portrait Gallery, Smithsonian Institution

Even this early, however, there were also the beginnings of a native culture of fine arts. The *South-Carolina Gazette*, the state's first newspaper, published in Charleston, printed an "Extract of a Poem, intitled INDICO" in its number for 25 August 1757. The *Gazette* had already been in existence for twenty-five years when it published the "Extract." Founded in January 1732 by **Timothy Whitmarsh (d. 1733)**, who had worked as a printer for Benjamin Franklin in Philadelphia and who established his Charleston press in partnership with Franklin, the *Gazette* continued to exist more or less continuously until December 1775. It continued to publish poetry throughout most of its lifetime too, but, as could be expected, much of this tended to be derivative and frequently topical. Whitmarsh's press and its continuation under his successor **Lewis**

Timothy (d. 1738), also a Franklin colleague from Philadelphia, published other works as well, but for the most part these were official legal documents, sermons, and religious tracts (McMurtrie 1933).

As the Royal Colony of South Carolina and its citizens became more firmly established, settled in, and eventually moved toward open conflict with Great Britain, the culture of the new society flourished as well. As Charleston emerged as one of the jewels of the British colonial and mercantile empire, it was only natural that it became an early literary center. Its leading citizens could afford to educate their children in the best colonial universities or, more commonly, abroad, usually in England; they could afford to stock their library shelves with the best English and classical authors; and they could devote substantial amounts of their increasing leisure time to literature and the other fine arts. Bookseller Ebenezer S. Thomas in fact imported 50,000 volumes for his shop in 1803 alone, and there were three other booksellers in Charleston at the time (Wallace, p. 350). It is no surprise that, steeped as they were in such a culturally rich environment, eventually some of the citizens of Charleston became authors, at first dilettantish amateurs but increasingly part-time professionals. In the end they produced the first consummately professional Southern man of letters: William Gilmore Simms.

Of course, historians played a prominent role during this period of increasing affluence. Ramsay's *History of the Revolution in South Carolina …* was soon followed by **William Moultrie's (1730-1805)** *Memoirs of the American Revolution so far as It Relates to the States of North and South Carolina and Georgia* (1802) and **John Drayton's (1767-1822)** *A View of South-Carolina, as Respects Her Natural and Civil Concerns* (1802) and *Memoirs of the American Revolution from Its Commencement to Year 1776, Inclusive* (1821). During this time too, **Louisa Susannah Wells**, **Eliza Wilkinson (b. 1757)**, and **Charles Woodmason (1720-ca.1777)** wrote letters and kept journals that have become a part of the literary legacy of the period, but they were not available to the general public at the time.

Of a decidedly more literary cast were the works of **Joseph Brown Ladd (1764-1786)** and **Washington Allston (1779-1843)**. Ladd, a native Rhode Islander who moved to Charleston in 1784 when he was twenty years old, died as the result of a duel just two years later as he was beginning to make a name for himself as a poet. His poetry reveals a light-handed mastery of technique that is at times reminiscent of the style of Alexander Pope, but his work remains largely the promise of a gifted youth; he is unanthologized today. Washington Allston, born near Georgetown on a Waccamaw River plantation, produced a collection of poetry early on, *The Sylphs of the Seasons, with Other Poems* in 1813, and subsequently published both a novel (*Monaldi: A Tale*, 1841) and a group of important *Lectures on Art* (with *Poems*, 1850). He is better known as a painter, however, addressing religious and allegorical subjects

William Moultrie
*Courtesy, Gibbes Museum of Art,
Carolina Art Association*

John Drayton
*Courtesy, Caroliniana Library,
University of South Carolina*

Washington Allston
*Courtesy, Caroliniana Library,
University of South Carolina*

and painting significant portraits of Benjamin West and the English poet Samuel Taylor Coleridge. He also spent most of his adult life abroad (1801-1809 and again 1811-1818) or in Boston and Cambridge, Massachusetts (from 1818 until his death in 1843), rather than in South Carolina. Still, poems like "On the Late S.T. Coleridge" and "To Michael Angelo" reveal a genuine sympathetic appreciation of the genius of others and, in the case of the apostrophe to Coleridge, genuine affection as well. Even more formal utterances like "Art," with its recognition of the necessity for inspiration alongside the adherence to established rules, and "America to Great Britain," which displays a true Anglophile's relish for "the language free and bold" of Shakespeare and Milton (Hungerpiller, p. 2), contain enough true sentiment in them to appeal to the modern reader.

The Antebellum Period

I use the term "antebellum" advisedly here, since there is a tendency to see the whole period from the successful conclusion of the American Revolution and the ratification of the Constitution of the United States to the opening hostilities at Fort Sumter in Charleston Harbor as one long prelude to the Civil War. Of course in one sense it was, and one may trace the issues underlying that conflict in the political and economic writings of **Thomas Cooper (1759-1840)** (*Letters on the Slave Trade*, 1787, and *Lectures on the Elements of Political Economy*, 1826); **William Crafts (1787-1826)** (*A Selection in Prose and Poetry, from the Miscellaneous Writings of the Late William Crafts*, 1828); **Hugh Swinton Legaré (1797-1843)** (*Writings*, 2 vols., 1845-6), **James Henry Hammond (1807-1864)** ("Slavery in the Light of Ethnography" in *Cotton Is King and Pro-Slavery Arguments*, edited by E.N. Elliott, 1860); and **John C. Calhoun (1782-1850)** (*Works*, 6 vols., 1883; *Papers*, 23 vols.,1959-1997). One may also examine these political, economic, and social issues cast poetically in **William John Grayson's (1788-1863)** *The Hireling and the Slave* (1856) where the plight of the Northern factory worker is portrayed as *worse* than that of the Southern slave who at least worked for a compassionate master who, according to Grayson, attended to most of his physical needs and saw to it that he would not starve or die from exposure. Most Southerners saw Grayson's poem as reasonably argued, mostly accurate, and persuasive; Northerners, who turned *Uncle Tom's Cabin* into a nineteenth-century bestseller, mostly ignored the poem

Thomas Cooper
*Courtesy, Caroliniana Library,
University of South Carolina*

intended as a rebuttal to Mrs. Stowe. Ironically, Grayson, a well-educated gentleman farmer who had been trained to the law and had served his state and country in a variety of elective and appointive positions, including a twelve-year stint as Collector of Customs at Charleston, was not a proponent of secession. In addition to writing publicly on the need for union, he also wrote a biography of another prominent Southern unionist, Charleston attorney James L. Petigru.

It remains true, however, that there was quite a bit of nonpolitical, nonmartial writing, both poetry and prose, being produced by South Carolinians during the period before the Civil War. Historian David Duncan Wallace observes in his history of South Carolina, "The number of persons who published trivial little volumes of verse is astonishing" (p. 479) and, Dr. Wallace's comments notwithstanding, some of it holds interest for us today. **William Crafts (1787-1826)**, for example, was a lawyer by trade and served in the state legislature, but he also published a collection of poems (*Sullivan's Island, the Raciad, and Other Poems*, 1820) and edited the Charleston *Courier*. Although Crafts's poetry is too obviously neoclassical in style, pregnant with phrases like "vernal bloom," "stormy wave," and "sedgy pillow," individual poems rooted in South Carolina places such as Sullivan's Island have an intrinsic appeal.

William Elliott (1788-1863), a longer-lived contemporary of Crafts, spent most of his time on the family plantation near Beaufort and, like Crafts, served in the legislature. His best-known work, *Carolina Sports by Land and Water: Including Incidents of Devil-Fishing*, published in 1856, was popular enough to receive a second printing in its American edition and was also published in England. The well-known and often-reprinted "Hunting the Devil-Fish" is compelling reading even today and anticipates a similar encounter with a devilfish in Pat Conroy's *Beach Music*. His short essay on "Sheepshead Fishing" gives the same instructions on how to catch this fish that my father gave to me in the 1950s. Elliott also wrote *Fiesco, a Tragedy* (1850) and *The Letters of Agricola* (1852).

William Elliott's uncle, **Stephen Elliott (1771-1830)**, another gentleman farmer, likewise pursued literary interests. He helped to found the Literary and Philosophical Society of South Carolina and edited *The Southern Review*. Stephen Elliott's most important contribution, however, lay in the sciences. A self-taught naturalist, he published his two-volume *Sketch of the Botany of South Carolina and Georgia* (1821-1824) near the end of his life.

Hugh Swinton Legaré (1797-1843) bears the burden of having been called variously "the man with the most cultivated mind in the South before the Civil War" (Martin, p. 57), "one of the most cultured and learned public men in America" (Wauchope, p. 240), and "perhaps the best linguist and most widely read man in America at the time of his death on June 20, 1843" (Guy Cardwell, in Bain et al., p. 278). A man so universally admired by both his contemporaries and subsequent students of the culture of the South

William Crafts
Courtesy, Caroliniana Library,
University of South Carolina

William Elliott

should have left more to interest the modern reader than he did. Although his diplomatic and political writings are important to the historian today, and although Legaré was influential through his co-founding of *The Southern Review* with Stephen Elliott in 1828, even as an editor and promoter of the literature of his region, he must have fallen short of the mark he set for himself: The *Review*, widely praised, was under-subscribed and failed in 1832 after a valiant four-year struggle. His two-volume *Writings*, edited by his sister after his death, in addition to containing diaries and correspondence, is largely devoted to classical learning; as might be expected, his style is formal and uninviting to the modern student although his private correspondence, journals, and even his commentaries on contemporary writers—for example, his comparisons of Walter Scott and Byron—are more accessible.

Hugh Swinton Legare'

Augustus Baldwin Longstreet (1790-1870), usually claimed with more justice by Georgia than South Carolina, is one of the true originals of antebellum Southern literature. He was born in Georgia and died in Mississippi, and spent only the three years of his presidency of South Carolina College (1858-1861) as a South Carolina resident. When the young men of South Carolina College— later the University of South Carolina—enlisted in the Confederate Army, Longstreet returned to Mississippi, where he spent the war years engaged in generating support for the cause of the Confederacy. Longstreet also served as president of Emory College in Georgia, Centenary College, Louisiana, and the University of Mississippi. His literary reputation rests upon the collection of local color stories called *Georgia Scenes* (1835) that deal with "phases of life among the simpler classes of the population" (Trent, p. 121). Longstreet's stories were the first of a group of similar collections by John Pendleton Kennedy, William Gilmore Simms, Johnson Jones Hooper, John Esten Cooke, and others—culminating ultimately in the work of Joel Chandler Harris and Mark Twain—to present with genuine affection and understanding slices of the real life of ordinary, often lower-class citizens. The frequently anthologized "The Horse-Swap" is typical in its rough-and-tumble, good-humored appreciation of natural-born shrewdness and the kind of frontier justice that could lead to the swindling of the swindler. In his later years, after he became a clergyman, Longstreet was embarrassed by the coarseness of his stories and never published another collection.

Although the fact is relatively unknown today, several South Carolina women writers gained varying degrees of prominence during the antebellum period. **Penina Moise (1797-1880)** in 1833 published her poetry collection *Fancy's Sketch Book*, the first book written by a Jewish woman in America. Often disregarded in studies of Southern literature, Moise was a leader of the Beth Elohim synagogue in Charleston and hosted a prominent salon as well. She began to publish locally in 1819 and continued to write for magazines as varied as *Godey's Ladies' Book* and the *Occident and American Jewish Advocate*, as well as for a wide range of newspapers,

Penina Moise

until the year before her death. Her poetry was groundbreaking in that it explored such typically "male" topics as states' rights, nullification, equal rights for Jews, and Zionism; she also wrote hymns, some of which are still in use today, and short fiction. Remarkable too is the fact that when Moise returned to Charleston after spending the Civil War years in Sumter, because she had gone blind she was forced to teach from memory in the school she opened there. She was inducted into the South Carolina Academy of Authors in March 1999.

Mary Elizabeth Lee (1813-1849) lived a "simple and uneventful life … devoted to home duties [in which she excelled] and to study and literature" (Wauchope, p. 235) and was a distinctly minor talent as a writer, but she attained popularity as an author of tales for youth and contributor to such magazines as *The Orion*, *The Southern Rose*, and *Graham's Magazine*, as well as *The Southern Literary Messenger*. Her poetry tended to be characterized by effusive gushings in nursery rhyme-like rhythms, but occasionally she produced verse of simple lyrical or exotic beauty, as in "An Eastern Love Song."

Two other women writers exhibited greater skill and appealed to a broader reading public. **Caroline Howard Gilman (1794-1888)** was probably South Carolina's best-known woman writer during her lifetime. A native Bostonian, Gilman moved to Charleston in 1819 as the wife of the Reverend Samuel Gilman, a prominent and popular Unitarian minister, and took naturally to the twin roles of wife/hostess and mother. She had written poetry in her teens and found her true authorial calling in 1832 when she founded the *Rose Bud*, according to George Armstrong Wauchope "the first weekly newspaper for children in the United States" (p. 165), as a source

Caroline Howard Gilman

for appropriate reading material for children. The *Rose Bud*, later the *Southern Rose Bud* and then, redirected to an adult audience, the *Southern Rose*, continued publication through seven volumes into 1839 and published well-known authors such as Simms and Nathaniel Hawthorne. Gilman published some two dozen books altogether, ranging from keepsakes (*The Ladies' Annual Register for 1838*, *The Rosebud Wreath*, and *The Little Wreath*) to domestic fiction (*Recollections of a New England Housekeeper and Recollections of a Southern Matron*) and collections of stories and poems for youth and adults. She also edited the *Letters of Eliza*

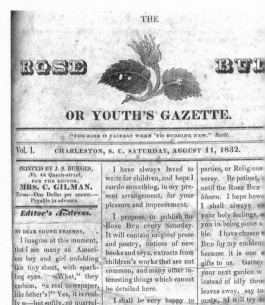

The first issue of Caroline Gilman's *Rose Bud*

Wilkinson, During the Invasion and Possession of Charleston, S.C. by the British in the Revolutionary War (1839). So industrious was she and so well received that one scholar has called her "clearly the best-known southern woman writer in the quarter century, 1833-1858" (Thompson, p. 177). Although her work now seems dated, as the work of most mid-nineteenth-century female writers probably would, it also provides ample evidence that it was not the men alone of "the Charleston school" that gave the port city its reputation as a center of culture. Gilman remained in Charleston for fifteen years following the death of her husband in 1858, and then lived another fifteen years in the North until her death in 1888. She was a 1990 inductee of the South Carolina Academy of Authors.

Susan Petigru King (1826-1875), a younger contemporary of Gilman, while not so prolific, wrote novels of manners based upon her knowledge of Charleston society. "Incisive in their often jaundiced view of the relations between the sexes in the South on the verge of the Great Divorce that came in 1861" (Johnson, 2003), they were extremely popular in their day. The younger daughter of the celebrated Charleston attorney James Louis Petigru, King married first Confederate Captain Henry C. King, also of Charleston, and later C. C. Bowen. Wauchope notes that she was conspicuous in Charleston's polite society, naming as the qualities that recommended her "gaiety," "conversational gifts," a "queenly presence," and "gracious courtesy" (p. 223). These same qualities are much in evidence in her novels, which include *Busy Moments of an Idle Woman* (1854), *Lily, a Novel* (1855), *Sylvia's World, a Novel* (1859), *Gerald Gray's Wife* (1866), and *An Actress in High Life* (1860), and in a collection of her short stories, *Crimes Which the Law Does Not Reach* (1859). Two of these novels were reissued by Duke University Press in 1993, and in 1994 King was inducted into the South Carolina Academy of Authors.

Along with these illustrious women, the name of **John C. Calhoun (1782-1850)** looms largest on the antebellum South Carolina literary horizon. Of course Calhoun was not a literary author at all, but his stature in the annals of South Carolina history and his undisputed importance as an antebellum politician and statesman, grappling almost daily with the issues that ultimately dissolved the Union in 1861, argue for his inclusion here. It is beyond both my intent and my abilities to assess Calhoun's historical legacy. Still, his words moved his contemporaries in a way that those of few of his colleagues did, and his name traditionally stands alongside those of Webster and Clay as one of the giants of the antebellum Senate. Also, a century after his death many members of another generation of white South Carolinians solemnly invoked Calhoun's philosophy as well as his fervor in defending their positions in the school desegregation battles of the state and in the broader realm of civil rights in all areas. His name continues to appear in the works of South Carolina writers of both fiction and nonfiction. Fortunately, the man left behind an ample and well-documented

John C. Calhoun
Courtesy, Gibbes Museum of Art, Carolina Art Association

record of his views on these and many other public issues.

Calhoun was educated at the legendary Willington Academy so successfully that he was able to matriculate directly into the junior class at Yale, as did many of his classmates at other colleges elsewhere in the states following the completion of their studies there. Willington, located in Abbeville District (modern McCormick County), was presided over by the renowned **Dr. Moses Waddel (1770-1840)** who, in addition to being Calhoun's older brother-in-law, was a schoolmaster trained for the Presbyterian ministry at Hampden-Sydney College. Waddel presided over up to 150 young students who lived in crude log cabins and studied five hours in the evening after a vigorous schedule of immersion in the classics during the day. Waddel's students included some of the wealthiest sons of blueblood Charleston as well as students of extremely modest means—in addition to Calhoun, Augustus Baldwin Longstreet, Preston Brooks, James L. Petigru and others among the most influential South Carolinians of their day. Charlestonian Thomas Horton has written an admirable modern study of Waddel and his Academy (*Moses Waddel: Nineteenth-Century South Carolina Educator* [USC Ed.D. Thesis, 1992]) as well as the script for a one-man theatrical presentation based on the master's pedagogical style. Waddel was also an early president of the University of Georgia.

William Gilmore Simms and the Charleston School

William Gilmore Simms

William Gilmore Simms (1806-1870) is the one name from the legion of eighteenth- and nineteenth-century South Carolina writers that the average citizen is most likely to know. Simms's only possible rival in terms of name recognition would be Henry Timrod, whose name is conceivably more familiar to some as the author of the official State Song, "Carolina." Still, although Simms was the grand old man of Southern letters at the outbreak of the Civil War, he has never received the full and impartial assessment that his body of work deserves. Lionized by South Carolinians, most of whom have never read anything he wrote, Simms was eclipsed in his own day by Northern contemporaries, especially James Fenimore Cooper, whose popular Leatherstocking Tales have much in common with Simms's Revolutionary and Border Romances. The staid *Cambridge History of English and American Literature* in fact wryly observes, in a commentary that sheds as much light upon Simms's milieu as upon the man himself and his works, that "...Simms has been, to a pathetic degree, the victim of attachment to his native state.... His best work was largely devoted to an heroic account of the Revolution in the Carolinas. But, whether his birth did not admit him to the aristocracy of Charleston, or because of a traditional disrespect for native books, South Carolina refused Simms the honour certainly due his powers." Ruined financially by the Civil War, Simms never regained his pre-war imaginative powers, and despite valiant efforts to revive it, his reputation has more or less languished ever since. Before the Civil War, however, Simms found a modest public on both sides of Mason and Dixon's line and was in fact praised by such northern reviews as *Godey's*, *Graham's*, *The Democratic Review*, and the *New York Mirror*.

Simms was born in Charleston in 1806, the son of an adventurer/vagabond father and a mother who came from one of the city's more prominent families. Largely privately educated and widely read, Simms trained to become a lawyer but early on turned his attention both to editing and to creating his own original works. His earliest work as an editor was for the *Album*, a Charleston journal, and over the years he also served as editor of the *Southern Literary Gazette*, the *City Gazette*, *The Magnolia*, *The Southern and Western Magazine*, and the *Southern Quarterly Review*.

Simms's novel *Martin Faber* (1833) brought him national fame at twenty-seven, and his output as a novelist thereafter was prolific. Altogether he wrote more than two dozen novels, the best known of which is probably *The Yemassee*, a little old-fashioned but still readable today. Not only does this historical narrative deal interestingly and, for the most part, accurately with the Yemassee War of 1732, but it also creates a sympathetic portrait of the Yemassee Indians. The masculine rhythms of "Mighty is the Yemassee" ring strong with the martial spirit of the Native American protagonist—"Mighty is the Yemassee,/Strong in the trial,/Fearless in the strife/Terrible in wrath—" and the novel as a whole displays an empathy for the Yemassee absent from other mid-nineteenth-century portrayals of Native American peoples.

William Gilmore Simms

Simms's poetry today seems hopelessly dated, mired in neoclassical diction and Latinate phrasings. Preferring both the rhythms and also the diction of everyday language, the modern reader has little patience for the artificiality and rehearsed posturing of such verse. This is unfortunate because the stories told in such Simms poems as "The Syren of Tselica" are authentically haunting, and poems like "The Edge of the Swamp" are deeply rooted in the South Carolina Lowcountry and fairly teem with alligators, butterflies, and similar native flora and fauna.

However, Simms's short narrative fiction is more rewarding to the modern reader than his poetry and novels. Sketches like the frequently anthologized "How Sharp Snaffles Got His Capital and Wife" come to life in the personalities of the real people who move through them and in the shrewd chicanery that often forms the basis of the plots, usually set in the Carolina backwoods at a time when the western border of South Carolina was part of the American frontier.

Simms also made a large mark as an editor. In addition to the many literary magazines he had a hand in, he edited *War Poetry of the South*, one of the last gasps of the lost cause in 1866.

A good deal of biographical and critical study of Simms has accumulated since his death, especially in the last twenty years or so. The William Gilmore Simms Society has been a prime mover in stimulating this activity. The society, founded in April 1993, has as its purpose "to offer scholars and other interested persons an opportunity to share in the study and appreciation of the life and works of William Gilmore Simms, one of the most significant literary figures in nineteenth-century America." Toward that end, the Simms Society maintains an exemplary website at www.westga.edu/~simms. Memberships, currently $15 for students and $50 for individuals, are available from Dr. James Kibler, Treasurer, English Department, Park Hall, University of Georgia, Athens, GA 30602.

Another intriguing source of information about the Simms family and Woodlands, the plantation home that Simms's wife brought into her marriage and that served as Simms's home for most of his working life, is the website *Shared History* at www.sharedhistory.org. This site is dedicated to preserving the histories and the relationships between Simms's immediate family and the families of the former slaves who lived at Woodlands. The project aims to "assist associated family members in learning more about their families' history and will create opportunities for family and non-family members to engage in cross-racial conversation toward better understanding the nature of race relations in this country." An overview and basic background information are already available together with photographs of surviving structures—an outbuilding, a dairy, and a remnant of the old house—and members of the families. The website serves as a cogent reminder of how inextricably twined together the lives of black and white South Carolinians have been during the last three hundred years. Simms was one of the first inductees into the South Carolina Academy of Authors, which was established in 1986.

Simms's work for the periodical press provided an outlet for the work of a sizable coterie of minor authors who were his friends in Charleston, some of whom continue to be read today, at least by Southern readers. Collectively, this group is often called...

The School of Simms

The so-called "school" of Simms, also known as the "Charleston school," can only in the loosest sense be called a "school," however. They shared a taste for such English authors as Milton, Dryden and Pope, Addison and Steele, Walter Scott and Fielding and Dickens, and to some extent Wordsworth and Tennyson. Largely members of a propertied and therefore complacent class, the school of Simms was more like something of a cultured and cultivated salon, a regular coming together, usually in the chambers of *Russell's Magazine* or of Simms's Charleston home, of a mostly young, mostly affluent, and decidedly eager and ambitious set of Charleston's brightest young gentlemen of parts. At various times, those in attendance might include Henry Timrod, Paul Hamilton Hayne, and Basil L. Gildersleeve, later renowned as a classicist at the University of Virginia and Johns Hopkins—who had all studied together at

James L. Petigru
Courtesy, Gibbes Museum of Art, Carolina Art Association

Christopher Cotes's Classical School in Charleston—together with older members of the club like Hugh Swinton Legaré and William John Grayson. Others less well-known today who were present from time to time included **John Dickson Bruns (1836-1883**, author of a biography of Henry Timrod), attorneys **Mitchell King (1783-1862)** and **James L. Petigru (1789-1863)**, physician **Samuel H. Dickson (1798-1872)**, U.S. Congressman **Samuel Lord**, and **William Porcher Miles (1822-1899)**.

Henry Timrod (1828-1867)

In some ways the life of Henry Timrod, who would come to be known as "the poet laureate of the Confederacy," mirrors that of his English predecessor John Keats. Like Keats, Timrod was born of good but primarily yeoman stock; his father was a bookbinder, albeit one who read widely and wrote poetry himself and at whose home others often gathered to discuss public affairs and literature. Like Keats, too, Timrod produced a good deal of amateurish early poetry, some of which shows promise but all of which would be forgotten today were it not for the mature accomplishment of such later poems as the Magnolia Cemetery "Ode," "Ethnogenesis," "Cotton," and a relatively small number of others. Finally, like Keats, Timrod died of tuberculosis, as well as of the ravages of the war he so soberly memorialized, as a relatively young man.

Henry Timrod

Born on December 8, 1828, Timrod showed early promise as a student of Latin in the Classical School of Christopher Cotes, where he also formed friendships with Paul Hamilton Hayne and Basil Gildersleeve. The future poet entered the University of Georgia in January 1845 but left about a year and a half later, and never received his degree. He studied law in the offices of the prominent Charleston attorney James L. Petigru, but this proved an uncongenial vocation, and Timrod spent most of his maturity combining a variety of tutoring and teaching positions with a very meager income from his writing. The university professorship he longed for, and for which he prepared by diligent reading and study on his own, never materialized.

Timrod also spent less than a year in the Confederate Army in 1862 and only one day in 1863, from both of which enlistments he was discharged because of an outbreak of the symptoms of the tuberculosis that was to take his life in 1867. The poet also found military service temperamentally unsuitable to his gentle nature, and one can only wonder at the mental torment he likely suffered from experiencing the horrors of mid-nineteenth-century warfare firsthand. Near the end of the war he worked as a newspaper editor in Columbia, but from 1865 until his death he was mostly unemployed, despondent over the loss of his infant son, and increasingly ill. Death, when it came, must have seemed a welcome release.

Timrod's work as an author can be conveniently classified into three categories: the derivative lyrics of the period before the Civil War; the Confederate odes and paeans to the South produced during the war years; and the criticism, which is substantive and important to the study of the development of American literary criticism. Timrod's early poetry is the product of schoolboy enthusiasm and adolescent romantic infatuation. This style was almost immediately put aside, however, when Timrod turned his mature reflection to what he perceived to be the great topical themes of the 1860s: the nobility of the South, the grandeur of its struggles, and the ultimate tragedy of its cause. Even the earliest of these poems, "The Cotton Boll" and "Ethnogenesis"—both written in 1861—rise above the merely sectional. When the speaker peers into the cotton boll at the beginning of the poem of the same name, he partakes of a vision reminiscent of that of Blake, who saw "infinity in a grain of sand" and "eternity in an hour." Timrod's persona intuits a "spell" in "the little boll" (Memorial Edition, p. 6) and a nearly mystical aura in the endless fields of cotton, from which "the whole landscape glows" (p. 7) under the benevolent blessings of an approving Deity. "Ethnogenesis," written during the first meeting of the Confederate Congress at Montgomery, Alabama, in February 1861, rises above the topical moment to roam symbolically as far as the Alps and the Arctic Ocean, and in the process its argument takes on an economic as well as a political cast. The great Magnolia Cemetery "Ode" itself, although it opens elegiacally remembering the "martyrs of a fallen cause" (Memorial Edition, p. 164), moves purposefully beyond the cause to sing of the "defeated valor" of the many thousands of men cut down in their prime and the "mourning beauty" that ennobles their memory (p. 165). The subject of the poem, in other words, is not the cause for which the men fought but the tragic waste of their sacrifice. Even "Carolina," a good poem cheapened somewhat by having been appropriated by the General Assembly as the officially endorsed "State Song" and accordingly trotted out on many occasions of varying merit, in the end looks not backward to the "glories of thy dead" so much as forward: "Then leave the future to thy sons, Carolina!" is the exhortation of the poem's concluding line (Memorial Edition, p. 144).

In these and his other best verses, the Civil War "had the result of giving a talented Southern poet the imaginative access to his own social and political experience as fit subject for literature," according to South Carolina-born literary critic Louis D. Rubin, Jr. (p. 206). The dirge-like majesty of "The Unknown Dead," insistent in its details—rain on the windowsill, spades of dirt on the coffin, the sound of the church bell muffled by the rain—and the realism of the images of Fort Moultrie in "Charleston" are powerful and immediate in a way the work of other Southern poets at the time is not. At his best in these poems, Timrod strikes a note that reverberates not only as recognizable in memory but also as memorably fresh and original. It was only when his mind engaged the tragic nature of the war that his verse became toughened and

Timrod's grave in Trinity Cathedral
churchyard, Columbia
Courtesy, Edwin Epps

elevated, and it is these later poems that we remember today. Rubin calls Timrod "the only other Southern poet [besides Poe!] whose best work can stand up to much objective literary scrutiny nowadays" (Rubin, 1989, p. 191).

What Timrod might have achieved had he lived longer is pure conjecture. What he has left behind is a small body of nearly great poetry and a handful of cogent critical essays. Many writers much older than he would have settled for less. Timrod was inducted into the South Carolina Academy of Authors in 1992. The induction speech on his behalf was made by James Dickey.

Paul Hamilton Hayne (1830-1886)

Paul Hamilton Hayne, Timrod's longer-lived friend, produced considerably more verse than his unfortunate schoolmate, but relatively less of it seems memorable today. Indeed, one modern anthology of Southern literature observed that critics were in general agreement that "Hayne wrote too much and revised his first drafts too infrequently" (Young *et al.*, p. 318). This is the dominant view today, although in his own lifetime Hayne was highly regarded by both his public audience and his fellow writers not only in the South but also in the Northeast.

Paul Hamilton Hayne

The descendant of a Revolutionary War hero, Hayne was born in Charleston on January 30, 1830. His father, a naval officer, died of yellow fever while Hayne was still an infant, and Hayne was subsequently reared under the protectorship of his uncle, U.S. Senator Robert Y. Hayne, the adversary of Daniel Webster in the debates over Nullification. The Senator died while the future poet was still less than ten years old, but he left enough of a mark on his nephew that several scholars have remarked on it since. Hayne did well at Christopher Cotes's Classical School, where he and Henry Timrod became fast friends, a lifelong relationship that is largely responsible for the high regard in which Timrod is held today. After graduating from the College of Charleston, Hayne briefly considered a career in law, read in the offices of James L. Petigru, and was admitted to the bar. But before long the muse of literature called, and Hayne remained her lifelong devotee even in the face of personal ruin after the Civil War.

Hayne contributed regularly to the *Southern Literary Messenger* during the years before the war, and he became editor of *Russell's Magazine* in 1855. He published three books before the outbreak of hostilities and was in regular correspondence with William Cullen Bryant, Henry Wadsworth Longfellow, and Oliver Wendell Holmes, all of whom remained his friends well after the conclusion of peace. During the war itself, Hayne, always physically frail, was limited to service as an aide to Governor Francis Pickens, but he nevertheless suffered a number of daunting personal reversals that would have defeated many men: His home and personal library in Charleston were destroyed during the Union bombardment of the city, and his family silver, having been sent to Columbia, was lost during the burning of that city. Less than forty years later, Ludwig Lewisohn would write that "when the war was over he had neither home, nor money, nor a profession." He was able to purchase a small tract of land in a Georgia pine forest near Augusta, where, inhabiting a modest house he built himself, he remained until his death in 1886.

Paul Hamilton Hayne

Although Hayne was never affluent after the war, he does seem to have achieved some small level of comfort while sustaining a remarkable literary career under extremely trying circumstances. He published four books after Gettysburg and in 1873 edited the work of his friend Timrod. He also continued to contribute in a variety of genres, including some still-readable short fiction, to literary magazines such as *Appleton's Journal*, *Lippincott's Magazine*, *Scribner's Monthly*, and *Harper's New Monthly*, and his work was praised in *The Atlantic* and elsewhere. He maintained his correspondence with his friends in the Northeast and even abroad— the latter group notably including Tennyson, Swinburne, Wilkie Collins, and the blind Pre-Raphaelite poet Philip Bourke Marston— and he found gratification in being named an honorary member of the literary societies at Princeton, Sewanee, Davidson, and The Citadel. In 1882 he received an honorary degree from Washington and Lee University in Virginia.

During his lifetime Hayne was regarded as a substantial member, even a leader, in the highest rank of post-Civil War American literary circles. He was called "the poet laureate of the South" (Moore, p. 145), and readers north of the Mason-Dixon line read him with pleasure as well. A few of Hayne's nature poems continue to strike responsive chords in the hearts of modern readers: those that benefit from his long residence at Copse Hill and the everyday proximity of the pine trees and the animals and birds that lived among them. At their best they bring a knowing smile of recognition. The opening of "Aspects of the Pines" arrays its forest "Tall, somber, grim, against the morning sky" (*Tricentennial Anthology*, p. 336), a sight familiar to any Southerner, and the slow-moving cadence of the verse underscores the majesty of "each tinted copse and shimmering dell." "The Mocking-Bird [At night]" opens with the truly inspired line "A golden pallor of voluptuous light" in which the sunlight is a palpable presence (*Tricentennial Anthology*, p. 337). And the first stanza of "Under the Pine," Hayne's elegy to his friend Timrod, is as sure in its handling of the rhythm of mourning as anything written by the more widely admired Georgian Sidney Lanier, who had the advantage of being a trained musician.

Hayne's contribution in the end was to sing enthusiastically but in what has come to be regarded as a minor key. As Warren Westcott puts it, "... it is most useful to read him as representative of the tastes and literary prejudices of the nineteenth century South—particularly the antebellum South since, despite his longevity, he never really felt himself to be in tune with New South industrialization" (*A Literary Map of South Carolina*, p. 23).

Mary Boykin Miller Chesnut (1823-1886) is remembered today as the chronicler of life in and about the homes, ballrooms, and offices of Confederate officialdom from the days leading up to South Carolina's secession from the Union to the crumbling of the rebel government in 1865. Born at Mount Pleasant, she was educated at private schools in Camden, Plane Hill, and later at Madame Talvande's French School for Young Ladies in Charleston. An apt and curious student, Mary Miller excelled at languages and loved literature, a lifelong passion evident in the pages of her "diary." At Madame Talvande's one of her friends was Mary Seren Chesnut Williams, whose uncle James Chesnut, Jr., soon became infatuated with the young girl from the Midlands. His courtship continued over an extended period of time, becoming more serious after Mary's return from Mississippi, where she had traveled with her mother in 1838 to settle her father's estate and where on an earlier trip she had attracted suitors not wholly to her parents' liking. James Chesnut's own affairs became complicated when his older brother John's health deteriorated. He accompanied John to specialists in France and then in the northeastern United States, but no one could provide a remedy, and the elder brother died in 1839. James suddenly became heir to one of the largest fortunes in South Carolina, and after his life began to return to normal, he and Mary Miller married on April 23, 1840.

Mary Boykin Chesnut
Courtesy, Caroliniana Library, University of South Carolina

James Chesnut prospered as a planter and as a lawyer, and he was soon recruited to represent his Camden neighbors in the General Assembly in both the House and the Senate. He was then elected to the United States Senate in 1858, where he served until his resignation after Abraham Lincoln's election and his state's preparations to secede from the Union. Chesnut served the Confederacy in a variety of official capacities during the war, and his service and the couple's life in the capital of Richmond and elsewhere provided his wife the raw material for her famous journal. C. Vann Woodward has summarized the writing and publication of the journal in his definitive edition of it, *Mary Chesnut's Civil War* (New Haven and London: Yale University Press, 1981).

Almost from the beginning, it seems, Mary Chesnut intended to publish a final, polished version of her work, and she labored at it off and on for years during the hardships she endured after the close of the war. Her magnum opus, called by her first two editors *A Diary from Dixie*, exists in two lengthy drafts from the 1860s and the 1880s as well as other variants and combines a journalist's keen observations with elements of autobiography and history. The later variants bear much evidence of careful reworking, and although Chesnut never finished her own work on it, she clearly conceived it as a conscious work of literary art. It is noteworthy not only for her firsthand accounts of important historical events and the personal tragedies that accompanied them but also for her unconventional views on slavery and women's roles in nineteenth-century Southern society. The completed version reconstructed and offered up by

Woodward runs to over eight hundred highly engaging pages. Few modern readers have been disappointed in their perusal of its narrative or its insights, and it has been consulted and mined by every leading scholar of Southern history since its publication.

Early African-American Writing from South Carolina

As might be expected, the roll of African-American writers who can also be called South Carolinians before Emancipation is a short one. The reasons are easily explained. For one thing, it was illegal in antebellum South Carolina to teach a slave to read and write, and while there are recorded instances of slave owners teaching favorite slaves these skills in defiance of the proscription, there are relatively few of these. Then, too, there would have been little, if any, market for works by African-American writers in the South and even fewer printers willing to take the substantial economic and—presumably—social and political risks of publishing their work. Finally, as war loomed and more and more free blacks who might have become authors or had been readers fled the state, especially the cultural center of Charleston, the number of individuals who might have either written or read such works dwindled to virtually nothing. There was, of course, a vital oral folk tradition in "the quarter" on most plantations and in other places where antebellum blacks could gather, and many folk tales, legends, and songs survive. These were generally collected later, however, and the names of their original authors are lost in the mists of time. So while the oral tradition flourished, the *literary* tradition was virtually nonexistent.

Daniel Alexander Payne

Still, there were a few antebellum African-American authors from the state. None of these writers, however, made an important or lasting contribution to Palmetto State literature other than in the sense that their lonely presence itself constitutes a telling commentary upon the state's history. One, **Daniel Alexander Payne (1811-1893)**, the son of free parents in Charleston, left the state while in his twenties after the General Assembly outlawed the education of slaves (he had been a teacher) and never returned. He subsequently became a bishop in the African Methodist Episcopal Church, worked and traveled throughout the North, and finally settled into the presidency of Wilberforce University in Ohio. His one volume of verse, *The Pleasures and Other Miscellaneous Poems* (1850), while pietistic and unremarkable, nevertheless witnesses to something of an early beginning to a black literary tradition in South Carolina.

A later poet, **Mary Weston Fordham (1845-1905)**, lived "in South and North Carolina" (Sherman, p. 441) and produced a lone collection, *Magnolia Leaves*, published in Charleston, ironically by Walker, Evans, & Cogswell, the former printers to the Confederacy, in 1897. Details of her life, including the dates of her birth and death, are uncertain. Her poetry, like Payne's, is undistinguished, but she did write an "Ode" on the Cotton States and International

Exposition held in Atlanta in 1895 that builds upon an address to the Exposition by Booker T. Washington, and Washington wrote an introduction to her book of poems.

Another book by an African-American, *My Life in the South* by **Jacob Stroyer (1849-1908)** of Richland County, was published two years before Fordham's poetry. It has the distinction of being the only known published autobiography by an ex-slave from South Carolina and is therefore of extraordinary value. Also, **Clarissa Minnie (Allen) Thompson (1859-1941)**, a native of Columbia, has the distinction of being the first known African-American from South Carolina to publish a novel, a serial story of forty chapters titled *Treading the Winepress* that appeared in *The Boston Advocate*, 1885-1886. She also wrote a novelette, *Only a Flirtation*, that appeared in *The Dallas Enterprise*. Finally, Charleston minister **George Clinton Rowe (1853-1903)** published two volumes of poetry before the turn of the twentieth century, *Thoughts in Verse: A Volume of Poems* (1887) and *Our Heroes: Patriotic Poems on Men, Women and Sayings of the Negro Race* (1890), both amazing for their candor and their revelation of the sensibility of an advantaged black man living in the South Carolina Lowcountry at the end of the nineteenth century.

Jacob Stroyer

The Postwar Malaise

Immediately following the Civil War, South Carolina literature suffered a precipitous decline that lasted well into the twentieth century. There were notably fewer writers, for one thing, since even those who were inclined to write were struggling against the demands of a harsh postwar economy in which much had been lost, and much more was at risk of being confiscated for delinquent taxes. All existence was constricted by the unaccustomed absence of slave labor and the difficult task of replacing that economic army with a new patchwork system dependent upon the family of the landowners, sharecroppers, day laborers, and—later, as northern industrialists began to bring the textile industry to the Piedmont and Midlands in the 1880s—mill workers displaced from even harder lives in the hardscrabble hills and mountains.

In such an economic environment few had sufficient leisure time to write. Just how bad was it? The 1860 Census recorded the total population of South Carolinians as 703,708; ten years later, in 1870, the population had grown only to 705,606. The human cost was horrific. The editors of *The Literature of the South* paint the picture with a broad brush: "Millions of people in the states which had comprised the Confederacy were without the necessities of life. Returning soldiers found their homes destroyed and their lands devastated. There was no money, little credit, and a serious shortage of manpower" (Young et al., p. 427). Historian Walter Edgar brings the statistics home to the Palmetto State when he observes that "between 31 percent and 35 percent of South Carolina's 1860 young adult white population died in the war" (p. 375), and that "[b]y 1867 land values had declined 60 percent" (p. 374). Small wonder, then, that as late as 1903 Ludwig Lewisohn was writing, "Since the close of the great war, South Carolina has produced but little in literature ... Since then, the difficult work for material goods, which necessarily precedes literary achievement, has been her inevitable fate. In this work her people have succeeded in large measure. The higher things are yet to come" (p. 65).

Thus, during the Reconstruction years and immediately thereafter there were fewer writers at work in South Carolina. Simms died in 1870, and although Hayne lived until 1886, much of his audience and even many of his friends were in the North. Other than Hayne, there was no South Carolina writer of importance in the immediate postwar period: His closest rival, and a better poet, was Sidney Lanier, a Georgian. Many of those who *were* engaged in the day-to-day or, more usually, occasional business of creating imaginative literature in South Carolina, primarily poetry and fiction, looked to the past for their subjects and, often, for their models as well. David Duncan Wallace again captures the essence of the situation when he writes: "Out of this calamity and helplessness there emerged a psychology of inferiority as injurious as ante-bellum delusions of grandeur. The heart took refuge in idealizing 'The Lost Cause'" (p. 608). Finally, as will be seen, those who chose to write about other topics and in other modes often did so by writing outside the state's borders or by finding audiences and publishers beyond them.

A number of the post-Civil War authors were already to be found in Simms's *War Poetry of the South* published in 1867, just three years before Simms's death. Among these are **Joseph Blyth Allston (1833-1904)**, an ex-Confederate officer, who saw his patriotic poems about the war published in a number of magazines and newspapers; **Samuel Henry Dickson (1798-1872)**, a physician who published poetry in the 1848 *The Charleston Book* as well as several medical treatises; and **Augustus Julian Requier (1825-1887)**, also the author of romances and dramas.

Other South Carolina writers noted by their contemporaries but forgotten today include **Clara Victoria Dargan (1841-1920)**, who wrote poetry about soldiers killed on the battlefield on their birthdays and similar subjects; **Robert Means Davis (1849-1904)**, political ally of Wade Hampton, who taught history and political economy at South Carolina College after the war and then wrote for a number of state newspapers; **James Wood Davidson (1829-1905)**, a Newberry County native who left the state following the Civil War and made his mark in New York and Florida, most especially for his *Living Writers of the South* (1869); **Anna Peyre Dinnies (1816-1888)**, Georgetown native and author of domestic poetry, who died after a long residence in New Orleans; **Alexander Gregg (1819-1903)**, Episcopal priest and historian of the Old Cheraws; **Laura Gwyn (b. 1833)**, wife of a Methodist Episcopal pastor in Greenville and author of pious poems such as "The Valley Flower" and "The Voyage of Life"; **John Henry Logan (1822-1885)**, a physician who wrote a *Digest of the Negro Law* and an early *History of the Upper Country of South Carolina*; **Louisa Susannah Cheves McCord (1810-1879)**, daughter of Langdon Cheves and wife of attorney David James McCord, the author of a collection of amateur verse and a tragedy, *Caius Gracchus*, as well as a large number of essays on social and political subjects in *The Southern Literary Messenger*, *The Southern Quarterly Review*, and elsewhere; historian **Edward McCrady (1833-1903)**, professor at The Citadel and a president of the Historical Society of South Carolina; **Carlyle McKinley (1847-1904)**, journalist and ultimately editor of *The News and Courier*, who wrote valuable accounts of the Charleston hurricane of 1885 and the earthquake of 1886; Huguenot poet **Catharine Gendron Poyas (1813-1882)**; and **William Hayne Simmons (1784-1870)**, who wrote a history of the Seminoles. In addition to the fact that these writers are no longer read today, they also have in common a predominantly backward-looking perspective. Most of what they wrote is of a generally historical character, and a great deal of it is about the Civil War. Therefore, although most of this body of work is of little interest to the literary historian, some of it is indeed of worth to the cultural, political, and social historian, especially those works published contemporaneously with the events they record.

Four additional postwar writers deserve more than cursory notice. Two, **Maximilian LaBorde (1804-1873)** and **Francis Lieber (1800-1872)**, were South Carolina College professors who produced most of their characteristic work—most of which was not belletristic in nature—before the war; a third, **George Herbert Sass (1845-1908)**, was yet another Charleston attorney with a literary bent who wrote under the name "Barton Grey"; and the fourth, **William Henry Trescot (1822-1898)**, was a United States diplomat known primarily for his writings on history and international relations.

La Borde was something of a polymath, having begun his public career as a student of the law before switching to medicine and graduating from the Charleston Medical College in 1826. He founded the *Edgefield Advertiser* ten years later, then dabbled in politics, and finally became successively professor of belles lettres, then metaphysics, and finally English at South Carolina College. His publications are relatively few, however, and he is usually remembered as author of the college's history; he is not anthologized among Southern writers.

Francis Lieber, a German by birth, by contrast had an international reputation as a political economist who wrote widely in the field. Persecuted for his liberal views in his native Prussia, he turned first to England and then to America for the political freedom that eluded him at home. He taught history and political economy at South Carolina College from 1835 to 1856 and thereafter taught at Columbia College, New York. His published works address a wide range of contemporary issues and include volumes of poetry, but his most enduring contribution was in the areas of civil liberty and political ethics. In 1835 he published *The Stranger in America: Comprising Sketches of the Manners, Society, and National Peculiarities of the United States, in a Series of Letters to a Friend in Europe.* He served as an archivist of the Confederacy's papers after the war, and in 1870 was a mediator between the United States and Mexican governments.

George Herbert Sass was educated privately and at the College of Charleston, became an attorney, and also served as local Master in Equity for more than twenty years. He began writing patriotic poetry while in his teens during the Civil War and later became a book and drama critic for the Charleston *News and Courier.* Writing as "Barton Grey," Sass produced a body of poetry that proved popular in its day. Among his better known pieces, "In a King-Cambyses Vein" possesses some of the exotically romantic preference for the East that one finds, for example, in Tennyson's *Sorab and Rustum,* but the elegies in memory of "Joan Mellish" and "Robert Edward Lee" and the memorial "The Confederate Dead," although sincere, are commonplace. His contemporary Stanhope Sams accorded him "the third rank among the poets of the South" (Hungerpiller, p. 244) after Timrod and Hayne.

Like Sass, William Henry Trescot trained as a lawyer in his native Charleston after graduating from the College of Charleston. He also grew cotton, but while still a young man he undertook a study of American diplomatic history and by age thirty was representing the United States in London. He served the United States government in a wide range of capacities both before and after the Civil War, and he negotiated on behalf of the Confederacy with England and France. From the 1870s he conducted what George Armstrong Wauchope calls "a brilliant diplomatic career" (p. 394) during which he was a party to many significant agreements between the United States and, among others, China and Mexico. After retiring from government service, he became a private litigator in cases involving foreign governments. In addition to his important writings on diplomacy, Trescot also delivered a number of widely read and appreciated addresses on the South and its old order. Walter Edgar has remarked that his words inscribed on the 1879 Confederate monument before the Capitol in Columbia "captured the essence of the Bourbon world-view" (p. 424). Among those words are the following:

> Let the Stranger,
> Who May in Future Times
> Read this Inscription,
> Recognize that these were Men
> Whom Power Could Not Corrupt,
> Whom Death Could not Terrify,
> Whom Defeat Could not Dishonor,

and Let their Virtues Plead
for Just Judgment
of the Cause in which they Perished.

The "Bourbon world-view" was that of Wade Hampton and his immediate successors in the governorship and other positions of power and influence after the end of what is sometimes called Congressional Reconstruction. These men, mostly aristocratic and mostly commissioned veterans of the Civil War who had watched their wealth, their power, and their vision of the future all vanish around them, managed to wrest control again for a couple of decades at the end of the nineteenth century. But theirs was only an Indian summer casting a fading glow onto a diminished society that was never truly to rise again. Ben Tillman was already rattling his pitchfork out in the hustings, and a new day—not necessarily a better one, to be sure—was about to be born. The old Bourbon society produced no lasting literature in its final incarnation, and it was soon to be swept away forever. In its wake, a new kind of South Carolina literature emerged.

4 CHAPTER

The Twentieth Century
Part One

Hervey Allen, John Bennett, DuBose Heyward, and the
Poetry Society of South Carolina

A number of trends, some national but some purely regional and local, combined to shake South Carolina and her authors out of their cultural doldrums as the state moved into the twentieth century. Long years of military occupation, begun in 1867, and the well-intentioned but poorly enforced Reconstruction policies of national and local Republican administrations came to an end in 1876 with the election of former Confederate General Wade Hampton to the governorship. Hampton's election was disputed, resulting in the brief occupation of the state Capitol by federal troops, and the campaign was preceded by race riots in which large numbers of black and white South Carolinians were killed at Hamburg, Ellenton, and Cainhoy. But Hampton's ultimate ascendancy to the office of governor and the withdrawal of federal troops led to at least a tenuous stability.

Of course the situation of black South Carolinians was very precarious. Although seventeen thousand had voted for Hampton, after his ascendancy to the governorship and for long decades afterwards, they saw their representation in elective offices and their presence on local voting lists substantially and increasingly diminished. The institution of legalized segregation and the passage of Jim Crow laws further marginalized this segment of the population. At the same time, although full equality for black South Carolinians was still almost a hundred years away, some progressive measures in relation to the former slave population of the state were initiated. Benedict Institute and Allen University were both founded in Columbia within sixteen years of the end of the Civil War, and State College for Negroes opened in Orangeburg before the turn of the century. In 1872 a South Carolinian, John Henry Conyers, became the first African-American student to enroll in the Naval Academy at Annapolis; and in 1875, the year before the tumultuous Chamberlain-Hampton election, Mary McLeod Bethune was born. Race riots were to continue into the next century, and opportunistic politicians like "Pitchfork" Ben Tillman and Cole Blease continued to exploit whites' fears of their black neighbors and to ignore the desperate plight, the economic straits, and the disfranchisement of black Carolinians; but the die had been cast and the state began to lurch, if fitfully at times, into the twentieth century. In January 1903 President Theodore Roosevelt appointed Dr. William D. Crum, an African-American, as Charleston Postmaster.

One concrete indication of the increasingly important role of African-Americans in South Carolina history *and* literature during this period is the inescapable presence of African-Americans both as authors themselves and as what librarian Tom Johnson, a keen observer of the state's literary scene, terms "a pervading theme in the work of South Carolina writers," both black and white. This theme is dealt with in reference to the works of individual authors in the remainder of this chapter and, significantly, in each chapter that follows this as well. Many, if not most, Palmetto State writers from this point forward deal either directly or indirectly with race relations in one way or another. The presence of this subject reflected an increasingly apparent national concern with race relations, especially in popular fiction. An extreme manifestation of this concern was the writings of North Carolinian Thomas Dixon (1864-1946), whose novel *The Clansman* (1905), one of a trilogy addressing themes of racial conflict and so-called "racial purity," gained particularly widespread attention when it was adapted as D.W. Griffith's film classic *The Birth of a Nation* (1915). Reaction to the film varied widely, from enthusiastic embracement by white audiences in the South to the issuance of a pamphlet by the National Association for the Advancement of Colored People that branded it "three miles of filth." Few viewers of the film remained strictly neutral. Less extreme treatments of the theme of black/white relations were legion, culminating in South Carolina during this period in works such as DuBose Heyward's *Porgy* and Julia Peterkin's *Scarlet Sister Mary*.

Strides were also finally being made in the realms of education and the economy in the early twentieth century. A General School Act was passed in 1871, and in 1907 the General Assembly authorized the state's first high schools. Thomas Green Clemson left Fort Hill, the Calhoun family ancestral home, to the state in 1889 for the establishment of the university that today bears his name. The school opened in 1893, and two years later Winthrop

Normal College was opened at Rock Hill. Cotton mills and the problems—some would say evils—attendant upon their spread and growth had become such a prominent feature of the industrial landscape that in 1892 the General Assembly found it necessary to limit the workweek to sixty-six hours, or eleven hours a day; and in 1903 child labor legislation was passed. Agricultural recovery also began, and although the price of cotton never returned to its pre-war highs, and Sea Island rice and cotton both were to be obliterated early in the new century by the combined forces of hurricanes and the boll weevil, farmers began to diversify, and it became possible again to make a meager living from the land. On December 1, 1901, the Interstate and West Indian Exposition began a six-month run in Charleston, and in 1916 an automobile factory owned by John Gary Anderson began production in Rock Hill.

The state clearly had a long way to go as the twentieth century opened, and South Carolina was hardly a scion of the New South envisioned by Henry Grady in his famous speech before the New England Society of New York in December 1886, but by the second decade of the twentieth century notable progress had undoubtedly begun. A new era was also beginning for the state's literature. At the end of the nineteenth century, the best-known writers of South Carolina were either dead like Simms and Timrod and Hayne, or they were academics (Gildersleeve and Lieber) or journalists (Sass) whose literary output was demonstrably secondary, a mere corollary to their real professional lives. Some of these writers were better known outside the state than within its borders, and some even traveled to other states to cap their professional careers. As the new century opened, however, the state produced the first of a growing number of genuinely professional *writers*, men—and women too—who made their livings by the pen. It should not be surprising that the first of these was the son of an old Charleston family down on its luck who found success by turning his knowledge of the rich history of his native city into something new.

DuBose Heyward (1885-1940), like Simms and Timrod and Hayne, is another of those South Carolina authors held in generally higher regard by his fellow Carolinians than by outlanders. While he had a national audience during his lifetime and produced one work of lasting importance in *Porgy* and its adaptations into both a play and an opera, Heyward today is often treated as a slightly embarrassing, paternalistic anachronism. His sympathetic mid-twentieth century biographer, Frank Durham, calls him "the trustee of a modest but admirable talent, one worthy of consideration in any study of Southern and American literature" (Rubin, p. 222). Another critic, Holly Westcott, herself a South Carolinian and a veteran educator dedicated to the state's literature, points out that *Porgy* was "the first American novel with black characters to find a national audience" (Spears, p. 44), and she concludes that Heyward is to be remembered "for creating serious dramatic material for black performers when such material was scarce, helping to

DuBose Heyward

integrate the black minority into the mainstream of American drama." She goes on to say that "he opened the minds of both black and white Americans to the literary possibilities inherent in black life and culture. And in Porgy, he gave to American literature and American theater one of its unforgettable characters" (p. 46).

James M. Hutchisson's expansive, revisionist assessment of Heyward, *DuBose Heyward: A Charleston Gentleman and the World of Porgy and Bess* (University Press of Mississippi, 2000), provides a fuller treatment both of Heyward's achievement and of his contribution. Hutchisson observes in his "Introduction" that the stage version of *Porgy* co-authored by Heyward and his wife, Dorothy, "revolutionized the American theater with its innovative use of black folk materials" (p. xiii). Hutchisson also stresses that through his prominence as a founder and chief promoter of the Poetry Society of South Carolina, Heyward was able to exert "a small but significant influence on the revival of southern literature during that region's cultural renaissance" and that in his later work Heyward in fact became "a major social critic" in *Mamba's Daughters* and *Brass Ankle* (p. xiii). Indeed, Hutchisson's fifth chapter, entitled "Evolution of a Social Critic," should be required reading for anyone who considers Heyward just another white conservative Charlestonian with a penchant for writing nostalgically about the good old days.

At his birth on August 31, 1885, however, future literary fame for their new son must have been the furthest thing from the minds of DuBose Heyward's parents. Although he was the great-great-great grandson of Thomas Heyward, one of South Carolina's signers of the Declaration of Independence, and recalled listening as a child to his great-grandfather's firsthand stories about his eminent forebear, Heyward and his family early on lived a modest existence that became dramatically precarious when his father was killed in a mill accident when the future author was only two. Thereafter, life for the family became for a time a genuine struggle to make ends meet. Heyward's mother, Janie Screven DuBose, herself a poet and public performer of local legends, sewed for others and rented out rooms. Heyward himself quit school at fourteen—he had attended his godmother Susan Hayne's private school and then Boys' High School—but already at age nine he had begun delivering the Charleston Evening Post to help his mother pay the family bills.

At fourteen Heyward became a clerk and stock boy in a Charleston hardware store, then at eighteen he contracted polio, followed two years later by typhoid fever and, after another year, pleurisy. At age 20 he became a cotton checker on a wharf in Charleston, where he daily observed and listened with a dialectician's ear to the laborers who became the models for characters who would later come to life in *Porgy*, *Mamba's Daughters*, and many of his poems. Heyward was also the beneficiary of his mother Janie's sharp ear for the nuances of Gullah in her own public renditions of local legends and folktales. A recurrence of pleurisy during this period sent him to Tryon, North Carolina, for rest and recuperation. At

Tryon he began to paint, and he continued to write the short stories and poems that had interested him for some time.

By 1920 in addition to embarking upon the literary career that his business success and convalescence had provided him the opportunity and leisure to pursue in earnest, Heyward had met two transplanted Northerners who were to be an immense influence upon him: **John Bennett (1865-1956)** and **Hervey Allen (1889-1949)**. Twenty years Heyward's senior and a native of Chillicothe, Ohio, Bennett was already a successful author with *Master Skylark*, *Barnaby Lee*, and *The Treasure of Peyre Gailliard* behind him and *Madame Margot* soon to appear. Allen, the author of *Anthony Adverse*, was a teacher at Charleston's Porter Military Academy. Before very long these three were holding "Wednesday-nighters" in support of each other's work, and at one of these Heyward suggested, "Let's organize a poetry society here in South Carolina" (Durham, *DuBose Heyward: The Man Who Wrote Porgy*, p. 24). The Poetry Society of South Carolina, the first state literary society in the nation, was born. Its first meeting took place in October of 1920, followed by the first regular meeting in January 1921, at which Heyward was elected secretary.

The influence of the Poetry Society at this point in South Carolina literary history can hardly be understated. Not only did it nurture and publish a wide range of contemporary poets—besides Heyward and Bennett, there were also Ellen Magrath Carroll, Richard Coleman, Elizabeth Durham, Robert Molloy, Chalmers S. Murray, Josephine Pinckney, Beatrice Ravenel, Herbert Ravenel Sass, and Katherine Mayrant Simons—but it also invited to Charleston some of the best-known and most-accomplished American poets of the day. Those who traveled to Charleston to read their own work included a veritable "who's who" of the world of verse: Frost and Sandburg, of course, but also Stephen Vincent Benét, Padraic Colum, Vachel Lindsay, Edna St. Vincent Millay, Louis Untermeyer, and Southerners Donald Davidson and John Crowe Ransom. The Society published its first *Yearbook* in 1921, even before the first issue of the Nashville *Fugitive* appeared, and Allen and Heyward's *Carolina Chansons* appeared the next year. In the preface to this slim but important volume, the two men proudly proclaimed, "If the only result of this book is to call attention to the literary and artistic values inherent in the South, and to the essentially unique and yet nationally interesting qualities of the Carolina Low Country, its landscapes and legends, the labor bestowed here will have secured its harvest."

At this period Heyward had been spending four months a year either resting in the Blue Ridge Mountains in Tryon or writing at the McDowell Colony in New Hampshire, and at the latter venue in 1921 he met his future wife, playwright Dorothy Kuhns. They married in the fall of 1923 and moved to Charleston. Kuhns encouraged Heyward in his literary ambitions, and soon he was writing full-time. A newspaper story about a crippled Charleston beggar named

Samuel Smalls gave Heyward the germ of *Porgy*, and the novel was published in New York in 1925, followed the next year by publication in England.

The story of *Porgy* and its subsequent publication history are familiar to many readers (see, for example, Westcott in Spears, *A Literary Map of South Carolina*, or the fuller treatment in Durham's

biography). The crippled beggar, the fallen Bess, the notorious Sporting Life, and the demonic Crown, together with the colorful milieu in which their tragedy works itself out, provided enough high melodrama and exotic but reality-based local color to ensure a wide appeal. The popularity of the novel created sufficient interest in New York that within two years the Theater Guild mounted a full-scale, black cast production of the play version Heyward wrote with the assistance of his wife. Not only did the play enjoy a run of nearly four hundred performances, but it also won Heyward and Dorothy the Pultizer Prize for *Porgy: A Play in Four Acts* published by Doubleday, Page in 1928. George Gershwin's interest in the play led to his and his brother Ira's collaboration with Heyward off and on during the next half-dozen years and resulted in *Porgy and Bess*, which was not an immediate hit but which, in revival not long after Heyward's death and henceforward, has become an American classic.

Although *Porgy* was to be the high-water mark of Heyward's popular reputation and commercial success, it was far from the culmination of his career. The year after the novel's appearance came *Angel*, a less successful tale of Appalachia, and in relatively quick succession the local color story "The Half-Pint Flask," the novel *Mamba's*

Heyward's novel *Porgy*, published in 1925

Daughters (which in its dramatic version in 1939 made Ethel Waters the first black woman star of the American theater), the failed play *Brass Ankle, Jasbo Brown and Collected Poems*, and others seldom remembered today. In the summer of 1940 Heyward was discussing with the composer Arthur Schwartz the creation of another opera to star Ethel Waters. Based upon his last novel, *Star Spangled Virgin*, the new work was to revolve around black characters in the Virgin Islands. Before work could begin, however, Heyward died of a heart attack on June 16, 1940, while traveling from Tryon to Hendersonville, North Carolina. Hutchisson summarizes his "varied array of contributions to southern literature" as follows:

> His was the first major southern voice to write realistically
> about African Americans as human beings rather than as
> comic or sordid stereotypes. DuBose and Dorothy Heyward

also worked hard to increase the opportunities for African Americans in theater and to elevate and recognize the state of African American art. Heyward's evolution into a social critic should also not escape notice, for his social attitudes matured and his views became more trenchant as he immersed himself deeper and deeper into the world of African Americans. (pp. 187-188)

Heyward was inducted into the South Carolina Academy of Authors in 1987.

While neither was a native of the state, Heyward's two friends who were also prime movers in the Poetry Society of South Carolina had substantial influence on the literary direction of the state's culture in the early twentieth century. Both had published beyond the South, and both had some acquaintance with the larger world of arts and letters. **John Bennett** had published three novels by the time he met Heyward: *Master Skylark* (1897), a romance of Elizabethan England once part of the parallel reading list at Harvard and Wellesley; *The Story of Barnaby Lee* (1902), set in Colonial America; and *The Treasure of Peyre Gaillard* (1906), a tale of Reconstruction. A novella, *Madame Margot*, the one most likely to be familiar to modern readers, was published soon after they met in 1921, and a book for young people, *The Pigtail of Ah Lee Ben Loo*, appeared in 1928. Bennett had been educated in Ohio and at the Art Students' League in New York City, and he had been a journalist, so it is not surprising that he brought to his friendship with Hervey Allen and DuBose Heyward a more cosmopolitan appreciation of the fine arts than was common in Charleston, a city still licking its war wounds and sending many of its more able sons and daughters far afield. Bennett became so much a fixture in the cultural life of Charleston that he lived there until his death in 1956 and was buried in Magnolia Cemetery. The recent publication of his correspondence with University of South Carolina professor Yates Snowden (ed. Mary Crow Anderson, Columbia: University of South Carolina Press, 1993) provides substantial information about his life and his work in Charleston. More recently, a second John Bennett has contributed to the literary culture of the state through his work with the Poetry Society of South Carolina and his good offices and hospitality to the South Carolina Academy of Authors, which inducted the first Bennett into its ranks in 1993.

Hervey Allen, younger than Bennett by two dozen years, was born in Pittsburgh, earned his Bachelor's degree at the University of Pittsburgh in 1915, and served at the Western Front during World War I after enlisting in the Pennsylvania National Guard in 1916. After the war he did graduate work at Harvard and came to Charleston to teach at Porter Military Academy. A published poet by 1921—his first book, *Wampum and Old Gold*, was issued in the Yale Series of Younger Poets—he quickly made friends with Heyward and Bennett. Initially it was poetry that formed the connection, especially between Allen and Heyward, and in 1922 the two published

The grave of DuBose Heyward in St. Philip's churchyard, Charleston
Courtesy, Edwin Epps

Carolina Chansons, a collection noteworthy for its use of the Gullah dialect and for its recreation of the characteristic natural beauty of the Lowcountry and of the life of Charleston's black citizens as Heyward had observed it while working on the wharfs. Allen and Heyward also guest-edited the April 1922 edition of *Poetry* at the invitation of Harriet Monroe. Despite his friendship with Heyward and Bennett, however, Allen's ambitions lay elsewhere. He taught at Columbia University and at Vassar, and later settled into a comfortable compound called the Glades in Dade County, Florida, where his visitors included Frost and other prominent writers. He produced *Israfel*, a still-consulted biography of Edgar Allan Poe, in 1926, and then embarked upon a series of well-received novels, the most popular of which, *Anthony Adverse* (1933), became a film starring Fredric March and Olivia de Havilland and won the 1936 Best Supporting Actress Oscar for Gale Sondergaard. At the end of his life Allen was still busy writing an historical saga of grand sweep. His personal papers, correspondence, and library are located at the University of Pittsburgh.

The official website of the Poetry Society of South Carolina describes its early meetings as follows: "Poetry Society functions were once held in stately South Carolina Society Hall. Admittance was by engraved invitation only, and dress was formal." This atmosphere of a deliberately cultivated, refined ambience has been remarked on by a number of observers. Still, while most of the new literature produced under the influence of the Society's mellow glow may be termed traditional, at least one of its poets wrote original, modern verse.

Beatrice Witte Ravenel (1870-1956) was well into middle age when the Poetry Society was organized. The daughter of a prominent German banker who was one of the few Charlestonians to make his fortune in the city *after* the Civil War during the throes of Reconstruction, Beatrice Witte was well educated in the city at Miss Kelly's Female Seminary and then departed for the female auxiliary of Harvard University known as the Society for the Collegiate Instruction of Women, later Radcliffe College. She earned no degree but studied under such professors as William James, George Lyman Kittredge, George Pierce Baker, and George Santayana; and she played an active role in a literary circle whose student members included the future poets William Vaughn Moody and Trumbull Stickney. While in Cambridge Witte contributed pieces to the *Harvard Monthly* and the *Advocate*, as well as poetry to the *Knight Errant*, stories to *Scribner's Magazine* and *Chap-book Magazine*, and a piece entitled "The Coming Man in Fiction," a reprint from the *Harvard Monthly*, to *The Literary Digest*. In 1900 Witte married Frank Ravenel, a member of a socially prominent family who, like many members of such families at that time, was, in the words of Louis Rubin, "very poor" (*The Yemassee Lands*, p. 11). Ravenel was also a poor businessman who could manage neither the affairs of the farm the family lived on south of the city nor the substantial

Beatrice Witt Ravenel

inheritance his wife received from her father when he died. As a result, the family's finances became depleted, and Witte began to write in earnest in order to help support her family. She contributed poetry to *The Atlantic Monthly* and fiction to *Ainslie's*, *Harper's*, and *The Saturday Evening Post*; and in 1919 she began to write editorials on foreign affairs for the Columbia *State*, which was edited by her brother-in-law. In 1920 her husband Frank died, and perhaps this event, combined with her absorption with international affairs in the early 1920s, her re-emergence into the world of letters, her acquaintance with modern poetry through the medium of *The Dial*, and her personal friendship with Amy Lowell (who had come to Charleston to read for the Poetry Society), caused a sea change in her verse.

Prior to the early twenties Ravenel's poetry had been competent but traditional, the sort of poetry that might have been written by almost any member of the Poetry Society but would have been of little interest to anyone except members of the Society. Now, however, her verse became more lean and concrete, more rooted in the specificity of immediate experience, more direct in its diction and its connection with the reader. "The Yemassee Lands" won the Poetry Society Prize in 1922. It was followed by a number of additional new poems, which appeared in a variety of periodicals and then were collected in *The Arrow of Lightning*, published in 1925. In 1926 Ravenel married again, to an attorney also named Ravenel but who had been born in Paris and lived for a time in Asheville. The poet no longer *needed* to write, and although she did compose a small collection of poems on West Indian subjects that Rubin regards as "among her best work" (p. 15), they were not published until 1969, thirteen years after her death. Not only are they "unlike anything else being written in Charleston at the time," Rubin claims, but they are also "among the more interesting work being done in American poetry of the period" (p. 25). There is very little poetry by any South Carolina poet of the 1920s that continues to be as *intrinsically* interesting today as Ravenel's. She was a 1995 inductee of the South Carolina Academy of Authors.

Another woman member of the Poetry Society, **Josephine Pinckney (1895-1957)**, produced a notable collection of poems, *Sea-Drinking Cities*, which in 1927 won the Carolina Sinkler Prize as the best book of poems published by a Southerner. One of the founding members of the Poetry Society, Pinckney was judged by a contemporary to be "one of the important South Carolina poets fostered by the new literary consciousness of the South" (Henry Bellamann in *The State*, quoted in Hungerpiller, p. 241), but time has not confirmed that judgment. Three of her poems made it into the *Tricentennial Anthology of South Carolina Literature 1670-1970*, but they lack the toughness and the strength of Ravenel's. "The Misses Poar Drive to Church," although its tone is playfully critical, is essentially a patrician piece. "Street Cries" contains picturesque images of African-American street scenes as conjured by a sleep-drugged white city dweller. And the title-piece of her book, "Sea-drinking Cities," with its "moon struck air," "loveliness, as of an old tale told," and "Towns that doze—dream—and never wake at all" (*Tricentennial Anthology*, pp. 417-418) suggests nothing so much as the dreamy, pastel-colored prints that are sold to tourists along Charleston's market. Pinckney's real fame during her lifetime came from a series of historical novels including *Hilton Head* (1941), *Three O'Clock Dinner* (1945), *Great Mischief* (1948), *My Son and Foe* (1952), and *Splendid in Ashes* (1958). *Hilton Head* is about the early settlement of South Carolina, and the plot of *Great Mischief* is set in the state two hundred years later. *Three O'Clock Dinner*, a Literary Guild selection and a bestseller, was optioned by Hollywood for $125,000. Miss Pinckney's induction into the South Carolina Academy of Authors took place in 1988.

One other member of the Poetry Society of South Carolina circle, **Herbert Ravenel Sass (1884-1958)**, deserves mention in these pages. Born into a literary family—his father was "Barton Grey," and his grandmother had written books about Charleston, Eliza Lucas Pinckney, and William Lowndes—Sass spent his entire life in Charleston, being educated at the College of Charleston and working first as assistant director of the Charleston Museum, then as an editor of the *News and Courier*, and finally as a freelance writer whose subject was usually his native state and its history. Although remembered today primarily for his historical and outdoors writing, during his lifetime Sass wrote many short stories, feature articles, and essays that appeared in prominent national publications like *The Saturday Evening Post*, *National Geographic*, *Harper's*, *The Atlantic Monthly*, and *The Saturday Review*. He also wrote three historical novels: *War Drums* (1928), *Look Back to Glory* (1933), and *Emperor Brims* (1941).

5 CHAPTER

The Twentieth Century
Part Two

Beyond the Poetry Society: E.C.L. Adams, Ambrose E. Gonzales, Julia Mood Peterkin, and Archibald Rutledge

Besides the Poetry Society of South Carolina group, the two early twentieth-century South Carolina writers who have garnered the most recent critical notice are Julia Mood Peterkin of Lang Syne Plantation and E.C.L. Adams of the Congaree Swamp in Lower Richland County. Both were white authors writing about the culture of black communities that they were intimately familiar with, but, of course, were not a part. Both enjoyed considerable popularity during their lifetimes but fell relatively out of favor as the twentieth century progressed and black writers themselves began to write about their own communities and cultures. Both also, however, have received renewed attention at the beginning of the twenty-first century, Peterkin because of a prize-winning biography, and Adams because of a new edition of his best-known works published by the University of North Carolina Press. There was a third South Carolinian also writing about similar subject matter at about the same time: Ambrose Gonzales, whose stories about what he called "the Black Border" have not fared as well as those of his two contemporaries. And, finally, there was Archibald Rutledge, "Old Flintlock," who grew up in the same milieu, but whose work is generally of a different nature.

Ambrose Elliott Gonzales (1857-1926), the grandson of the author of *Carolina Sports by Land and Water*, was born at Adams Run in rural Colleton District, one of the way stations along the

A.E. Gonzales

road from Charleston to Edisto Island. After working there as a telegrapher in his mid- and late teens and after similar jobs in New York City and New Orleans, Gonzales returned to his native state to become a reporter for the *News and Courier*, a position he maintained until founding *The State* in Columbia with his brother N.G. Gonzales in 1891. After time off as a captain in the Spanish-American War, also with his brother, he settled back into the safer life of a writer and in 1922 published *The Black Border*, followed in quick succession by *With Aesop Along the Black Border* (1924), *Laguerre: A Gascon of the Black Border* (1924), and *The Captain: Stories of the Black Border* (1924). While Gonzales's folktales are strongly paternalistic in style and tone, they do preserve material that has not otherwise survived, and they continue to be serviceable as a written transcription of the Gullah dialect. On balance, however, there is too much evidence that the tales' narrator is a privileged white recording with condescending bemusement the humorous failings of a people he regards as simple and childlike.

Edward C. L. Adams (1876-1946) was born a quarter century after Gonzales and at the edge of the Congaree Swamp rather than near Charleston, but he began to publish his tales of Midlands blacks at about the same date that the older man began to publish his tales of the "Black Border." Like Gonzales, Adams came of distinguished South Carolina lineage. His father was a descendant of one of the early leaders of old Charles Towne, and his mother's forebears included a colonial Massachusetts governor; later ancestors included college presidents and planters who were influential members of their communities. Adams himself attended public schools in Columbia and then went to Clemson for his undergraduate education. After service on the home front during the Spanish-American War, he undertook his medical education in Charleston and also studied in Baltimore, Philadelphia, and Dublin, Ireland. While in Dublin during 1908 and 1909 Adams established a lasting friendship with the Irish writer Padraic Colum, whose interest in portraying authentic Irish life in his writing influenced Adams in the early stages of his own desire to portray the authentic lifestyle of his black neighbors in "the Congarees."

Marriage to Pennsylvanian Amanda M. Smith in 1910 allowed Adams to use some of her family's money to purchase land that had belonged to his family in former times but which had in the interim passed into other hands. From then on, although he maintained an increasingly casual medical practice in Columbia, Adams led the life of a country squire, experimenting with crop varieties, milling grain for others, studying the wildlife on his extensive property—even becoming the first president of the state affiliate of the National Audubon Society—and entertaining friends and guests, who included the fan dancer Sally Rand and the poet Edgar Lee Masters. He also ran twice for lieutenant governor, losing both times by large margins, and volunteered to serve overseas during World War I while in his forties. Thereafter Adams retired from medicine, even sending sick workers from his own property to other physicians for treatment.

As the owner of an extensive estate, Adams oversaw the working lives and participated in various ways in the everyday social lives of several hundred African Americans who lived on his property. The relationship that Adams had with Tad Goodson and his friends by the Congaree Swamp was something other than simply that of employer and employee, and this fact may well account for one of the differences between Adams's sketches of black life and those of Ambrose Gonzales: the relative absence not only of white characters but also of a condescending white narrator.

Some of Adams's sketches were first published in *Dublin Magazine* early in 1926, and his first book, *Congaree Sketches*, was published the following year by the University of North Carolina Press. Most reviewers, black and white, praised the book and its realistic portrayals of life among plantation blacks. Among the qualities praised were the depth of the characterization of black folk life, the unobtrusive presence of the white author, and the tales' frequent tone of grim and sardonic realism, qualities absent from the work of many whites in this genre, who tended merely—and, of course, objectionably—to present the humorous follies of a childlike people. In Adams's work, Tad and Scip exhibit a shrewdness and a clarity of vision uncharacteristic of most so-called black folk tales of the era.

Maxwell Perkins, Scribner's legendary editor, so liked *Congaree Sketches* that he offered to reissue it in a Scribner's edition. It never appeared, but in 1928 the company did publish a book of all new sketches, unfortunately titled *Nigger to Nigger* at Maxwell Perkins's suggestion as a means of emphasizing the authentic "Negro-ness" of the tales. Perhaps foreseeably, the book did not do well, and although Adams refurbished an earlier tale as a play and issued it under the title *Potee's Gal* during the next year, the majority of his work as a writer was by then behind him.

All in all, Adams's work is important but must be read with caution. As Robert G. O'Meally rightly points out in his introduction to *Tales of the Congaree*, the narrator of the Congaree sketches wears a number of masks during his tale telling, often simultaneously, and Adams himself was not without prejudice. At the same time, however, his relationships with his black friends and neighbors were very different from those of most of his white friends in Columbia, and thus he genuinely shared a large part of his life with Thaddeus Goodson and the other laborers on his land. He therefore saw more of the black folk life that he wrote about than most whites did, and he regarded it more sympathetically as well. Thus in a significant sense he is more trustworthy literarily than most of his peers. He *was* a white man, however, and this fact inherently limited both the degree of his participation in the world he recorded and his ability to record it with absolute verisimilitude. The truth of this observation is demonstrated in a literary anecdote from 1931. In that year Langston Hughes gave a poetry reading in

Columbia, after which Ned Adams, who was in the audience, invited him to a visit out at his farm. Hughes accepted the invitation and enjoyed a "wonderful time" that afternoon with the doctor and some of his field hands. Neither Hughes nor the doctor felt uncomfortable or self-conscious during the meeting. At the end of the afternoon, Hughes took his leave of Adams and rejoined his driver for the occasion, an African-American doctor from Columbia who had remained in his car the whole time because of the reprisals he feared if white Columbians learned that he had also visited with the white Adams. Adams himself could afford to be a maverick because of the security of his own position in Columbia society, but a respected member of the black middle class in the same city could not.

After visiting with Ned Adams, Langston Hughes intended to spend some time at Lang Syne Plantation with **Julia Peterkin (1880-1961)** who, he believed, had invited him at the New York City home of Joel Spingarn, the president of the National Association for the Advancement of Colored People. Hughes arrived unexpectedly, however, and was told that the writer was not at home by a white man who either did not recognize his name or deliberately turned him away on Peterkin's instructions. In either event, the incident led to gossip, criticism of Peterkin's actions, and embarrassment before her literary friends outside the South.

The daughter of a successful doctor, Julius Mood of Sumter, Peterkin was reared in Beaufort and Manning by her grandfather, Methodist minister Henry Mood, after the death of her mother, Alma Archer Mood, when she was only a year old. She did not get along well with her stepmother, and she was more her grandfather's child than her father's. From her grandfather, whose denomination actively opposed slavery, she apparently learned discipline, good manners, and sympathy for her African-American neighbors. In 1896 she graduated from Converse College, and in 1897, the year in which her grandfather died, she received her Master of Arts degree. Subsequently she taught for two years at Fort Motte, where she met and then in 1903 married Willie Peterkin, thus becoming the mistress of Lang Syne Plantation, the source of much of her later fiction. Peterkin became pregnant with her son, Bill, almost immediately, and after a difficult delivery and to avoid future complications, her father and her husband decided on their own to remove her ovaries, a decision for which she never fully forgave either man. The combination of the stresses of her delivery, postpartum depression, and her anger at what had been done to her—together with servants and family too eager to minister to her every need—drove her to bed for two years afterward. When she finally arose from her bed, Peterkin was determined to become both the knowledgeable mistress of her plantation, a position for which her earlier life had left her poorly prepared, and a leader in the polite society of Calhoun County, a position for which her upbringing and education had well suited her.

Peterkin learned the duties required of her station at the elbow

Julia Peterkin
Courtesy, Converse College

The Peterkin silhouette, which hangs at Converse College's Mickel Library

of Lavinia Berry, a longtime family servant who was born a slave and had observed the fortunes and misfortunes of a procession of mistresses at Lang Syne. When economic conditions and Willie Peterkin's fortunes took a turn for the worse, Julia Peterkin found herself the mistress of a plantation empire on the verge of collapse. Determined not to become destitute and with the example of her successful, indeed flourishing, physician father before her, Peterkin sought both escape and an alternate source of income. She found them through the agency of a piano teacher.

Peterkin approached Henry Bellamann, dean of the School of Fine Arts at Chicora College in Columbia, after she learned that a friend on a neighboring plantation had been taking lessons at Chicora. Quickly convinced that she had little real aptitude for the piano, Peterkin found herself passing more and more of her time with Bellamann by telling him tales of the lives of the field hands and servants at Lang Syne. Bellamann was himself a published poet and incipient novelist, and he belonged to the newly founded Poetry Society of South Carolina. He encouraged Peterkin and began to help her develop and polish her stories into a form that might be publishable. In addition, Bella-mann and his wife introduced Peterkin to Daniel Reed, the director of a community theater group in Columbia, and his wife Isadora Bennett. Bennett had been a reporter for the *Chicago Daily News*, and there she had known Carl Sandburg, so when the Reeds learned that Sandburg was to read before the Poetry Society in Charleston, they invited him to Columbia on the following day, the seventeenth of February 1921. Sandburg accepted, and when he and Peterkin subsequently met they became friends on the spot. He then made a trip out to Lang Syne, and Peterkin's literary career was launched.

From left, **Havilah Babcock, Elizabeth Boatwright Coker, Julia Peterkin and Mr. and Mrs. Edison Marshall**
Courtesy, Converse College

Susan Millar Williams, in her exemplary biography of Peterkin, *A Devil and a Good Woman Too: The Lives of Julia Peterkin* (University of Georgia Press, 1997) describes Peterkin's publishing history in detail. To summarize, it combined the luck of presenting a subject matter that dovetailed nicely into the new interests and energies of the Harlem Renaissance and the Jazz Age with the shrewdness of a woman on a personal mission, the winning charm of a redhead, the good offices of friends and acquaintances, and no small degree of real talent. Her earliest sketches were published in *The Richmond Reviewer* in its issue for October 1921, and over the years more of her tales appeared in the *Reviewer*'s pages than anywhere else. Others appeared in H.L. Mencken's *Smart Set*—and Mencken became one of Peterkin's early champions as well—and in *The Borzoi 1925*, the *American Magazine*, *Century*, and even *The Saturday Evening Post*, *Ladies' Home Journal*, and *Good Housekeeping*. Some made their way into Harriet Monroe's *Poetry* as free-verse monologues.

Peterkin's first book appearance was as author of the group of sketches collected as *Green Thursday* in 1924. Peterkin had taken a summer writing course at Winthrop College in 1923, followed by a meeting with publisher Alfred A. Knopf and his wife Blanche arranged by Mencken. Blanche Knopf provided editorial expertise to make the collection more of a unified whole, and two thousand copies of the book were issued in the fall of 1924. These stories of Kildee and Rose Pinesett and their family and neighbors recall those of Ned Adams in that their central concern is the lives of the blacks themselves, not the relationships between them and any white characters, and the themes involve suffering and endurance in the face of often hostile and inexplicable forces. The Northern press generally liked the book as did some of the era's black reviewers. Others, however, were equivocal, and the Columbia *State*, where Ambrose Gonzales worked, was less than enthusiastic. Most reviewers, though, recognized that *Green Thursday* represented something new—in the words of Frank Durham, "a truthful, non-stereotyped portrayal" of Southern plantation blacks as characters in their own right, not just as stereotypes filtered through the perspective of a superior white narrator ("Introduction," *The Collected Stories of Julia Peterkin* [University of South Carolina Press, 1970], p. 25).

Although the critics generally liked *Green Thursday*, it was not a commercial success, and Peterkin was uncertain where to turn next. Although she continued to send her sketches to the periodicals, her next book began as an attempt at a thinly autobiographical novel. Mencken didn't like it, though, and neither did Knopf, and Peterkin finally transformed it entirely. *Black April*, reshaped and refined by her new editor, Hudson Strode, at her new publisher, Bobbs-Merrill, was a huge success, commercially and for the most part critically as well. Most reviewers found it to be, in Joel Spingarn's words, "an extraordinary book, born of unusual insight into the hearts of black folk" (Williams, p. 112). Although Ambrose Gonzales still demurred, and a few other Southern editors were cool in their appraisal, *Black April* was widely praised, even among black critics who lamented the absence of similar fiction by black authors. In the end, the literary editor of *The State* also wrote a laudatory notice, but only after five months and only after Peterkin had visited him personally at his home.

In the interim, Peterkin was becoming a celebrity, the subject of feature articles and profiles in a number of prominent magazines, and it was becoming hard for her to write at home. So when she received an invitation from Mrs. Edward MacDowell to attend her famous artists' colony in Peterboro, New Hampshire, Peterkin gratefully accepted—after all, her editor Hudson Stode, DuBose Heyward, Edwin Arlington Robinson, and the composer Aaron Copland were all there or soon would be. At the MacDowell Colony, she worked hard on *Scarlet Sister Mary*, which was published barely a year after *Black April* and was well received even in Columbia. Her alma mater had paid homage to her with an honorary degree in 1927, and *Scarlet Sister Mary* won the 1929 Pulitzer Prize and became a bestseller, but all was not well. In addition to temporary financial straits, Peterkin was experiencing doubt and uncertainty over the affair she was carrying on with the writer Irving Fineman, and the dramatic version of *Scarlet Sister Mary*, starring Ethel Barrymore and a cast composed largely of her relatives, all in blackface, closed after a mere thirty-four performances. These and other personal concerns made it difficult for the author to work, and her next book and final novel, *Bright Skin*, did not appear until 1932.

Bright Skin was a departure, looking forward instead of backward and abandoning the familiar, somewhat nostalgic tone that adhered to her other books. As Susan Millar Williams describes it, "*Bright Skin* portrays the grandchildren of slavery uneasily evolving from dirt-poor field hands into urban bootleggers, slumlords, bail bondsmen, and chorus girls" (*A Devil and a Good Woman Too*, p. 205). It was not what her readers expected, and the critics' reviews were also lukewarm. The book did sell, but unspectacularly, and Peterkin found herself having to repay her publisher $6,000 of her advance and other miscellaneous expenses. Disappointed with this book's performance, unhappy in her personal life, and increasingly disconsolate over the passing of the old world of which Lang Syne had stood as the central symbol, Peterkin began to withdraw from the public and eventually stopped writing. *Roll, Jordan, Roll* (1933), an unhappy collaboration with her photographer friend Doris Ullman, was marred by poor-quality reproductions of the photographs in the trade edition. Its distinctly paternalistic and condescending tone offended some readers, and the book was not a success. Peterkin still had one book in her—a recasting of "A Plantation Christmas," an illustrated essay that had first appeared in *Country Gentleman* in 1929—and it was popular, but in more than one sense it was too little and too late (1934). Although she would write occasional reviews and teach at Yaddo, Bread Loaf, and Bennington in the years to come, her career, her impact, and her influence on other writers were essentially behind her. When she died on August 1, 1961, of congestive heart failure, it had been twenty-seven years since her last book had been published. The final verdict is still out concerning Peterkin's lasting importance, but Joseph M. Flora presents a reasonable overview when he says that her portrayals of black Carolinians, as important as they were for their time, have not met the needs of later generations. "Her interest in the primitive aspects of Gullah life has seemed too exclusive," he writes. "But Peterkin unquestionably pioneered in portraying the black as human being; she broadened the scope of modern fiction" ("Fiction in the 1920s: Some New Voices," in Rubin *et al.*, *The History of Southern Literature*, p. 283). Julia Peterkin was inducted into the South Carolina Academy of Authors in 1986, as one of the organization's first inductees.

A. J. Verdelle, in his foreword to the University of Georgia's 1998 edition of *Scarlet Sister Mary*, agrees that "Peterkin's work was considered fresh and new in her time. Many of her readers were encountering the lives of African Americans for the first time" (p. xxviii). Verdelle goes on to point out also that "Peterkin portrayed African Americans as people and was stuck nonetheless in the racism of her day" (p. xxxii). This fact may help to explain why, when *Bright Skin* seemed to puzzle her loyal readers when it appeared, she was unable to carry her fiction further into the changing twentieth century.

Henry Bellamann (1882-1945) was not born in South Carolina, did not write primarily about South Carolina, and when he is thought of at all in connection with South Carolina literature, it is usually as the muse and promoter of Julia Peterkin, whose career he was instrumental in launching. This view of Bellamann is shortsighted, however, in light of his friendship with a number of important Palmetto State literary figures and his influence as a reviewer for *The Columbia Record* and *The State*. Bellamann was born in Fulton, Missouri, in 1882, and although he never earned an undergraduate degree, much less a Ph.D., he taught music at a number of colleges, including Juilliard and Vassar. In 1907 after his marriage to Katherine Jones of Carthage, Mississippi, Bellamann moved to Greenville to accept a position at Chicora College. He moved to Columbia with the college in 1915 and lived at 1522 Blanding Street until 1924, when he moved to New York as head of the Juilliard Foundation.

Although he was a music teacher by profession, Bellamann was active in many aspects of Columbia's cultural life, notably as a member of the Columbia Stage Society and of the Quill Club, the literary group that met regularly at Gittman's Book Store. During his years in the city, Bellamann and his wife entertained Carl Sandburg, Amy Lowell, and Charles Ives. In 1923 Bellamann accepted a position as editor of the fine arts section of *The Columbia Record*, an office he held even after moving to New York the following year, and in 1929 he accepted the same position at *The State*.

Bellamann wrote three books of poetry in an Imagist vein—*A Music Teacher's Notebook* (1920), *Cups of Illusion* (1923), and *The Upward Pass* (1928)—and seven novels, two of which may be singled out as of interest here. *Kings Row* (1940), the story of a psychiatrist's search for identity and an orderly life, was made into a popular

1942 film. *The Gray Man Walks* (1936) is a mystery set on a sea island off the South Carolina coast and draws upon the Lowcountry for ambience and a backdrop of local color. Bellamann's role in literary South Carolina has been examined most completely in a series of publications by Harry Bayne, associate professor of English at Brewton-Parker College in Mount Vernon, Georgia; his "Henry Bellamann: The Columbia, SC, Years at Chicora College" is available online at www.geocities.com/lrampey/henrysc.htm.

While **Archibald Rutledge (1883-1973)** did not restrict his subject matter to African-American folklore and folklife as did his colleagues in this chapter, a significant number of his books and shorter pieces do deal with the lives of the blacks on his beloved Hampton Plantation near McClellanville and their relationship with the Rutledge family. Rutledge undeniably had a deep and abiding affection for the people he grew up among, especially the family of Prince Alston, his childhood companion. He also presented these simple country people in a generally sympathetic light. At the same time, however, although he did live among them and hunt and fish with them regularly and on occasion even overnighted with them in their cabins or in simple hunting camps along the Santee River, he was in a significant sense not *of* them, and it is as an outsider that he views and presents their lives in his writing. In this, he is much like Ned Adams in his portrayals of his African-American neighbors among the Congarees. Still, unlike Adams, Rutledge also produced a large body of work—some of it writing about the outdoors, and some of it primarily inspirational and motivational in purpose—that is free from the kinds of paternalistic time- and place-bound references that make modern readers uncomfortable.

Archibald Rutledge,
the state's first poet laureate

Archibald Rutledge was born in 1883 in his family's summer retreat cabin in McClellanville, sometimes called Little Hampton, where he was also to die almost ninety years later. This fact in many ways epitomizes the man and his life, since for as long as he lived he was attempting to return in one way or another to the life into which he was born. He was a child of Hampton Plantation; he was the son of a Confederate colonel who struggled manfully to preserve his birthright after the Civil War; he was the descendant of Middletons and Pinckneys and Rutledges, all storied names in South Carolina history; and he was always more at home walking the fields and forests and swamps of the Lowcountry than he was anywhere else. In a very real sense he could not escape his heritage, which in turn became his most frequent subject and endeared him to the state that was to make him its first poet laureate for life in 1934, a full thirty-nine years before his death.

Rutledge spent his childhood rambling among the lush plant and wildlife at Hampton Plantation before the lower reaches of the Santee River had been changed forever by the Santee Cooper dam and diversion project. For a child like Rutledge, it was an idyllic existence, and he learned the ways of deer and wild boar, otter and foxes, possum and raccoons, and the great bull alligators that were a constant reminder of the primeval wildness of the land itself. His earliest teachers were his father and mother and the adult blacks at Hampton whose ancestors had tamed the wild land in the eighteenth century.

When Rutledge was ten years old, he witnessed at close hand the death of his brother Hugh, who was killed by an unexpectedly fast-moving locomotive that surprised the two boys as they were playing on railroad tracks near their summer home in Flat Rock, North Carolina. Covered in his brother's blood, Rutledge ran to tell his family what had happened, only to overhear a sister's remark, "Oh, if it could only have been Archie instead." Rutledge had been a less-than-model pupil in school, and one of his teachers called him "willful Archie," a sobriquet readily adopted by the family of this dreamy boy often lost in his own thoughts. Still, his sister's unfeeling, unthinking bestowal of guilt and shame marked the young boy for the rest of his life.

Rutledge's earliest schooling was at home, followed by lessons from Miss Anne Ashburn Lucas in a small schoolroom on a neighboring plantation. He also read and was read to—at this time Hampton had no electricity so there was not even the diversion of the radio to interfere with quieter leisure pursuits—discovering a special affinity for Sir Walter Scott and Edgar Allan Poe, who had supposedly visited Hampton. Later Rutledge attended Porter Military Academy in Charleston, where he distinguished himself in Latin, French, and English but struggled in mathematics; he also began to write poetry, which appeared in local newspapers and magazines even before his graduation from Porter.

At age sixteen Rutledge moved on from Porter to Union College in Schenectady, New York, where he lived on a strict budget and was received at first with some curiosity by his Northern schoolmates as "Johnny Rebel." He also found work as a sort of zookeeper for the exotic animals kept by Charles Proteus Steinmetz of General Electric and worked for a time as an armature winder at GE. He continued to write at Union, and by the time he graduated as valedictorian in 1904 he had been both editor of the college paper and class poet. Unsure of what to do with his life but needing work, he served briefly as a telephone salesman, a patent attorney's assistant, and a reporter for *The Washington Post*, and then he interviewed for a temporary teaching position at Mercersburg Academy in Mercersburg, Pennsylvania. There he found his true profession and remained until his retirement in 1937.

At Mercersburg Rutledge found a congenial occupation, an appreciative community, a wife—he married Florence Hart, the sister of his headmaster's wife, in 1907—and sufficient leisure time both to continue his beloved hunting and fishing and to write about these and other subjects. His position at Mercersburg provided him easier access to the publishers and editors to whom he would submit his work. Visitors to the campus during Rutledge's early years there included the editors of *Outlook* and *Outdoor Life* as well as Henry

Van Dyke, the widely published Princeton professor, and all of these encouraged him. Soon he was writing for *Virginia Quarterly* and *The Georgia Review*, and then *The Saturday Evening Post*, *Reader's Digest*, *Good Housekeeping*, and *Field and Stream*. His first book of poetry, *Under the Pines, and Other Poems*, was published in 1906, soon to be followed by the first of his outdoors volumes: *The Banners of the Coast* (1908), *Days Off in Dixie* (1924), *Children of the Swamp and Wood* (1927), and *Wild Life of the South* (1935). At the same time Rutledge was beginning his series of highly popular inspirational titles: *Life's Extras* (1928), *The Flower of Hope* (1930), *Peace in the Heart* (1930), *The Angel Standing*; or, *Faith Alone Gives Poise* (1948) and others. To these over the years were added a variety of other titles such as his tribute to his parents, *My Colonel and His Lady* (1937); *Home by the River* (1941), the story of his return to Hampton; and even a group of stories from the Bible, *Voices of the Long Ago: Bible Stories Retold* (1973).

From the very beginning Rutledge's poetry and prose struck a deeply responsive chord in the hearts of his reading public, which included as many Northerners as Southerners. Henry Ford purchased twenty-five thousand copies of *Life's Extras* to present to his factory workers; another ten thousand copies were distributed by the Seventh Day Adventists; and any number of schools gave copies to their graduates. In 1930 Rutledge won the John Burroughs Memorial Association's medal for the best nature writing of the year, and four years later the South Carolina General Assembly named him the state's first poet laureate. Other recognitions followed, including two nominations for the Pulitzer Prize, a double handful of honorary degrees, membership in the American Society of Arts and Letters and in the Neucomen Society, and a Distinguished Service Award from *Reader's Digest*. By the time of his death Rutledge had published more than fifty books and over a thousand poems and articles in a wide variety of popular magazines.

Rutledge's first wife died in 1934, and in 1936 he married Alice Lucas, his childhood sweetheart who was also the sister of his teacher of many years before. He retired from Mercersburg shortly thereafter and, with his pension from the Academy, his annual stipend as poet laureate, and the income from his books and magazine pieces, he returned to Hampton Plantation to accomplish the dream of the remainder of his life: the restoration of the great house and grounds. This task he largely accomplished, and then, realizing that the upkeep of the place was beyond the resources of his own now dispersed family, in 1970 he and his sole surviving son, Irvine, deeded the property to the state, which maintains and showcases it today. Rutledge himself continued to live at Hampton for a large part of each year until he was struck by a car in the spring of 1967 and became bedridden. His wife died a year later, and Rutledge moved to a nursing facility in Spartanburg, where his sisters-in-law lived and where he and his wife had visited frequently in the years before her death. When the family's former cabin at McClellanville came onto the market in the same week that Hampton was sold to the state in 1970, Rutledge purchased the land along Jeremy Creek and spent his remaining years there attended by nurses. He died in September 1973, a few weeks before his ninetieth birthday, and was buried beside his son Archibald, Jr., at Hampton Plantation.

The years since his death have not treated Rutledge's critical reputation as a poet kindly. In an era whose ear is more sympathetic to the tough meters and often demanding style of a James Dickey, the classical tone and diction of most of Rutledge's poetry are not in favor. He is seldom anthologized. Still, at least at home in South Carolina, Rutledge is a popular poet. The feelings that stirred his heart still move the hearts of his neighbors, and his verse is eminently approachable to an audience not bound by the constraints of academic criticism. His prose likewise is popular if, like the man himself, a little formal in its bearing. No one else has ever written more affectionately of the Lowcountry of South Carolina; nor has anyone else better seemed to encompass in his or her writing all of the many facets of the Lowcountry and life along its rivers and swamps that appeal to so many. Rutledge was inducted into the South Carolina Academy of Authors in 1999.

The best general introduction to Rutledge the man—other than his own work, much of which is still available in reprint—is Idella Bodie's biography for young readers, *A Hunt for Life's Extras: The Story of Archibald Rutledge*, published by Sandlapper Publishing, Inc., in 1980. His son Irvine also wrote a memoir of his father, containing family photographs and reproductions of letters and other documents, entitled *We Called Him Flintlock* (The R.L. Bryan Co., 1974). Another helpful resource is *Hidden Glory: The Life and Times of Hampton Plantation, Legend of the South Santee* by Mary Bray Wheeler, published by Rutledge Hill Press of Nashville in 1983.

6 CHAPTER

The Twentieth Century
Part Three

Beyond Charleston and into the Modern World
—The Maturation of Literary South Carolina

As the United States as a whole moved from the false promise of the Jazz Age into the deep doldrums of the Great Depression in the 1930s, South Carolina discovered that she had become more of a part of the mainstream and that she marched confidently or faltered together with the industrial rhythms of the rest of the country. When the nation turned to Franklin Delano Roosevelt and the Democrats for help, so, largely, did South Carolina. When World War II began, the state also sent its sons off to fight for democracy with the sons of the Northeast, the Midwest, and the West Coast. Many of these sons from all sections had black faces, and their experiences of the war and the expectations they brought home with them from Europe and the Far East changed the social and economic landscape of the nation, including now more fully than ever before the South, forever.

Times were changing fast. More Sandlappers than ever worked in the booming textile industry, and the numbers of civil servants increased with the demands upon, and then the responses of, local and state governments. Local booms were also fueled by Army training bases at Camps Wadsworth (World War I) and Croft (World War II) in Spartanburg County and Camp, later Fort, Jackson in Columbia, the Marine Corps air station and training base at Port Royal near Beaufort, the Myrtle Beach Air Force Base, and the Charleston Naval Base. More citizens were staying in school longer, and the state's institutions of higher education were beginning to make their influence genuinely felt. In 1941, W.J. Cash, a South Carolinian, even called into question the very validity of the plantation myth of the Old South itself in the landmark book, *The Mind of the South*. And in December 1950 forty black parents initiated legal action in Clarendon County that challenged racial segregation of public schools, ultimately leading to the end of that practice in South Carolina.

During this period of growth and ferment, the state's cultural center—really, more properly now, centers—finally moved in and up from the coast. Charleston continued to be an important locus of activity, of course, but so was Columbia, the center of state government and home of the University of South Carolina, Allen University, Benedict College, the energetic Town Theatre, and an impressive art museum containing a surprisingly large number of important Renaissance paintings. So, too, were Spartanburg, the home of Wofford and Converse Colleges and the eastern end of the busiest two-lane concrete highway in the state in 1941; Greenville, the western terminus of this highway and the seat of Furman University and of more textile mills than anyone could shake a stick at, many of whose owners were beginning to exercise a profound philanthropic influence upon their region's culture; Clemson, where the college was nearly bursting at the seams with droves of returning servicemen after World War II and emerging as a university; Sumter, where both Claflin and Morris Colleges served the African-American population; and even much smaller towns like Newberry (Newberry College), Hartsville (Coker College), Due West (Erskine College), Gaffney (Limestone College), and Clinton (Presbyterian College), all of which boasted brave little centers of academe struggling fiercely to push, pull, shove, and, when necessary, wrench a formerly backward state into the full promise of the twentieth century. All of these institutions helped produce a significantly more literate and cultured population across the state, and this fact, coupled with increasing affluence and increased leisure time, was a powerful stimulus to a native literature. Not only did the larger number of college graduates increase the demand for good literature, but they also produced many of the authors of this new flowering of literary endeavor, both from among the ranks of their own faculty and from the numbers of a large body of professional men and women who fancied and then proved themselves to be authors as well. Thus, when the post-Poetry Society generation of South Carolina writers began to emerge, it was not accidental that they came from a variety of locations in the Palmetto State.

The Journalists

South Carolina has always had its share of journalist authors, and the early- to mid-twentieth century produced its share. An early representative of this period, **Carlyle McKinley (1847-1904)**,

William Watts Ball
*Courtesy, Caroliniana Library,
University of South Carolina*

actually served in the Confederate Army against Sherman outside Atlanta, and is remembered today for his backward-looking *An Appeal to Pharaoh* (1889), an argument for the deportation of former slaves, and occasionally for his nostalgic verses in praise of the conquered South of yesterday. Another journalist whose influence lingered longer was **William Watts Ball (1868-1952)**, born during Reconstruction, who spent much of his professional life championing conservative causes and opposing forces of change such as Roosevelt's New Deal and integration. Over the years he served as editor of the Columbia *Journal*, the Greenville *Daily News*, the Charleston *News and Courier*, and *The State*; During the 1920s he spent four years as dean of the School of Journalism at the University of South Carolina. *The State That Time Forgot* (1932) is his memoir of his family, his own life, and his state; it belongs to the old school of personal memoirs, graceful and easy-paced and speaking confidently of and for his community. **Robert Lathan (1881-1937)**, the youngest editor of any nationally known newspaper when he became editor of *The News and Courier* in 1910, also bears the distinction of being South Carolina's first recipient of the Pulitzer Prize for his editorial "The Plight of the South" in 1924; he further distinguished himself by his opposition to the policies of Governor Cole Blease.

From left, **Robert Lathan** and **Roger Peace**

Glenn Allan (1899-1955) was born in Summerville, received his B.S. from The Citadel in 1920, and also studied at Columbia University and Harvard University. He worked as a journalist for the *Greenville Piedmont* and the *Asheville Citizen* before joining the sports staffs of *The Atlanta Journal* and *The Atlanta Georgian*; later he was an editor for the Associated Press Feature Service and a sportswriter and columnist for the New York *Herald-Tribune*. He wrote short stories, many about the outdoors, for *Southern Golfer*, *Outdoor Life*, *The Saturday Evening Post*, and *Country Gentleman*. He was also the author of three novels: *Boysi Himself* (1946), *Little Sorrowful* (1946), and *Old Manoa* (1932).

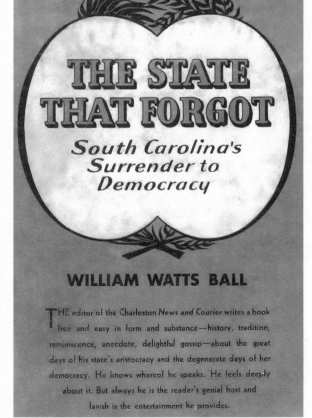

THE STATE THAT FORGOT

South Carolina's Surrender to Democracy

WILLIAM WATTS BALL

THE editor of the Charleston *News and Courier* writes a book free and easy in form and substance—history, tradition, reminiscence, anecdote, delightful gossip—about the great days of his state's aristocracy and the degenerate days of her democracy. He knows whereof he speaks. He feels deeply about it. But always he is the reader's genial host and lavish is the entertainment he provides.

Ball's memoir, *The State That Forgot*
Courtesy, Converse College

The South Carolina journalist to make the largest mark outside his region was unquestionably **Wilbur Joseph Cash (1900-1941)**. Born in Gaffney, where his father was the manager of the Limestone Mills company store, Cash was educated at Wake Forest College, worked briefly as a teacher and small-town reporter, and joined the staff of *The Charlotte News* in 1926. In addition to his work for the News, Cash produced a handful of essays for H. L. Mencken's *American Mercury* from 1929 to 1935. Altogether he wrote more than 1,300 articles, reviews, and editorials. Cash's *magnum opus*, of course, was the seminal *The Mind of the South*, which he worked on throughout the 1920s and 1930s. To say that the book caused a sensation would be an understatement; it was widely praised by the mainstream press of the North and South, by the NAACP, and the Guggenheim Foundation. From the moment it appeared until the present, it has been the one book that any serious student of the South must read and take account of. Cash was one of the few progressive newsmen of his generation in the South, and his hard-nosed examination of the impact of slavery upon Southern society as well as his critique of its religion of "primitive frenzy" and "blood sacrifice" and his shrewd recognition of the importance of the frontier as an influence upon Southerners resulted in a book that few readers, in 1941 or today, could accept passively. Following the publication of *The Mind of the South* in February of 1941, Cash departed for Mexico City with a new wife and a Guggenheim Fellowship, planning to write a novel. There he suffered a sudden, inexplicable mental collapse and on July 1 committed suicide. His book remains in print to this day. Cash was a 1995 inductee into the South Carolina Academy of Authors.

In contrast to McKinley and Ball and in some ways like Cash, **Ben Robertson (1903-1943)** made his mark as a consummately modern newspaperman. Born in Calhoun in Pickens County and educated at nearby Clemson, where he majored in botany, and the University of Missouri School of Journalism, Robertson worked for the Charleston *News and Courier* and the New York *Herald-Tribune*, as

THE MIND OF THE SOUTH

W. J. CASH

The philosophy, temperament, and social customs of the South brilliantly analyzed and interpreted, explaining how and why they developed and what their future is likely to be. It is a highly significant contribution toward our understanding of American life and manners.

ALFRED·A·KNOPF PUBLISHER·N·Y·

Cash's seminal book, which remains in print to this day

well as several newspapers overseas and the Associated Press, and then returned to his home in the Upstate to write a novel, *Travelers' Rest* (1938). Chastened by the lack of success of his novel, which he had had to publish himself, Robertson returned to journalism on the eve of World War II as overseas correspondent for *PM* magazine. When he returned home on leave, he spent his downtime writing *I Saw England* (1941), an account of the early stages of the German attack against the British. Unlike the earlier novel, *I Saw England* was widely praised, and, thus encouraged, Robertson wrote his best-known book, the Upcountry memoir *Red Hills and Cotton*, which was published in 1942. At the height of his creative powers, Robertson was en route to London to take charge of the New York *Herald-Tribune's* London bureau when his plane crashed in Portugal and he was killed. He was inducted posthumously into the South Carolina Academy of Authors in 1992.

Jonathan Worth Daniels (1902-1981) was born in Raleigh, North Carolina, but died on Hilton Head Island, where he was the founding editor of the *Island Packet* newspaper. He was educated at the University of North Carolina (A.B., 1921; M.A., 1922) and at Columbia University Law School (1923) before beginning a distinguished journalism career at the *Louisville Times* (1922-23). The majority of his time as a journalist was spent with the Raleigh *News and Observer*, where he was a reporter and Washington correspondent from 1923 to 1928, executive editor from 1947 to 1948, editor from 1948 to 1969, and editor emeritus from 1969 until his death in 1981. He also worked as an official of the U.S. Office of Civilian Defense (1942), as President Franklin Roosevelt's administrative assistant and press secretary (1943-1945), and was active in Democratic Party politics. His many books include the novel *Clash of Angels* (1930); the biographies *Stonewall Jackson* (1959)—which won the 1960 American Association of University Women Juvenile Award—*Mosby, Gray-Ghost of the Confederacy* (1959), and *Robert E. Lee* (1960); and the nonfiction titles *A Southerner Discovers the South* (1938), *A Southerner Discovers New England* (1940), *The Devil's Backbone: The Story of the Natchez Trace* (1962), *The Time Between the Wars: Armistice to Pearl Harbor* (1966), *The Randolphs of Virginia* (1972), and *White House Witness: 1942-1945* (1975).

Jonathan Worth Daniels

William Watts Ball's philosophical successor was **W.D. Workman, Jr. (1914-1990)**, journalist, politician, and spokesman for states' rights in the political upheavals of the 1950s, 1960s, and 1970s. Workman served as a reporter and capital reporter for the Charleston *News and Courier*, as assistant editor and then editor of *The State* in Columbia, and as a columnist and freelance writer for *Newsweek*, the Hall Syndicate, WIS radio and television, and others. His major legacy, however, is as one of the leaders of the modern Republican Party in South Carolina, under whose banner he ran for the United States Senate seat held by Olin Johnston in 1962. Although Workman lost the race, he demonstrated the viability of the Republican Party and thus laid the groundwork for its subsequent successes. His best-known books are *The Case for the South* (1960), a defense of the region's stand on integration, and *The Bishop from Barnwell* (1963), a study of state Senator Edgar A. Brown's impact upon state government.

The Palmetto State journalist who stood most squarely in the midst of the new progressivism that began to appear at mid-century was born at roughly the midpoint of William Ball's life but represents a dramatic departure in attitude. **Harry S. Ashmore (b. 1916)**, born in Greenville, became sensitized to the issues surrounding race relations in his native South while working on a cotton farm and delivering newspapers in a black neighborhood during his youth. After graduating from Clemson Agricultural College in 1937, Ashmore worked for the Greenville *Piedmont* and *News* and *The Charlotte News*, and then attended Harvard as a Nieman Fellow in Journalism. After distinguished service during World War II, Ashmore returned to *The Charlotte News* but left the paper in 1947 at the request of J.N. Heiskell, the publisher of the *Arkansas Gazette*. Ashmore then became the editorial conscience of the region as he penned an influential series of editorials on the subjects of equality of education, civil rights, and race relations in the South. His *The Negro and the Schools* (UNC Press, 1954) was followed by the equally important *An Epitaph for Dixie* in 1958 and two Pulitzer Prizes in the same year: the editorial award to Ashmore and the Public Service Award to the paper. "The newspaper's fearless and completely objective news coverage," wrote the Pulitzer committee, "plus its reasoned and moderate policy, did much to restore calmness and order to an overwrought community, reflecting great credit on its editors." This was no mean feat, of course, during the era of school desegregation in which the Arkansas governor defiantly resisted federal court orders in front of national television news cameras.

Ashmore continued to speak out against injustice during the course of his career. *Hearts and Minds: The Anatomy of Racism from Roosevelt to Reagan* (1982) brought his analysis into the Republican eighties on a cautiously optimistic note, but the larger perspective of his 1997 volume from the University of South Carolina Press, *Civil Rights and Wrongs: A Memoir of Race and Politics, 1944-1996*, cast a coldly realistic eye upon the relative lack of progress made by poorer blacks since the early days of desegregation. In 1989 Ashmore was honored by his alma mater by being named one of Clemson's "most distinguished alumni," and in 1995 he was inducted into the South Carolina Academy of Authors.

Among other twentieth-century journalists who have made a lasting mark in South Carolina and beyond were **Kyle Haselden (1913-1968)**, **Louis Cassels (1922-1974)**, and **Bob Talbert (1936-1999)**. Haselden, a native of Florence County, attended Furman University (B.A., 1943) and Colgate Rochester Divinity School (B.D., 1937). After serving a number of pastorates, he became a staff member and then managing editor of *The Christian Century*, which

Louis Cassels

during his tenure spoke out boldly in favor of civil rights and against the war in Vietnam; he was the author of six books. Cassels wrote for United Press, later United Press International, and eventually rose to become the religion editor of UPI. His column "Religion in America" appeared in more than 400 newspapers, and he was the author of more than a dozen books, mostly on religious subjects. Born in Spartanburg in 1936, Talbert graduated from the University of South Carolina with a degree in journalism in 1958 and began his career as a sportswriter in Spartanburg. From there he moved to Columbia where he wrote a popular column for both *The State* and *Columbia Record* before he was recruited away by the *Detroit Free Press* in 1968. Widely popular in Detroit, Talbert hit his stride with a column combining personal openness with an unusual ability to find topics of interest to the ordinary citizens of his adopted city. As a result, he was eulogized by his colleagues as a "beloved columnist" who "was always the ringmaster of whatever circus he was part of" when he died in 1999 of complications following heart surgery after thirty-one years with the newspaper. A collection of his columns, *Good Moanin'*, was published by the paper in 1984.

Bob Talbert

One magazine journalist deserves mention in this space. **John Shaw Billings (1898-1975)**, a native of Beech Island, began his career as a reporter for the Bridgeport, Connecticut, *Telegram* after returning from World War I. He then worked for the *Brooklyn Eagle* and *Time* magazine, where by 1933 he became managing editor. When *Life* magazine debuted in 1936, Billings was prevailed upon to become its managing editor, a position he retained until 1944, when he became editorial director of Time, Inc. After his death in 1975, Billings's estate provided the first endowment ever received by the then-new Thomas Cooper Library at the University of South Carolina; the South Caroliniana Library at USC is the repository of Billings's papers.

A businessman and a businessman's wife

Few figures cut as wide a swath in twentieth-century South Carolina as **Elliott White Springs (1896-1959)**, who had distinct careers as a flying ace in World Wars I and II, as the chairman of one of the most successful textile firms in the state, and as the popular author of nine books and dozens of widely published short stories. Springs was born in Lancaster in 1896 and educated at a private academy in Asheville, at Princeton, and at the Oxford School of Military Aeronautics during World War I. By the end of the war, when he was only twenty-two years old, Springs had become a captain and a squadron commander who had earned both the British Flying Cross and the American Distinguished Service Cross.

Elliott White Springs
Courtesy, Springs Industries

Between the World Wars, Springs discovered his talent as a writer, most notably as author of *War Birds: The Diary of an Unknown Aviator* (1926), an acknowledged classic, but also of *Nocturne Militaire* (1927), *Above the Bright Blue Sky* (short stories, 1928),

The Rise and Fall of Carol Banks (1931), *Clothes Make the Man* (1949), and others. His story "Fed Up" appeared in anthologies of *Best Short Stories of the War* (1931) and of aviation stories: *This Winged World* (1946). When Springs's father died during the depths of the Depression and the young man found himself the head of the family firm at age thirty-five, he quickly set about reorganizing the company. Combining a top-to-bottom mastery of textiles with a shrewd business sense and uncanny marketing ability, he turned Springs Cotton Mills into an industry leader. Although taking time off during World War II to again serve in the Air Force, Springs devoted most of the remainder of his life to his business. A respected philanthropist and friend of governors, he left a notable void at his death in 1959; in 1985 he was inducted into the South Carolina Business Hall of Fame. And in 2000 he was honored with induction into the South Carolina Academy of Authors.

Another South Carolina writer from a family of wealth and privilege, **Elizabeth Boatwright Coker (1909-1993)** was a friend of Elliott White Springs and shared his fondness for fast sports cars. She even featured him as a thinly disguised character, the aviator

Elizabeth Boatwright Coker
Courtesy, Converse College

son Aaron, in her novel *The Bees*. Born in 1908 in Darlington, Coker was educated in the public schools of that city and at Converse College. Having begun to write while she was in high school, Coker was editor of the Converse literary magazine, *Concept*, and she won prizes awarded by the Poetry Society of South Carolina while in college as well. Encouraged by these successes, Coker traveled to New York City after her graduation and in 1929 applied for a job with *The New York Times*. "They laughed at me," the author told Patti Just in her 1993 interview for *The Writers' Circle of South Carolina*, and "I became a model." Her prospects seemed to have improved when the *Times* reversed itself and expressed interest in her in October of the same year, but on the same day that she received the notice from the newspaper, her father called from Darlington—the Depression had begun—to say that his bank had failed and to ask her to come home. The die was cast: she returned home and subordinated her own literary ambitions first to the needs of her father and then to the demands of her own family. Although she continued to write during the next twenty years, and although Robert Frost praised a story of hers at the Middlebury Writers Conference in 1939 and told her that she should turn it into a novel, her first book, *Daughter of Strangers*, was not to appear until 1950. When it did, it became an instant hit at the annual meeting of the National Association of Manufacturers in Hot Springs, Virginia, which Coker attended with her husband, James Lide Coker III, a business executive. In October of the same year she found herself introduced at the Coker College Literary Festival by none other than James A. Michener and began to suspect that she had a hit. She did: *Daughter of Strangers* remained on *The New York Times* bestseller list for six months and became the largest bestseller ever in South Africa.

Other successes followed. By the time of her death she had written eight more historical romances which, together with her personal grace and charm, endeared her to South Carolinians throughout the state. After her husband's death she continued to live in their home in Hartsville, venturing out from time to time to address book clubs, university audiences, and other groups. Invariably she talked about "the three me's: corporate wife, doting mother, and closet writer." A member of *Who's Who In America* and *Who's Who In the World*, she was also a 1991 inductee in the South Carolina Academy of Authors.

The Academics

In the twentieth century as at other times in the state's history, writers identified primarily as members of the academic community played a large role in South Carolina's literary life. Among the earliest and most interesting of these was **Ludwig Lewisohn (1882-1955)**, who was born in Berlin but grew up and was educated in Charleston, where his family had moved in search of a better life. A convert to Methodism in his teens, Lewisohn enthusiastically entered into the life of his adopted home city and in 1901 graduated from the College of Charleston with a B.A. in English Literature. He received a M.A. from Columbia University in 1903 and thereafter spent his professional life in other parts of the country, serving variously as a publisher's editor, a freelance writer, a German instructor, drama editor and then associate editor of *The Nation*. He was also a successful novelist, a spokesman for the Zionist movement as editor of the magazine *New Palestine*, and finally an English professor at Brandeis University. Discriminated against over the years for his Jewish heritage, his opposition to World War I, and his German background, and constrained by an unhappy youthful marriage, Lewisohn's early adulthood was a time of turmoil and change. His personal transformations during these years are reflected in the themes of his novels *The Case of Mr. Crump* (1926) and *The Island Within* (1928). His interest in the larger worlds of cultural and world history is evident in nonliterary works like *Israel* (1925), *The Answer: The Jew and the World* (1939), and *The American Jew: Character and Destiny* (1950). Lewisohn also made original contributions to German and American literary history.

Of special relevance to literary South Carolina is Lewisohn's own "Books We Have Made: A History of Literature in South Carolina," a newspaper series that appeared in the Charleston *News and Courier* between July 5 and September 20, 1903. This series, which runs to more than sixty double-column pages in photographic facsimile, is remarkable for its breadth, its depth, and the independence of its author's viewpoint. Although he was only twenty-one when the series appeared, Lewisohn was well read enough in the literature of South Carolina to survey the writings of the early historians, to write at length about the publishers of the Confederacy and about the literary periodicals of mid-nineteenth-century Charleston, and to offer modern-sounding judgments of some of the "classical" authors of the state. He maintained, for example, that "...Timrod is not a great poet, not even of the second order" (p. 57). Of Simms he wrote, "Simms's prose style is a style of the coarsest texture" (p. 46) and "'Atalantis,' the most ambitious poem of Simms, deserves to be mentioned only because it was dear to him" (p. 49). But Lewisohn also recognized that Simms had made a significant contribution in *The Yemassee*, a view that has been sustained by modern criticism: "*The Yemassee*, Simms's masterpiece and a truly remarkable book to have been written by a self-trained man of 29 ... bears witness to the original strength of Simms's talent" (p. 48). The young Lewisohn had an intuitive understanding of literature and a facile way of discussing it. We are the poorer for not having a modern scholarly edition of his series today.

Kelly Miller (1863-1939) was one of four prominent African-American academicians from the Palmetto State whose influence extended far beyond the state's boundaries. Together with Benjamin Brawley, Nick Aaron Ford, and Benjamin Mays, he became a spokesman for and chronicler of the issues facing his people. The son of a free African-American father and a slave mother, Miller was born near Winnsboro, and was educated at Fairfield Institute, a Presbyterian school for former slaves, and Howard University, which he attended on a scholarship. While at Howard, Miller also worked at the U.S. Pension Office, a position which, combined with his tenacious frugality, enabled him to purchase the land that his family farmed and to present it to them as a graduation gift to the family. After graduating from Howard, Miller studied at Johns Hopkins University and taught at Washington High School until he returned to Howard as a member of its faculty. At Howard, Miller became the dean of the College of Arts and Sciences and embarked upon a writing career that was to see him become published in most of the major magazines and newspapers of his era. In addition to his own column, "Kelly Miller Speaks," which was published in more than a hundred papers, Miller published articles in *Popular Science*, *Atlantic Monthly*, *Crisis*, *The Independent*, *The Journal of Negro History*, and elsewhere. His subjects were race relations and social equality, religion, education, and morality. He was a member of the American Negro Academy and was a 1993 inductee of the South Carolina Academy of Authors.

Kelly Miller

Benjamin Griffith Brawley (1882-1939) was perhaps South Carolina's most prolific African-American writer. Through his many books and articles he did much both to legitimize and to popularize the works of other African-American writers, especially Paul Laurence Dunbar. Brawley was born in Columbia and educated at Atlanta Baptist College (the former name of Morehouse), the University of Chicago, and Harvard. He taught at Morehouse from 1902 to 1910 and again from 1912 to 1920, at Howard University (1910-1912 and 1931-1939), and at Shaw University in Raleigh (1923-1931). An ordained Baptist minister like Benjamin Mays, Brawley also served a congregation in Brockton, Massachusetts, for a year and took another year off from teaching to undertake a sociological and educational survey in Liberia. It was as a scholar and a teacher that Brawley made his mark. A moralist, a conservative, and a traditionalist, his *The Negro in Literature and Art in the United States* (1918) and *A Social History of the American Negro* (1921) were important early manifestations of and influences upon the Harlem Renaissance. The range of his interests is indicated by the titles of his works: *The Problem and Other Poems* (1905), *A Short History of the American Negro* (1913), *The Seven Sleepers of Ephesus* (1917), *Africa and the War* (1918), *A New Survey of English Literature* (1925), *Freshman Year English* (1929), *A History of the English Hymn* (1932), *Negro Builders and Heroes* (1937), and *The Negro Genius* (1937). *Paul Laurence Dunbar: Poet of His People* (1936) and *The Best Stories of Paul Laurence Dunbar* (1938) helped to reintroduce Dunbar to a generation unfamiliar with the work of the writer who had died more than thirty years earlier. Brawley is an inductee of the South Carolina Academy of Authors.

John Andrew Rice (1888-1968), a native of Lynchburg, was educated at Tulane and at Queen's College, Oxford University, which he attended as a Rhodes Scholar. After serving brief tenures at the University of Nebraska and at Rollins College, Rice achieved the stature that was to give him his claim to fame when he and other disaffected faculty members and students left Rollins and founded the experimental Black Mountain College in the mountains near Asheville. The story of the Black Mountain experiment is told in detail and with understanding by Martin Duberman in *Black Mountain: An Exploration of Community* (Dutton, 1972). In spite of attracting some of the most original and influential artists and thinkers of the day—including, at various times, Josef and Anni Albers, Eric Bentley, Robert Creeley, Charles Olson, Francine du Plessix Gray, John Wallen, John Cage, Merce Cunningham, Robert Duncan, Joel Oppenheimer, and R. Buckminster Fuller—the College ultimately failed in 1956, although much of its vision and its innovative concept of a closely-knit community of scholars, artists, and students living and working and learning together survive today in a variety of manifestations. Always a difficult personality, Rice left Black Mountain in the late thirties under the cloud of an affair with a student. Rice's inimitable memoir, *I Came Out of the*

Eighteenth Century, which contains a chapter on his Black Mountain experience, is a classic that reveals both an original mind and the passing of the way of life that nurtured it in its formative years. Rice was also an accomplished writer of short fiction, which appeared in *Harper's, Collier's, The New Yorker*, and several prize collections. His own collection is titled *Local Color*, and one of its stories, "Miss Hattie," is reprinted in *South Carolina in the Short Story*.

James McBride Dabbs

James McBride Dabbs (1896-1970) wrote more and had a larger, if different, influence than did Rice. Educated in Sumter County where the family plantation, Rip Raps, was located, Dabbs settled into a college teaching career after being educated at the University of South Carolina, at Clark University, and at Columbia University. He also served in the American Army in France during 1918. Dabbs taught briefly at USC and then moved on to Coker College, where he ended his career after serving as chairman of the English department from 1925 to 1937. Dabbs then entered into a new career as a gentleman farmer and freelance writer. He wrote publicly and with a sense of moral rectitude—as well as with wit and a sense of humor—about civil rights and race relations at a time when few other white Southerners were doing so, speaking as the conscience of his community although many members of that community would have rejected the title. His most eloquent works were *The Southern Heritage* (1958) and *Who Speaks for the South?* (1964). *The Road Home* (1960), a memoir of his spiritual and intellectual pilgrimage, has come to be considered by many to be a modern Southern classic in the genre. He himself regarded *Haunted by God*, published after his death by his second wife, Edith Mitchell Dabbs, his most important book. Few South Carolinians have written so powerfully about the subjects Dabbs felt genuinely compelled to write about; as a result, Dabbs has been called "South Carolina's most distinguished resident essayist" by Tom Johnson, a serious student of Dabbs's work and author of a doctoral dissertation on Dabbs's life and work. Dabbs was a 1990 inductee of the South Carolina Academy of Authors.

Benjamin Mays

Benjamin Elijah Mays (1895-1984) exerted a significant influence upon the civil rights movement in this country, especially in the 1950s and 1960s. Born in Epworth in Greenwood County, he received his undergraduate degree from Bates College and his Master's and doctorate from the University of Chicago. He taught at Morehouse and South Carolina State Colleges, was dean of religion at Howard University, and served for twenty-seven years as president of Morehouse. An ordained Baptist minister, Mays exerted his moral conscience upon every endeavor in which participated. He acted to quell extremist actions in the conflict between the races, and he advised the Reverend Martin Luther King, Jr., a former student of Mays's at Morehouse, who called the older man "my spiritual mentor." His publications include the first sociological study of African-American religion, *The Negro's Church* (1933), as well as *The Negro's God* (1938), *Disturbed About Man* (1969), and the memoir *Born to Rebel* (1971). In 1982 the NAACP awarded him its Spingarn Medal. In 1997 Mays was inducted into the ranks of the South Carolina Academy of Authors.

Havilah Babcock (1898-1964), a contemporary of both Rice and Dabbs, wrote a more genial variety of prose about less weighty subjects. During his lifetime he was beloved by hundreds of students who passed through his classes at the University of South Carolina. A native Virginian, Babcock attended Elon College, the University of Virginia, Columbia University, and the University of South Carolina. He taught at Elon, the College of William and Mary, and the University of South Carolina. His undergraduate vocabulary course was a perennial favorite, and his *I Want a Word* is still cited by his former students as one of the most influential books in the entire course of their higher education. During his lifetime Babcock contributed nearly two hundred stories of the outdoors to a wide range of national sporting magazines, and collections of these stories—*My Health is Better in November* (1947) and *Tales of Quails 'N Such* (1951)—remain in print. Babcock is a 2001 inductee of the South Carolina Academy of Authors.

Havilah Babcock

Alexander Sprunt, Jr. (1898-1973), like Babcock, is remembered as a writer of the outdoors, but more as a naturalist than a sportsman. His *South Carolina Bird Life* (1949) is still the classic in its field. Sprunt was born in Charleston and educated there, at Porter Military Academy and Smith School, before matriculating at Davidson College. A staff member of the National Audubon Society, Sprunt was a Fellow of the American Ornithologists Union and Honorary Curator of Ornithology at the Charleston Museum. In addition to his major work on the state's birds, Sprunt also wrote stories and sketches for magazines such as *Nature Magazine*, *Bird Lore*, and *Audubon Magazine* as well as for popular publications like *St. Nicholas Magazine*, *Ladies' Home Journal*, and *Good Housekeeping*. Many of his stories are collected in *Dwellers of the Silences* (1931). "The Hunters of the Moonlight," selected for *South Carolina in the Short Story*, is typical in its easy narrative flow combined with passages of almost poetic description.

Nick Aaron Ford (1904-1984), like Kelly Miller, was born in a small South Carolina town, was educated outside the South, and lived his professional life elsewhere. Ford's formative years were spent in South Carolina: he was born in Ridgeway and educated as an undergraduate at Benedict College in Columbia. From there he went to the University of Iowa, where he received an M.A. in 1934 and a Ph.D. in 1945. His professional life began in small Southern colleges—Florida Memorial College in St. Augustine and St. Philips Junior College in San Antonio—but came to fruition at Langston University in Oklahoma and then at Morgan State College in Baltimore. Early on he developed a scholarly interest in African-American literature, publishing *The Contemporary Negro Novel* in 1936 and editing the important early anthology *Best Short Stories by Afro-American Writers, 1925 to 1950* in 1950. A poet himself,

Ford also edited texts for undergraduates (*Extending Horizons: A Freshman College Reader*, 1967; and *Language in Uniform: A Reader on Propaganda*, 1967) and wrote a personal memoir, *Seeking a Newer World: Memoirs of a Black American Teacher* (1983). He served as president of the College Language Association (1960-1962) and was a member of the board of directors of the National Council of Teachers of English (1964-1967).

Lodwick Charles Hartley (1906-1979) received his B.A. from Furman University (1927), his M.A. from Columbia University (1928), and his Ph.D. from Princeton University (1937). He served as the chairman of the English department at North Carolina State University from 1940 until he retired in 1971, during which time he wrote biographies of the English writers Laurence Sterne and William Cowper and dozens of scholarly articles on eighteenth-century English literature and Southern literature in journals such as *PMLA*, *The Sewanee Review*, *Texas Quarterly*, and *Bibliographic Society of America*.

Louis B. Wright (1899-1984), one of the most erudite of South Carolina's twentieth-century writers, capped a long and distinguished academic career by serving as the director of the Folger Shakespeare Library in Washington from 1948 to 1968. Born in Greenwood, Wright was educated at Wofford College (B.A., 1920) and at the University of North Carolina at Chapel Hill (M.A., 1924; Ph.D., 1926) after brief service during World War I. He taught at North Carolina and worked as a research scholar at Johns Hopkins and then as a visiting scholar and a member of the permanent research group at the Huntington Library in San Marino, California, before assuming his duties at the Folger. He also taught as a visiting professor at a number of large universities across the country. His primary research interests were Colonial American and Renaissance English history, and his numerous scholarly publications were largely concentrated in these areas as well. He edited many of Shakespeare's plays for the Folger, and he edited the diary of William Byrd of Virginia (1941) as well as an important anthology of American literature (1955). Although he was a scholar and not a writer of imaginative fiction or poetry, few South Carolinians of any era have had as large an influence as Louis B. Wright upon the reading and study of American and English literature and history. In addition, two of his books—*Barefoot in Arcadia* (1974) and *Of Books and Men* (1976)—are models of a kind of urbane, gentlemanly prose that is all too rare.

Columbia native **Francis Marion (Frank) Durham (1913-1971)** played a significant role in literary South Carolina not only as the author of original plays but also as a biographer, editor, and critic of the works of two of the state's most important writers, Julia Peterkin and DuBose Heyward. After being educated at the University of South Carolina, the University of North Carolina, and Columbia University, Durham taught at Clemson University, at The Citadel for more than twenty years, and at the University of South Carolina

Louis B. Wright
Courtesy, Wofford College

from 1964 until his death. While at The Citadel he was a Fulbright visiting professor in Australia (1958-1959) and a Smith-Mundt lecturer in Vietnam (1961-1962), the latter an experience that moved him deeply and about which he wrote in depth in a number of periodicals after his return to this country. His books include the plays *Fire of the Lord* (1937) and *My Late Espoused Saint* (1937), *Government in Greater Cleveland* (1963), and *Studies in Cane* (1971); but his major works are his biography of DuBose Heyward, *DuBose Heyward: The Man Who Wrote Porgy* (1954) and his edition of *The Collected Short Stories of Julia Peterkin* (1970). Durham also played a significant role in the founding and early success of *The South Carolina Review*, and upon his death the current editor wrote, "When we thought about founding this *Review*, we went at once to the only man of letters in the state who had the experience to help us make it succeed. ... With Frank Durham's death in October, the state has lost one of its finest wits and most versatile men of letters. We have lost a co-editor. And many of us have lost a friend" (Volume 4, number 1 [December 1971], p. 3).

C(larence) Hugh Holman (b. 1914) is one of the "North Carolina expatriates," the name applied by archivist and librarian Tom Johnson to that important group of South Carolinians—including Holman, W.J. Cash, Louis B. Wright, Louis D. Rubin, Jr., and Max Steele—who established their professional lives and reputations in the Tarheel State. Holman was born in Cross Anchor, received both B.S. (1936) and A.B. (1936) degrees from Presbyterian College, and then went on to study at the University of North Carolina (Ph.D., 1949). He held a variety of administrative positions at Presbyterian and at UNC, including, at the latter, chairman of the Board of Governors of the University Press (1959-1962), dean of the graduate school (1963-1966), provost (1966-1968), and special assistant to the chancellor (1972-1978). Early in his career Holman wrote a series of mystery novels including *Death like Thunder* (1942), *Trout in the Milk* (1946), *Up This Crooked Way* (1946), *Another Man's Poison* (1947), and *Small Town Corpse* (1951), the latter writing as "Clarence Hunt." As a scholar, his interests ranged widely over the field of Southern literature but especially prose fiction. His titles in this area include *Thomas Wolfe* (1960), *The Thomas Wolfe Reader* (1962), *The Letters of Thomas Wolfe* (with Sue Fields Ross, 1968), *Studies in Thomas Wolfe* (1975), and *The Immoderate Past: The Southern Writer and History* (1977). He is the co-author, with W.F. Thrall and Addison Hibbard, of the popular *Handbook to Literature* (1960) and also co-authored important studies with Louis D. Rubin, Jr., and others; again with Rubin, he was a founding editor of the *The Southern Literary Journal*. He has served on the advisory boards of a number of encyclopedias and journals and has been an officer of the South Atlantic Modern Language Association, the Modern Language Association of America, and the Southeastern American Studies Association. His awards include a Guggenheim Fellowship (1967), the Thomas

From left, **James Dickey**, **Betty** and **Monroe Spears**. At back, **Charles Israel**
Courtesy, Thomas L. Johnson

Jefferson Award (1975), an honorary D.Litt. from Presbyterian College (1963), and a fellowship in the American Academy of Arts and Sciences. His journal publications are legion.

Monroe K. Spears (1916-1998) grew up in Darlington, where his high school teachers included William Stanley Hoole, later to become dean of the libraries at the University of Alabama, and M.A. Owings, who received his M.A. and Ph.D. from Vanderbilt. Spears himself went on to the University of South Carolina (A.B., A.M., 1937), Princeton University (Ph.D., 1940) and a teaching career that took him to the University of Wisconsin (1940-1942), to Vanderbilt University (1946-1952), to the University of the South (Sewanee, 1952-1964), and, finally, to Rice University, where he was Moody Professor of English. At Vanderbilt he became friends with Robert Penn Warren and Allen Tate and even "sat in on Donald Davidson's classes" (*South Carolina Review*, Volume 26, number 1, p. 183). Among his students there were James Dickey and Madison Jones. At Sewanee he was a colleague of Andrew Lytle and taught, among others, the writer Richard Tillinghast. Spears was both a poet (*A Word in Your Ear*, 2002, and *The Levitator and Other Poems*, 1975) and an important editor responsible for the publication of some of the best American poets of the twentieth century during his editorship of *The Sewanee Review*. He was also a critic who published shrewd analyses of the work of modernists W.H. Auden (*The Poetry of W.H. Auden: The Disenchanted Island*, 1963) and Hart Crane (*Hart Crane*, 1965) and a textual editor of the work of the eighteenth-century English poet Matthew Prior (with H. Bunker Wright, 2 vols., 1959). His influential *Dionysus and the City* (1970) is a broad study of modern poetry and its contexts, and the volumes *American Ambitions* (1987) and *Countries of the Mind* (1992) collect his best essays. Spears was inducted into the South Carolina Academy of Authors in 1993.

One of the grand old men of South Carolina letters when this volume was being written, **Max Steele (b. 1922)** has long had a reputation as a master of fiction, especially short fiction. Born in Greenville, Steele attended Furman University before transferring after two years to the University of North Carolina at Chapel Hill. His university education was interrupted by military service during World War II, but even then he attended Vanderbilt and UCLA as a cadet in the Air Corps. Steele received his degree from North Carolina in 1946 and almost immediately won a fellowship from the Eugene F. Saxton Memorial Trust, which allowed him to write the novel *Debbie*, published in 1950, the recipient of both the Harper Prize Novel Contest and the Mayflower Award. After studying

Max Steele

painting and French abroad during a stint as advisory editor to the *Paris Review*, Steele settled into a university teaching career, all but two years of which he served at North Carolina as writer-in-residence and later director of the creative writing program. During his long and distinguished career, Steele won multiple O. Henry Prize Story awards, fellowships from the National Foundation on the Arts and Humanities, and recognition for excellence as a classroom teacher. His stories appeared in the best magazine fiction markets, including *Harper's Magazine*, *The Atlantic Monthly*, *Collier's*, and *Cosmopolitan*, and he collected a number himself for his *Where She Brushed Her Hair*. He was inducted into the South Carolina Academy of Authors in 1992.

Novelists (including a politician)

Two late nineteenth-early twentieth-century South Carolina novelists who did not find a wide readership until later were **Orlando Benedict Mayer (1818-1891)** and **Zach McGhee (1872-1911)**. Mayer, a physician from Newberry, wrote sketches of life in the Dutch Fork area of Richland County that have been published as *The Dutch Fork* (The Dutch Fork Press, 1981), as well as the longer *John Punterick: A Novel of Life in the Old Dutch Fork* (The Reprint Co., 1981). During his lifetime he published *Mallodoce the Briton: His Wanderings from Druidism to Christianity* (E. Waddey Co., 1891). McGhee is remembered primarily for *The Dark Corner* (The Grafton Press, 1908), about northeastern Greenville County. He also published the less highly finished *Life at The Citadel: A Sketchbook Containing a Collection of Verse, Comic Essays, Parodies, Humorous Delinquent Reports, and Amusing Incidents, Illustrative of the Life of a Cadet at the South Carolina Military College* (Walker, Evans, & Cogswell, 1891).

Orlando Benedict Mayer

Marie Conway Oemler (1879-1932), born in Savannah and an approximate contemporary of McGhee, was educated at private and convent schools and at home. She lived most of her life in Savannah, where her husband was also from, but is buried in Charleston. She published her novel *Johnny Reb* in 1929, three years before her death.

A curious but inescapably appealing figure in the history of South Carolina literature, **Bernard Adolph Rodrigues Ottolengui (ca. 1861-1937)** was born to parents who were both writers in Charleston, where he was reared but which he left for New York City in 1877. In New York he practiced dentistry and orthodontics, making major contributions to both and also laying the groundwork for the field of forensic dentistry, which figures in some of his mystery stories and novels. His novels include *Conya: A Romance of the Buddhas*, *An Artist in Crime*, *Conflict of Evidence*, and *A Modern Wizard*. Ottolengui's story "The Nameless Man" appears in *The Death of the Clever Criminal: Isaac Asimov Presents the Best Crime Stories of the Nineteenth Century* (Knightsbridge Publishing, 1990). He also published *Methods of Filling Teeth* (1899) and *Table Talks on Dentistry* (1935) and was an expert on butterflies and moths.

Elliott White Springs and Elizabeth Boatwright Coker were not the only South Carolina novelists to find a readership in their native state in the first part of the twentieth century. **Elliott Crayton McCants (1865-1953)** was born at Silent Hill, the family plantation near Ninety Six, and graduated from The Citadel. After teaching in a number of schools throughout the Southeast, McCants became Superintendent of Education in Anderson, where he also wrote a column for the *The Daily Mail* and the *Independent*. McCants wrote some two hundred short stories and published many in *National Magazine*, *The People's Home Journal*, *Everybody's Magazine*, and elsewhere. His published books include three novels set in and around Ninety Six—*In the Red Hills: A Story of the Carolina Country* (1904), *White Oak Farm* (1928), and *Ninety Six* (1930)—a textbook for fourth graders (*History, Stories, and Legends of South Carolina*, 1927), and a collection of short stories. He received honorary degrees from The Citadel and the University of South Carolina and was inducted into the South Carolina Academy of Authors in 1996.

Thornwell Jacobs (1877-1956) was born and reared in Clinton, the home of the orphanage that today bears his name. He attended Presbyterian College (A.B., 1894; A.M., 1895), Princeton University (A.M., 1899), and Princeton Theological Seminary (1899), and became an ordained Presbyterian minister in 1899. He was the founder of Oglethorpe University in Atlanta, which he served as president from 1915 onwards. During his lifetime he published a variety of religious and fictional works as well as poetry. Among his many books are two collections of poems; *The Midnight Mummer, and Other Poems* (1911) and *Islands of the Blest, and Other Poems* (1928)—the novels *The Law of the White Circle* (1908), about race riots, *Red Lanterns on St. Michael's*, a Civil War story, and *Drums of Doomsday* (1942); and *The New Science and the Old Religion* (1927), a treatise on evolution.

Octavus Roy Cohen (1891-1959) was another mystery writer from Charleston. He graduated from Clemson College (1911) and Birmingham Southern College (1927) and practiced law briefly before turning to a career in journalism and freelance writing. He worked for *The Birmingham Ledger*, the Charleston *News and Courier*, *The Bayonne Times*, and *Newark Morning Star*, but he was best known as an author of detective mystery novels and short stories and of paternalistic comic stories featuring simple black characters that do not sit well with modern sensibilities. His character Florian Slappey, featured in *Florian Slappey Goes Abroad* (1928) and *Florian Slappey* (1938), was one of the first fictional black private eyes; while Jim Hanvey, the hero of *Jim Hanvey, Detective* (1923) and *Detours* (1927) and others, was sort of a knee-slapping, white cracker detective. Altogether, Cohen published more than fifty books and wrote more than twenty screenplays. His short stories appeared frequently in *The Saturday Evening Post* as well as *Collier's* and elsewhere. The 1937 Republic Pictures film *Jim Hanvey, Detective*, was based upon Cohen's 1923 novel. His play, *Come Seven*, featuring the character Florian Slappey, appeared on Broadway in 1920; and the novel, *The Crimson Alibi* (1919) was also adapted for the stage.

Samuel Gaillard Stoney, Jr. (1891-1968) was born in Charleston into an established family who owned three plantations along the tidewater rivers. Educated at Porter Military Academy, the University of the South, and the College of Charleston (B.S., 1912), he served in the South Carolina militia during the Mexican War and briefly in the United States Army in France at the end of World War I. After attending Georgia Tech, where he received his architecture degree in 1923, he established a successful practice in New York City. Professional and social contacts in the city led to his friendship with Martha Bensley Bruere, an illustrator, who provided Stoney both entry into the publishing world and the pictures for his first book, *Black Genesis* (1930), a collection of Gullah tales and sketches. His second book, the Lowcountry Huguenot novel *Po' Buckra*, appeared the same year. Today, however, Stoney is more likely to be remembered for his work on Charleston architecture, history, and historic preservation. His three books, *Charleston: Azaleas and Old Bricks* (photographs by Bayard Morgan Wooton, 1937), *Plantations of the Low Country* (1938), and *This Is Charleston* (1944), have all been frequently reprinted. *This Is Charleston*, an historical architectural survey, remains especially important today. After the failure of his marriage to the poet Frances Frost in the 1930s, Stoney gave up the practice of architecture and devoted the remainder of his life to writing and to promoting the preservation of the architectural and cultural heritage of his native city. He taught classes in the history of art at the College of Charleston until two years before his death in 1968. He received an honorary Doctor of Letters degree from the college, and in 1991 he became a posthumous inductee into the South Carolina Academy of Authors.

Paul Hyde Bonner (1893-1968), a native New Yorker, graduated from Phillips Exeter Academy (1911) and Harvard University (1915), served in the United States Army during World War I, and worked for a dozen years for the Stehli Silks Corporation. After service in the United States Army Air Corps in World War II, he accepted appointments with the United States State Department in Paris and Rome. Drawing upon these experiences, in the 1950s and 1960s he wrote a series of novels set against the Cold War background of post-World War II Europe. Among these are *S.P.Q.R.* (1953), *Hotel Talleyrand* (perhaps his best-received book, 1954), *Excelsior!* (1955), *With Both Eyes Open* (1957), *Amanda* (1958), *The Art of Llewellyn Jones* (1960), and *Ambassador Extraordinary* (1962). Bonner also published two collections of hunting and fishing stories—*Aged in the Woods* (1959) and *The Glorious Mornings* (1956)—many of which had previously appeared in *Sports Illustrated*, *Esquire*, and *Holiday*. Other sketches and stories appeared in *The*

Atlantic and *The New Yorker*. Bonner died in Charleston, where he was a member of the Carolina Yacht Club.

Nell S. Graydon (1893-1986), a native of Pineville, North Carolina, and a graduate of Elizabeth College in Charlotte, became interested in the history of South Carolina during stays in her summer home on Edisto Island. This interest led first to the publication of stories in *The State Magazine* and then to her first book, *Tales of Edisto* (1955). The immediate and widespread success of this title encouraged Graydon to write more, with the result that she eventually published nine additional volumes. These included novels—*Another Jezebel* (1958), the fictionalized story of the life of a Confederate spy, and *Eliza of Wapoo: A Tale of Indigo* (1967), based on the life of Eliza Lucas Pinckney—as well as further collections of ghost stories and tales—*Tales of Beaufort* (1963) and *Tales of Columbia* (1964)—the cookbook *From My House to Your House* (1968), and even a garden book, *South Carolina Gardens* (1973).

Chalmers Swinton Murray (1894-1975) was born on Edisto Island and attended The Citadel and the University of South Carolina. He was a newspaperman, editing the *Georgetown Times* from 1926 to 1931, and was admitted to the South Carolina Bar in 1927, but he served as district director of the Federal Writers Project from 1938 to 1940 and became a freelance writer in the mid-1940s. He wrote a series of newspaper pieces on Sea Island Gullah lore and the novel *Here Comes Joe Mungin* (1942), which featured a black character very different from the smiling Uncle Toms who populated much popular fiction of the day. He also wrote *This Is Our Land: The Story of the Agricultural Society of South Carolina* (1949).

Kate Lily Blue was born in Marion and was educated privately, sometimes with tutors. Active throughout her life in the civic and cultural affairs of her hometown, she was a member of the Daughters of the American Revolution, the United Daughters of the Confederacy, and the American Legion Auxiliary; she also oversaw the operations of several farms. In 1895 she published *The Hand of Fate: A Romance of the Navy*. She also wrote *The History of Marion County, South Carolina, and the Background of Her Present and Future Development*, a radio address for WBT, Charlotte, in November 1933; and prepared the "Historical Background of Marion County" for the University of South Carolina *Bulletin* (1923).

Katharine Ball Ripley (1898-1955), born in Charleston and educated in Virginia and at Converse College, began writing while she was still in school and had published two memoirs, *Sand in My Shoes* (1931) and *Sand Dollars* (1933), by the time her novel, *Crowded House*, appeared in 1936 and was praised by DuBose Heyward for the "universality" of its characters' appeal. By this time, too, Ripley was collaborating with her husband, **Clements Ripley (1892-1954)**, a native of Washington state, on Hollywood treatments of some of the adventure stories he was selling to pulp magazines as well as to such mainstream publications as *The American*

Magazine, *Argosy*, *Collier's*, *Cosmopolitan*, *The Philadelphia Inquirer*, *Redbook Magazine*, *The Saturday Evening Post*, and *This Week*. Clem Ripley worked on film adaptations of his own novels—he wrote seven, from *Dust and Sun* in 1929 through *Mississippi Belle* in 1942—as well as others, including *Jezebel*, starring Bette Davis, in 1938, *Pioneer Woman* in 1940, and *Buffalo Bill* in 1943. As the native Charlestonian, Katharine Ripley was inducted into the South Carolina Academy of Authors in 1998.

Katherine Drayton Mayrant Simons (1899-1969) was born in Charleston and educated at Converse College in Spartanburg. Writing under the pseudonyms of Drayton Mayrant and Kadra Maysi, she published nine historical novels, including two set in the Palmetto State; three books of verse (*Shadow Songs*, *The Patteran*, and *White Horse Leaping*); and two collections of historical sketches (*Roads of Romance* and *Stories of Charleston Harbor*). Simons also served as contributing editor of *Names in South Carolina*, one of the most interesting and entertaining little journals ever published in the state. She was a 1997 inductee into the South Carolina Academy of Authors.

Annie Greene Nelson (1902-1993), one of South Carolina's first African-American female novelists, was born in Cartersville, Darlington County, to parents of little means who nevertheless possessed a strong moral sense and instilled this, together with an appreciation for the virtues of hard work and good behavior, in their thirteen children. Nelson was educated on Parrott's Plantation and then at Benedict and Voorhees Colleges, from the latter of which she received a degree in education and nursing in 1923. Nelson worked in several capacities for the Works Progress Administration during the New Deal and then worked for twenty years as a nurse; she also served as a community activist, as founder of Columbia's first kindergarten for black students, and, later, as a popular speaker, reader, and performer of her own work. Her novels—*After the Storm* (1942), *The Dawn Appears* (1944), *Don't Walk on My Dreams* (1961), and *Shadows in the Southland*, published serially in *The Palmetto Leader* in 1952—celebrate the everyday lives of ordinary black Americans. Her plays, *The Weary Fireside Blues* and *On Parrott's Plantation*, written after she returned to the University of South Carolina to study drama in her eighties, contain much autobiographical information. Nelson was the recipient of the Columbia Community Drama Award (1980) and the J. Scott Kennedy Award for dedication to black theater.

Gwen Bristow (1903-1980) was born in Marion and attended Anderson College, Judson College in Alabama (A.B., 1924), and the Columbia University College of Journalism (1924-1925). She worked as a reporter for the New Orleans *Times-Picayune* from 1925 to 1934 and then devoted herself to full-time freelancing. As a novelist she worked first in partnership with her husband Bruce Manning, the two of them together producing four novels: *The Invisible Host* (1930), *Gutenberg Murders* (1931), *Two and Two*

Gwen Bristow

Make Twenty-Two (1932), and *The Mardi Gras Murders* (1937), all published by the Mystery League. In 1937 she published the first of her own books, also the first in her Plantation trilogy, *Deep Summer*, followed quickly by *The Handsome Road* (1938) and *This Side of Glory* (1940). These novels, each set on a different Louisiana plantation, were uniformly praised for their historical accuracy and for their realistic re-creation of a sense of place. They have been reprinted as recently as 1979 and, with others of her books, have been translated into German, French, Spanish, Dutch, and Swedish. Her next two novels, *Tomorrow Is Forever* (1943) and *Jubilee Trail* (1950), were made into films by RKO (1946) and Republic (1953), respectively, as had been her first novel with her husband in 1931. Her final books were the novels *Celia Garth* (1959), *Calico Palace* (1970), and *Golden Dreams* (1980). Early in her career Bristow also published *The Alien and Other Poems* (1926). She was a 2000 inductee into the South Carolina Academy of Authors.

Robert Molloy (1906-1977) was born in Charleston and was reared there and in Philadelphia, where his family moved when he was twelve; he graduated from George Washington High School in New York City in 1922. After high school Molloy was largely self-educated, reading widely, especially in music and foreign languages. By the 1930s he was translating European novels for New York publishers and writing for encyclopedias and other reference publications. He also became a book reviewer, and from 1936 to 1945 he served as assistant to the literary editor of the New York Sun and then as literary editor himself. Molloy had begun writing novels while still a schoolboy, and in 1945 his first novel, *Pride's Way*, set in a fictional Charleston, appeared. Thereafter he wrote nine more novels, among them *Uneasy Spring* (1946), *A Multitude of Sins* (1953), *The Reunion* (1959), and *The Other Side of the Hill* (1962). He also wrote *Charleston, a Gracious Heritage* (1947), praised at the time by *The New York Times Book Review* for getting in "an unusual amount of solid history (which he mostly slips in painlessly) together with a great deal of amusing lore and legend."

Mary Dodgen Few (1912-1992), a native of Spartanburg, was educated at Spartanburg High School, the Fontaine School (Cannes, France), and Converse College, where she received her M.B. In addition to being a teacher and proprietor of Few's Pen Shop in Anderson she wrote three historical novels—*Carolina Jewel* (1970), *Under the White Boar* (1971), and *Azilie of Bordeaux* (1973)—two of which are set in South Carolina. She is also the author of *The Dodgen Story: An Account of a Truly American Family* (1985).

Barbara Ferry Johnson (1923-1989), a popular instructor at Columbia College in the state capital, came to writing relatively late but made the most of her time in the limelight. A native of Grosse Pointe, Michigan, she received her B.S. from Northwestern University (1945) and her M.A. from Clemson University; she also studied at Oxford University. She worked as associate editor of *American Lumberjack* magazine in Chicago and as a high school

Robert Molloy

74

teacher in Myrtle Beach before settling into a twenty-five-year career at Columbia College. Her first book, *Lionors* (1975), the account of a youthful love affair by King Arthur, established her among the first ranks of popular paperback novelists and received good critical notices. *Delta Blood* (1977), her second, won the Palmetto Fiction Award. Four others followed: *Tara's Song* (1978), *Homeward Winds the River* (1979), *The Heirs of Love* (1980), and *Echoes from the Hills* (1982).

Ferdinan Backer "Nancy" Stevenson (1928-2001), in addition to being the first woman in South Carolina to hold statewide office, was co-author of a popular mystery series, writing under the name **Daria Macomber** with **Patricia Colbert Robinson (1922-1998)**. Together the two women published three books: *A Clearing in the Fog* (1970), *Hunter, Hunter Get Your Gun* (1966), and *Return to Octavia* (1967). Before entering politics, Stevenson was active in theater and historic preservation. She served first in the General Assembly as a representative from Charleston and then as lieutenant governor of South Carolina from 1979 to 1983;. After her term expired, she opened the Winston Gallery, specializing in contemporary art, in Washington, D.C. In 1993 she retired to Floyd, Virginia, where she died. Robinson also created, produced, and directed a number of plays, several of which were produced in Charleston during the Spoleto Festival, and wrote books under her own name, including *Something to Hide* (1990) and *Love and Death in Charleston* (1998).

Young Adult and Children's Book Authors

Eleanor Frances Lattimore (1904-1986), born in Shanghai, China, was a prolific author and illustrator of books for children whose work, much of which is about Chinese and other minority characters, has not weathered changing fashions and standards for what constitutes authenticity in the depiction of ethnicity particularly well. Still, she produced over sixty books as author and/ or illustrator over a period of more than forty years—in the mid sixties she lived at Indigo Hill on Edisto Island—and also contributed to such children's magazines as *Jack and Jill*, *Story Parade*, and *Trailways*. Among her books are *Little Pear: The Story of a Little Chinese Boy* (1931) and its three sequels; *Junior, a Colored Boy of Charleston* (1938), *Storm on the Island* (1942), *Bayou Boy* (1946), *Holly in the Snow* (1954), *The Youngest Artist* (1959), and *The Taming of Tiger* (1975). *The Chinese Daughter* (1960) is an early story of mixed-race adoption. Lattimore's artwork was exhibited in galleries in New York, Boston, and Charleston, and may be found in the collections of many American libraries.

Eleanor Frances Lattimore

Anne Christensen Morse (1915-1968), writing under the pseudonym **Ann Head**, was born into a family long active in progressive educational and human rights causes in Beaufort and attended Antioch College for three years. She began her career as a

Anne Morse,
who wrote as "Ann Head"

freelance fiction writer for magazines in 1943, contributing many stories and serialized novels over the years to *The Saturday Evening Post*, *Cosmopolitan*, *Redbook*, *Ladies' Home Journal*, *McCall's*, and *Good Housekeeping*. She also wrote four novels for young adults, one of which, *Mr. and Mrs. Bo Jo Jones*, has become a modern classic that tells the story of a teenage couple who unexpectedly become parents and must cope with all of the resultant changes in their suddenly complicated lives. Morse died in Beaufort.

Matthew F. Christopher (1917-1997) helped to instill a love of reading in several generations of young readers, especially boys, from the 1950s to the 1990s. Born in Bath, Pennsylvania, he graduated from Ludlowville, New York, High School (1935), and worked in business and industry for nearly thirty years before becoming a full-time writer in the early 1960s. He also played semipro baseball, and his love for this sport spawned more than two dozen baseball books among his nearly fourscore novels for young readers. He also wrote a number of books for adults, penned the "Chuck White" adventure comic strip in *Treasure Chest* magazine from 1967 to 1973, and published almost three hundred pieces of short fiction and nonfiction. He won five awards from *Writer's Digest* and the 1957 Junior Book Award certificate from Boys' Clubs of America for *Basketball Sparkplug*. He spent his last years in Rock Hill, where he died of a brain tumor in 1997.

Among the South Carolina writers most beloved by her readers was **Margaret C. (Peggy) Parish (1927-1988)**, creator of the literal-minded but indomitable Amelia Bedelia, a favorite of elementary-age readers for more than thirty years. A native of Manning, Parish acquired a love of reading while convalescing from illnesses as a child and not unexpectedly became a teacher after receiving her B.A. in English from the University of South Carolina in 1948. She taught in Oklahoma, in the coal mining hills of Kentucky, and finally in Manhattan at the progressive Dalton School. Her complete output totaled more than thirty different titles, including a dozen Amelia Bedelia books; *Dinosaur Time*, which was named one of *School Library Journal's* Best Books of Spring 1974; craft books like *Costumes to Make*; and adventure stories like *Granny and the Desperadoes* (1970), *Good Hunting, Little Indian* (1962), and *Hermit Dan* (1977).

Dawn Langley Pepita Simmons (1937-2000) was born Gordon Langley Hall in England at Sissinghurst, the estate of Vita Sackville-West, whose chauffeur was Simmons's father. In his teens he moved to Ontario, Canada, where he worked among the Ojibwa Indians and wrote the memoir *Me Papoose Sitter* (1955). Simmons also became a journalist during this period, working for the *Winnipeg Free Press* and then the *Nevada Daily Mail*. Also around this time in New York City he met the actress Margaret Rutherford, who, together with her husband, adopted Simmons; and the painter Isabel Whitney, who, according to Simmons, left him a legacy of two million dollars upon her death in 1962. Simmons subsequently moved to

Charleston, underwent sex reassignment surgery at Johns Hopkins University in 1968, and then in 1969 married her twenty-two-year-old black butler in what has been claimed to be the first documented interracial marriage in the city's history. Opposition to the wedding, scandal attending the announced birth of a daughter to the couple, and turmoil within the family resulted in Simmons's move to Hudson, New York, where she lived for some twenty years until her return to Charleston, where she died of Parkinson's disease. Near the end of her life she published the memoir *Dawn: A Charleston Legend* (1995).

In his National Public Radio profile of Simmons after her death, Robert Siegel called her "a writer whose most remarkable creations were her own identity and lifestyle," and many who knew her in Charleston would likely agree. Still, the author achieved not inconsiderable success, publishing more than twenty books altogether and supporting her family, if frugally, with her income. In addition to her memoirs, she also wrote *Dear Vagabonds: The Story of Roy and Brownie Adams* (1964), *The Sawdust Trail: The Story of American Evangelism* (1964), *Osceola* (1964), *Vinnie Ream: The Story of the Girl Who Sculptured Lincoln* (1963), *Golden Boats from Burma* (1961), and profiles of Jacqueline Kennedy, Lady Bird Johnson, and others. The majority of her books were written for young readers.

Poets and playwrights

Ohio native **Dorothy Hartzell Kuhns Heyward (1890-1961)** is too often remembered only as the wife and collaborator of DuBose Heyward, but she had a successful career as an author in her own right. Educated at the National Cathedral School in Washington, D.C., she also attended the Harvard Drama Workshop and the MacDowell Colony, where she met her future husband. Her first play, *Nancy Ann* (1927), won the 1924 Harvard Prize, and she published nearly a dozen additional plays: *The Lighted House* (1925), *Love in a Cupboard* (1926), *Porgy* (with DuBose Heyward, 1927), *Three-a-Day* (1930), *Jonica* (with Moss Hart, 1930), *Cinderelative* (with Dorothy DeJagers, 1930), *Little Girl Blue* (with Dorothy DeJagers, 1931), the play version of her husband's *Mamba's Daughters* (with DuBose Heyward, 1939), *South Pacific* (with Howard Rigsby, 1943), *Set My People Free* (1948), and *Babar the Elephant* (1953). She also wrote the novel *Pulitzer Prize Murders* (1932). After her husband's death Mrs. Heyward spent considerable time in court defending his and her rights to the operatic and film versions of *Porgy and Bess*. She died in New York City in 1961 and is buried in St. Phillips Cemetery in Charleston.

Although most of her work was produced during the thirties and forties, **Gamel Woolsey (1895-1968)** has only recently become widely known, especially in her native state. Born at Breeze Hill Plantation near Aiken, Woolsey, her mother, and her siblings moved to Charleston in 1910 after the death of her father. There she contracted tuberculosis, which was to recur throughout her life, and a portion of one lung was removed. In the early 1920s Woolsey moved to Greenwich Village, where she met and then in 1923 married the New Zealand journalist and novelist Rex Hunter after becoming pregnant with his child; the pregnancy was terminated because of her tuberculosis, and although she never divorced, her marriage to Hunter failed after four years. While in New York in 1927 she met the English writer J.C. Powys and, through him, his brother Llewelyn, with whom she fell passionately in love. Powys returned her affection, apparently encouraged by his own wife, Alyse, and she became pregnant by him and suffered a miscarriage. Woolsey subsequently moved to England in 1929 to be near the Powyses, where she later met and fell in love with the writer Gerald Brenan in the summer of 1930. Although never divorced from Hunter, she agreed to "marry" Brenan. She moved with him to Spain, where she lived the remainder of her life, almost forty apparently happy years.

During her lifetime Woolsey published one volume of poetry, *Middle Earth* (1931), which may be the most original and accomplished verse published in the early twentieth century by any South Carolinian other than Beatrice Ravenel. It was published in England, however, and remained virtually unknown in her own country. She also wrote a novel, *One Way of Love*, based upon her marriage to Hunter, but although this book was accepted by Gollancz and actually typeset in 1932, it was not issued due to the publisher's concerns about its supposed sexual explicitness in light of recent obscenity cases in the English courts. She did publish two other works during her lifetime: *Death's Other Kingdom* (1939), a memoir of the Spanish Civil War recently reissued by Zalin Grant, a neighbor of the Brenans in Spain, under the title *Malaga Burning*; and *Spanish Fairy Stories* (1944). In the late seventies and early eighties the English poet Kenneth Hopkins published new editions of Woolsey's poetry, and her *Letters to Llewylyn Powys* appeared in 1983; Penguin Books issued their Virago Modern Classics edition of *One Way of Love* in 1987. In retrospect, the totality of Woolsey's output establishes her as a significant voice of literary South Carolina calling back to her homeland from across the Atlantic and over the span of years.

Helen von Kolnitz Hyer (1896-1983) was South Carolina's first woman poet laureate, appointed in 1974 by Governor John West. Hyer early on developed a taste for adventure and the Lowcountry during summer visits with her grandfather in Mt. Pleasant. This bore early fruit as well when she was published in *Romance Magazine* at age seventeen. Poems in *Adventure Magazine* followed and then appearances in *Poet Lore*, *Argosy*, the *Christian Science Monitor*, and elsewhere. Her first book, *The Magnificent Squeak*, appeared in 1902; her last, *What the Wind Forgets: A Woman's Heart Remembers*, in 1975. Hyer's subjects are typically drawn from history and the nostalgically romantic imagery of the antebellum South, but they also include poems set in Ireland, Michigan, and Canada. Her poem "Fish Boat" is about the recently resurrected Confederate submarine, the Hunley.

Louise Jones DuBose (1901-1994) was born in Georgia but lived most of her life in South Carolina and contributed substantially to the cultural life of the state as longtime director of the University of South Carolina Press. Educated at Agnes Scott, Chicora, and Presbyterian Colleges, DuBose received her A.B. and M.A. degrees from the University of South Carolina. In addition to a number of historical and biographical studies, DuBose wrote plays (*The Woman from Off*, 1934, and several unpublished one acts) and poetry (*Windstar*, 1943). She also served as director of the South Carolina Writers' Project from 1935 to 1941 and edited *South Carolina Lives: The Palmetto Who's Who, A Reference Edition Recording the Biographies of Contemporary Leaders in South Carolina, with Special Emphasis on Their Achievements in Making It One of America's Greatest States*. Mrs. DuBose was a 2001 inductee of the South Carolina Academy of Authors.

Louise Jones DuBose

A popular poet of the second half of the twentieth century, **Grace Beacham Freeman (1916-2002)** was born in Spartanburg and graduated from Converse College with a B.A. in English. A syndicated columnist, she was also poet laureate of South Carolina (1985-1986). Her Quaker religion informed the spirit and tone of much of her verse, and she was dedicated to promoting poetry in the public schools. *Remembering a Gentle Father* (1996) and *This Woman Called Mother* (1992), perhaps her best-known books, honor her parents. She was also the author of *Children Are Poetry* (1951), *Midnight to Dawn* (1981), and *Stars and the Land* (1983). Her work appeared in *St. Andrews Review*, *Red Clay Reader*, and elsewhere. In 1983 she received an honorary doctor of letters degree from St. Andrews Presbyterian College.

Alice Childress (1920-1994) was born in Charleston but grew up and was educated in Harlem, where she lived most of her life, working as an actress, technician, and then director of the American Negro Theatre. Not university educated, Childress learned from her grandmother, who raised her, from her own voracious reading, and from her rich store of life experiences, which included jobs as an apprentice machinist, a governess, a sales clerk, and an insurance agent. During 1966 to 1968 she also enjoyed an appointment from Harvard University as a scholar-writer at Radcliffe. Her first play, *Florence*, was performed in 1949 and published the following year. In 1950 *Just a Little Simple*, based on Langston Hughes's collection of stories *Simple Speaks His Mind*, was produced at the Club Baron Theatre. Other plays followed, including *Trouble in Mind*, which in 1956 was the first play by an African-American woman to win an Obie award. Childress was also the first black woman to have a play produced on Broadway. Her *A Hero Ain't Nothin' but a Sandwich* won the 1974 Jane Addams Award for a young adult novel and both

Grace Beacham Freeman,
poet laureate (1985-86)

the 1975 ALA Best Young Adult Book award and the 1975 Lewis Carroll Shelf Award. *Rainbow Jordan*, another young adult novel, was a Coretta Scott King Award Honorable Mention book for 1982. Other honors bestowed on Childress include the Sojourner Truth Award of the National Negro Business and Professional Women's Clubs and the Black Filmmakers first Paul Robeson Medal of Distinction. Childress's other works include *Young Martin Luther King*, produced by the Performing Arts Repertory Company in 1969-1972, and *Sea Island Song*, commissioned by the South Carolina Arts Commission and first produced by Stage South in Charleston during Alice Childress Week in 1977. She was inducted into the South Carolina Academy of Authors in 1990.

Bennie Lee Sinclair (1939-2000), appointed poet laureate of South Carolina for life by Governor Dick Riley in 1986, was one of those rare poets who appealed to both a popular audience and an academic audience of her peers in the universities. Born in Greenville, Sinclair received her B.A. from Furman University and was married to potter Don Lewis, with whom she lived in a quiet corner of the southern Appalachian Mountains near Cleveland, South Carolina, that she called "Wildernesse." The mountains around her and her relationship with her husband were both strong influences on her work; her "simplicity and directness of statement" she attributed to him. During the 1970s and 1980s Sinclair devoted much of her time to being a Poet-in-the-Schools and also taught at Furman University and the Greenville Fine Arts Center. She read widely before university audiences.

Sinclair's poetry was often the product of close encounters with the natural world around her and has an immediacy of impact that is often startling. She was capable of imagining herself crawling into the blossom of a flower and "becoming powder fine as pollen" ("Metamorphosis"), of affectionately memorializing "my schizophrenic friend, the cat/I am temporarily feeding" ("My Schizophrenic Friend"), and of apotheosizing the race car driver Fireball Roberts whom, she suspects, "died for us, a prolonged/and national sacrifice/of green and checkered madness, vomitable dust ...," all in the same volume, the early *Little Chicago Suite* (1971). Never sentimental as a poet, near the end of her life Sinclair, who suffered from multiple seriously limiting physical ailments, confronted her own mortality and the struggle of daily existence head-on. "Life has dealt me blows you can only deal with with poetry," she said. After her own kidneys failed, Sinclair received a kidney from a young Georgia woman and wrote of the donor, "... a mere/ biological trace, like the remnant/of a Siamese twin," and of the transporting helicopter, "casting her forfeited loveliness/like that of a desiccated angel/to far-flung operating rooms" in the remarkable poem "The Dying. The Donor. The Phoenix." And only Sinclair could have written the blunt "Butterflies Eat Dung and Carrion," which combines in its five short lines images of butterflies, dung, carrion, "gospel glass," flowers, and wedding rice into a

Bennie Lee Sinclair,
poet laureate (1986-2000)

statement of belief in only the *possibility* of harmony, the uncertainty of relationships.

Dorothy Perry Thompson (1944-2002), born in Springfield, was reared in the Wheeler Hill neighborhood of Columbia, which later became a prominent setting in her verse. She graduated from Booker T. Washington High School in Columbia (1962), Allen University (B.A., 1968), and the University of South Carolina (M.A.T., 1974). After teaching at Riverside High School, Lower Richland High School, and Dreher High School, she returned to the University of South Carolina, where she received her Ph.D. in English in 1987. She was the second African-American to earn a Ph.D. in English from USC and the first to complete a dissertation in creative writing; she studied under James Dickey. She then taught at Winthrop University, where she coordinated the African-American Studies program. Her dynamic presence and genuinely warm humanity made her a popular reader of her own work, and she traveled widely throughout the United States. She also published widely in academic journals and was in demand as a conference speaker.

Dorothy "Dot" Thompson

Thompson's poetry deals with race, gender, place, and the love that binds people together. Her first book, *Fly with the Puffin*, appeared in 1995, followed by *Out of the Rough: Women's Poems of Survival and Celebration* (2001), *Priest in Aqua Boa* (2001) and *Hurrying the Spirit: Following Zora* (2002). She was also published widely in little magazines and journals, including among many others *African-American Review*, *Black American Literature Forum*, *Crucible*, *Catalyst*, *Southern Poetry Review*, and *Sucarhochee Review*; and in the anthologies *Poems from the Green Horseshoe: Poems by James Dickey's Students* (1987) and *45/96: The Ninety-Six Sampler of South Carolina Poetry* (1994). She served as a member of the Board of Governors of the South Carolina Academy of Authors and was posthumously inducted into the Academy itself in 2002.

7 CHAPTER

Post-World War II
New Directions

As South Carolina emerged from the dislocations of World War II and the Korean War, it was inevitable that her literature would begin to blossom into all sorts of new and luxuriant directions. For one thing, her writers had a solid tradition behind them upon which to build. It was no longer a novelty that good literature should spring from the state's nurturing sand and red clay regions, and her writers no longer had to prove themselves to a skeptical reading public. Moreover it began to be possible for South Carolina authors to explore the *contemporary* quirks and idiosyncrasies of some of her native inhabitants and to ramble along the byroads beyond the main drags and into the dark corners. Although Charleston and Beaufort and Georgetown and the rest of the Lowcountry remained important settings, the state's readers discovered places like Dixiana and Salley and more often than not found themselves cruising through the fifties and sixties in the coaches of the Southern Railroad or the back seats of Chevy convertibles instead of jouncing along moss-covered avenues in rickety carriages.

The state's writers during this period were also a better-educated lot than ever before. Most had university degrees to go along with their military experience, and increasingly fewer numbers of the men as well as the women had seen military service of any kind. Some of these new-breed writers had advanced degrees, including M.F.A.'s, and, as had authors elsewhere, many of them profited from and came to depend upon the largesse of governmental and private arts organizations. Some of them also displayed an intellectual sophistication and breadth of learning rare since the days of Hugh Swinton Legaré and demanded an equally attentive audience schooled with equal rigor. Finally, some of the state's most gifted writers emigrated to other states while at the same time the state opened her arms wide to accept talented newcomers from other parts.

All of these characteristics and tendencies are evident in the careers of six accomplished contemporary writers who have produced a substantial share of the best of the state's writing in the second half of the twentieth century. **William Price Fox** grew up on the outskirts of Columbia and after stints in the military and the business world made a name for himself with a cast of improbably outrageous fictional characters. He then left for Hollywood but returned after a relatively short sojourn to become a writer-in-residence at the University of South Carolina. His features and sketches continue to be published in the best magazines in the country. **Guy Davenport** left the state early on to settle into a distinguished university career at the University of Kentucky, where he produced admirable translations of the Greek classics, highly regarded short fiction embodying a sort of neoclassical vision of how to lead a good and happy life, and engaging essays on a wide variety of subjects. **Ennis Rees**, another academic writer, moved *into* South Carolina in 1954 after teaching at Duke and Princeton universities. He became a noted translator of *The Iliad* and *The Odyssey* and other tales from the Greeks, a poet, and a successful author of books for young readers. **John Jakes**, who, like many other outlanders, was lured to South Carolina by the lifestyle and beauty to be found on Hilton Head Island, toiled in the world of business for twenty years before ultimately abandoning it for the writing life he had led simultaneously as his second vocation during his entire business career. The "Kent Family Chronicles" and the "North and South Trilogy" brought him wealth and fame beyond anyone's reasonable expectations, and lately the critics have praised him as well. Finally, two native Georgians, **James Dickey** and **Pat Conroy**, struck deep roots in the fertile creative soil of their adopted state and rose to an eminence and popularity seldom equaled by any authors identified so closely with a specific locale.

William Price Fox, Jr., was born in Waukegan, Illinois, on April 9, 1926. Two years later his parents moved to Columbia, where Fox attended Logan Elementary School, Wardlaw Junior High School, and the old Columbia High School before leaving in the tenth grade to join the Army Air Corps. He left the service in 1946, completed high school in Columbia, and then entered the University of South Carolina, where he graduated in 1950 with a B.A. in history. Fox then moved to Miami, where he bellhopped, delivered singing telegrams, and briefly coached football at Miami Military Academy before hitchhiking to New York City. In New York he worked at a variety of sales jobs into his mid-thirties but also began to write. He met and became friends with Norman Mailer, Shel Silverstein, and

William Price Fox

Village Voice writer Bill Manville. His contact with Manville resulted in the publication of a couple of pieces in the *Voice* and brought him to the attention of Fawcett editor Knox Burger. A similar acquaintance with Southern novelist Caroline Gordon, from whom he was taking a course in writing fiction at the New School for Social Research, secured him an agent as well. He began writing for major magazines like *The Saturday Evening Post* and *Harper's*, and within a year he had sold his first book, *Southern Fried* (1962), a highly entertaining collection of stories about an outrageous cast of characters who frequented hamburger drive-ins, used car lots, and trailer parks. As Fox told interviewer Patti Just, "I tried to do everything I thought was amusing and fun in this first book." Readers recognized an original, and the book sold well. This was followed by *Dr. Golf* (1963), a less-than-bestseller that nonetheless still has "fan clubs who swear to this day that it's the truest, not to mention funniest, book on golf ever written" (Deno Trakas in *A Literary Map of South Carolina*, p. 84).

By this time Fox had acquired enough of a reputation for his work that Hollywood beckoned with offers to create scripts for film and television, and he enthusiastically answered the call, working for a time, among others, on the popular sitcom *The Beverly Hillbillies*. While in California he also continued to write for the magazine market, and at the conclusion of his tenure with the studios he traveled to Europe to do more work for the periodical press. On his return he accepted a position at the University of Iowa Writers' Workshop at the instigation of his friend, Kurt Vonnegut. Fox stayed at Iowa for seven years, from 1968 to 1975, and when the work there began to overwhelm the creativity and fun that were the hallmarks of his writing, he found a more congenial home at the University of South Carolina, where he accepted the position of writer-in-residence. In between the appearance of *Doctor Golf* and his return to Columbia, Fox had written two novels, *Moonshine Light, Moonshine Bright* (1967) and *Ruby Red* (1971), and reissued his first book with a half-dozen new stories as *Southern Fried Plus Six* (1968). Each of these books contains the usual Fox stable of engaging misfits and rednecks who tell their stories in their own inimitable voices and with a characteristic zest for life that is irresistible.

At USC, Fox continued to publish, beginning with the novel *Dixiana Moon* (1981), a send-up of Southern canvas-tent evangelism featuring a character based in part upon Fox's own moonshining father. The collection, *Chitlin' Strut and Other Madrigals* (1983), came next, showcasing some of the best magazine pieces from the Columbian's typewriter, including an affectionate sketch about Satchel Paige and an hilarious re-creation of Jack West's unforgettable performance of the Chitlin Strut, "shimmying like a '54 Ford with a bad front end" at the 1971 festival of the same name in the small town of Salley. Having honed his sportswriting abilities in the pages of *Sports Illustrated* and *Holiday*, Fox turned next to books on local sports: *How 'Bout Them Gamecocks!* (1985) and *Golfing in the Carolinas* (1990). Then Hurricane Hugo heaved its fury against the South Carolina coast just north of Charleston, and Fox applied his novelist's skills to the retelling of the event in *Lunatic Wind: Surviving the Storm of the Century* (1992), a book that for many Sandlappers accurately recaptured the drama and terrifying reality of the event. Depite the fact that the book took him three long years of concentrated labor to complete—"I've never really liked nonfiction because you can't get inside like I've wanted," he observes—*Lunatic Wind* remains one of his most popular titles. More recently, Fox has written *South Carolina Off the Beaten Path* (1996), dedicated "To my brother Bob, who sells the best Christmas trees in Lexington County" and full of tidbits of useful information like "the town of Pocataligo is the compression of 'poke a turtle's tail and he will go'" and "Myrtle Beach is the Putt-Putt Capital of the known world."

The essence of Fox's appeal is his ability to spin yarns, and he spins 'em better than just about anybody else. His outlandish characters and their impossible dilemmas fairly leap from the page to declare their authenticity, and all of us have met them up and down the Main Streets of our cities and towns. But this is just part of his appeal. Of equal importance is the fact that whatever their failings and foibles may be, Fox's characters are, in the words of Harold Woodell, "good people who win in the end" (*Contemporary Southern Writers*, p. 142). We *want* these people to win their battles, large and small, and when they do, we stand up and cheer right along with them. In this, Fox stands squarely in the mainstream of a tradition that stretches all the way back to Mark Twain.

Ennis Rees followed a more conventional path to the halls of academe at the University of South Carolina. Born in Newport News, Virginia, in 1925, Rees attended the College of William and Mary (A.B., 1946) and Harvard University (M.A., 1948; Ph.D., 1951). While at William and Mary, he wrote for the campus literary magazine and took two years of Greek, thus beginning a lifelong dedication to the study of the classics, especially *The Iliad* and *The Odyssey*, a fascination initially stimulated by his third-grade teacher's oral readings from *The Iliad*. After completing his studies, Rees served as an instructor at Duke for three years (1949-1952) and at Princeton for two more (1952-1954). In 1954 he accepted the position that he would hold until retirement at the University of South Carolina, becoming a full professor of English in 1963.

Rees devoted six years in the late fifties and early sixties to his translations of *The Odyssey* and *The Iliad*, which were published in 1960 and 1963, respectively, by Random House. The task of translating "the lean, spare, and yet very rich language of Homer" (quoted by Israel in Spears, *A Literary Map of South Carolina*, p. 79) was clearly a congenial one. It inspired Rees's own verse and led to further explorations of the ancient Greeks, especially the *Fables* of Aesop, which he translated for Oxford University Press in

Ennis Rees,
poet laureate (1984-1985)

85

1966. The translations of Homer were well received, having been called by James Dickey "among the finest of our times" (Israel, p. 80), and they have worn well over the years, being reissued in the early nineties by MacMillan and Oxford.

Rees's work was not confined to the classics, however, even early on. Soon after the publication of *Fables from Aesop* came his retelling of *Brer Rabbit and His Tricks*, illustrated by Edward Gorey (1967); this, too, was well received, and a second selection from Aesop, also illustrated by Gorey, followed as *Lions and Lobsters and Foxes and Frogs: Fables from Aesop* (1971). Altogether Rees produced a dozen books for young readers, some originals and some retellings of older stories but all fortunate enough to be illustrated by some of the best book artists of the time. These titles included *Riddles, Riddles Everywhere*, illustrated by Quentin Blake (1964); *The Song of Paul Bunyan and Tony Beaver*, illustrated by Robert Osborn (also 1964); *Pun Fun*, another collaboration with Quentin Blake (1965); *Windwagon Smith*, with pictures by Peter Placentia (1966); *Teeny Tiny Duck and the Pretty Money*, illustrated by Paul Freeman (1967); *The Little Greek Alphabet*, illustrated by George Salter (1968); *Gillygaloos and Gollywhoppers*, a third title with Quentin Blake (1969); and *Potato Talk*, illustrated by Stanley Mack (1973).

Rees was writing his own poetry during these years as well. Pithy, aphoristic, often outright funny, his work has been described as essentially optimistic. It often celebrates the everyday and the ordinary: housecats, for example, or the unfortunate and ironically named Happy the Tiger, consigned to live most of his life on display in an animal trailer beside a well-known Columbia car wash, or a lifeguard making it through the day with hashish and beer. Believing that the message of "good poets from Homer to Yeats and Auden" has been simply "Rejoice" (*Conversations with South Carolina Poets*, p. 75), Rees's poems sing of the happiness of ordinary existence and "the natural and growing and green" world around us all (p. 81).

Rees's poetry also found an audience. It appeared in *The Southern Review*, *Arion*, *Prairie Schooner*, *Red Clay Reader II*, *Outposts*, *The Sewanee Review*, and *The New Republic*. The University of South Carolina Press issued both a collected edition, *Poems*, and *Selected Poems* in 1973. In 1984 Governor Richard Riley recognized his achievement with a one-year appointment as the state's poet laureate. Rees retired from USC in 1988. He was made a member of the South Carolina Academy of Authors in 1999.

Guy Davenport, the son of an express agent, was born in Anderson and educated at Duke University (B.A., 1948), Merton College of Oxford University (B.Litt., 1950), and Harvard University (Ph.D., 1961). At Merton College, which he attended as a Rhodes Scholar, Davenport studied James Joyce's *Ulysses*, and at Harvard he wrote his dissertation on Ezra Pound's *Cantos*. Both Joyce and Pound, among the toughest of the moderns, have continued to be

Guy Davenport

major interests of his over the years. He has published a major study of Pound, *Cities on Hills: A Study of I-XXX of Ezra Pound's Cantos* (1983), and a number of the essays in his collection *The Geography of the Imagination: Forty Essays* (1981), deal with Joyce or Pound or both, often in far-reaching explorations that range over wide expanses of cultural landscape.

After completing his B.Litt. at Merton College, Davenport served for two years in the Army Airborne Corps and then accepted a position as an English instructor at Washington University in St. Louis. This was followed by two years as assistant professor of English at Haverford College in Pennsylvania, then an appointment in 1963 to a position in the English department at the University of Kentucky, where he taught for twenty-seven years, retiring as Distinguished Alumni Professor of English in 1991, the year he received a MacArthur Fellowship.

Davenport's first book, *The Intelligence of Louis Agassiz*, was published in 1963, the same year he accepted his appointment at the University of Kentucky. From then until his retirement, and even beyond, he published on the average a book a year on a staggering variety of subjects that reveal both an agile and actively curious mind and a depth of learning rare among all except a handful of the most erudite scholastics. The essays in *The Geography of the Imagination* (1981) are characteristic. They range chronologically from a consideration of 50,000-year-old cave art to the teaching of poetry in late twentieth-century classrooms. They cover the disciplines of literary and cultural history, archaeology and anthropology, natural history, Irish art and French sculpture, modern music, classicism, and philosophy—and often lessons from several of these disciplines are marshaled together in support of wholly fresh insights into literature or other works of art that scholars have studied for decades or, in some cases, centuries. The book contains significant appreciations of Pound, Poe, and Whitman, but there is also a chatty reminiscence of J.R.R. Tolkien, whom Davenport remembers as "mumbling and pedantic" (p. 337), and a charming depiction of Irish portraitist Jack Yeats the Elder. Moreover, no matter what material he turns his attention to, Davenport remains both convincing and understandable. He communicates honestly and competently on an immense range of difficult and occasionally abstruse subjects. The essays as a whole are a tour de force and, more, are immensely readable. A second collection of essays by Davenport, *The Hunter Gracchus and Other Papers on Literature and Art* (1996), is equally demanding and rewarding, as is the book-length rumination *Objects on a Table: Harmonious Disarray in Art and Literature* (1998).

A second genre at which Davenport has proven to be a master is translation from the ancient Greek and other ancient languages. The first of these was *Carmina Archilochi: The Fragments of Archilochos* (1964), followed in a year by *Songs and Fragments of Sappho* (1965). Three more translations from the Greek appeared in the early 1980s: *Herakleitos and Diogenes* (1980); *Archilochus, Sappho, Alkman: Three Greek Poets of the Late Greek Bronze Age* (1980); and *The Mimes of Herondas* (1981). Davenport has also published translations from the Egyptian, *Maxims of the Ancient Egyptians*, (1983) and, with Benjamin Urritia, the essential sayings of Jesus, *The Logia of Yeshua* (1996). Davenport's translations have twice been nominated for American Book Awards, in 1980 and 1981.

Davenport is equally at home writing original short fiction of his own; in fact, it is in this area that his work has attracted the most critical attention and no inconsiderable body of praise. His first story collection, *Tatlin!*, published by Scribner's in 1974, includes "The Aeroplanes at Brescia," the bravura story in which Franz Kafka, Giacomo Puccini, Gabriele D'Annunzio, and Ludwig Wittgenstein appear as characters at the 1909 Paris air show. *Da Vinci's Bicycle: Ten Stories* (1979) features, in addition to Leonardo Da Vinci and the Wright Brothers, a recurring series of symbols in which flight represents freedom, an important theme in much of Davenport's work. *Eclogues: Eight Stories* (1981) demonstrates the validity of the pastoral ideal for the twentieth century, and *Apples and Pears and Other Stories* (1984) applies the Biblical motif of fall and loss to the modern world but also offers the hope of recovery of what was lost. In a postscript to *12 Stories* (1997), Davenport writes that "I tried to be as inventive as I could, obeying the injunction 'in letters of gold on T'ang's bathtub' to 'yet again make it new' that Thoreau quotes in *Walden* and Ezra Pound used as a battle cry." This effort is visible everywhere in his fiction, where the combination of lyrical passages with philosophical reflections and visions of a recoverable golden age mark a distinctive approach to narrative technique.

In addition to the collections mentioned above, Davenport has written five other story collections and two novellas, *The Bicycle Rider* (1985) and *Jona* (1986). Recurrent themes include a longing for the lost innocence of childhood; the capacity for personal fulfillment in small, close communities dedicated to the pastoral ideal and pleasures of both the body and the mind; and the need to turn outward, beyond the self, rather than restrictively inward in searching for happiness. These ideas and others are also explored in four volumes of poetry: *Flowers and Leaves: Poema vel sonata, carmina autumni primaeque veris transformationum* (1966); *The Resurrection in Cookham Churchyard* (1982); *Goldfinch Thistle Star* (1983); and *Thasos and Ohio: Poems and Translations, 1950-1980* (1986). In addition to winning the Thomas Carter Award for his literary criticism in 1987, Davenport has won awards for his fiction and poetry: the Anne Flexner Creative Writing Award (1948), the Blumenthal-Leviton Prize (1967), and the Morton Dauwen Zabel Award for fiction from the American Academy and Institute of Arts and Letters (1981).

A final arena in which Davenport has excelled has been that of the visual arts. He has illustrated two of his own books, *Da Vinci's*

Bicycle and *Apples and Pears and Other Stories*, and a collection of his work, *The Balance of Quinces: The Paintings and Drawings of Guy Davenport*, was issued in 1996 under the editorship of Eric Anderson Reece. He has also written studies of the art of Lafcadio Hearn (1983), Paul Cadmus (1990), and Charles Burchfield (1994).

In the final analysis, Guy Davenport's impact upon the world of twentieth-century letters may be larger than that of any other South Carolina writer. Certainly his interests are broader and the depth of his understanding more comprehensive than most; indeed, the only other South Carolina writer whose work seems anywhere nearly as audacious as Davenport's is James Dickey. Both Davenport and Dickey look to the stars for much of their inspiration, but both are ultimately grounded in a world of consummately human experience. Both experiment in their fiction, and both speak with distinctive voices.

If Guy Davenport is the most erudite of South Carolina writers, the one most likely to wear his education on his sleeve, then **John Jakes** is the one most adept at matching his material to his audience. Another best-selling writer from the Lowcountry, Mickey Spillane, is fond of calling his readers his "customers," emphasizing the commercial relationship between the writer/seller and reader/buyer. While Jakes is less blatant in defining the author as businessman or huckster, he is clearly a master at understanding it. He told Patti Just in his interview for *The Writers' Circle of South Carolina* that his first rule as a writer is "be a good storyteller" since that is the only way to get the reader to turn the first page.

John Jakes

Jakes was born in Chicago in 1932 and earned an A.B. from Depauw University (1953) and an M.A. in American literature from Ohio State (1954). Lacking the funds and, he came to realize, the interest to pursue studies for a doctorate and already married for three years, Jakes became a copywriter and later promotion manager for Abbott Laboratories in North Chicago in 1954. He subsequently worked in a variety of positions in business and advertising in the industrial Upper Midwest until becoming a full-time writer in 1971. In spite of his hours at the office, however, Jakes wrote throughout this period. Like Ray Bradbury and Stephen King before him, he had begun writing as a teenager, selling his first story, "The Machine," about a diabolical toaster, to *The Magazine of Fantasy and Science Fiction* for twenty-five dollars in 1951. He wrote his first novel, *The Texans Ride North* (1952), a story for children, while studying for exams in college. It sold between three and four thousand copies.

During the next twenty years Jakes was to write approximately fifty works in the genre condescendingly called "pulp fiction," mostly Western and science fiction paperbacks. He was pretty good at it, and his books sold steadily, if unspectacularly, producing what he himself calls "indifferent results." He wrote westerns and historical fiction under his own name and the pen name Jay Scotland, mystery novels as Alan Payne, and send-ups of the fantasy-adventure genre like *Brak the Barbarian* (1968), *Brak the Barbarian Versus the Sorceress* (1969), and *Brak Versus the Mark of the Demons* (1971). Writing came easily to him, and he enjoyed the challenge of writing in a variety of forms. He even wrote some nonfiction—*Tiros: Weather Eye in Space* (1966), for example, and *Great Women Reporters* (1969)—and in the early seventies began to write plays, some, like *Wind in the Willows* (1972), based upon works of fiction by other writers.

Jakes's big break came in the early seventies when a friend who had been asked to write a series of novels about an American family to celebrate the upcoming Bicentennial had to decline but recommended Jakes as his replacement. The rest, as they say, is history. The "Kent Family Chronicles," originally planned as five books, became huge bestsellers and expanded to eight volumes. The series to date has altogether sold more than fifty million copies, and as of this writing the first volume, *The Bastard*, is in its sixty-first printing. The series has also become a popular group of miniseries film adaptations from Universal Studios. Never one to rest on his laurels or sit idly, Jakes followed the last volume of the "Kent Family Chronicles" (*The Americans*, 1980) with the first volume of his "North and South Trilogy," *North and South* (1982). This series, too, captured the public imagination. To date there are ten million copies of the three books in print, and the ABC miniseries adaptation of *North and South* (David L. Wolper Productions) is ranked seventh among the top ten highest rated miniseries *of all time*.

Until recently Jakes has not been a favorite of the critics. The first volumes of the "Kent Family Chronicles" were not even reviewed in the newspaper press, depending instead upon word of mouth for their initial popular surge. As their popularity became apparent, however, critics took notice, comparing the series in its sweep and technique to Alex Haley's *Roots* and its televised permutations. More recently he has received the National Cowboy Hall of Fame's Western Heritage Literary Award for his short story "Manitow and Ironhand" (1995), the Cooper Medal of the University of South Carolina's Thomas Cooper Library (2002), the Career Achievement Award of the South Carolina Humanities Association (1998), and the Celebrity and Citizen's Award of the White House Conference on Libraries and Information (1995). In 1996 he became the tenth living inductee into the South Carolina Academy of Authors. In the summer of 2002 Jakes's novel *Charleston*, the saga of the Bell family from the American Revolution to the fall of Charleston during the Civil War, became his fifteenth consecutive *New York Times* bestseller. John Jakes has lived on Hilton Head Island since 1978, where he takes an active part in the cultural life of the permanent community. He has written stage adaptations of works by Charles Dickens for the Self Family Arts Center and from time to time makes an appearance on stage himself, continuing an interest in the amateur theatre that began when he was an undergraduate. Jakes is a member of the Authors Guild, American P.E.N., and Western Writers of America; and he serves on the board of the Authors Guild Foundation.

The John Jakes Web Site, the author's official home on the Internet, is at www.johnjakes.com/index.html.

Leviathan and Behemoth

When considering what to do with **James Dickey** and **Pat Conroy** in this study, I was faced with a number of dilemmas. The first was where to put them. Dickey clearly stood apart from other twentieth-century authors from the Palmetto State because of the sheer audacity as well as the breadth and depth of his accomplishments. Not only was he the best known and most highly regarded serious poet the state had ever produced, but he was also a serious and best-selling novelist, with one book that became a classic, another that was a failed masterpiece, and a third that told a bold story with more panache than most critics allowed it. On top of those accomplishments must be added Dickey's solid achievement as a critic of the work of his contemporaries, many of whom disagreed with him but few of whom wrote so memorably themselves. Then there were the two children's picture books and an impressively weighty stack of coffee table tomes intended to generate income as much as to puff the poet's reputation. Clearly few writers ever set such grandly ambitious goals for themselves. Dickey seemed to demand a chapter of his own.

Then there was the question of Pat Conroy. To begin with, he was not even a native South Carolinian, having been born in Atlanta and traveling up and down the East Coast of the United States during his youth. He actually spent more time growing up in North Carolina than in South Carolina although, as he has said more than once, North Carolina was the one state that did not claim him as one of her own. Still, Conroy had been shaped into a man during his junior and senior years at Beaufort High School and his four years as a cadet at The Citadel, and all of his books were set completely or largely in his adopted state. Moreover, he spent and still spends considerable time in South Carolina on Fripp Island and is obviously a child of the Lowcountry. In addition, more South Carolinians probably look forward to each new Conroy title with greater expectation than that generated by any other contemporary author. He seems to swagger through the muck of Beaufort County's marshes with such an ambitiously braggadocio style that he seems to be one with it. His readers sensed this early on, and they turn to him with a deeply rooted devotion that is absolutely unique. True, Conroy is not so prolific as Dickey was. Nor does he embrace as wide a fictional swath as John Jakes. Nor is he such a workmanlike craftsman as mystery writer Mickey Spillane, still cranking out thumping good reads in his eighties at Murrells Inlet. Yet Conroy commands the state's attention as no one else currently does, and he has done so now for thirty years. And whatever the faults of his plotlines may be—and they are not negligible, as more than one reviewer has pointed out—Conroy can turn a phrase and sustain its beautiful magic like no one else. His epic romances strike powerfully the basic intuitive and emotional chords that characterize the South Carolina and Southern psyche. He is undeniably a Writer with a capital "W."

So Dickey and Conroy seem to me larger than life, both literally and metaphorically. Their largeness is not of the same type: Conroy's prose can be even more poetic than the poet's, for example, and the masculine toughness of Dickey's best poetry is alien to Conroy's style, even in such "masculine" books as *The Great Santini* and *The Lords of Discipline*. Still, they are undeniably "large" writers of a type unlike the others the state has produced. They seem to demand, if not a full chapter of their own, a shared prominence as something like a culmination of various trends, tendencies, and strivings—a grand end product of the Palmetto Muse's strivings thus far.

Dickey was born in Buckhead, then a suburb of Atlanta, on February 2, 1923, and grew up during the Great Depression, but he has said that the family did not suffer as many did from the economic dislocation characteristic of the time. His father, Eugene Dickey, was an attorney and his mother, Maibelle Swift Dickey, was a bed-ridden sufferer from heart disease. He had "lots of good fun" as a child, according to his interview with Patti Just for SCETV's *Writers' Circle of South Carolina*, attended public schools in Atlanta, playing football at North Fulton High School, and then attended Clemson, where he also played football, eventually starting as a freshman. His undergraduate career was then interrupted by service during World War II in the 418th Night Fighter Squadron, after which he transferred to Vanderbilt, where he began to feel like a writer and first published his poetry in *The Gadfly*, the student literary magazine. At Vanderbilt, too, he came under the important formative influence of another South Carolinian, Monroe Spears, who influenced and helped to shape his work. Dickey received both a B.A. and an M.A. from Vanderbilt and was teaching at Rice

James Dickey
Courtesy, Mark Olencki

University in Texas when he was recalled into service during the Korean War.

Dickey came back to Rice after Korea and taught freshman composition for a couple of years. He and his wife also separated, but after living in Europe for a year under the terms of a *Sewanee Review* fellowship, the two resurrected the marriage and Dickey felt even more like a writer. Dickey next took a job at the University of Florida in 1956 but left of necessity after scandalizing Gainesville's P.E.N. Women with a poem about a boy's discovery of his father's and his own maleness in the shower one day. Dickey had a chance to salvage the situation by apologizing but could not bring himself to do so, was released by the university, and ended up in New York City writing advertising copy for the McCann-Erickson agency. He worked in advertising for five years, eventually making his way back to Atlanta, but all the while he was writing and publishing poetry and reviewing the work of others. Slowly but surely he was building a solid reputation as a poet.

James Dickey
Courtesy, Mark Olencki

The 1960s was Dickey's miraculous decade. He received a Guggenheim Fellowship after *Into the Stone* was published and traveled to Italy for a second time during 1961 and 1962. In quick succession came *Drowning with Others* (1962), *Helmets* (1964) and *The Suspect in Poetry* (prose, also 1964), the National Book Award-winning *Buckdancer's Choice* (1965), *Poems 1957-1967* (1967), and *Babel to Byzantium: Poets and Poetry Now* (1968). The solid corpus of work represented in *Poems 1957-1967* convinced whatever doubters there still were at that point that Dickey was indeed a poet of the first order. As companion to this achievement Dickey then offered up *Deliverance* (1970), a solid novel that first won a substantial audience in its own right and then a cult following to boot after it was made into a film in 1972 starring Jon Voigt (also the star of Pat Conroy's *Conrack*), Burt Reynolds, Ned Beatty, and Dickey himself as the frowning but ultimately quiescent sheriff at the end.

The remainder of the 1970s saw Dickey extend his reach and his reputation in all directions. Having already served as writer-in-residence at a number of colleges in the mid- to late sixties—and as Consultant in Poetry at the Library of Congress from 1966 to 1968—Dickey settled into his dual role as professor of English and writer-in-residence at the University of South Carolina beginning in 1969. Ever mindful of his public persona, Dickey continued to read publicly before a wide variety of audiences, and many of these occasions have become legendary because of the poet's mental state before, during, or after his performance. At one of his readings in Atlanta Dickey regaled a predominantly artsy and collegiate audience in his most cultivated poet-as-hunter-and-metaphysician pose, clad in a magnificently fringed buckskin jacket and leather-brimmed Western scout hat. A show it was, but that fact did not matter to anyone in the audience. Or, rather, it mattered to some, that being the reason they had come in the first place, but the poetry he launched into the audience that evening more than made up for the shilling huckster he had dressed up to become, and even the most academic members of the audience came away impressed—sadder, too, perhaps, but they had received their money's worth.

Dickey continued to produce substantial works during this period. Following *Deliverance* in 1970 were *The Eye-Beaters, Blood, Victory, Madness, Buckhead and Mercy*, and the Mailer-esque *Self-Interviews; Sorties* in 1971; and the visionary *The Zodiac* in 1976. The seventies also saw his two grand coffee table volumes: *Jericho: The South Beheld*, with Hubert Shuptrine's paintings, in 1974, and *God's Images*, with engravings by Marvin Hayes, in 1977. The late seventies brought change: the death of his wife Maxine in 1976, followed by his remarriage to Deborah Dodson the same year; *The Strength of Fields*, composed for and read at Jimmy Carter's Presidential inauguration in 1977; and *Tucky the Hunter*, Dickey's first children's book in 1978.

Ever the innovator, Dickey published *Puella*, a book that puzzled some reviewers but that included a group of Levinson Prize-winning poems, in 1982. In 1986 *Bronwen, the Traw, and the Shape-Shifter: A Poem in Four Parts*, written for the daughter of his second marriage, appeared; as did *Alnilam*, a sprawling and ambitious novel that disappointed most critics, the following year. A new miscellany, *Night Hurdling: Poems, Essays, Conversations, Commencements, and Afterwords*, which collected a few important pieces not found elsewhere, was published in 1983.

The nineties saw the appearance of *To the White Sea* (1993), a frighteningly insistent book that redeemed the false promise of *Alnilam* and demonstrated that Dickey could still write compelling prose even if his best poetry was now behind him. Pat Conroy, writing the rear cover blurb for the dust jacket, put it succinctly: "Dickey is incapable of writing a sentence in which he is not totally involved." His public, relieved that the great man had recovered his voice, confirmed the judgment with its wallets. A further confirmation was *The Whole Motion: Collected Poems 1945-1992*, which offered the whole smorgasbord of the poet's achievement as his body began to fall final prey to liver disease and emphysema. Never one to give in easily, Dickey rallied near the end to make his peace with his son Christopher, whose memorial *Summer of Deliverance* (1998) is as frank and moving a literary post mortem as has ever been written, as well as with his estranged wife, his daughter, and his personal demons. He taught almost until the day he died, wheeling himself and his oxygen tent to class, a last assertion of will against those forces seeking to silence him.

Like Dickey, Pat Conroy was born in Atlanta. Unlike Dickey, Conroy spent a peripatetic childhood journeying up and down the

East Coast and beyond as his father was assigned to one Marine Corps base after another during a highly successful and often decorated career as a fighter pilot. Colonel Don Conroy was from Chicago, and his toughness was just what might have been expected in a Marine from the Windy City. He fought with distinction in both Korea and Vietnam and was one of the Corps's most honored pilots. He took great pride in his prowess in the cockpit and swaggered across the landscape and through the lives of his wife and children with a largeness and grandeur that are hard for most secondhand observers to imagine; to a very great degree he was the creature of his own mythmaking.

Conroy's mother, the other hugely formative presence during his youth, was by contrast a product of the South. She apparently always wished she had been born into a more genteel background than was the actual fact. This desire was both reflected in and fueled by her love for Margaret Mitchell's *Gone with the Wind*, a book she read dozens of times and which she read aloud to her son Pat. She created her own personal mythology around this dream, and when her imagined self encountered that of Don Conroy across a cosmetics counter in Atlanta, their mutual fate was sealed. The

Pat Conroy
Courtesy, Doubleday Publicity

Conroys' marriage was productive if tempestuous. They had seven children, a diverse lot who were devoted to one another and who became, in addition to a best-selling novelist, teachers and poets and social workers. The children also became cowering observers of the frequent battles between their parents, and occasionally they as well as their mother became their father's targets. It is therefore small wonder that, in spite of her loyalty to her family and her husband and the Marine Corps, Peg Conroy sought escape in divorce as soon as her husband retired. Ultimately, she found something like vindication as well as happiness in a second marriage.

Conroy emerged from his torturous childhood the product of contradictory influences. Physically tough himself and dedicated to the Marine virtues of loyalty, duty, and honor, he also developed a fierce devotion to fairness, a sensitivity to and appreciation of the beauty and power of language, and an emotional brittleness that was to cost him personally in his adulthood. When the family moved to Beaufort, and he entered Beaufort High School, Conroy began both to form a new set of lifelong friendships and to think of himself as a writer.

The strongest Lowcountry influence on Conroy was probably that of Gene Norris, his junior English teacher. Conroy has immortalized Norris as the slightly wacky but beloved, chain-smoking, paisley tie-festooned Ogden Loring in his novel, *The Great Santini*, as well as in an affectionate remembrance in a collection of celebrity tributes to teachers published by the National Council of Teachers of English. Norris was apparently a born teacher, gifted at being able to stimulate his students' imaginations and to motivate them to learn the finer points of American literature and English grammar. He performed two immeasurably important services for Pat Conroy: he recognized and nurtured his talent as a writer, and he introduced him to the work of Thomas Wolfe, a lifelong model for the younger man.

Two other adults strongly influenced Conroy while he was at Beaufort High. One, his senior English teacher, Millen Ellis, attended to the critical skills of Conroy the writer and helped him further to hone his wordcraft; he also modeled the pedagogical use of magazines, art prints, and visiting artists in the English classroom, all techniques Conroy himself would later adopt. The other adult mentor that Conroy found at Beaufort High, Bill Dufford, was the school's principal and must have seemed like a second father on those Saturdays when he and Conroy worked side by side on the school's landscaping and other projects. He and Conroy remained close after the latter's graduation; it was Dufford who invited Conroy to participate in the human relations workshop that ultimately gave the school district a rationale for dismissing him at the end of his tenure on Daufuskie Island in the fall of 1970. Additional inspiration was provided for Conroy by the predominantly young teaching staff at the high school and by liberal friends in the community, notably the Christensens, descended from a Danish immigrant who served in the Union Army during the Civil War and remained in Beaufort after Reconstruction. The Christensens entertained a broad cross section of Beaufort society in their home, and there in the mid- to late sixties blacks and whites socialized together to an extent rare in South Carolina in those days.

From Beaufort High Conroy traveled to The Citadel, his father's choice, for college. At The Citadel he sometimes felt himself at odds with the excesses and perversions of the military system he encountered, but he also found an environment that strongly appealed to his innate sense of justice and personal loyalty. Never ambitious for a traditional military career and unconvinced that his duty to his country required his active service as a member of the military, Conroy was nonetheless named Best Senior Private and also served proudly on the Honor Court. He was poetry editor of the literary magazine, *The Shako*, as well, played basketball and baseball—the former well enough to be named Most Valuable Player—and belonged to the Newman Club and Block "C." Faculty and staff who influenced Conroy at The Citadel included Colonel John Robert Doyle, Jr., another English instructor who recognized and encouraged the writer in the undergraduate; Charles Martin, a history instructor; and Colonel Thomas Nugent Courvoisie, "The Boo," a legendary figure on the campus whose story Conroy told in the book about him that he self-published not long after his graduation. Conroy impressed Colonel Doyle with the range of his pre-college reading experience—he had read moderns like Alan Paton, John Hersey, William Styron, W.H. Hudson, and John Dos Passos, for example, together with classic Southern writers like Margaret Mitchell, Katherine Anne Porter, and Eudora Welty, and time-honored standards like the Brontës, Dickens, Walter Scott, and R.L. Stevenson—as well as with his special writing ability.

From The Citadel Conroy returned to Beaufort, where he taught English and psychology and coached basketball for two years at his alma mater. As a teacher at Beaufort High School, Conroy again displayed competitiveness and combativeness. His methods were at least partially nontraditional, and he was known as a champion of the underdog and the unconventional. His friendship with Gene Norris continued, and he found new friends in Mike Jones, George Garbade, and Bernie Schein. Their common immersion in issues of the day, particularly civil rights and Vietnam, and their mutual sense of educational mission were strengthened in frequent nighttime discussions. Conroy became, if anything, more liberal and more experimental. Then his friend Bernie, the principal of a nearby elementary school, told Conroy about the opening on Daufuskie Island, and the rest, as they say, is history.

By the time he arrived on Daufuskie, Conroy was a dedicated teacher who believed he could change the world, or at least his small part of it. The unique combination of the inadequate facilities, materials, and instruction provided for the island children; the district's apparent unwillingness to compromise with a teacher who had deliberately placed it in a virtually untenable position; Conroy's moral outrage; the remote locale and quasi-exotic Gullah culture; and a cast of real characters better than any novelist could create from imagination alone—all of these factors interacted to produce a volatile situation and then a story that begged to be written for a wider audience. Conroy was up to the task: he became a novelist. The road was not an easy one, of course. It required the moral support of a large number of friends and acquaintances in Beaufort and as far afield as Virginia. It also required time and a little money, both of which were provided by a brief graduate-studies interlude and a small grant. When *The Water Is Wide* was published, it attracted widespread attention. By then it was 1972 and the country was awash in a maelstrom of civil rights successes and failures, the debacle in Vietnam, the increasingly obvious ebbing of psychedelic flower power and brotherly goodwill among men, and a newly discovered and disturbing undercurrent of violence. In some ways *The Water Is Wide* rode the crest of these cultural waves; in other ways it contributed in some measure to them. Senator Fritz Hollings and Dr. Donald Gatch made America aware of poverty in Beaufort County, and the photographs that Billy and Paul Keyserling took of Pat Conroy and his students on Daufuskie appeared not only in a photo spread in the book itself but had also been featured in *Life*. The plight of Conroy's students and their families became a veritable *cause celebré*, and the new author became, first, famous and then, at least in his adopted home state, infamous. The novel became the film *Conrack*, starring Jon Voigt, and people began to wonder what might come next from the pen of young Pat Conroy.

They did not have long to wait. *The Great Santini*, whose protagonist, Bull Meecham, suggested a thinly veiled portrait of Colonel Donald Conroy to many readers, appeared in 1976, and *The Lords of Discipline*, often misunderstood as a frontal attack upon The Citadel, followed in 1980. Many friends of Conroy and his family were alienated by these two books; indeed many had already been scandalized that characters in *The Water Is Wide* bore uncomfortably close resemblances to their friends and neighbors. The local communities of Beaufort and Charleston hunkered down to lick their wounds and display protective shields. Others, however, were struck by Conroy's frankness and his fearlessness in facing up to his personal demons. Still others were titillated by the books and their relationship to real life. Through it all, the books themselves sold well, and both became feature films. The legend of Pat Conroy grew. So, seemingly, did his personal pain. It was six years before *The Prince of Tides* appeared, and it too contained close parallels to the author's own life. His marriage also fell apart, and he wrote about it publicly in *Reader's Digest*. His beloved mother died, and he wrote a powerful nonfiction tribute to her—"Mama and Me: The Making of a Southern Son" in the collection *The Prevailing South: Life and Politics in a Changing Culture* (Longstreet Press, 1988)—that revealed new depths of pain and also unexpected reservoirs of strength to his faithful readers. He and his father reconciled. There was well-publicized therapy. The long-awaited fifth novel, *Beach Music*, was published: to some, it seemed to fulfill an anticipated promise; to others, it was a disappointment.

With each new book it became increasingly apparent that Pat Conroy was an exceedingly complicated artist and an even more complicated man. The public found it hard to separate the two. In some ways it seemed that each new book was both more personal *and* less personal. Alongside the familiar angst, the expected plot twists, and the presence of characters who always suggested Conroy himself, each new book also cut across a broader swath of human experience and geographical territory. The characters became deeper and their concerns more human than merely "Southern." And always there was the beautiful language. No other South Carolina writer has ever *wanted* to write *beautifully* as much as Pat Conroy has, and none has surpassed him in the sheer gorgeousness to be found in sustained passages of his prose. *That*, more than the swaying palmettos and pluff mud marshes, is why readers return to his books again and again and continue to be satisfied, even enriched, by the experience. His latest book, *My Losing Season* (2002), about his senior-year basketball team at The Citadel, continues the Conroy tradition: Called a "literary slam-dunk" by *Newsweek* reviewer Malcolm Jones, it received favorable reviews in most major newspapers. He has long been rumored to be working on a book about Thomas Wolfe, and he is thought to have a cookbook in him. His readers—be they businessmen who graduated from The Citadel or veterans of the Marine Corps or the wives of veterans or housewives curling up with a book at the beach or bankers on Wall Street—all want to read each of the books he has in him and can barely wait for the next one to appear.

The Current Crop

A Who's Who and Directory of South Carolina Writers at the Beginning of the Third Millennium

As will be clear from the entries that follow, the universe of South Carolina writers is a large and ever-expanding one. Indeed, altering the criteria for inclusion here just a little could easily have doubled the size of this list. Obviously there was a need to impose limits, and I have tried to do so in a way that is inclusive enough to embrace all major figures as well as most minor ones. I realize that even using the terms "major" and "minor" is likely to cause offense somewhere, however, so let me be as specific as possible: writers whose names appear below have in most cases published at least one book, and their work generally falls into one or more of the categories of fiction, poetry, drama, and creative nonfiction. Therefore, writers whose profession is primarily journalism have been omitted, although some journalists who have published books of wide appeal and a general nature are represented. Likewise, historians who write primarily for an academic or scholarly audience are not included, but others who write for a general audience and/or whose work has had a profound and extensive influence are. Nature writers who are university academicians are likewise absent from these pages unless they write with a "literary" style for a wide audience, and many English department faculty members whose work is primarily critical in nature are similarly left out.

If any common term can be applied to the works listed below, I suppose it would be "belletristic," a term that connotes conscious attention to issues of art and style and a desire to be thought of as a "writer" rather than, say, a "professor" or a "journalist" or a "critic" or an "historian." I am, of course, well aware that members of these non-writerly professions also attend to style, but I think they do so less perhaps as a matter of "art" than as a matter of necessity.

In the end, of course, at least some of the reasons for inclusion in and exclusion from this list must be attributed to my own personal sense of literary taste, and I am the first to admit that my taste is as susceptible to prejudice and fallibility as anyone's. Still, I have launched out into this murky sea with the best of intentions, and I solicited input from a large number of sources early on in this project. Among others whose assistance I have benefited from in this regard are Tom Johnson at the South Caroliniana Library, Sara June Goldstein of the South Carolina Arts

Commission, the South Carolina Writers Workshop, Harlan Greene of the Charleston Public Library, Patti Just of SCETV, and, of course, John Lane and Betsy Teter of the Hub City Writers Project. I also sent a mailing to English department chairpersons at the state's public and private institutions of higher education, and that mailing turned up a number of writers' names that I had been otherwise unaware of. I am deeply indebted to all of these individuals and organizations, but the final praise or blame for a given writer's inclusion or exclusion is mine alone. In any case, I am certain that future editions of this list shall be longer, not shorter. And that is as it should be.

Aarnes, William (b. 1947). Educated at Oberlin College (B.A.), Catholic University (M.A.), and The Johns Hopkins University (Ph.D., 1979), Aarnes is the author of two volumes of poetry, both published by the Ninety-Six Press: *Learning to Dance* (1991) and *Predicaments* (2001).
Address: Department of English,
Furman Hall 109B, Furman University,
3300 Poinsett Highway, Greenville, SC
29613; (864)294-3159
Email: bill.aarnes@furman.edu

Abramo, J. L. (b. 1947). Abramo, a native of Brooklyn, New York, is a long-time educator, theater producer and director, stage and screen actor and arts journalist; he now lives and writes in Columbia. His first novel, *Catching Water in a Net* (St. Martin's Minotaur, 2001), about a private eye who reads Dickens and drives a 1963 Chevrolet Impala, begins, "The phone on my desk rang so unexpectedly that I nearly spilled the Mylanta onto my only unstained necktie." It won the St. Martin's Press/PWA Award for Best First Private Eye Novel. His second Jake Diamond mystery, *Clutching at Straws* (Thomas Dunne/St. Martin's), was released in early 2003.
Website: www.jlabramo.com
Email: jakediamond@att.net

Allen, Gilbert (b. 1951). Allen was born in Rockville Centre, New York, grew up on the

Gilbert Allen

south shore of Long Island, and received his B.A., M.F.A., and Ph.D. from Cornell University. Since 1977 he has taught at Furman University in Greenville, where he is one of the two editors of the Ninety-Six Press. He has published four volumes of poetry: *Commandments at Eleven* (Orchises, 1994); *Second Chances* (Orchises, 1991); *In Everything* (Lotus, 1982); and *Driving to Distraction* (Orchises, 2003). He was co-editor of 45/96: *The Ninety-Six Sampler of South Carolina Poetry* (Ninety-Six Press, 1994). His work appears in a wide variety of respected journals, including *The Cortland Review, Cumberland Poetry Review, The Florida Review, The Georgia Review*, and *Southern Review*.
Address: Department of English, Furman University, 3300 Poinsett Highway, Greenville, SC 29613; (864) 294-3152
Email: gil.allen@furman.edu

Paul Allen

Allen, Paul (b. 1945). An associate professor of English at the College of Charleston, Allen was educated at Huntingdon College (B.A., 1967), Auburn University (M.A., 1971), and the University of Florida (M.A., 1976). His books of poetry include *American Crawl* (University of North Texas Press, 1997), and *The Clean Plate Club* (forthcoming in 2004 from Salmon Publishing Ltd.). He has also issued a CD, *The Man with the Hardest Belly: Poems and Songs* (Glebe Street Productions, 2000). He

has published widely in journals such as *Northwest Review, Southern Poetry Review, Cimarron Review*, and *New England Review/ Bread Loaf Quarterly*; and in anthologies including *45/96: The Ninety Six Sampler of South Carolina Poetry*. He is also the editor of the Charleston-based literary journal, Crazyhorse, and the director of the College of Charleston Writers and Songwriters Series. Allen's awards include two Individual Artist Fellowships from the South Carolina Arts Commission, the Mary Roberts Rinehart Award for a first book of poetry in progress (George Mason University), and the 1996 Vassar Miller Poetry Prize (University of North Texas Press).
Address: Department of English,
College of Charleston, Charleston, SC 29424;
(843) 953-5659
Email: allenp@cofc.edu

Allison, Dorothy (b. 1949). The product of an abusive and otherwise-dysfunctional family, Allison grew up in Greenville and found her voice as a writer in a lesbian feminist collective community in Tallahassee, Florida. She is a National Merit Scholarship graduate

Dorothy Allison

of Florida Presbyterian College and of the New School of Social Research. She has written widely for the gay and women's movement press. Her first book, *The Women Who Hate Me* (Long Haul Press, 1983), a collection of poetry, was followed in 1988 by the story collection *Trash* (Firebrand Books), which won Lambda Literary Awards as both Best Small Press Book and Best Lesbian Book. *Trash* was also the basis for the partly autobiographical novel *Bastard Out of Carolina* (Dutton, 1992), which was a Finalist for the National Book Award. Since *Bastard Out of Carolina*, Allison has published a second novel, *Cavedweller* (Dutton, 1998); a memoir, *Two or Three Things I Know for Sure* (Dutton, 1995); and a collection of essays, *Skin: Talking About Sex, Class & Literature* (Firebrand Books, 1994).

Autrey, Kenneth M. (b. 1945). A professor in the Department of English at Francis Marion University in Florence, Autrey received his B.A. in English from Davidson College (1967), his M.A. from Auburn University (1973), and his Ph.D. from the University of South Carolina (1986), where he studied with James Dickey and majored in rhetoric and composition. He is currently coordinator of freshman composition at Francis Marion; in 1996-1997 he was visiting professor at Hiroshima University, Hiroshima, Japan; and he has also taught at the University of South Carolina and Tougaloo College. He has twice been a member of the Reader's Circuit of the South Carolina Arts Commission, has won first-prize competitions sponsored by *The Devil's Millhopper* and *Portfolio* (University of South Carolina), and has been honored for his teaching by the University of South Carolina and Tougaloo College. A frequent contributor of features and book reviews to *The State* and *The State Magazine*, Autrey has also published dozens of poems in journals like *The Devil's Millhopper*, *Midwest Poetry Review*, *Emrys Journal*, *Savannah Literary Journal*, *The Chattahoochee Review*, and T*he South Carolina Review*. He has been a member of the board of editors of both the J*ournal of Teaching Writing* and the *Journal of Visual Literacy*, and he was an early inspiration to the leaders of the South Carolina Writing Project network.
Address: Department of English, Francis Marion University, Florence, SC 29501; (803) 661-1512
Email: kautrey@fmarion.edu

Bailey, Jan (b. 1944). The director of the creative writing program at the South Carolina Governor's School for the Arts and Humanities, Bailey was born in Charlotte and grew up in the Appalachian foothills of South Carolina. She holds an M.F.A. in creative writing from Vermont College and is the author of three collections of poetry: *Paper Clothes* (Emrys Press, 1995); *Heart of the Other: Island Poems* (Two Fish Press, 1998); and the forthcoming *Midnight in the Guest Room* (Leapfrog Press, 2004). Her verse has also appeared in a variety of journals, including *The Kenyon Review*, *Ploughshares*, *Chicago Review*, *The South Carolina Review*, *Prairie Schooner*, *The Greensboro Review*, *Indiana Review*, and *Willow Springs*. In 1993 she was named a South Carolina Arts Commission Poetry Fellow, and in 2003 she won the Elinor Benedict Poetry Prize from *Passages North*.
Address: South Carolina Governor's School for the Arts and Humanities,
15 University Street, Greenville, SC 29601; (864) 282-3708

William Baldwin

Baldwin, William (b. 1941). One of the long list of contemporary Southern writers discovered by Algonquin Books of Chapel Hill, Baldwin received his undergraduate education and a master's degree at Clemson University, then spent most of his life designing and building houses. He also taught agriculture, ran a seafood company for a year, fished for almost a decade, and spent a week as a film scriptwriter. This varied background, a love for Faulkner and Marquez, and a lifetime of stories gathered at the knees of old-timers in his native McClellanville coalesced in the early 1990s in the novel *The Hard to Catch Mercy* (Algonquin Books of Chapel Hill, 1993). As Baldwin told Patti Just, he "... heard these stories all my life. Ten or eleven years ago I began waking in the middle of the night with these characters talkin' inside my head." The result, after at least four versions had been written and cast aside, was a novel called by *Publishers Weekly* "a sly but loving send-up of Deep South gothic mythology." Baldwin has also written four nonfiction titles: *Plantations of the Low Country* (Legacy Publications, 1986), *The Visible Village: A McClellanville Scrapbook, 1860-1945* (self-published, 1984), *Lowcountry Day Trips: Plantations, Gardens, and a Natural History of the Charleston Region* (Legacy Publications, 1993), and *The Loggerheads of Cape Romain* (McClellanville Village Museum, 1999). A second novel, *The Fennel Family Papers: A Novel* (Algonquin Books of Chapel Hill), appeared in 1996. Baldwin appears in two interviews in Patti Just's *Writers' Circle of South Carolina* series: Program Numbers 302 and 802.
Address: c/o Algonquin Books of Chapel Hill, P.O. Box 2225, Chapel Hill, NC 27515-2225; (919) 967-0108

Ball, Edward (b. 1959). Ball is the descendant of a landed family that had owned numerous plantations along the Cooper River in the South Carolina Lowcountry. Reared in the Southern parishes served by his father, an Episcopal priest, he moved with his family to South Carolina when he was nine years old. He graduated from Brown University, became a magazine and newspaper correspondent for, among others, *The Village Voice* newspaper, and ultimately moved back to Charleston to research the history of his family. The result of that work, *Slaves in the Family* (New York: Farrar, Straus & Giroux, 1998), an unsentimental, uncompromising saga including the details of his ancestors' affairs with their slaves and the subsequent stories of the two sides of his family, won the National Book Award. *Slaves in the Family* has been widely praised in both the scholarly and the popular press, and Ball has appeared widely on television to discuss his book and its implications for American society today.
Address: c/o Farrar, Straus & Giroux, Inc., 19 Union Square West, New York, NY 10036

Ballard, Mignon Franklin (b. 1934). Ballard was born in Calhoun, Georgia, and now lives in Fort Mill. She received a degree in journalism from the University of Georgia. She is the author of twelve published novels. Her first book, *Aunt Matilda's Ghost* (Aurora Publishers, 1978), a mystery for young readers, was based on a story about her great-great-grandfather. It received the Excellence in Writing Award at the Winthrop College Writers' Conference for the best novel for children by a South Carolina writer. Subsequent mysteries for adult readers are: *Raven Rock* (Dodd Mead, 1986), *Cry at Dusk* (Dodd Mead, 1987), *Deadly Promise* (Carroll & Graf, 1989), *The Widow's Woods* (Carroll & Graf, 1991), *Final Curtain*

(Carroll & Graf, 1992), and *Minerva Cries Murder: An Eliza Figg Mystery* (Carroll & Graf, 1993). St. Martin's Minotaur published the Augusta Goodnight Mysteries beginning with *Angel at Troublesome Creek* (1999), followed by *An Angel to Die For* (2000), *Shadow of an Angel* (2002) and T*he Angel Whispered Danger* (2003). *The War in Sallie's Station*, a novel about growing up during World War II, was published by Five Star Thorndike in 2001. Ballard has belonged to the same writers' group that has been meeting regularly for almost thirty years. Her interview with Patti Just is Program Number 308 in *The Writers' Circle of South Carolina*.
Website: www.mignonballard.com

Meg Barnhouse

Barnhouse, Meg (b. 1955). Born in Philadelphia to parents who were students at Princeton Seminary, the Reverend Meg Barnhouse grew up in both Philadelphia and North Carolina as her father worked first for Billy Graham, then as a commentator for the Philadelphia CBS affiliate. She graduated *summa cum laude* from Duke University, touring on vacations with a Christian rock and roll band. She spent a semester in Jerusalem learning Hebrew, traveling on her own around the Mediterranean and through Europe. After leaving Duke, she completed her seminary work at Princeton, where she won the Grier-Davies Preaching Prize. A job offer as chaplain at Converse College brought her to Spartanburg in 1981, where she has preached, taught, and for fifteen years was in private practice as a pastoral counselor. She became the minister of the Unitarian Universalist Church of Spartanburg in the summer of 2002. Barnhouse has written essays, meditations, and humorous pieces for a variety of secular and religious publications over the years. She has been a commentator for NC Public Radio since 1993, and is the author of two collections of those

commentaries: *The Best of Radio Free Bubba* (Hub City Writers Project, 1998), which includes pieces by Barnhouse and three colleagues; and *The Rock of Ages at the Taj Mahal* (Skinner House Books, 1998), a UU Meditation Manual. A second book from Skinner House, *Waking Up the Karma Fairy*, was published in the spring of 2003.
Address: Unitarian Universalist Church, 251 East Henry Street, Spartanburg, SC 29306; (864) 585-9230
Website: www.megbarnhouse.com
Email: dearmegb@aol.com

Bass, Jack (b. 1934). One of the elder statesmen in the world of journalism and public affairs, Bass received his A.B. and master's degree from the University of South Carolina and his Ph.D. from Emory University; he also studied constitutional law as a Nieman Fellow at Harvard University. Bass covered South Carolina as governmental affairs editor for *The State* and then Columbia bureau chief for *The Charlotte Observer*, during which time he was South Carolina non-staff correspondent for The New York Times, *Washington Post*, and *Newsweek*. His work as an observer and interpreter of the Southern Civil Rights and political scenes is legendary. His widely admired books include *The American South Comes of Age* (Knopf, 1986); *Ol' Strom: An Unauthorized Biography of Strom Thurmond* (with *Washington Post* editor Marilyn W.

Jack Bass

Thompson, Longstreet, 1998); *The Orangeburg Massacre* (with Jack Nelson, World Publishing Co., 1970); *Porgy Comes Home: South Carolina After 300 Years* (R.L. Bryan Co., 1972); *Taming the Storm: The Life and Times of Judge Frank M. Johnson and the South's Fight Over Civil Rights* (Doubleday, 1993); *The Transformation of Southern Politics: Social Change and Political Consequence Since 1945* (Basic Books, 1976);

and *Unlikely Heroes: The Dramatic Story of the Southern Judges of the Fifth Circuit Who Translated the Supreme Court's Brown Decision into a Revolution for Equality* (Simon and Schuster, 1981). His *Taming the Storm* was the 1994 winner of the Robert Kennedy Book Award grand prize. Bass taught journalism for more than a decade at the University of Mississippi and currently serves as professor of humanities and social sciences at the College of Charleston.
Address: College of Charleston, 96 Wentworth Street, Room 310, Charleston, SC 29401; (843) 953-7018
Email: bassj@cofc.edu

Bateman, Claire (b. 1956). Bateman received her B.A. from Kenyon College (1978) and her M.F.A. from Vermont College (1993). She has

Claire Bateman

taught at Clemson University and Chattanooga State University and at summer writing conferences such as Bread Loaf and Mount Holyoke; currently she is an instructor at the Fine Arts Center, Greenville County's Public School for the Literary, Performing and Visual Arts. Bateman is the author of four books of poetry: *The Bicycle Slow Race* (Wesleyan University Press, 1991), *Friction* (Eighth Mountain Press, 1999), *At the Funeral of the Ether* (Ninety-Six Press, 1998), and *Clumsy* (New Issues Press, 2003). Her work has been awarded a Pushcart Prize, and she has received awards from the Tennessee Arts Commission and the National Endowment for the Arts.
Address: The Fine Arts Center, 1613 West Washington Street, Greenville, SC 29601; (864) 241-3327
Email: Bateman7@juno.com

Battle, Lois (b. 1942). A native of Australia, Battle attended junior college in California, the American Academy of Dramatic Arts in New

York City, and UCLA, then acted, taught, worked as a probation officer and held "every minimum-wage job known to woman" (*Writers' Circle of South Carolina* Program Number 303). She began writing after she followed a boyfriend to Wofford College "just to try something different," scored a surprise hit with *War Brides* (Berkeley, 1983), and has written five novels since: *Southern Women* (St. Martin's Press, 1984), *A Habit of the Blood* (St. Martin's Press, 1987), *The Past Is Another Country* (Viking, 1990), *Bed & Breakfast* (Viking, 1996), and *Storyville* (1993). Most of her books "tend to be about three women" and their relationships. Battle has lived in Beaufort since the late 1980s. She is the subject of Program Number 303 of *The Writers' Circle of South Carolina*.

Beamguard, Betty Wilson (b. 1947). A writer of Southern women's fiction, poetry, and essays, Beamguard has published a humorous novel, *Weej and Johnnie Hit Florida* (2000). Her work has won three Carrie McCray Literary Awards from the South Carolina Writers Workshop.
Address: 13671 W. Hwy. 55,
York, SC 29745-8756; (803) 222-4208
Email: bbeamguard@earthlink.net

Bernardin, Libby (b. 1934). A native of Mobile, Alabama, Bernardin grew up in Georgetown and now lives in Columbia. She graduated from the University of South Carolina, where she was a member of Phi Beta

Libby Bernardin

Kappa and where she currently teaches in the College of Hospitality, Retail and Sport Management. She also works with public school students and their teachers through the South Carolina Writing Project and other educational and arts organizations. An award-winning poet, she is also the author of the novel, *The Stealing* (McGraw-Hill, Inc., College Custom Series, 1993), and the co-editor, with Linda Kirszenbaum, of two widely praised anthologies of poetry by South Carolina teachers: *Rhythms, Reflections, and Lines on the Back of a Menu: Writing by South Carolina Teachers/1988* (Bench Press, 1989), and *Out of Unknown Hands: Writing By South Carolina Teachers/1990*, Volume II (R.L. Bryan, 1990). Bernardin's poetry has appeared in *Negative Capability*, *The Devil's Millhopper*, *Notre Dame Review*, *The MacGuffin*, and the anthologies *From the Green Horseshoe: Poems by James Dickey's Students* (University of South Carolina Press, 1987), *You, Year* (Harbinger Publications, 1996), and *Negative Capability Press Anthology*. Her nonfiction prose has been featured in *South Carolina Wildlife*, *Charleston Magazine*, and *The State Magazine*. Bernardin has held a South Carolina Arts Commission Literary Fellowship, has been a member of the Arts Commission's Readers' Circuit and is a former chairman and member of the board of directors of the South Carolina Academy of Authors. Bernardin is interviewed by Patti Just in Program Number 504 of *The Writers' Circle of South Carolina*.
Address: 4 Myrtle Court,
Columbia, SC 29205
Email: ebernardin@sc.rr.com

Blanton, Gail (b. 1941). Born in Gastonia, North Carolina, Blanton has lived in Mauldin since 1971. She has published six drama collections—*And the Race Goes On...*, *The Sheople Incidents*, *Sarah Mae and Her Kinfolk*, *Seniors CenterStage*, *Eve's Daughters* and *All the Best Sketches II*, all published by Lillenas Publishing—as well as more than 100 dramatic sketches and articles on drama. Her sketches have twice won the Christians in Theatre Arts Writing Contest: 1995 (Drama) and 2000 (Comedy). She has also edited two collections of sketches: *Scripts to Reach In and Out and Sharing the Hope*.
Address: 800 Central Avenue,
Mauldin, SC 29662; (864) 963-8273
Email: gblanton2@aol.com

Bodie, Idella (b. 1925). One of South Carolina's most successful authors of books for young people, Bodie began writing in 1985 after retiring from a full career as a high school English teacher. She is a native of Ridge Spring and attended Mars Hill Junior College, Columbia College, and the University of South Carolina. Her books are mostly intended for ages 10-14, but Bodie prides herself in not writing with a controlled vocabulary, preferring to treat her young readers with the respect they deserve and to help them build their own vocabularies through reading her books. The majority of her books are published by Sandlapper Publishing Company, Inc., and include both novels and nonfiction; among them are *Carolina Girl: A Writer's Beginning*,

Idella Bodie

Ghost in the Capitol, Ghost Tales for Retelling, A Hunt for Life's Extras: The Story of Archibald Rutledge, The Mystery of Edisto Island, The Mystery of the Pirate's Treasure, The Secret of Telfair Inn, South Carolina Women, Stranded!, Trouble at Star Fort, Whopper, and ten books in a Revolutionary War series geared toward elementary students. Featured are Francis Marion, Thomas Sumter, unheralded black heroes of the Revolution, and others.

Bodie's contributions to the literature and history of her state have been recognized by many public organizations. Three of her books were nominated for the South Carolina Book Award, and she has received the Wil Lou Gray Educator Award (Columbia College), first place in fiction and poetry in the Anderson Writers Workshop, the Toastmasters International Communication Award, lifetime membership in the South Caroliniana Library for preservation of South Carolina's literary heritage, and inclusion in the American Association of University Women's 1999 calendar of significant South Carolina Women. The Idella Bodie Creative Writing Award is presented annually in her honor by South Aiken High School. She frequently speaks before educational, literary, and public service groups. Her biography of Archibald Rutledge is the most readily accessible introduction to the man and his work, and she takes his literary credo as her own: "Find something worth writing about. Make it simple and clear. Make it reach the heart. Make it beautiful."

Bodie is featured in Program Number 111 of *The Writers' Circle of South Carolina*.
Address: 1113 Evans Road, Aiken, SC 29803; (803) 649-2912
Email: bodieevans@ddminc.net

Boggs, Johnny D. (b. 1962). Born in Timmonsville, Boggs moved to Texas after graduating from the University of South Carolina College of Journalism in 1984 to begin a newspaper career with the *Dallas Times Herald*. After that paper ceased publication in 1991, he worked for the *Fort Worth Star-Telegram* from 1992 until 1998, when he became a full-time writer and photographer. Boggs's first Western story appeared in *Portfolio*, the USC student literary publication, in 1983, and he has since written a steady stream of stories for *Boys' Life*, *Wild West*, *True West*, and similar publications. His Western novels include *Hannah and the Horseman* (Avalon Books, 1997), *This Man Colter* (Avalon, 1997), *Riding with Hannah and the Horseman* (Avalon, 1998), *Ten and Me* (Avalon, 1999), and *The Lonesome Chisholm Trail* (Five Star, 2000). Among his nonfiction titles are *The Big Fifty* (Five Star, 2003), *Spark in the Prairie* (Signet, 2003), *Great Murder Trials of the Old West* (Republic of Texas Press, 2002) and *That Terrible Texas Weather: Tales of Storms, Drought, Destruction, and Perseverance* (Republic of Texas Press, 2000). Boggs currently lives in Santa Fe, New Mexico, and can be reached c/o his publisher.
Five Star, an Imprint of the Gale Group, P. O. Box 159, Thorndike, ME 04986; (800) 223-6121
Website: www.johnnydboggs.com
Email: jdboggs@aol.com

Boling, Katharine (b. 1933). Born in Florence, Boling traveled extensively growing up as the child of an officer in the United States Army. She received her A.B. in English from Coker College, her M.A. in English from the University of North Carolina at Chapel Hill, and her M.A. in children's literature from Hollins University. She has worked in radio and taught in high school and at Francis Marion University. She is a contributor to *The Cambridge Guide to Children's Books in English* and has published widely as a freelance writer, poet, and newspaper columnist. Her books are *A Piece of the Fox's Hide* (Sandlapper Press, 1972), a true legend of the Pee Dee; *Country Bunnies* (Boling, 1973); and *New Year Be Coming: A Gullah Year* (Albert Whitman & Co., 2002), poetry illustrated by Daniel Minter.

Address: Department of English, Francis Marion University, Box 100547, Florence, SC 29501; 800-368-7551
Email: kboling@fmarion.edu

Cathy Smith Bowers

Bowers, Cathy Smith (b. 1949). A native of Lancaster, Bowers graduated from Winthrop College and returned to teach at Lancaster High School for ten years. In 1983 she became an instructor and later poet-in-residence at Queens College in Charlotte. She has published two books of poetry: *Traveling in Time of Danger* (Iris Press, 1999) and *The Love that Ended Yesterday in Texas* (Texas Tech University Press, 1992; Iris Press, 1997). *Traveling in Time of Danger* won the 1992 Texas Tech University Press First Book Award. Bowers's poetry has appeared in *The Atlantic Monthly*, *The Georgia Review*, *Poetry*, *Shenandoah*, *The Southern Review*, and elsewhere. Her family's wrenching experiences with alcoholism, brown lung disease, and AIDS have been the stimuli for much of her writing.
Address: Department of English, Queens College, 1900 Selwyn Avenue, Charlotte, NC 28274; (704) 337-2334
Email: Bowerscs@queens.edu

Boyd, Blanche McCrary (b. 1945). A native of Charleston, Boyd received her B.A. from Pomona College and her M.A. from Stanford University (1971). An author of long and short fiction and nonfiction, she has written four novels: *Nerves* (Daughters, Inc., 1973), *Mourning the Death of Magic* (Macmillan, 1977), *The Revolution of Little Girls* (Knopf, 1991), and *Terminal Velocity* (Knopf, 1997). Her novels deal with life in her native region, with relationships among women, and with change. In 1981 Boyd published *The Redneck Way of Knowledge: Down-Home Tales* (Vintage Books), a collection of cheeky essays about aspects of the South that attracted widespread

attention and praise. She also writes for a variety of magazines, including *Esquire*, *The New York Times Magazine*, *Premiere*, *The Village Voice*, *Voice Literary Supplement*, *Ms.*, and *Oxford American*. Her awards include the Southern Book Award, two Lambda Awards for Lesbian Fiction, and fellowships from the Guggenheim Foundation, the National Endowment for the Arts, the South Carolina Arts Commission, and Stanford University. Boyd is writer-in-residence and Roman and Tatiana Weller Professor of English at Connecticut College.
Address: Department of English, Connecticut College, 270 Mohegan Avenue, New London, CT 06320; (860) 447-1911
Email: bboyd@conncoll.edu

Brewton, Butler. Born in Spartanburg County, Brewton received his Ph.D from Rutgers University. He was a tenured professor of English for twenty-five years at Montclair State

Butler Brewton

University in New Jersey, retiring as professor emeritus. During that period he served as poet-in-residence for the New Jersey State Council on the Arts. Brewton has more than seventy-five poetry publications in literary journals and magazines, including *Pulpsmith*, *Lips*, *Footwork*, *Midway Review*, *Nimrod* and *Essence*. In 1995 he moved back to the Upstate, first to Spartanburg, then to Greenville. He published the collection of poems *Rafters* (Sunbelt Books) in 1995 and *Indian Summer* (Sunbelt) in 1997. He is currently serving as an adjunct professor of English at Furman University.

Bruccoli, Matthew J. (b. 1931). Few scholars have had as deep or as broad an impact upon the worlds of American literature, American literary criticism, and American literary biography as Bruccoli, who has served as the

Jefferies Professor of English at the University of South Carolina since 1976. Educated at Yale University (B.A., 1953) and at the University

Matthew Bruccoli

of Virginia (M.A., 1956; Ph.D., 1960), Bruccoli is an internationally recognized expert on the life and work of F. Scott Fitzgerald and has written or edited major texts on writers as varied as Raymond Chandler, James Gould Cozzens, Ernest Hemingway, and John O'Hara. In addition, in 1962 he became one of the founding partners of Bruccoli Clark Layman, a specialty publisher of limited first editions that in 1976 evolved into the corporation producing the *Dictionary of Literary Biography*, the preeminent work in the field. Among the important works he has produced are *The Composition of Tender Is the Night* (University of Pittsburgh Press, 1963), *Reader's Companion to F. Scott Fitzgerald's Tender Is the Night* (with Judith S. Baughman, University of South Carolina Press, 1996), *The Profession of Authorship in America, 1800-1879* by William Charvat (editor, Ohio State University Press, 1968), *Ernest Hemingway, Cub Reporter: Kansas City Star Stories* (editor, University of Pittsburgh Press, 1970), *By Love Possessed* by James Gould Cozzens (editor, Carroll and Graf, 1998); *Crux: The Letters of James Dickey* (co-editor with Judith S. Baughman, Knopf, 1999), and *O Lost by Thomas Wolfe* (co-editor with Arlyn Bruccoli, USC Press, 2000). Bruccoli is director of the Center for Literary Biography, Thomas Cooper Library, University of South Carolina; editorial director of Fitzgerald Centenary Home Page (www.sc.edu/fitzgerald/index.html); editorial advisor to *The Paris Review*; and series editor of the *Pittsburgh Series in Bibliography* (University of Pittsburgh Press), the *Dictionary of Literary Biography* (Bruccoli Clark Layman/Gale Research), *Understanding Contemporary American Literature* (USC Press), *Understanding*

Contemporary British Literature (USC Press), and *Gale Study Guides* (Manly/Gale Group). He also edited the journals *Fitzgerald Newsletter (1958-1968)*, *Fitzgerald/Hemingway Annual (1969-1979)*, *The New Black Mask (1985-87)*, and *A Matter of Crime: New Stories from the Masters of Mystery and Suspense (1988-89)*. He is the curator and donor of the Matthew J. and Arlyn Bruccoli Collection of F. Scott Fitzgerald and of the Joseph M. Bruccoli Great War Collection at the University of South Carolina, and he is the Literary Personal Representative for the Estate of James Dickey. Among his honors are the Thomas Cooper Medal of the University of South Carolina (1999), USIS lectureships in Italy (1996) and Norway (1999), NEH Summer Institute lectureships at Illinois State University (1997 and 1998); and induction into the South Carolina Academy of Authors (2001).

Address: Department of English, University of South Carolina, Columbia, SC 29208; (803) 777-8193
Email: bruccoli@gwm.sc.edu

Buckless, Andrea (b. 1968). A National Board Certified Teacher from Simpsonville, Buckless has published two well-received picture books for young readers: *Class Picture Day* (Scholastic, Inc., 1998) and *Too Many Cooks* (Scholastic, 2000).

Address: 37 Summer Glen Drive, Simpsonville, SC 29681; (864) 963-2692
Email: andibuckless@yahoo.com

Burns, Russ (b. 1937). A charter member of the South Carolina Writers Workshop, Burns has edited its newsletter, *The Quill*, and co-edited its annual anthology, then known as *Horizons*. Since retiring as a public school administrator in 1995, he has been engaged in his "serious" writing, which amounts to short stories, nature essays, and poetry in addition to nonfiction features on a wide range of subjects. His chapbook, *Seasongs*, is in the works, and his other current projects include a popular book on archaeology in South Carolina to be published in 2004 and *Synergy in the Treatment of Cancer*.

Address: 2806 Metric Road, Laurens, SC 29360; (864) 682-7387
Email: rusburns@aol.com

Burroughs, Franklin G. (b. 1942). Burroughs was born in Conway and educated at the University of the South (B.A. *magna cum laude*, 1964) and Harvard University (A.M., 1965; Ph.D., 1970). After serving for two years

Franklin Burroughs

(1966-67) as a teaching fellow at Harvard, Burroughs taught for more than thirty years in the English department of Bowdoin College, from which he retired in 2002. His publications consist of two books—*Billy Watson's Croker Sack: Essays* (W.W. Norton, 1991) and *The River Home: A Return to the Carolina Low Country* (University of Georgia Press, 1998)—and a variety of essays published in literary quarterlies over the past twenty years. His writing reflects on conjunctions of human history, natural history, and personal experience. His essays have been included in *Best American Essays* (1989 and 1999) and won a Pushcart Prize in 1989.

Byars, Betsy (b. 1928). The most successful children's book author currently from South Carolina, Byars was born in 1928 in Charlotte, attended Furman University, and graduated from Queens College, and began to write while her husband was a graduate student in Illinois "to have something to do and to make money." Her first book, *Clementine*, a collection of seven short stories about three characters, was rejected by numerous publishers before finally making its way into print in 1962. Her classic, *Summer of the Swans*, made her reputation when it was chosen as the 1971 Newbery Medal winner. At the time the book, which was the first book for young readers to deal honestly with learning disabilities, had sold only about 5,000 copies. Since then, Byars has written more than fifty books for young people; her works have been translated into nineteen languages. In addition to the 1971 Newbery Medal, her books have also won the American Book Award (1981: *The Night Swimmers*), the Edgar for the best mystery for young people (1992: *Wanted ...Mud Blossom*), and the Regina Medal from the Catholic Library Association for the body of her work.

Many of Byars's books are based upon her

Betsy Byars

life and the lives of her son and daughters, and many are set in states where she once lived, notably North Carolina, West Virginia, and Ohio. The roll call of characters she has created that are beloved by students and former students of all ages is a familiar one: the ineptly lovable Golly Sisters, traipsing and blundering their way along the trails of the Old West; Bingo Brown, intrepid hero of four books whose male admirers write to the author, "I'm just like Bingo Brown except I'm not afraid to hold a girl's hand"; the Pinballs, a band of foster children in a book by the same title (Bantam, 1988); Cracker Jackson, would-be juvenile rescuer of a woman abused by her husband (Viking, 1985); and, of course, McMummy, a giant plant pod shaped like a mummy. *The Pinballs* and five other books by Byars have been adapted for television as "After School" and "Saturday Specials."

Readers interested in learning more about Byars should read her entertaining memoir, *The Moon and I* (Messner, 1992), or check out Program Number 313 in *The Writers' Circle of South Carolina*, a cozy interview conducted by SCETV's Patti Just.
Website: www.BetsyByars.com

Cabaniss, Alice (b. 1934). Born in Ulmer, Allendale County, Cabaniss received her B.A. in journalism from Winthrop College (1955), her M.A.T. in the teaching of English from The Citadel (1974), and her Ph.D. in English from the University of South Carolina (1987). A longtime presence on the South Carolina arts scene, Cabaniss has taught at the University of South Carolina Spartanburg, Trident Technical College, the College of Charleston, and several Charleston high schools. For a number of years she traveled across the state as poet-in-residence in public schools under the auspices of the South Carolina Arts Commission. She was the founding editor of

Tinderbox (1978-1982), and from 1978 to 1988 she coordinated the Sundown Series of poetry readings for Piccolo Spoleto. Her own poetry and prose have appeared in *South Carolina Review*, *Kudzu*, *South Carolina Magazine*, *Southern Voices*, *The New South*, *Sandlapper*, and the anthologies *From the Green Horseshoe: Poems by James Dickey's Students* (University of South Carolina Press, 1987), *45/96: The Ninety-Six Sampler of South Carolina Poetry* (1994), and *You, Year: New Poems by Point Poets* (Harbinger Publications, 1996). She has published one collection: *The Dark Bus and Other Forms of Transport* (Saltcatcher Press, 1974). Cabaniss lives at Edisto Beach.

Card, Orson Scott. Although he was born in Richland, Washington; grew up in California, Arizona, and Utah; holds degrees from Brigham Young University and the University of Utah; and lives in Greensboro, North Carolina, Card deserves brief mention because at one time he spent four months a year writing at Myrtle Beach. Best known for his science fiction and fantasy novels, Card is distinguished for having won the Hugo and Nebula Awards for two years running for *Ender's Game* and *Speaker for the Dead*. His career began inauspiciously as a playwright, copywriter, and editor, but he became a fiction writer after incurring theatrical debts of $20,000 while still a student. Today he is widely admired for his fiction, and he frequently speaks to educational groups promoting the seriousness of science fiction as a literary genre. Card is also a devout Mormon whose work has been the target of critics hostile to the Church of Jesus Christ of Latter-Day Saints; as a result he is a champion of free speech and an opponent of censorship. An individualist's individualist, Card has a large and devoted following that is still growing. His interview with Patti Just is Program Number 407 of *The Writers' Circle of South Carolina*.

Mary Cartledgehayes

Cartledgehayes, Mary Jo (b. 1949). A full elder of the South Carolina Conference of the United Methodist Church since 1993, Cartledgehayes received her B.A. *magna cum laude* from the University of South Carolina (1983), her M.D. *magna cum laude* from The Divinity School of Duke University (1994), and her M.F.A. in creative nonfiction from Goucher College (2000). She is writer-in-residence with World Connections for Women, Morganton, North Carolina, and a former director of the mentor program of the Creative Nonfiction Foundation. Her nonfiction and poetry have appeared in many journals and magazines including *The Christian Science Monitor*, *Ms.* magazine, *The Upper Room*, *The Christian Century*, and *Welcomat of Philadelphia*. A commanding presence in the pulpit and before secular audiences, Cartledgehayes's sermons and meditations have appeared in anthologies such as *The Wisdom of Daughters: Twenty Years of the Voice of Christian Feminism* (Innisfree Press, 2001) and *Women at the Well: Meditations on Healing and Wholeness* (Judson Press, 1996). Her own books are a memoir, *Grace* (Crown Publishing, a division of Random House, 2003), and *To Love Delilah: Claiming the Women of the Bible* (LuraMedia, 1990). Address: 600 Crystal Drive, Spartanburg, SC 29302; (864) 573-7647
Email: MJCSP@aol.com

Casada, Jim. Casada in recent years has almost single-handedly managed to keep the best writing of Archibald Rutledge in print and before the public, although his own professional writing is in the area of history. He attributes his dedication to the deceased outdoorsman's work to a lifelong love of the writing of Archibald Rutledge, who, he maintains, combines elements of romance and of "oneness with nature" with an ability to carry the reader "vicariously directly to the scene." The result has been his editions of *Bird Dog Days and Wingshooting Ways*,*Hunting and Home in the Southern Heartland: The Best of Archibald Rutledge*, *Tales of Whitetails*, and *America's Greatest Game Bird*, all published by the University of South Carolina Press; and four books of his own, one an appreciation of fly-fishing. Casada also serves on the editorial staff of *Sporting Classics*, and he is editor-at-large of *Turkey and Turkey Hunting* magazine. He is interviewed by Patti Just in Program Number 312 of *The Writers' Circle of South Carolina*. Address: 1250 Yorkdale Drive, Rock Hill, SC 29730.
Email: jimcasada@comporium.net

Chapman, Wayne K. Chapman's primary contributions to the universe of literary South Carolina have been made as editor (2001-) and co-editor (1996-2001) of *The South Carolina Review*, Clemson University's fine journal that specializes in publishing both original poetry and short fiction by South Carolina writers and critical evaluations of the works of major figures from the state. As founding executive editor of Clemson University Digital Press, he has directed publication of several monographs, in print and online, including a book of poetry and a short-story collection. A full professor in the Clemson Department of English, Chapman received his B.S. (1972) and M.A. (1977) degrees from Portland State University and his Ph.D. from Washington State University (1988). His areas of professional specialization include Victorian through twentieth-century British and Anglo-Irish literature, American writers from 1855 to the present, W.B. Yeats and his circle, and Leonard and Virginia Woolf and the Bloomsbury group. He has received a National Endowment for the Humanities Summer Stipend (1993), a Fulbright Research Grant (1990), a Huntington Library Fellowship (1988), and numerous other awards.
Address: Department of English, Strode Tower, Box 340523, Clemson University, Clemson, SC 29634; (864) 656-5399.
Email: cwayne@clemson.edu

Chepesiuk, Ron. An accomplished freelance journalist with close to 3,000 articles in more than 370 different publications, Chepesiuk received his B.A. in history and political science from Minnesota State University at Moorhead, his M.L.S. in library science from Clark Atlanta University, and his D.A.S. in archival studies from the National University of Ireland. In addition to his many credits in print and electronic publications, including such major outlets as *USA Today*, *The New York Times*, *The Los Angeles Times*, *Modern Maturity*, *Writer's Digest*, and others, Chepesiuk has authored eight books on investigative journalism and the U.S. war on international drug trafficking. Of particular interest to aficionados of South Carolina literature and related subjects is "South Carolina Story," a weekly newspaper column co-authored by Chepesiuk that appeared from 1980 to 1989. Chepesiuk is adjunct professor in the journalism department, extension division, for UCLA, and was a Fulbright Scholar and visiting professor of journalism of the Chittagong University, Chittagong, Bangladesh in 2003.

He has also taught at Queens College, UCLA, Winthrop University, York Technical College, and for several professional organizations, including the Society of Professional Journalists and Investigative Reporters and Editors.
Address: 782 Wofford Street, Rock Hill, SC 29730; (803) 366-5440
Email: dmonitor1@yahoo.com

Childers, Max (b. 1947). A native of Mount Holly, a small North Carolina factory town, the source of his wry, quirky sense of humor—"The kind of humor that comes from there is often violent, it's excessive, and it's built around storytelling" (interview with Patti Just, Program Number 412 in *The Writers' Circle of South Carolina*)—Childers did not begin writing fiction until around age thirty. He earned a Ph.D. in American literature from the University of South Carolina (1978) and later a law degree, and in 1982 went to Winthrop University, where he still teaches. His first novel, *Things Undone* (Wyrick & Co., 1990), the saga of a quasi-mystic wreck survivor who hires a broken-down lawyer as his representative against the insurance company, was praised by *The New York Times Book Review* as "a good sharp dose of literary vinegar." His second novel, *Alpha and Omega* (Wyrick, 1996), tells the story of a guitar player who learns to play from a burned-out rhythm-and-blues star, his prison-mate, and who then founds the Elvis Presley-inspired Graceland by the Sea. Childers sees Elvis as the iconic embodiment of "all the possible bad taste in American culture"; the book exemplifies this belief and takes the reader on a rollicking good tour of the high and low points of this culture. Childers is a state treasure whose work deserves to be more widely known.

Cinelli, Joan. The editor and publisher of the poetry journal *Timelapse*, Cinelli's poems and articles have appeared in *Good Housekeeping*, *Christian Century*, *Jack and Jill*, and other national publications. A native of Virginia, she has made Anderson her home for many years.
Address: P.O. Box 834, Anderson, SC 29622
Email: tljoan@carol.net.

Coburn, Randy Sue (b. 1951). Coburn grew up in Greenville and is a Phi Beta Kappa graduate in journalism of the University of Georgia (1973). She has written the screenplay for *Mrs. Parker and the Vicious Circle* (1994), which was nominated for an Independent Spirit Award for best screenplay. She also wrote

and co-produced the television movie *Snap Decision* (2001). She is a former staff writer for *The Washington Star*, and her work has appeared in *Esquire*, *Smithsonian*, *The Washington Post*, *Premiere*, and *Interview*. She is also the recipient of a Hedgebrook Cottages residency, which allowed her to work on *Remembering Jody* (Carroll and Graf, 1999), her debut novel dealing with schizophrenia, set in Seattle against a backdrop of the main character's South Carolina childhood. Coburn lives in Seattle and teaches screenplay writing at the University of Washington.

Coggeshall, Rosanne (b. 1946). A native of Hartsville, Coggeshall currently lives and writes in Pittsboro, North Carolina. Her poetry and short fiction have appeared in *Epoch*, *Southern Review*, *New Virginia Review*, and—frequently—*The South Carolina Review*. One of her stories, "Lamb Says," was selected by John Gardner to appear in *Best American Short Stories* for 1982. She has taught at Hollins University and in the continuing education department at Duke. Her poetry is characterized by vivid imagery and uncompromising emotional confrontation, as well as both mastery of traditional forms and experimentation with forms of her own. Annie Dillard has called her "a modern Metaphysical poet" and her work "absolutely stunning monuments." She has published three collections: *Hymn for Drum* (Louisiana State University Press, 1978), *Traffic, with Ghosts* (Houghton Mifflin, 1984), and *Fire or Fire* (LSU Press, 2000).
Address: 159 Windstone, Pittsboro, NC 27312; (919) 542-5205

Conroy, Carol. Like her brother Pat, the poet Carol Conroy was born in Atlanta. Her two books of poetry, *The Beauty Wars* (W.W. Norton, 1992) and *The Jewish Furrier* (Old New York Book Shop Press, 1980), are notable for their uncompromising honesty and willingness to embrace even the most painful of emotions in public. Now living in New York City, she works with the Online Poetry Classroom of the Academy of American Poets, meets monthly with the Poems by Heart memorization circle at Poets House, and helps the Teachers and Writers Collaborative create special events like its James Wright Birthday Reading. She has been the recipient of two Twin Elms Writers Center fellowships (1993) and a New York State Fellowship for Individual Artists (1990). Her work has appeared in *The Paris Review*, *Agni Review*, *Ark/Angel*, and elsewhere. Conroy was the model for Savannah Wingo in Pat Conroy's *The Prince of Tides*. Additional information is to be found at the website of the Teachers and Writers Collaborative, www.twc.org/writers/pp_cconroy.htm.

Stephen Corey

Corey, Stephen (b. 1948). Poet, editor, and teacher Corey was born in Buffalo, New York, and received his B.A. and M.A. from the State University of New York at Binghamton and his Ph. D. from the University of Florida in Gainesville. In Gainesville he founded the journal, *The Devil's Millhopper*, which he continued to edit after being appointed assistant professor in the College of Applied Professional Sciences at the University of South Carolina in Columbia in 1980. Three years later he accepted an appointment as the assistant editor of *The Georgia Review*, where he has worked ever since. Although he is no longer a South Carolinian, Corey keeps his finger to the pulse of literary South Carolina and frequently returns to the state to participate in readings, panels, and workshops. His poetry has appeared in a wide range of journals; his books of verse include *11 Poems* (Renaissance Press, 1977), *The Last Magician* (Water Mark Press, 1981), *Fighting Death* (State Street Press, 1983), *Gentle Iron Lace* (The Press of the Night Owl, 1984), *Synchronized Swimming* (Swallow's Tale Press, 1985), *All These Lands You Call One Country* (University of Missouri Press, 1992), *Mortal Fathers and Daughters* (Palanquin Press, 1999), *Greatest Hits, 1980-2000* (Pudding House Publishers, 2000), and *There is No Finished World* (White Pine Press, 2003). He also compiled *Spreading the Word: Editors on Poetry* (2001) with editor/publisher Warren Slesinger of The Bench Press in Beaufort. Among Corey's awards are residencies at the Winthrop Writers' Conference and the Governor's School for the Arts, a John Atherton Fellowship in Poetry at

the Bread Loaf Writers' Conference, and a Fellowship in Poetry from the South Carolina Arts Commission. There is an engaging interview with Corey conducted by William B. Thesing in *Conversations with South Carolina Poets*, in which the poet discusses the role of poetry in relation to technology and the modern world.
Address: The Georgia Review,
The University of Georgia, Athens, GA 30602-9009; (706) 542-3481
Email: scorey@arches.uga.edu

Cox, Wayne (b. 1960). An associate professor of English at Anderson College, Cox is the author of *The Things We Leave Behind*, a book of original poetry with subjects ranging from the Falklands War to climbing Table Rock Mountain, published by Ninety-Six Press in 2000. Along with Lourdes Manye i Marti, he translated and published a bilingual edition of Miquel Marti i Pol's *Vacation Notebook* with Lang Press in 1996. This marked the first book-length appearance in English of one of the most widely-read poets in contemporary Catalan literature. Cox was educated at the University of Maine (B.A., 1984) and the University of South Carolina (M.A., 1989, and Ph.D., 1991). Cox's poetry has appeared in such journals as *Shenandoah*, *Yemassee*, *Southern Humanities Review*, *Southern Poetry Review*, and *The Chattahoochee Review*.
Address: Department of English,
Anderson College, Anderson SC 29621;
(864-231-2155)

Côté, Richard N. (b. 1945). A native of Waterbury, Connecticut, Côté studied political science and journalism at Butler University and served for six years in the U.S. Air Force. He moved to South Carolina in 1979 and worked on the staff at the South Carolina Historical Society in the 1980s. His vanguard book was *Safe House* (National Press Books, 1995), the autobiography of Edward Lee Howard, the first CIA agent to accept political asylum in Russia. Three South Carolina-based books followed. *Mary's World: Love, War, and Family Ties in Nineteenth-Century Charleston* (Corinthian Books, 1999) describes the tumultuous life of Charleston's Mary Pringle, her husband, thirteen children, and 337 slaves before, during, and after the Civil War. The best-selling biography was showcased on Patti Just's SC Educational Television show, *The Writers' Circle of South Carolina* in 2002. Dr. Walter Edgar read the book in segments when his SC Educational Radio show, *The Southern*

Reader, premiered in March 2003. *The Redneck Riviera* (Corinthian Books, 2001) is a contemporary novel about the healing power of a mother's love, set against the gaudy backdrop of tourist-crazed Myrtle Beach. *Theodosia Burr Alston: Portrait of a Prodigy* (Corinthian Books, 2003) is the biography of Aaron Burr's talented and mysterious daughter, who married a wealthy South Carolina rice planter and served as South Carolina's First Lady for 21 days before she and her ship disappeared at sea in 1813. A *Writers' Circle of South Carolina* program about Theodosia aired in 2003. Côté is interviewed by Patti Just in the fall 2001 season of *The Writers' Circle of South Carolina*.
Address: The Côté Literary Group,
P.O. Box 1898, Mount Pleasant, SC 29465;
(843) 881-6080
Email: dickcote@corinthianbooks.com

Wilbur Cross

Cross, Wilbur Lucien (b. 1918). A resident of Hilton Head, Cross received his undergraduate education at Yale University and served almost four years during World War II as an Army captain in the Pacific, then started his writing career as a copywriter in a New York advertising agency. He was an editor of Life magazine for eight years; during that period he also contributed to Time/Life books. His fifty-plus books include a wide range of subjects: history, biography, adventure, military affairs, entrepreneurship, retirement, education, self-help, and travel. *Choices with Clout: How to Make Things Happen by Making the Right Decisions Every Day of Your Life* was a bestseller and has been published in eight foreign countries. *Disaster at the Pole* is an account of the crash of the airship Italia in 1928, which launched the most extensive search for survivors in polar history. *Wooly Bear and the Reticent Menehunes* is a fantasy novel.

Damron, Carla (b. 1957). Born in Sumter, she currently lives in the woods outside of Columbia with her husband and their blended family of assorted animals. She draws upon her own experience as a clinical social worker in her first novel, *Keeping Silent* (Write Way Publishing, 2001; Worldwide Publishing mass market paperback, 2002). *Spider Blue*, her second Caleb Knowles novel, is in the works. Damron's interview with Patti Just for *The Writers' Circle of South Carolina* occurs in Program 9 of the 2003 season.
Address: 124 Fox Run Drive,
Hopkins, SC 29061
Email: carladamron@yahoo.com

Davidson, Phebe (b. 1944). One of South Carolina's most distinguished contemporary poets, Davidson holds the G.L. Toole Chair in English at the University of South Carolina

Phebe Davidson

Aiken. She earned her B.A. from Trenton State College (1967), and her M.A. and Ph.D. from Rutgers University (1991). In addition to teaching a broad range of English and film courses, she manages the Palanquin Poetry Press, of which she is the founding editor. Her own poems appear widely in literary magazines including *The Kenyon Review*, *The Literary Review*, *Poetry East*, *The Southern Poetry Review*, *The Journal of New Jersey Poets*, and *The Atlanta Review*. Her published collections include *Milk and Brittle Bone* (Muse-Pie Press, 1991), *Two Seasons* (Muse-Pie Press, 1993), *The Silence and Other Poems* (Mellen Poetry Press, 1995), *The Artists' Colony* (Mellen Poetry Press, 1996), *Dreameater* (Delaware Valley Poets, 1998), and *Reaching for Air* (Mellen Poetry Press, 2000).

Among Davidson's awards are the Soundpost Press Prize for 1999 for her chapbook, *The Plumage of Swans*, the Amelia Chapbook Prize for 2000 for *The Night That*

Eddy Died, the Kinloch Rivers Chapbooks Prize for 2002 for *Lying Down with Grief*, the Ledge Chapbook Prize for *A Note on Demographics*, the Johanna Burgoyne Poetry Award, the Yemassee Prize, the Porter Fleming Award, and the Poetry Society of South Carolina's Society Prize. In her poetry, her academic writing, and her editorial practice, Davidson is devoted "to clarity and to the belief that our daily language holds incalculable riches." Others seem to agree: she has received four Pushcart Prize nominations and is an artist-fellow of the Virginia Center for the Creative Arts. She is interviewed by Patti Just in Program Number 805 of *The Writers' Circle of South Carolina*.
Address: Palanquin Press,
Department of English, University of South Carolina Aiken, Aiken, SC 29801
Email: phebed@usca.edu

Dawes, Kwame Senu Neville (b. 1962). A native of the African nation of Ghana, Dawes grew up in Jamaica and attended Jamaica College and the University of the West Indies. He received his Ph.D. in 1992 from the University of New Brunswick in Canada, and since that time he has taught at the University of South Carolina in Columbia, where he is currently an associate professor of English. One of South Carolina's most accomplished and most prolific contemporary authors, Dawes has written more than fifteen plays, most of which have been produced in the Caribbean and elsewhere, including the Bristol Old Vic and Lyric Hammersmith in London. The play *One Love* has been published by Methuen Books (UK, 2001), and *Stump of the Terebinth* was the winner of Trinidad and Tobago's National Schools Festival in 2001. Dawes is also an award-winning poet, having published nine collections of verse: *Progeny of Air* (Peepal Tree, 1994), *Resisting the Anomie* (Goose Lane, 1995), *Prophets* (Peepal Tree, 1995), *Jacko Jacobus* (Peepal Tree, 1996), *Requiem* (Peepal Tree, 1996), *Shook Foil* (Peepal Tree, 1998), *Mapmaker* (Smith Doorstop, 2000), *Midland* (Ohio State University Press, 2001), and *New and Selected Poems* (Peepal Tree, 2003). *Progeny of Air* won the Forward Poetry Prize for Best First Collection (UK), and *Midland* won the 2001 Hollis Summers Poetry Prize of the Ohio State University Press. Dawes also won a 2001 Pushcart Prize for poetry. *Requiem* is a sequence of poems based upon the illustrations of South Carolina-based African-American artist Tom Feelings in his award-winning book, *Middle Passage: White Ships/ Black Cargo* (Penguin Putnam Books for Young

People, 1995).

Dawes is also known as a researcher and student of Caribbean and post-Colonial

Kwame Dawes

literature. He has edited *Talk Yuh Talk: Interviews with Caribbean Poets* (University of Virginia Press, 2000) and *Wheel and Come Again* (Peepal Tree Books/Goose Lane Editions, 1998), an anthology of reggae poetry.

Dawes has also written *Natural Mysticism: Towards a New Reggae Aesthetic* (Peepal Tree, 1999) and *Bob Marley: Lyrical Genius* (Sanctuary, 2003), the first in-depth study of the lyrics of Bob Marley. The novel *Bivouac* (Peepal Tree) is scheduled to appear in 2004, and the short-story collection *A Place to Hide* (Peepal Tree) was published in 2002. His essays and reviews on the literature and culture of Africa and its diaspora have appeared in a variety of American and international journals. In 1987 Dawes became an Honorary Fellow of the University of Iowa's writing program, and in 1997 he was named an Associate Fellow of the University of Warwick. He is the editor of a series of Caribbean plays for Peepal Tree Books, the director of the Poetry Initiative at the University of South Carolina, and criticism editor of *Obsidian III*, a leading African-American literary journal. Dawes frequently gives readings from his works, conducts writing workshops, and addresses a variety of educational groups on a range of literary and cultural topics. Dawes's interview with host Patti Just appears in Program Number 605 of *The Writers' Circle of South Carolina*.
Address: Department of English, University of South Carolina, Columbia, SC 29208;
(803) 777-2096
Website: www.kwamedawes.com
Email: dawesk@gwm.sc.edu

Dorrell, Linda (b. 1962). Novelist Dorrell has lived in the rural Florence County community of Effingham her entire life. She was educated at Francis Marion University and turned to fiction after jobs as a journalist and public relations specialist. She has also been a regular contributor to *Pee Dee Magazine*, and her work has appeared in *Southern Living* and *Ancestry*. Dorrell's first novel, *True Believers* (Baker Book House, 2001), was praised by *Library Journal* as "historical fiction with a kick and some devious surprises"; her second novel, *Face to Face*, was issued in December 2002 by Baker Books.
Website: www.lindadorrell.com
Email: lindorrell@aol.com

Bernie Dunlap

Dunlap, Benjamin Bernard (b. 1937). A native of Columbia, where he became a legendary professor of English and the humanities at the University of South Carolina, Dunlap is a *summa cum laude* graduate of the University of the South (1959). He was a Rhodes Scholar and received his Ph.D. from Harvard University in 1967. A true man for all seasons, Dunlap is the author of poetry, essays, opera *libretti*, anthologies, and film scripts; he has been a Fulbright professor in Thailand and a Japan Society Leadership Fellow in Japan. He is also a frequent moderator for the Aspen Institute Executive and C.E.O. Seminars as well as the Institute's Executive Seminar Asia. As writer-producer for public television, he has been responsible for more than 200 programs, for which he has won numerous national and international awards, and he is the author of op-ed pieces in newspapers across the state and region. He is the former Chapman Family Professor in the Humanities and currently the tenth president of Wofford College. He has recently completed his first novel, *Famous Dogs of the Civil War*.
Address: Office of the President,

Wofford College, Spartanburg, SC 29301; (864) 597-4010
Email: dunlapbb@wofford.edu

Dupree, Nathalie. Cookbook author Nathalie Dupree has "thrown parties on rooftops and in tiny apartments from San Francisco to Rome to Social Circle, Georgia," and has "entertained as a young professional on a tight budget, a television personality, and cooking teacher; planned galas for hundreds and put on last-minute get-togethers." She has clearly learned a great deal along the way because her many cookbooks have sold over half a million copies. She has also hosted six 26-part series on PBS and 130 shows on the Food Network. Her books include *Cooking of the South* (Irena Chalmers Cookbooks, 1984); *New Southern Cooking* (Knopf, 1986); *Nathalie Dupree Cooks for Family and Friends* (William Morrow, 1991); *Nathalie Dupree's Comfortable Entertaining: At Home with Ease and Grace* (Viking Press, 1998); and *Savoring Savannah: Feasts from the Low Country* (Ten Speed Press, 2001). Currently Dupree lives in Charleston where she writes for the food page of the *Post and Courier*, a column that is also syndicated by the *Los Angeles Times*.

Durban, Pam (b. 1947). Aiken native Durban arrived at literature via a circuitous route after graduating from the University of North Carolina-Greensboro. She worked on a small newspaper in Seneca, then on Atlanta's independent *Great Speckled Bird*, and later as a staff writer for *The Atlanta Gazette*. In the late seventies she attended the University of Iowa Writer's Workshop. "That's where," she says, "I made a commitment to writing ... I began to think of myself as a writer." She graduated from Iowa in 1979 and taught in New York, Kentucky, and Ohio. Her collection of stories, *All Set About with Fever Trees and Other Stories* (David R. Godine), was published in 1985; this and the appearance of her stories in the prize anthologies *New Stories from the South* and *The Best American Short Stories of the Century* brought her to the attention of an increasingly large and appreciative audience. *The Laughing Place* (Scribner's, 1992) won the 1994 Townsend Prize for Fiction, and *So Far Back* (Picador, 2000) won the 2001 Lillian Smith Book Award for Fiction. Durban has also won the 1988 Whiting Writer's Award, the 1984 Rinehart Award in Fiction, and a National Endowment for the Arts Fellowship. Her work is published in *Tri-Quarterly*, *Crazyhorse*, *The Georgia Review*, and

elsewhere. She teaches at the University of North Carolina at Chapel Hill, where she is the Doris Betts Distinguished Professor of Creative Writing. Durban is interviewed by Patti Just in Program Number 405 of *The Writers' Circle of South Carolina*.
Address: Department of English, University of North Carolina, Chapel Hill, NC 27599; (919) 962-4006

Earle, Garet W. See Wilton Earle Hall, Jr.

Earle, Wilton. See Wilton Earle Hall, Jr.

Edgar, Walter (b. 1943). "South Carolina is the most fascinating but one of the most misunderstood places in the world," according to Edgar, who has devoted most of his professional life to rectifying that fact. The Claude Henry Neuffer Professor of Southern Studies at the University of South Carolina and director of the Institute for Southern Studies, Edgar received his B.A. from Davidson College (1965) and his M.A. (1967) and Ph.D. (1969) degrees from the University of South Carolina. His *magnum opus* to date has been *South Carolina: A History* (University of South Carolina Press, 1998), the first comprehensive history of the state in fifty years. Praised by Charles Joyner for his "careful scholarship, insightful interpretation, and graceful writing," Edgar has been able to combine scholarly excellence with popular appeal in a

Walter Edgar

manner few historians have been able to achieve. *South Carolina: A History* went through five printings in its first three years, and its audiotape edition became a popular item in the catalog of South Carolina Educational Television.

Among Edgar's other noteworthy studies of South Carolina history are *South Carolina in the Modern Age* (USC Press, 1992), *A Guide* for the Teaching of South Carolina History and its Relationship with United States History (SC Dept. of Education, 1989; rev. ed., Institute for Southern Studies, 1991), *Columbia: Portrait of a City* (with Deborah K. Woolley, The Donning Company, 1988), *History of Santee Cooper, 1934-1984* (The R.L. Bryan Company, 1984), and *Partisans and Redcoats: The Southern Conflict that Turned the Tide of the American Revolution* (William Morrow, 2001). He has also edited or co-edited biographical dictionaries of the South Carolina House of Representatives, *The Papers of Henry Laurens Vol. VI* (USC Press, 1974), *The Letterbook of Robert Pringle* (USC Press, 1972), and other works.

As *Literary South Carolina* went to press, Edgar was hard at work as editor of another major work, *The South Carolina Encyclopedia*, a project of the Humanities Council^SC, the Institute for Southern Studies, and USC Press. Billed as "the first comprehensive reference source of the people, places, events, things, achievements, and ideals that have contributed to the ongoing evolution of the Palmetto State," *The South Carolina Encyclopedia* will consist of more than 2,500 entries, hundreds of illustrations, and more than one million words. Its unique contribution to a fuller understanding of all aspects of the history and culture of South Carolina is hard to overestimate. Edgar is profiled in Program Number 406 of *The Writers' Circle of South Carolina*.

Address: Institute for Southern Studies, Gambrell Hall 107, University of South Carolina, Columbia, SC 29208; (803) 777-2340
Email: edgar@gwm.sc.edu

Ely, J. Scott (b. 1944). Novelist and short-story writer Ely received his B.A. (1968) and M.A. (1973) from the University of Mississippi and his M.F.A. from the University of Arkansas (1986). He taught at Snead State Junior College (Alabama) and the University of Arkansas before arriving at Winthrop University in 1987, where he remains today as associate professor of English. A prolific author of short fiction, his stories have appeared in the *Antioch Review*, *The Southern Review*, *Shenandoah*, *The Ohio Journal*, and elsewhere. His story collections include *Pulpwood* (forthcoming, The University of West Alabama, 2004), *The Angel of the Garden* (University of Missouri Press, 1998), and *Overgrown With Love* (University of Arkansas Press, 1993). He has also written two novels:

Pit Bull (Widened and Nicolson, 1988), an exploration of the effects of violence on human beings, and *Starlight* (Widened and Nicolson, 1987), a Vietnam War story based on his own experiences in Southeast Asia.

Ely has received fellowships from the National Endowment for the Arts (1992) and the Rockefeller/Bellagio Fellowships (1990). His works have been included in *New Stories from the South* (1998). In 2001 he was appointed contributing and advisory editor to *Shenandoah*. Patti Just interviews Scott Ely in Program Number 307 of *The Writers' Circle of South Carolina*.

Address: 330 Marion Street, Rock Hill, SC 29730; (803) 328-9207
Email: sely@comporium.net

Edwin Epps

Epps, Edwin C. (b. 1948). A harmless drudge, Epps lives in Spartanburg where he is a National Board Certified Teacher of English at Spartanburg High School. He is a graduate of Emory University (B.A. with Highest Honors in English, 1970) and the University of South Carolina (M.A., 1973; Ed.D., 1993). His poetry has appeared in *Point*, the *Savannah Literary Journal*, *Drift*, and a number of anthologies. He has published on a variety of bibliophilic and pedagogic topics in journals such as *Conradiana*, the *Virginia English Bulletin*, the *Journal of Pre-Raphaelite Studies*, *Carolina English Teacher*, and *South Carolina Writing Teacher*, of which he is former editor. He has been a student and devotee of South Carolina literature since his childhood, and his previous work in this area includes *South Carolina Literature: A Reading List for Students, Educators, and Laymen* (Woodspurge Books, 1989) and essays on Pat Conroy; his freelance essays have appeared in *Sandlapper* and *Creative Loafing*.

Address: P.O. Box 18404, Spartanburg, SC 29318; (864) 529-0180
Email: eppse@ bellsouth.net

Percival Everett

Everett, Percival (b. 1956). The author of nearly a dozen books, Columbia native Everett is a graduate of the University of Miami and of the graduate writing program at Brown University. A lover of books from his boyhood, he majored at Miami in philosophy; he has taught at the University of Kentucky, Notre Dame, the University of California Riverside, and the University of Southern California, where he is currently a professor in the English Department.

Everett is known for his experimental approach to fiction. Among his works are *Erasure* (University Press of New England, 2001), about a black novelist's encounters with racism; *Glyph* (Graywolf Press, 1999), whose protagonist is an eighteen-month-old prodigy; the sensationalist *Cutting Lisa* (Tickner and Fields, 1986); and *Walk Me to the Distance* (Tickner and Fields, 1985), in which a Vietnam veteran undertakes a journey of self-discovery. Everett's other novels include *Grand Canyon, Inc.* (Versus Press, 2001), *Frenzy* (Greywolf Press, 1997), *God's Country* (Faber and Faber, 1996), *For Her Dark Skin* (Owl Creek Press, 1993), *Zulus* (Permanent Press, 1992), and his debut book, *Suder* (Viking Press, 1983). He has also published two story collections: *Big Picture* (Graywolf, 1998) and *The Weather and Women Treat Me Fair* (August House, 1987).

Everett's awards include the Pen/Oakland-Josephine Miles Award for Excellence in Literature for *Big Picture*, 1997; the Lila Wallace-Readers Digest Fellowship and Woodrow Wilson Foundation, 1994; the New American Writing Award, for *Zulus*, 1990; the D.H. Lawrence Fellowship, University of New Mexico, 1984; the Hillsdale Prize from the Fellowship of Southern Writers; and the Hurston/Wright Legacy Award. He is married to the Assyriologist Francesca Rochberg Everett.

Address: Department of English,

University of Southern California,
University Park, Los Angeles,
CA 90089-0354; (213) 740-3743
Email: peverett@usc.edu

Ezell-Schmitz, Doris. A native of York County, Ezell-Schmitz has been teaching language arts at Chester Middle School since 1978. Educated at Winthrop (B.A. and M.A. degrees), she spent six weeks in England during the summer of 1996 on a DeWitt Wallace Reader's Digest fellowship awarded through the Bread Loaf Rural Teacher Network. The victim of a blood clot in her brain when she was a teenager, Ezell began writing poetry in the eighth grade but "got serious" about it at Winthrop, where she was published in the college's literary journal. She has since published four books of poetry, including *A Teacher Testifies* and *Beyond Superlatives: Encounters in Indonesia.* Her work has appeared in *English Journal, Point, The Vermont Literary Review,* and elsewhere.
Address: Chester Middle School, 1014 McCandless Road, Chester, SC 29706; (803) 377-8192

Farley, Benjamin Wirt (b. 1935). Retired Erskine College professor Farley published widely in the field of Reformation studies during his twenty-six-year career; he has ten books to his name and served as president of the Calvin Studies Society. He is the author of a novel, *Corbin's Rubi-Yacht* (Sandlapper Publishing, 1992), about loss, love, sailing, and the Vietnam War. He also has written three collections of short stories: *The Hero of St. Lo: Stories of Abbeville and the Upcountry* (Jacobs Press, 1983; republished by Cherokee, 1986, reprinted 1997), *Mercy Road: Stories of South Carolina, Virginia, and Georgia* (Cherokee, 1986), and *Son of the Morning Sky: Reflections on the Spirituality of the Earth* (University Press of America, 1999). Farley lives with his wife in Irmo. He is interviewed in Program Number 211 of *The Writers' Circle of South Carolina.* Email: aag@infoave.net.

Farrow, David A. (b. 1952). Lowcountry editor and author Farrow moved to Charleston when he was adopted on April 2, 1953. He attended Christ School, George Washington University, and the College of Charleston, where he received his B.A. in 1978. After more than twenty years as an author and tour guide in Charleston, Farrow decided to concentrate on writing when he turned forty and "my mortality slapped me flat in the face. It was

time to fish or cut bait." Since then he has been past editor of *Carolina Style* magazine and the current managing editor of the *Charleston Mercury.* He is also the author of *Charleston, South Carolina: A Remembrance of Things Past: A Walking Tour Book for Literate People* (Tradd Street Press) and of the popular novel *The Root of All Evil* (Wyrick & Co., 1997), a horror/detective novel set in Charleston featuring demonic possession, a reunion of three old friends, a series of tourist murders, voodoo-like religious talismans, and a main character with the undeniably Lowcountry moniker "Andrew Rutledge." Farrow is also the author and host of the film *Charleston, SC: 1860-1865: The War for Southern Independence* (SunCoast Media Productions, 2002) and the tour guide for the online *Magical History Tour of Charleston* (www.charlestonliving.com). In 1990 he was co-producer, with Pete Peters, of a tour video called *Charleston, S.C.: A Magical History Tour.* He is working on another novel.
Address: 2073 Clayton Street, Charleston, SC 29414; (843) 763-8945
Email: housebios2@aol.com

Gene Fehler

Fehler, Gene (b. 1940). One of South Carolina's most prolific poets, Fehler lives in Seneca and teaches poetry writing in the schools through South Carolina's Artist in Education program. His books include *Center Field Grasses: Poems from Baseball* (McFarland & Co., 1991), *Dancing on the Basepaths* (McFarland & Co., 2001), *I Hit the Ball: Baseball Poems for the Young* (McFarland & Co., 1996), *Tales from Baseball's Golden Age* (Sports Publishing, 2000), *More Tales from Baseball's Golden Age* (Sports Publishing, 2002), and *Let More Poems Begin* (forthcoming from McGraw-Hill). Little Simon, a division of Simon & Schuster, will publish *The Little Goblin Book of Poems* in 2004. He has also published more than 1,800 poems and stories in more

than 300 magazines and anthologies including *Christian Living, Connecticut River Review, Ellery Queen's Mystery Magazine, Minneapolis Review of Baseball, Poet Lore, Point, Spitball, The Writer,* and *Writer's Digest.* Fehler has won numerous local, state, and national poetry contests and has been nominated for three Pushcart Prizes.
Address: 106 Laurel Lane, Seneca, SC 29678; (864) 882-8574
Email: fehler@earthlink.net

Nikky Finney

Finney, Nikky (b. 1957). A native of Conway, Finney grew up in a household in which the importance of heritage and the issues of the Civil Rights movement of the 1950s and 1960s were of equal importance. Her father—attorney and then judge Ernest Finney, Jr.—played an important role in a number of important South Carolina desegregation cases. She began writing at age ten in response to her parents' involvement in the Civil Rights movement. Finney graduated from Talladega College in Alabama (B.A., 1979) and also studied at Atlanta University from 1979 to 1981. Her mentors include the writers Richard Long, Toni Cade Bambara, Nikki Giovanni, and the actress Ruby Dee. From 1984 to 1986 she worked as a writer, editor, and photographer for *Vital Signs Magazine,* and she has taught at the University of Kentucky and Berea College. Currently she is associate professor of creative writing at the University of Kentucky. She has published a collection of short stories, *Heartwood* (University Press of Kentucky, 1998) and three volumes of poetry: *On Wings Made of Gauze* (William Morrow, Inc., 1985), *Rice* (Sister Vision Press, 1995), and *The World Is Round* (InnerLight, 2002). *Rice,* in particular, is a collection notable for its interweaving of the rice culture of the South Carolina Lowcountry with the lives of those who worked in the rice fields and their descendants. Finney's poetic voice has been compared to "cool jazz" by the *Library Journal*. Her interview with Patti Just is Program Number 402 of *The Writers' Circle of South Carolina*.

Address: Department of English,
University of Kentucky, Lexington, KY
40506; (859) 257-6997
Email: finney@uky.edu

Floyd, Carlisle Sessions, Jr. (b. 1926). One of the nation's most celebrated living composers, Floyd was born in Latta, studied for two years at Converse College, and received his B.M. (1946) and M.M. (1949) degrees at Syracuse University. He studied further at the Aspen Institute before accepting teaching positions at Florida State University (1947-1976) and then the University of Houston. Floyd's best-known composition is the opera *Susannah* (1955), followed closely by *Of Mice and Men* (1970), which is based upon the John Steinbeck novel. Other well-known works include *Bilby's Doll* (1976), *Willie Stark* (1981, based upon Robert Penn Warren's *All the King's Men*), and *Cold Sassy Tree* (2000, based upon Olive Anne Burns's novel); Floyd has also written a large number of non-operatic scores, including a song cycle based upon the poems of Emily Dickinson. Floyd has won virtually every major award in his profession, notably the National Opera Institute's Award for Service to American Opera and major commissions from the Ford Foundation, the Kennedy Center Foundation, and from the New York, Santa Fe, Houston, and Greater Miami opera companies.

Flythe, Starkey, Jr. (b. 1935). A native of North Augusta, South Carolina, Flythe graduated from the University of the South (B.A.) and the University of Georgia (M.A.). After summer graduate work at Harvard, he served in the United States Army in East Africa

Starkey Flythe

and later attended night law school in Augusta while teaching in public schools in Beaufort and North Augusta. He worked with the Curtis Publishing Company, where he was re-founding and managing editor of *The Saturday Evening Post*, edited *Holiday* and *The Country Gentleman*, and supervised the production of books on popular serial fiction and American illustration. Lately he has been a manuscript screener at *The Georgia Review* and a summer teacher at the SC Governor's School for the Arts and Humanities. Flythe's books include the short story collection *Lent: The Slow Fast* (University of Iowa Press, 1990), an anthology that explores relationships and religion; and the poetry collections *Paying the Anesthesiologist* (1995) and *They Say Dancing* (2000), both from Ninety-Six Press. His stories have appeared in the *Best American Short Story* and *O. Henry Prize* annuals, and he has won a PEN/Syndicated Fiction prize, an NEA fellowship, and a University of Iowa Press Prize for *Lent: The Slow Fast*. Flythe is interviewed by Patti Just in Program Number 410 of *The Writers' Circle of South Carolina*.

Address: 1220 Georgia Avenue,
North Augusta, SC 29841

Frank, Dorothea Benton (b. 1951). Charleston native Frank grew up on Sullivan's Island, graduated from the Fashion Institute of America in Atlanta, and attended the Art Student's League in New York and Bloomfield College in New Jersey. During her career she worked in New York's fashion industry, importing women's knitwear and collection sportswear from Hong Kong, Korea, Japan, and Taiwan. She retired upon the birth of her daughter and became a volunteer fundraiser for various arts and educational organizations in the metropolitan New York area, serving appointed positions on the New Jersey State Council on the Arts, the Drumthwacket Foundation, and the New Jersey Cultural Trust. She has held numerous board positions with other nonprofit organizations at the Margaret Mitchell House (Atlanta), the Bill T. Jones/Arnie Zane Dance Company (New York), the Montclair Art Museum (New Jersey), and the New Jersey Chamber Music Society and Whole Theater (New Jersey). She began writing as a way of coping with her grief after the death of her mother in 1993 and has since penned three best-selling novels set along the contemporary South Carolina coast: *Sullivan's Island* (Berkley Publishing, Inc., 2000), *Plantation* (Berkley, 2001), and *Isle of Palms* (Berkley, 2003). Her engagingly human

narrators and warm sense of humor and good fun have ingratiated her with a large and devoted reading public, especially, but not limited to, Southerners. She is at work on her fourth novel, *Shem Creek*. She lives in the New York area with her husband, Peter, and their two teenagers, Victoria and William.

Website: www.dotfrank.com
Email: dot@dotfrank.com

Frazier, Charles (b. 1950). North Carolina native Frazier received his Ph. D. from the University of South Carolina in 1986. While subsequently living in Colorado, he wrote *Adventuring in the Andes: The Sierra Club Travel Guide to Ecuador, Peru, Bolivia, the Amazon Basin, and the Galapagos Islands* (Sierra Club Books, 1985), but it was not until he moved back to North Carolina that he wrote and published *Cold Mountain* (Atlantic Monthly Press, 1997), winner of the National Book Award and a bestseller. *Cold Mountain* became a true sensation, not only capturing the attention of the reading public but also drawing the admiring praise of fellow authors such as Kaye Gibbons, Ann Beattie, Willie Morris, and Larry Brown. United Artists purchased the film rights to the novel for $1.25 million, and Frazier received an unprecedented advance for his second novel.

Keller Cushing Freeman

Freeman, Keller Cushing (b. 1934). Freeman, a native of Asheville, North Carolina, was educated at Radcliffe and Erskine Colleges (A.B., *magna cum laude*, 1958), at Rhodes House, Oxford (Woodrow Wilson Fellow, 1960-1961), and the University of Georgia (Ph.D., 1963). She has taught at Furman and Clemson universities, Greenville Technical College, and the Greenville Museum Art School. In addition to *Shadow of Suribachi*, a book on the Iwo Jima campaign during World War II (with Parker Bishop Albee, Jr., Praeger Publishers,

1994), she has published two volumes of poetry: *Walking Like a Waterspider* (Ninety-Six Press, 1996) and *Trespass of Venus* (Emrys Press, 2000). She is a co-founder of the Emrys Foundation and *Emrys Journal* and is a frequent reader before a large variety of public audiences; she has also won a number of civic service and humanitarian awards.

Address: 118 Crescent Avenue, Greenville, SC 29605; (864) 242-5632
Email: dlfreeman10@charter.net

Friddle, Mindy (b. 1964). A native of Greenville and former newspaper reporter, Friddle earned her bachelor's degree from Furman University and an M.A. in teaching/English from the University of South Carolina. Her first novel, *A Garden Angel*, which celebrates women's friendships in a down-at-the-heels Southern town, was due to be published by St. Martin's Press in spring 2004. Of that work, Pulitzer Prize winner Richard Russo says, "Mindy Friddle has a great comedic touch, and her novel is a touching, heartfelt debut." Friddle is a two-time winner of the South Carolina Fiction Project and the Piccolo Spoleto Fiction Open and was named alternate for the 2004 South Carolina Arts Commission's Artist Fellowship for Prose.

Gardner, Stephen (b. 1948). A past president of the board of governors of the South Carolina Academy of Authors, Gardner is professor of poetry, modern literature, and creative writing at the University of South Carolina Aiken, where until recently he also edited *The Devil's Millhopper* and was publisher of TDM Press. He received his B.A. and M.A. in English from the University of South Carolina in Columbia, where he studied with Ennis Rees and George Garrett. His Ph.D. in English and creative writing is from Oklahoma State University, where he generated the first creative writing dissertation in poetry while also pursuing the traditional degree track in literature. His poetry has been published in *California Quarterly, Cimarron Review, Cincinnati Poetry Review, Connecticut Review, The Devil's Millhopper, The Mexico Humanities Review, New Orleans Review, Poetry Northwest, The Southern Review*, and elsewhere. He is the author of *This Book Belongs to Eva* (Palanquin Press, 1996) and plans to collaborate with Steve Corey and Jim Peterson on a twenty-five-year retrospective of work published in *The Devil's Millhopper*. His interview with Patti Just is Program Number 805 of *The Writers' Circle of South Carolina*.

Address: Department of English, University of South Carolina Aiken, 471 University Parkway, Aiken, SC 29801; (803) 648-6851
Email: steveg@usca.edu

George Garrett

Garrett, George (b. 1929). Novelist Garrett qualifies for inclusion in this volume by virtue of his tenure as writer-in-residence and professor of English at the University of South Carolina in Columbia from 1971 to 1974. Born in Orlando, Florida, Garrett was educated at Sewanee Military Academy and the Hill School. His B.A. (1952) and M.A. (1956) are from Princeton, with military service in the U.S. Army intervening. He has taught, successively, at Wesleyan University (1956-1960), Rice University (1961-62), the University of Virginia (1962-67), Princeton University (1964-65), Hollins College (1967-1971), USC, Florida International University (1974), Princeton University again (1975-77), Columbia University (1977-78), the University of Michigan at Ann Arbor (1979 and 1982-84), Bennington College, Virginia Military Institute, and the University of Virginia (since 1984). The author of more than two dozen novels, plays, and poetry collections, Garrett is best known for his Elizabethan trilogy: *Death of the Fox: A Novel About Raleigh* (Doubleday, 1971), *The Succession: A Novel of Elizabeth and James* (Doubleday, 1983), and *Entered from the Sun* (Doubleday, 1990). A rarity among major modern novelists in that his devout Christianity strongly influences his fiction, Garrett has been widely praised for his short stories as well as his longer fiction. In the summer of 2002, he was named poet laureate of the state of Virginia.

Geraty, Virginia Mixson (b. 1915). A lifelong student of the Gullah language and the people who speak it, Geraty lived for fifty years in the Yonges Island/Edisto region of the Lowcountry. She is the author of five books: *Bittle En' T'Ing: Gullah Cooking with Maum Chrish'* (Sandlapper Publishing, 1992); *Porgy: A Gullah Version* (Wyrick & Co., 1990); *Gulluh Fuh Oonuh/Gullah for You: A Guide to the Gullah Language* (Sandlapper, 1998); and *Gullah Night Before Christmas*, illustrated by James Rice (Pelican Publishing, 1998). She has also published *A Teacher's Guide to the Gullah Language*, a manual to help close the achievement gap between African-American and Caucasian students. Geraty has written scholarly papers on Gullah and is a frequent presenter before educational organizations. She received a Doctor of Humane Letters from the College of Charleston in 1995, the Governor's Award for Lifetime Achievement in the Humanities in 1998, a nomination for the poet laureate of South Carolina in 1984, and membership in Kappa Delta Pi International Honorary Society in Education at the Citadel. She maintains an active Web presence.

Address: 1252 Sunset Drive, Charleston, SC 29407; (843) 556-4701 (10 am-7 pm only)
Website: http://members.aol.com/_ht_a/drgeraty/Gullah.htm
Email: DrVGeraty@aol.com

Sarah Gilbert

Gilbert, Sarah (b. 1959). After exploring the world of work as a hairdresser, bank teller, bartender, model, hostess at a hamburger restaurant, and adult diaper salesperson, Gilbert began to write her first novel, *Hairdo* (Warner, 1990), initially a short story, in response to a writing prompt from her instructor, William Price Fox, whom she later married. The book struck an immediately resonant chord with Southern readers because of its unpretentious heroine and her no-holds-barred approach to life. Like the protagonist of her second novel, *Dixie Riggs* (Warner, 1991), whom she describes as "a redneck version of myself," Gilbert sees herself as "kind of a woman child with a great sense of humor," a persona much in evidence in her interview with Patti Just in Program Number 103 of *The Writers' Circle of South Carolina*. She has written two other novels—*A League of Their Own* (Warner Books, 1992), about a women's baseball team, and *Summer Gloves* (Warner Books, 1993)—and magazines pieces for, among others, *Allure*, *Glamour*, and *Self*.

Glazener, Mary (b. 1921). A resident of Central, South Carolina, Glazener returned for her degree at Clemson University after time off to have a family. Strongly influenced by Dietrich Bonhoeffer's *Letters and Papers from Prison* during a crisis in her own faith, Glazener researched Bonhoeffer's life and then wrote her novel, *The Cup of Wrath: A Novel Based on Dietrich Bonhoeffer's Resistance to Hitler* (Smyth & Helwys Publishing, 1992). Patti Just's interview with Glazener is featured in Program Number 408 of *The Writers' Circle of South Carolina*.

Goding, Cecile (b. 1951). A native of Florence, Goding now lives in Iowa City, Iowa. She is a past winner of *Poetry Northwest*'s Theodore Roethke and Richard Hugo awards (1990, 1992), the State Street Press Chapbook Contest (1991), the South Carolina Fiction Project (1990, 1994), and the Fellowship in Poetry from the South Carolina Academy of Authors (1993). Her chapbook *The Women Who Drink at the Sea* was published by State Street Press in 1992. Her essay "Six Degrees of Fluency" won the Gold Star 2000 award from the Georgia Magazine Association. Her most recent work has appeared in *Ploughshares*, *The Gettysburg Review*, *The Georgia Review*, *Kestral*, and the fiction collection *Inheritance* (Hub City, 2001) and the nonfiction collection *In Brief: Short Takes on the Personal* (Norton, 1999).
Address: 811 Brown Street,
Iowa City, IA 52245
Email: cecile-goding@mchsi.com

Godwin, Rebecca T. (b. 1950). Born in Charleston, Godwin graduated from Coastal Carolina Community College *summa cum laude* in 1977 after marrying, becoming a mother, and working as a secretary in a steel mill. She has also been a real estate broker, an advertising agency writer, and editor. She received her M.A. from Middlebury College's Bread Loaf School of English in 1988, and is currently a faculty member at Bennington College, where she also has taught in the

M.F.A. writing program. Godwin's short fiction has appeared in *The South Carolina Review*, *Epoch*, *The Crescent Review*, and *The Paris Review*. Her first novel, *Private Parts* (Longstreet Press, 1992) received enthusiastic reviews; for portions of her second novel, *Keeper of the House* (St. Martin's Press, 1994), she received a National Endowment for the Arts fellowship. Other honors include a South Carolina Fiction Project award and a MacDowell Colony fellowship.
Address: Bennington College,
One College Drive, Bennington, VT 05201;
(802) 442-5401
Email: rgodwin@bennington.edu

Goldman, Judy Ann (b. 1942). Rock Hill native Goldman now lives in Charlotte where she is a local commentator for National Public Radio. She is the author of two volumes of poetry—*Holding Back Winter* (St. Andrews Press, 1987) and *Wanting to Know the End* (Silverfish Review Press, 1993)—as well as *Collected Essays* (Warren Publishing, 1994) and *The Slow Way Back* (Morrow, 1999), a novel about family secrets that was nominated for the Southeastern Booksellers Association Fiction Award and which won the Sir Walter Raleigh Award for Fiction and the Mary Ruffin Poole First Work of Fiction Award. Goldman has also won the Fortner Writer and Community Award. She teaches at writers' conferences throughout the Southeast.

Gould, Scott (b. 1959). Born near the black water swamps of Williamsburg County, Gould graduated from Wofford College and the University of South Carolina. His stories have appeared in *Kenyon Review*, *Kansas Review*, *Carolina Quarterly*, *Black Warrior Review*, *Crescent Review*, *New Stories from the South*, and the Hub City anthology *New Southern*

Harmonies: Four Emerging Writers (1998). He is also the author of the chapbook *Jukebox Love: Poems* (Holocene Publishing, 1996). The winner of awards for his fiction, poetry, screenwriting, and teaching from the South

Scott Gould

Carolina Arts Commission and the South Carolina Academy of Authors, among others, he taught at the Greenville Fine Arts Center and the Governor's School for the Arts and Humanities. He now teaches creative writing at Presbyterian College.

Greene, Harlan (b. 1953). A native of Charleston, Harlan Greene received his B.A. from the College of Charleston in 1975 and spent a large part of his professional life in that city as archivist and assistant director of the South Carolina Historical Society from 1976 to 1989. In the 1990s he was director of the North Carolina Preservation Consortium in Durham, and today he is manager of special collections at the Charleston County Public Library. He is the author of two novels, *Why We Never Danced the Charleston* (St. Martin's Press, 1984) and Lambda Literary Award-winner *What the Dead Remember* (Dutton, 1991), both of which explore the relationships between gay protagonists and the larger worlds, both straight and homosexual, of which they are a part. Greene is also the author of four works of nonfiction: *Charleston: City of Memory*, with photographs by N. Jane Iseley (Legacy Publications, 1987); *Mr. Skylark: John Bennett and the Charleston Renaissance* (University of Georgia Press, 2001); *Renaissance in Charleston: Art and Life in the Carolina Low Country* (edited with James Hutchisson, University of Georgia Press, 2003); and, with Harry S. Hutchins, Jr., and Brian E. Hutchins, *Slave Badges and the Slave-Hire System in Charleston, South Carolina, 1783-1865* (McFarland, 2003). He has essays in the collections *Hometowns: Gay Men Write About Where They Belong*, edited by John Preston (Dutton, 1991), and *A Member of the Family: Gay Men Write About Their Closest Relations*, edited by John Preston (Dutton, 1992). He has also compiled an index to the 1970-1980 decade of issues of the *South Carolina Historical Magazine*. Greene is widely known for his knowledge of and expertise in South Carolina Lowcountry culture and documentary history. A new novel from his pen, as yet unnamed, is expected in 2004.

Address: 133+ Wentworth Street, Charleston, SC 29401; (843) 805-6801
Email: greeneh@ccpl.org

Greer, Ben (b. 1948). A native of Spartanburg, Greer worked his way through college as a prison guard, experience that stood him in good stead when he wrote the novel *Slammer* (Atheneum, 1975), called "the best first novel to come out of the South since *Deliverance*" by *The New Republic*. Greer's other novels are *Halloween* (Macmillan Publishing Co., 1978), *Time Loves a Hero* (Doubleday, 1986), and *The Loss of Heaven* (Doubleday, 1988). He is also the author of *Presumed Guilty: The Tim Wilkes Story* (Wyrick & Co., 1995). Greer received his B.A. from the University of South Carolina and his M.A. from Hollins College (1973). He was a speechwriter and consultant to both Governor Richard Riley, a Democrat, and Governor Carroll Campbell, a Republican. From 1990 to 1991 he was senior political consultant to South Carolinian Lee Atwater, the Chairman of the Republican National Committee.

Address: Department of English, University of South Carolina, Columbia, SC 29208; (803) 777-2174
Email: greerb@gwm.sc.edu

Greiner, Donald (b. 1940). A native of Baltimore, Greiner received his B.A. in English from Wofford College (1962) and his M.A. (1963) and Ph.D. (1967) from the University of Virginia. In 1967 he began a long and distinguished career at the University of South Carolina, where in 1986 he was named Carolina Distinguished Professor of English. In addition, Greiner has been director of undergraduate studies (1970-75) and of graduate studies (1978-1982) in the department of English and in 1993 was appointed interim associate provost of the University. He currently holds the position of associate provost and dean of undergraduate affairs. His research interests include American

Donald Greiner

literature, modern American poetry, and contemporary fiction. Among his fourteen published books are *Adultery in the American Novel* (University of South Carolina Press, 1986), *Comic Terror: The Novels of John Hawkes* (Memphis State University Press, 1973), *Domestic Particulars: The Novels of Frederick Busch* (USC Press, 1988), *John Updike's Novels* (Ohio University Press, 1984), *Robert Frost* (American Library Association, 1974), *Women Enter the Wilderness: Male Bonding and the American Novel of the 1980s* (USC Press, 1991), and *Women Without Men: Female Bonding and the American Novel of the 1980s* (USC Press, 1993). Greiner has also published nearly one hundred essays. Among his many awards are an AMOCO Teaching Award and the Educational Foundation Award for Distinguished Research in the Liberal Arts.

Address: Office of the Provost, University of South Carolina, Columbia, SC 29208; (803) 777-2808
Email: greiner@gwm.sc.edu

Griffith, Michael (b. 1965). A native of Orangeburg, Griffith attended school in that city until his senior year, which he spent at Phillips Exeter Academy in New Hampshire. He received an A.B. in Germanic languages and literatures, *summa cum laude* and Phi Beta Kappa, from Princeton University (1987) and an M.F.A. from Louisiana State University (1992). At Princeton he studied with Joyce Carol Oates and at LSU with Vance Bourjaily. After leaving Princeton, Griffith worked briefly at LMPM Advertising in New York City but decided to return South for graduate school. In 1992 he began to work for *The Southern Review*, and in early 1994 he eventually became full-time associate editor. Since 2002 he has been assistant professor of English and comparative literature at the University of Cincinnati. Griffith's short fiction and essays

have appeared in *New England Review*, *Oxford American*, *The Southern Review*, *The Virginia Quarterly Review*, *The Southern Literary Journal*, *The Southern Quarterly*, *Southwest Review*, *The Washington Post*, and elsewhere. Griffith's first novel, *Spikes* (Arcade, 2001), described as a "literary golf book," tells the story of a lower-echelon golfer forced to confront the reality that he never will be quite good enough to become the pro he envisioned himself to be. *Bibliophilia: A Novella and Stories* about, among other things, "a postmenopausal university librarian who's pressed into duty as a sex cop," appeared from Arcade Books in July 2003. Another novel is in the works. Griffith's awards include fellowships from the Sewanee Writers' Conference, the Louisiana Division of the Arts, and the University of Cincinnati.

Address: Department of English, The University of Cincinnati, 2624 Clifton Avenue, Cincinnati, OH 45221; (513) 556-6000
Email: griffimc@ucmail.uc.edu

Vertamae Grosvenor

Grosvenor, Vertamae (b. 1938). Lowcountry native Grosvenor is a correspondent on National Public Radio's Cultural Desk and a renowned culinary anthropologist whose cookbooks combine the best folk recipes with folk narratives of the culture they spring from. *Vertamae Cooks in the Americas' Family Kitchen* was published by Bay Soma Publishing in 1996; *Vertamae Cooks Again: More Recipes from the Americas' Family Kitchen* followed from Bay Books in 1999. She is or has been the host of NPR's *The Americas' Family Kitchen*, *Seasonings*, and *Horizons*, for which she won the Robert F. Kennedy Award for the program "Daufuskie: Never Enough Too Soon." She has also won a duPont-Columbia Award for "AIDS and Black America: Breaking the Silence" (1990), a National Association of Black Journalists

Award, and a 1991 CEBA Award for "Marcus Garvey: 20th Century Pan-Africanist." Grosvenor's first book was *Vibration Cooking, or, The Travel Notes of a Geechee Girl* (Doubleday, 1970); her second, *Thursdays and Every Other Sunday Off: A Domestic Rap* (Doubleday) appeared two years later. Currently she is working on a food folk opera and a novel about black expatriates in Europe.

Hall, Wilton Earle, Jr. (b. 1930). A native of Anderson, Hall graduated from the University of Georgia and worked for a dozen years in Latin America as a print, radio, and television journalist before turning to script and play writing and nonfiction. His first play was an adaptation of George Orwell's *1984* written with the approval of the novelist's widow. Since then, he has written three plays and fifteen books, among them *Terilynn, America's Youngest Female Serial Killer; The Coming;* and *Final Truth: The Autobiography of Mass Murderer/Serial Killer Donald "Pee Wee" Gaskins* (Adept/Pinnacle, 1992). For *Final Truth*, Hall collaborated over a period of fifteen months with Gaskins. Hall works on a contract basis as a script-consultant to motion picture producers and directors in the United States, Latin America, and Europe. His work also appears under the pseudonyms "Wilton Earle," "Garet W. Earle," and "Ashley Thirleby." His literary representation is by Albert Zuckerman, Writers House, New York. Hall is the subject of Program Number 205 in *The Writers' Circle of South Carolina*.
Address: 750 Wilton Hall Road,
Starr, SC 29684
Email: wearle@wiltonearle.com

Hansen, Joyce (b. 1942). New Yorker Hansen has been a South Carolina resident since her retirement in 1995. Inspired first by her parents in her native Bronx and then by her students during her twenty-two-year career as a public school teacher, Hansen writes "about what I know and what moves me deeply." Her books, perennial favorites of young readers across the nation, include *The Gift-Giver* (Houghton Mifflin/Clarion, 1980), *Which Way Freedom?* (Walker, 1986), *Yellow Bird and Me* (Clarion Books, 1986), *Out From This Place* (Walker, 1988), *Between Two Fires: Black Soldiers in the Civil War* (F. Watts, 1993), *The Captive* (Scholastic, 1994), *I Thought My Soul Would Rise and Fly: The Diary of Patsy, A Freed Girl* (Scholastic, 1997), *Breaking Ground, Breaking Silence: The Story of New York's African Burial Ground* (Henry Holt, 1998), *Women of*

Hope (Scholastic, 1998), *The Heart Calls Home* (Walker, 1999), *"Bury Me Not in a Land of Slaves" African Americans in the Time of Reconstruction* (Scholastic, 2000), *One True Friend* (Clarion, 2001), and *Freedom Roads: Searching for the Underground Railroad* (Cricket Books, 2003). Hansen's books deal with the African-American experience in historical and contemporary novels. They have won numerous awards, including six Notable Children's Trade Book in the Field of Social Studies awards, four Coretta Scott King Honor Book Awards, two ALA Notable Book Awards (1986, for *Which Way Freedom?*, and 1988, for *Out From This Place*), the 1995 African Studies Association Children's Book Award (*The Captive*), the 1998 National Parenting Publication Gold Award (*Women of Hope*), and a 1986 Parent's Choice Award (*Yellow Bird and Me*).
Address: c/o Stephanie Wimmer,
Scholastic Inc., 555 Broadway, New York,
NY 10012-3999. Fax: (212) 389-3063
Email: hansnels@aol.com

Hardy, Frances L. (b. 1960). A native of Spartanburg, poet Hardy was educated at Wofford College (B.A.), Converse College (M.Ed.), and the University of South Carolina (Ed.D.). Her dramatic skits and one-act plays have been performed by local drama troupes such as the Inspirational Players, and her

Frances Hardy

essays have appeared in *Education Issues*. She has written two books of poetry: *Risings* (Vision Unlimited Press, 1993) and *Peace Weaving: Poetic Reflections* (Vision Unlimited Press, 2002). Hardy's poetry celebrates family, heritage, and the power of independent women and speaks with a firm, no-nonsense voice. It continues to inspire new poets every year in the persons of the students fortunate to sit in her classes at Spartanburg High School.

Address: Department of English,
Spartanburg High School, 500 DuPre Drive,
Spartanburg, SC 29307; (864) 594-4410
Email: fhardy@spart7.k12.sc.us

Harper, Linda Lee (b. 1950). A graduate of the M.F.A. program at the University of Pittsburgh, Harper is the author of *Toward Desire*, winner of the 1995 Washington Prize for Poetry; *A Failure of Loveliness*, winner of the William and Kingman Page Award; *Cataloguing Van Gogh*, winner of the Hibiscus Award; and *The Wide View*, winner of the Fall Open Reading Award. *Blue Flute* and *Buckeye* are out from Adastra Press and Anabiosis Press, respectively. Her work has appeared in *Nimrod, The Journal, Crazyhorse, Ascent, Massachusetts Review, The Southern Poetry Review, The Seneca Review,* and *The Texas Review*. She was nominated for a Pushcart Prize by Stephen Corey of *The Georgia Review* in 2000. Harper lives in Augusta with her family and teaches at USC Aiken; her interview with Patti Just is a part of Program Number 805 of *The Writers' Circle of South Carolina*.
Address: Department of English,
University of South Carolina Aiken,
471 University Parkway, Aiken, SC 29801;
(803) 648-6851
Email: lindah@usca.edu

Harper, Meredith Annette (b. 1949). The daughter of a South Carolina farmer, Harper earned a B.F.A. in painting from Tulane University and then accompanied her boyfriend to New York City, where she became a window dresser for Hallmark Cards's Fifth Avenue corporate gallery. From there she moved into production design and stage management for several off-Broadway companies, pop music writing, and the creation of musical plays for children. At that point, Harper says, she "could no longer interest herself in painting and so returned to New Orleans to write." Her first novel, *For the Love of Robert E. Lee* (Soho Press, 1992), appeared thirteen years later. Its 1960s female protagonist comes to terms with her own heritage through a fixation on Southern general Robert E. Lee and his conception of honor. Her second novel, *The Worst Day of My Life, So Far* (Hill Street Press), appeared in 2001; her third, a ghost story set in Louisiana, will also be published by Hill Street. Harper is interviewed by Patti Just in Program Number 211 of *The Writers' Circle of South Carolina*.
Email: AnnetteHarper@aol.com

Hart, Carolyn G. (b. 1936). Prolific mystery writer Hart is the first writer to win all three major mystery awards (the Agatha, the Anthony, and the Macavity) for her novels. She has written more than thirty of them, including a half-dozen "Henrie O" mysteries, fourteen popular "Death on Demand" mysteries, and five novels for children and young adults. A stand-alone novel, *Letter From Home*, was published in 2003. A former president of Sisters in Crime, she was born and currently lives in Oklahoma City, but she has vacationed at Hilton Head Island since the mid-1970s. Her "Death on Demand" series, featuring the crime-solving proprietor of a mystery bookshop, is set in Broward's Rock, a barrier island off the South Carolina coast that bears suspicious resemblances to Hilton Head.
Website: www.carolynhart.com
Email: carolynghart@juno.com

Hayes, Terrance (b. 1971). Born in Columbia, Hayes received his B.A. from Coker College and his M.F.A. from the University of Pittsburgh. His poetry appears in *The Beloit Poetry Journal*, *Chelsea*, *Callaloo*, and *Crab Orchard Review*; in the anthologies *Giant Steps: The New Generation of African American Writers* (ed. Kevin Young, 2000) and *American Poetry: The Next Generation* (eds. Gerald Costanzo and Jim Daniels, 2000); and on the website of the

Terrance Hayes

Academy of American Poets (www.poets.org) His second collection, *Hip Logic* (Penguin Books, 2002), was a National Poetry Series Open Competition selection, a finalist for the Los Angeles Times Book Award, and runner-up for the James Laughlin Award. His inaugural collection, *Muscular Music* (Tia Chucha Press, 1999), won the Kate Tufts Discovery Award and was followed by a Whiting Writers Award. Hayes has received fellowships from the Bread Loaf Writers Conference and the Provincetown

Summer Writing Program and has served on the staff of the Cave Canem Retreat for African American Poets. Currently he teaches at Carnegie Mellon University in Pittsburgh, where he is associate professor of creative writing.
Address: Department of English, Carnegie Mellon University, Pittsburgh, PA 15213-3890; (412) 268-9195
Email: thayes@andrew.cmu.edu

Hays, Tommy (b. 1955). A native of Greenville, Hays received his undergraduate degree from Furman University and his M.F.A. from Warren Wilson College. He is executive director of the Great Smokies Writing Program and the creative writing chair for the honors program of the South Carolina Governor's School for the Arts and Humanities. He also reviews books for *The Atlanta Constitution*. Hays's second novel, *In the Family Way* (Random House, 1999), won the Thomas Wolfe Memorial Literary Award, was a selection of the Book-of-the-Month Club, and was praised by Bret Lott, Reynolds Price, and Josephine Humphreys among others. Its ten-year-old protagonist must cope with a variety of changes in the life of his family, which includes a mother recently converted to Christian Science and a father described as a "Waffle House mystic." His first novel, *Sam's Crossing*, published by Atheneum in 1992, was praised by *The New York Times Book Review* and the *San Francisco Chronicle*.
Address: The Great Smokies Writing Program, University of North Carolina at Asheville, One University Heights, Asheville, NC 28804

Hembree, Mike (b. 1951). Born in Spartanburg, where he also currently lives, Hembree graduated from the University of South Carolina (B.A., 1973) and has worked since 1978 as a staff writer for *The Greenville News*. He has written three books on auto racing: *The Driving Force* (J. Countryman, 1999), *NASCAR: The Definitive History of America's Sport* (HarperCollins, 2000), and *Dale Earnhardt Jr.: Out of the Shadow of Greatness* (Sports Publishing, 2003). Three of his stories were included in *Taking Stock* (Brassey's, 2002), a compilation book about auto racing. He also has written a profile of Spartanburg resident, gardener, and human-rights activist Harold Hatcher, *The Seasons of Harold Hatcher* (Hub City, 1999). He has co-authored and self-published important local titles about the Clifton, Glendale, and Newry mill communities and a history of the Lake Jocassee and Lake

Mike Hembree

Keowee region of northwestern South Carolina. Also, he is one of the authors of the nostalgic *Journey Home* (Greenville News-Piedmont, 1988). A frequent contributor to Hub City publications, *The Sporting News*, *Winston Cup Illustrated*, and *Stock Car Racing*, he was the National Motorsports Press Association Writer of the Year in 1982, 1992, 1995, and 2002, and the South Carolina Sports Writer of the Year in 1977 and 1982.
Address: 531 Heritage Hills Drive, Spartanburg, SC 29307
Email: Paperinker@aol.com

Hospital, Janette Turner (b. 1942). Anyone following in James Dickey's footsteps as writer-

Janette Turner Hospital

in-residence at the University of South Carolina has a difficult assignment, but Hospital seems up to the task. A native of Queensland, Australia, Hospital received her B.A. from the University of Queensland (1965) and began her teaching career in public high schools of her native state. She received her M.A. in Medieval English literature from Queen's University (Canada) in 1973 and since then has taught at Queen's University, Massachusetts Institute of Technology, and a succession of other institutions in the United States, the United Kingdom, Canada, and Australia. In 1999 she was appointed professor and distinguished writer-in-residence in the English department at the University of South Carolina.

Hospital's first novel, *The Ivory Swing* (Dutton, 1983; Bantam paperback, 1984), won Canada's Seal Award (a $50,000 prize) and has been followed by five more novels and three short-story collections published in twelve languages. Four of her short stories appeared in Britain's annual "Best Short Stories in English"; "The End-of-the-Line End-of-the-World Disco" was selected for "The Best of the Best," an anthology of the decade. Her novel, *Oyster* (Norton, 1998; Norton paperback, 1999), was a finalist for the Miles Franklin and National Book Awards (Australia) and the Trillium Award (Canada); it was also a *New York Times* "Notable Book of the Year" and one of the *Observer's* "Best Books of the Year." The *Observer* has called her "one of the best female novelists writing in English," and Bill Ott in *Booklist* called *Oyster*, her novel about a strange cult figure in a remote opal-mining community, "a genuinely hypnotic novel."

Hospital's work has not achieved bestseller status, but it has a large following among those who might be called "serious" readers: she is a writer's writer. Together with *The Ivory Swing* and *Oyster*, her novels include *The Tiger in the Tiger Pit* (Dutton, 1984; Bantam paperback, 1985), *Borderline* (Dutton, 1985; Bantam paperback, 1986), *Charades* (Bantam, 1987; Bantam paperback, 1988), and *The Last Magician* (sometimes called her masterwork, Holt, 1992; Ballentine paperback, 1993). Her story collections are *Dislocations* (LSU Press, 1987; Norton paperback, 1988), *Isobars* (LSU Press, 1990), and *Collected Stories, 1970-1995* (UQP, 1995). She has also written a crime thriller, *A Very Proper Death* (Scribner's, 1990), under the pseudonym "Alex Juniper," an alternate selection for the Mystery Book Club in its publication month. Her newest novel, *Due Preparations for the Plague*, was published as Norton's lead title in 2003, and her new collection of short stories, *North of Nowhere, South of Loss*, was published in 2003 in Australia, and in the United States by Norton.
Address: Department of English,
University of South Carolina,
Columbia, SC 29208; (864) 777-4203

Humphreys, Josephine (b. 1945). One of South Carolina's most popular and most widely

Josephine Humphreys

respected writers, Humphreys was born in Charleston and attended Ashley Hall, Duke University (A.B., 1967), Yale University (M.A., 1968), and the University of Texas at Austin. She taught for seven years at the Baptist College at Charleston, leaving in 1977 to become a full-time writer. As she told Patti Just, she "bought the paper and pen and sat down to write." She was thirty-three; five years later, her first novel, *Dreams of Sleep*, appeared (Viking, 1984). It won the PEN American Center's Ernest Hemingway Award.

Three years later, *Rich in Love*, (Viking, 1987), a sensitive story about the initiation of a tough young girl from the Lowcountry and her dysfunctional family, appeared to nearly universal praise. It became a Richard and Lili Fini Zanuck film starring the English actor Albert Finney. Humphreys's other novels are *The Fireman's Fair* (Viking, 1991), a book she finished before Hurricane Hugo and then rewrote in light of the changes wrought by the storm, and *Nowhere Else on Earth* (Viking, 2000), the story of a young Lumbee Indian woman and the relationships among the peoples in her community near Lumberton, North Carolina. Humphreys was also instrumental in bringing into print *Gal: A True Life* (Harcourt Brace, 1994), Ruthie Bolton's best-selling story of abuse and ultimate survival.

Humphreys and her husband live on Sullivan's Island, and she writes in downtown Charleston in the Old Confederate Home. She is a 1994 inductee of the South Carolina Academy of Authors and was featured in Program Number 106 of *The Writers' Circle of South Carolina*.

Hunter, Gwen (b. 1956). Novelist Hunter began to think of herself as a writer when her work was praised by her tenth-grade English teacher, Carol Kohler. She immediately became

a devoted reader of *Writer's Digest* magazine and embarked upon a writing career while working as a laboratory technician to pay her bills. Her first two books, the Garrick Travis mysteries *Death Warrant* (Warner Books, 1990) and *Death Sentence* (Warner Books, 1992), were written under the pen name Gary Hunter in collaboration with police officer Gary Leaveille, whom she met early one morning on duty in the hospital where she worked. Since then she has written a string of successful mysteries under her own name: *Betrayal* (Pocket Books, 1994), translated into French, Dutch, and German, and the winner of the WH Smith Fresh Talent award in the United Kingdom; *False Truths* (Pocket Books/ Hodder & Stoughton, 1995); *Ashes to Ashes* (Hodder & Stoughton/New English Library, 1996); *Law of the Wild* (Hodder & Stoughton, 1997/Coronet Books, 1998); *Delayed Diagnosis* (Mira Books, 2001); *Prescribed Danger* (Mira Books, 2002); and *Deadly Remedy* (Mira Books, 2003). Harper's books are about "women who are flawed, weak, and have problems to overcome" and "that thin flame of heroism that burns in each of us." Her interview with Patti Just is Program Number 608 of *The Writers' Circle of South Carolina*.
Website: www.gwenhunter.com

Hutchisson, James M. (b. 1961). A native of Washington, D.C., James Hutchisson received his B.A. from Radford University (1982), his M.A. from Virginia Polytechnic Institute and State University (1984), and his Ph.D. from the University of Delaware (1987). He has taught at Washington and Jefferson College in Pennsylvania (1987-1989) and at The Citadel, where he teaches a course in Southern literature and pursues scholarly research in American literature and the culture of Charleston. He has been textual editor of the University of Pennsylvania edition of the works of Theodore Dreiser and has published biographical and critical studies of Sinclair Lewis. He has contributed to literary South Carolina as author of *DuBose Heyward: A Charleston Gentleman and the World of Porgy and Bess* (University Press of Mississippi, 2000), now the standard treatment of the subject; *A DuBose Heyward Reader* (University of Georgia Press, 2003); and as co-editor with Harlan Greene of *Renaissance in Charleston: Art and Life in the Carolina Low Country, 1900-1940* (University of Georgia Press, 2003).
Address: Department of English, The Citadel, Charleston, SC 29409; (843) 953-5143
Email: hutchissonj@citadel.edu

Sue Lile Inman

Inman, Sue Lile (b. 1936). A native of Little Rock, Arkansas, Inman received her B.A. from Agnes Scott College (1958) and her M.A. from Clemson University (1978). She has taught composition and literature at Clemson and Furman universities and writing courses at Greenville Technical College, the Greenville County Museum School of Art, and Furman University Learning in Retirement. She was founding editor of *Emrys Journal* and *Upcountry Review* and has edited *Upstate Magazine*. Her poetry has been published in a variety of journals and little magazines including *The South Carolina Review*, *The Devil's Millhopper*, and *Kennesaw Review*. Her collection *Voice Lessons* was published by Emrys Press in 1998.
Address: 408 West Faris Road, Greenville, SC 29605; (864) 242-6555

Irvin, Wilmot B. (b. 1950). Columbia attorney Irvin lives on a farm in rural Lower Richland County where he writes novels strongly influenced by his professional life and by his Christian faith and commitment to values that strengthen the family. He has written three novels, all published by Greatunpublished: *Jack's Passage*, a novel of initiation; *There Is a River*, the story of the brutal abduction of an innocent and charming teenage girl and of the triumph of faith over despair; and *The Storytellers*, a novel of family and change.
Address: 2930 McCord's Ferry Road, Eastover, SC 29044
Email: irvinlaw@scbar.org

Israel, Charles M. Professor of English at Columbia College, Israel received his B.A. from Wofford College, his M.A. from Emory University, and his Ph.D. from the University of South Carolina. His novel, *Love Is Where You Find It*, was his Ph.D. thesis at the

University of South Carolina. He has also written a history of Columbia College (Arcadia, 2001), and his work has appeared in *The South Carolina Review*, *The Crescent Review*, *Sandlapper*, *The State Magazine*, and *Charleston Magazine*.
Address: Department of English, Columbia College, 1301 Columbia College Drive, Columbia, SC 29203; (803) 786-3704

Jackson, Dorothea M. (b. 1932). One of South Carolina's most accomplished nature writers, "Dot" Jackson worked for fifteen years as a columnist and environmental specialist for *The Charlotte Observer*, then "went from paper to paper like a lumberjack from camp to camp." She has worked for the *Anderson Independent* and the *Greenville News* and has edited several weeklies. Her book credits include *The Catawba River* (Gardner-Webb Press, 1983), *Keowee: The Story of the Keowee River Valley in Upstate South Carolina* (with Mike Hembree, 1995), *One Hundred Years of Appalachian Visions, 1897-1996* (with Billy F. Best and Bennie Lee Sinclair, Appalachian Imprints, 1997), and *Journey Home* (again with Mike Hembree and others, Greenville News-Piedmont Co., 1988). She also publishes frequently in magazines of the outdoors, including *South Carolina Wildlife*. Her honors include National Conservation Writer of the Year (Trout Unlimited, 1980) and the Alicia Patterson Foundation Fellowship (1991). Currently Jackson is working on a history of Appalachian music for Chicago Review Press; in addition, she is working hard with a group of writers to establish Birchwood, an arts and folk life center at the foot of Table Rock.
Address: 187 Birchwood Road, Pickens, SC 29671; (864) 898-1418
Email: dotjackson6mile@aol.com

Pat Jobe

Jobe, Pat. (b. 1954). Folksy country preacher

Jobe hit the public radio airwaves of WNCW in Spindale, North Carolina, with "Radio Free Bubba" in 1989. Ten years later, along with three other writers, he parlayed those commentaries into the book *Radio Free Bubba* (Hub City Writers Project, 1999). Next came a short novel, *365 Ways to Criticize the Preacher* (Smyth & Helwys, 2001). Born in Rutherford County, Jobe has a B.A. from High Point University and studied theology at Erskine Theological Seminary. As a journalist, he worked for *The McDowell News* and freelanced for *The Charlotte Observer* and *Asheville Citizen-Times*.
Address: 112 Scruggs Lane, Gaffney SC 29341; (864)706-1676
Email: patjobe@chesnet.net

Dianne Johnson

Johnson, Dianne (b. 1960). A graduate of Spring Valley High School, Johnson received her A.B. in English/creative writing from Princeton University in 1982, her M.A. in Afro-American studies from Yale University in 1984, and her Ph.D. from Yale University in 1988. She is a professor in the English department of the University of South Carolina, where her areas of specialization are children's and young adult literature, African-American literature, and multi-ethnic autobiography. Her publications include *Presenting Laurence Yep* (Twayne, 1995), an introduction to the celebrated Chinese-American author, and The *Best of the Brownies' Book* (Oxford, 1996), an anthology of pieces from the early twentieth-century black children's magazine edited by Jessie Fauset and W.E.B. DuBois. Under the name Dinah Johnson, Dr. Johnson is also the author of four books for children: *All Around Town* (Henry Holt, 1998), a narrative to accompany the photographs of Richard Samuel Roberts; *Sunday Week*, illustrated by Tyrone Geter (Henry Holt, 1999); *Quinnie Blue*, illustrated by James Ransome (Holt, 2000);

and *Sitting Pretty: A Celebration of Black Dolls*, photographed by Myles Pinkney (2000). She frequently speaks before educational and community groups.

Address: Department of English,
University of South Carolina,
Columbia, SC 29208; (803) 777-2345
Email: dianne@sc.edu

Johnson, Dinah. See *Dianne Johnson*.

Johnson, Thomas L. (b. 1935). Recently retired as the assistant director of the South Caroliniana Library at the University of South Carolina in Columbia, Johnson has been the guardian spirit of literary South Carolina for more years than anyone except himself actually knows. A life member of the board of governors of the South Carolina Academy of Authors, Tom was also editor of the "365 Degrees" poetry page of *Point*, the independent Columbia news monthly, and for many years taught a popular course on South Carolina writers at the University of South Carolina.

Johnson's non-belletristic work includes contributions to a number of important publications documenting neglected aspects of South Carolina's cultural history, among which are *Camera Man's Journey: Julian Dimrock's South* (co-edited with Nina Root, University of Georgia Press, 2002), *Conflict and Transcendence: African-American Art in South Carolina* (Columbia Museum of Art, 1992), *James McBride Dabbs: A Life Story* (Ph.D. Thesis, USC, 1980), four volumes of *South Carolina Postcards* (co-edited with Howard Woody, Arcadia Publishing, 1997), and *A True Likeness: The Photographs of Richard Samuel Roberts, 1920-1936* (Bruccoli Clark/Algonquin, 1986). The latter, co-edited with Philip Dunn, received the Southern Regional Council's Lillian Smith Award. Johnson also edited *You, Year: New Poems by Point Poets* (Harbinger Publications, 1996) and contributed the introduction to a modern edition of John Bennett's *The Doctor to the Dead: Grotesque Legends and Folktales of Old Charleston* (University of South Carolina Press, 1995). His own poetry has appeared in *From the Green Horseshoe: Poems by James Dickey's Students* (USC Press, 1987) and in a number of volumes of the Poetry Society of South Carolina Yearbook. He is a multiple winner of the South Carolina Fiction Project and of various prizes awarded by the Poetry Society of South Carolina. He functioned as the primary research editor for the new literary map of South

Carolina issued by the Palmetto Book Alliance in 2003.

Address: 124 Highridge Drive,
Spartanburg, SC 29307

Jones, Lewis P. (b. 1916). A native of Laurens, beloved historian, teacher, and popularizer of South Carolina history, Jones retired as chairman of the Wofford College history department in 1987 after a productive career that spanned forty-one years. He has been called the conscience of Wofford College and "one of the most respected minds in the

Lewis P. Jones

state's academic community" by Gary Henderson (Spartanburg *Herald-Journal*, 9 December 2001). He unquestioningly influenced untold hundreds of Wofford students and ordinary South Carolinians through his love for the state and its history. *South Carolina: One of the Fifty States* (Sandlapper Publishing, 1985), perhaps Jones's most familiar work, has been used as an eighth-grade history textbook in the state's public schools and went into a second, revised edition in 1991. Among his other works are *Books and Articles on South Carolina History* (University of South Carolina Press, 1991), *Books and Articles on South Carolina History: A List for Laymen* (USC Press for the South Carolina Tricentennial Commission, 1970), *South Carolina: A Synoptic History for Laymen* (Sandlapper Press, 1971), *The South Carolina Civil War of 1775* (Sandlapper Store, 1975), and *Stormy Petrel: N.G. Gonzales and His State* (USC Press for the South Carolina Tricentennial Commission, 1973). For many years Jones wrote a regular feature on South Carolina history in *Sandlapper: The Magazine of South Carolina*, and his articles ran in many local newspapers as well.

Address: c/o Denny Jones, 400 Webber Road, C-2-3, Spartanburg, SC 29307

Jordan, Robert. See *James Oliver Rigney, Jr.*

Joyner, Charles W. (b. 1935). Another of South Carolina's exemplary modern historians, Joyner is the Burroughs Distinguished Professor of South Carolina History and Culture at Coastal Carolina University. A graduate of Presbyterian College, he holds a Ph.D. in history from the University of South Carolina and a Ph.D. in folklore and folklife from the University of Pennsylvania; he also held a postdoctoral fellowship in Comparative Slave Societies at Harvard University.

Joyner's *magnum opus*, *Down by the River-side: A South Carolina Slave Community* (University of Illinois Press, 1984), won the National University Press Award and has been called "the finest work ever written on American slavery." A study of All Saints Parish in the South Carolina Lowcountry, *Down by the Riverside* explores the "creolization" of the whole culture of the area in a style of written history informed by techniques usually employed by novelists. Joyner's other works include *Shared History: Southern History and Folk Culture* (University of Illinois Press, 1999), *Remember Me: Slave Life in Coastal Georgia* (Georgia Humanities Council, 1989), and *Folk Song in South Carolina* (University of South Carolina Press, 1971). He is co-author of *Before Freedom Came: African-American Life and Labor in the Antebellum South* (University Press of Virginia, 1992) and *Southern Writers and Their Worlds* (Louisiana State University Press, 1998); and he has edited modern editions of *A Woman Rice Planter's Diary* (USC Press, 1992) and Julia Peterkin's *Green Thursday* (University of Georgia Press, 1984). His essays are too numerous to mention.

Joyner is featured in an interview with Patti Just in Program Number 208 of *The Writers' Circle of South Carolina*.

Address: Department of History,
Coastal Carolina University,
P.O. Box 261954, Conway, SC 29528-6054;
(843) 347-3161
Email: cjoyner@coastal.edu

Kelly, Angela. Spartanburg resident Kelly received her B.A. in English literature from the University of South Carolina Spartanburg and has published three award-winning chapbooks of poetry: *Weighing the body back down* (Middle Tennessee State University, 1996), *those banded and coherent* (Pudding House Publications, 1994), and *Being the Camel* (Pearl Editions, 1990). Her work has appeared in a number of journals, including

Angela Kelly

Asheville Poetry Review, *Nimrod*, *Slipstream*, *Southern Poetry Review*, and *Rhino*. She has won the South Carolina Arts Commission's Literary Fellowship (1998-99), the Southern Women Writers Conference Emerging Voices Award (1998), and the Gwendolyn Brooks Poetry Award (1990).
Address: P.O. Box 8395,
Spartanburg, SC 29305; (864) 894-5310

Kibler, James Everett, Jr. (b. 1944). Prosperity native Kibler was educated at the University of South Carolina (B.A., 1966; Ph.D., 1970). After teaching as a graduate student in the English department at USC from 1966 to 1970, Kibler has taught for more than

thirty years in the English department at the University of Georgia. In addition to his academic publications, Kibler has written a number of books dealing with South Carolina social history and culture. These include: *Fireside Tales: Stories of the Old Dutch Fork* (Dutch Fork Press, 1984), *A Carolina Dutch Fork Calendar* (Dutch Fork Press, 1986), *A Guide to Confederate Columbia* (Mary Noel Kershaw Foundation, Cultural and Educational Institute of the Southern League, 1996), and *Our*

Fathers' Fields: A Southern Story (University of South Carolina Press, 1998). Kibler has also contributed to literary South Carolina by editing a number of the works of nineteenth-century man of letters William Gilmore Simms. *Our Fathers' Fields* won the Fellowship of Southern Writers' 1999 Award for Non-Fiction. His short-story cycle *Child to the Waters* (Pelican Press) was published in 2003. He has just completed a novel entitled *Walking Toward Home*.
Address: 211 Peters Creek Road, Whitmire, SC 29178

Kidd, Sue Monk (b. 1948). Although she now lives on a marsh near Charleston, nonfiction

Sue Monk Kidd

memoirist and novelist Kidd "grew up in the 1950s and '60s in a tiny town tucked among the pine-lands and peanut fields of Southwest Georgia." Her B.S. from Texas Christian University in 1970 led her into a nursing career in spite of an English professor's assessment that she was a "born writer." Only in her thirties did she begin writing personal-experience pieces, becoming a contributing editor at *Guideposts*. She has published three nonfiction books: *God's Joyful Surprise* (Harper, 1988), *When the Heart Waits* (Harper, 1990), and *The Dance of the Dissident Daughter* (Harper, 1996). *The Secret Life of Bees*, her first novel, was published by Viking Press in 2002 and became a *New York Times* bestseller. Josephine Humphreys called it "a rich, lovely novel, brimming with energy and humor and hope."

Kidd has won many awards, among which are the South Carolina Arts Commission's 1993-1994 Fellowship in Literature (Fiction), 1994 and 1996 Fellowships in Fiction from the South Carolina Academy of Authors, the 1994 Isak Dinesen Creative Nonfiction Award, and a 1995 Bread Loaf Scholar award.

Contact: c/o Cindy Hamel at Viking Penguin, chamel@penguinputnam.com
(212) 366-2754
Website: www.suemonkkidd.com

James Kilgo

Kilgo, James (1941-2002). Born in Darlington, Kilgo graduated from Wofford College (A.B., 1963) and received his M.A. (1965) and Ph.D. (1972) from Tulane University. His entire teaching career of more than thirty years was spent at the University of Georgia. His belletristic writing consists primarily of three elegant works about the natural world—*Deep Enough for Ivorybills* (Algonquin Books, 1988), a sustained narrative about white-tailed deer hunting; *Inheritance of Horses* (University of Georgia Press, 1994), a collection of essays; and *Colors of Africa* (University of Georgia Press, 2003), a reflection on an African safari—and *Daughter of My People*, a widely admired novel. Kilgo also published in journals and literary magazines including *The New York Times Book Review* and the *Sewanee Review*. He died in December 2002 as *Literary South Carolina* was undergoing revision.

Kilpatrick, James J. (b. 1920). Oklahoma native Kilpatrick has lived in Charleston since 1989. He began his newspaper career in 1941 as a reporter with the *Richmond News Leader*, where he "had to cover all the beats, one at a time." He succeeded well enough that seven years later, he followed Douglas Southall Freeman as that paper's editorial page editor. Widely known for his column, "A Conservative View," Kilpatrick has also written syndicated columns on "The Writer's Art" and "Covering the Courts," the latter appearing in more than 500 local newspapers; and he is the author of eleven books, among which are *Fine Print: Reflections on the Writing Art* (Andrews and McMeel, 1993), *The Writer's Art* (Andrews,

McMeel & Parker, 1984), *The Foxes' Union: And Other Stretchers, Tall Tales, and Discursive Reminiscences of Happy Years in Scrabble, Virginia* (EPM Publications, 1977), and *The American South: Four Seasons of the Land* (with photographer William A. Bake, Oxmoor House, 1980). He has also written for *Nation's Business* and *The National Review*, and he served a nine-year term as conservative point man on the CBS television series *Sixty Minutes'* "Point/Counterpoint" debates. His honors include the University of Missouri Medal for Distinguished Editorial Writing and the William Allen White Award for Distinguished Service to Journalism. His interview with SCETV's Patti Just is Program Number 401 in *The Writers' Circle of South Carolina*.
Email: kilpatjj@aol.com

Kitt, Eartha Mae (b. 1928). Born in North, South Carolina, Kitt's early life was poverty-stricken and abusive;. After age eight she spent her formative years in New York City, where she developed the characteristic toughness and talent that enabled her to become a distinguished actor, singer, dancer, nightclub entertainer, and social activist. Among her many credits are the role of Helen of Troy in Orson Welles's *Faust*, touring companies of *The Skin of Our Teeth* and *The Owl and the Pussycat*, television appearances on *The Ed Sullivan Show*, *Colgate Comedy Hour*, and *Batman*, and numerous recordings for RCA Victor and others. She has also been a community activist and in January 1968 gained national notoriety for her remarks on the relationship between crime in inner city ghettos and the war in Vietnam at a luncheon hosted by Lady Bird Johnson; she was subsequently blacklisted in the entertainment community and was investigated by the Secret Service and the CIA. Her claim to literary distinction lies in her authorship of two impassioned memoirs: *Thursday's Child* (Duell, Sloan & Pearce, 1956) and *Alone with Me: A New Autobiography* (H. Regnery Co., 1976). She continues to live in New York City.
Website: www.earthakitt.com

Knight, Marilyn B. (1951). Assistant professor of English at the University of South Carolina Spartanburg, Knight received her B.A. from the University of South Carolina-Spartanburg (1978), her M.A. from Clemson University (1991), and her Ph.D. from the University of Georgia (1997). Her novel *Babydoll* was published by Zebra/Kensington in 1988, and she has published poetry and

Marilyn Knight

fiction in journals including *The South Carolina Review* and *Lonzie's Fried Chicken*. She is currently at work on *Blood and Water*, another novel.
Address: 232 West Hampton Avenue, Spartanburg, SC 29306; (864) 583-2088
Email: mknight@gw.uscs.edu

Koon, George William (b. 1942). A long-time editor and/or member of the editorial boards of *The South Carolina Review*, Longstreet Press, Peachtree Publishers, and Books for Children at Clemson University, Koon received his A.B. in English from Newberry College (1964), his M.A. from Auburn University (1966), and his Ph.D. from the University of Georgia (1973). During a long and distinguished career at Clemson University, which began in 1972, his research interests have ranged over a wide variety of subject matter from eighteenth-century English literature and Southern American literature to humor and popular culture. He has also received substantial grants from the National Endowment for the Humanities, the Bingham Trust, and the South Carolina Committee for the Humanities among others. His books include two volumes on Hank Williams—*Hank Williams: A Bio-Bibliography in Popular Culture* (Greenwood Press, 1983) and *Hank Williams, So Lonesome* (The University Press of Mississippi, 2002)—two books, as editor, on Southern humor—*A Collection of Classic Southern Humor* (Peachtree Publishers, 1984) and *A Collection of Classic Southern Humor II* (Peachtree Publishers, 1986)—and *Old Glory and the Stars and Bars: Stories of the Civil War* (University of South Carolina Press, 1995). He is the interview subject of Program Number 804 of *The Writers' Circle of South Carolina*.
Address: Department of English, Clemson University, Clemson,

SC 29634-0523; (864) 656-5411
Email: BADK@clemson.edu

Kostoff, Lynn B. (b. 1954). Associate professor of English at Francis Marion University, Kostoff received his M.F.A. from Bowling Green State University. His novel, *A Choice of Nightmares*, a tale of double-dealing and drug-dealing in central Florida, was published in 1991 by Crown Publishers. His new novel, *The Long Fall* (Carroll and Graf), was published in 2003. It has been described as a "smart, funny, troubling, and thoroughly original neo-noir crime thriller." Kostoff is interviewed by Patti Just in Program Number 107 of *The Writers' Circle of South Carolina*, where he discusses the "tension between a literary novel and a page-turner" during the process of composition of the novel.
Address: Department of English, Francis Marion University, P.O. Box 100547, Florence, SC 29501; (843) 661-1509
Email: Lkostoff@fmarion.edu

Lamb, Robert. A former feature writer for *The Atlanta Constitution*, Lamb was born in South Carolina, grew up in Georgia and California, and was educated at the University of Georgia. His first novel, *Striking Out* (Permanent Press, 1991), was inspired by his childhood in the Frog Hollow section of Augusta, Georgia. It depicts the conflicts between the communities of Milltown and "the Hill," especially as represented by the girls who live there. His second novel, tentatively titled *Atlanta Blues*, is based upon his work in Atlanta among the homeless, the prostitutes, and other misfortunates. Lamb's interview with Patti Just is Program Number 112 of *The Writers' Circle of South Carolina*.

Lane, John Edward (b. 1954). Lane is the author of two full collections of poetry and a number of chapbooks, including *Thin Creek* (Copper Canyon, 1978), *Quarries* (Briarpatch, 1984), *As the World Around Us Sleeps* (Briarpatch, 1992), *Body Poems* (New Native, 1991), *Against Information and Other Poems* (New Native, 1995), and *The Dead Father Poems* (Holocene Publishing/Horse & Buggy Press, 2000). His nature writing includes *Weed Time: Essays from the Edge of a Country Yard* (Briarpatch, 1993; reprinted by Holocene, 1995), *Waist Deep in Black Water* and *Chattooga: Descending into the Myth of Deliverance River* (both University of Georgia Press, 2002 and 2004), and, as editor with Gerald Thurmond, *The Woods Stretched for*

John Lane

Miles: New Nature Writing from the South (University of Georgia Press, 1999). Lane is also a founder and editor for the Hub City Writers Project in Spartanburg. The books he has edited for Hub City include the award-winning *New Southern Harmonies: Four Emerging Writers* (1998).

Born in Southern Pines, North Carolina, Lane was reared in his mother's hometown, Spartanburg, where he graduated from Wofford College with a B.A. in English and Religion; his M.F.A. is from Bennington College. Lane describes his own journey as an author in these words: "Ten years on the road: Bread Loaf, Belize, Port Townsend, Copper Canyon Press, pizza and beer in a dark pool bar on Water Street. Then Virginia: UVA, Hoyns Fellow, cooking in Charlottesville, and on to cook in wilderness, Cumberland Island. Finally back to South Carolina and North Carolina piedmont and mountains, kayaking, writing. Back to Spartanburg, teaching at Wofford College: literature, creative writing, and film."

At his best, John Lane is an original and challenging writer. *The Dead Father Poems* is a remarkably imagined series of conversations between the poet and his father, a suicide who returns to enact scenes that never happened in his son's actual life. *Against Information* is the poem Allen Ginsberg's *Howl* would have been if it had appeared in the nineties instead of the fifties. *Weed Time* is a sort of conversational Appalachian *Walden*, and *Waist Deep in Black Water* and *Chattooga* are worthy companions to the work of Wendell Berry and Walker Percy, both of whom are acknowledged as influences. Lane's interview with Patti Just is Program Number 708 of *The Writers' Circle of South Carolina*.
Address: Box 101, Wofford College, Spartanburg, SC 29303; (864) 597-4518
Email: laneje@wofford.edu

Lindsay, Nick (b. 1927). Lindsay married a DuBose from Greenville (1945) and received his B.A. in French and Spanish from the University of South Carolina (1950). At various times he has worked as a steelworker, a machinist, a carpenter, an electrician, and a brick mason. Since 1955 he has made a living for himself and his ten children building and repairing boats and houses on Edisto Island. He has taken all the family onto the mainland from time to time so he could study Russian literature and linguistics at Columbia University, the University of West Virginia, Fordham University, and Indiana University. From 1969 until his retirement in 2000, he served as both part-time and full-time instructor and later poet-in-residence at Goshen College in Indiana, where he also established the Pinchpenny Press, a chapbook publisher that now boasts a board of directors and an extensive academic book list. In the late 1970s Lindsay came back to Edisto to stay. He reads his own work, lectures, and participates in programs about his father, the poet Vachel Lindsay, in the United States, Canada, and Europe. Some of his writings have been first performed at the Spoleto Festival in Charleston. He is the author of eight volumes of poetry, one novel in verse, a double handful of broadsides, and a well-received oral history of Edisto. His poetry has been described as incantatory, mystical, rhythmical, direct, sensuous—all of the things one might expect from a student of Whitman, a lover of Blake, Hopkins, and Vachel Lindsay. His works published by the Pinchpenny Press include *Prince of Glory, Prince of Darkness* (1969), *Sweat, Bread, and Money* (1972), *Ma Donna of the Brickbats* (1973), *Words and the School* (1973), *Tree with the Broken Rim* (1975), *Hope Is a Condor* (1975); *An Oral History of Edisto Island: The Life and Times of Bubberson Brown* (1975), *An Oral History of Edisto Island: Sam Gadsden Tells the Story* (1977), *The Cowtail Whip* (1995), and *Magnificent Storm: Selected Poems, 1960-2000* (2000). His other works include *And I'm Glad: An Oral History of Edisto Island*, with photographs by Julia Cart (Tempus Publishing, 2000), *Bien Que De Nuit* (self-published in brass, Plexiglas and cypress, Edisto Boat Works, 1999), *Esau Lanier* (a verse novel in Pushkin stanzas, self-published, Bloomington, IN, 1969), and *Yes* (the first book by Pinchpenny Press, 1967).
Address: 8555 Peters Point Road, Edisto Island, SC 29438;
phone/fax (843) 869-2244

Littlejohn, C. Bruce (b. 1913). A native and long-time resident of Spartanburg, Littlejohn enjoyed a distinguished and productive career, first as a state legislator and then as a justice of the Seventh Circuit and South Carolina Supreme courts; he retired as chief justice of the state Supreme Court in 1985. Although his contributions in the area of jurisprudence are beyond the scope of this volume, Littlejohn was known throughout his career as a fair-minded judge who worked hard to reform the inefficiencies of the judicial system; nationally, he promoted the overhaul of the system of law school accreditation. He has written three popular books about his experiences in the General Assembly and on the bench: *Laugh with the Judge: Humorous Anecdotes from a Career on the Bench* (Sandlapper Store, 1974), *Littlejohn's Half Century at the Bench and Bar (1936-1986)* (South Carolina Bar Foundation, 1987), and *Littlejohn's Political Memoirs: 1934-1988* (Bruce Littlejohn, 1989). Judge Littlejohn's interview with Patti Just is Program Number 105 of *The Writers' Circle of South Carolina*.

Long, Melinda Kay Brown (b. 1960). Greenville teacher and storyteller Long got her start as an author writing stories about television cartoon characters "when it was raining outside and there was nothing good on TV." During her childhood she lived in Spartanburg (her birthplace), Columbia, Greenville, Nashville, and Travelers Rest. She attended Furman University, where a poem of hers was published in the school literary magazine and where she received her B.A. in elementary education. It took her twelve years to publish her first story, and then in 1996 she found an agent for her work. *When Papa Snores* (Simon and Schuster) appeared in 2000 and, in 2001, *Hiccup Snickup* (Simon and Schuster) followed. Her third children's book, *How I Became a Pirate*, illustrated by award-winning artist David Shannon, was published by Harcourt Brace in 2003.
Address: 100 Sewanee Avenue, Greenville, SC 29609
Email: story39@hotmail.com

Lott, Bret (b. 1958). One of South Carolina's most popular and respected novelists, Lott has been embraced by both the critical community and the television community represented by Oprah's Book Club. Reared in California, Lott received his B.A. from California State University Long Beach (1981) and his M.F.A. from the University of Massachusetts at

Amherst (1984). At Amherst he studied writing under Jay Neugeboren and the late James Baldwin. After teaching at Ohio State University from 1984 to 1986, he accepted a position at the College of Charleston, where he is currently writer-in-residence and professor of English.

Lott is the author of five novels—*The Hunt Club* (Villard Books of Random House, 1998), *Reed's Beach* (Simon and Schuster, 1991), *Jewel* (Simon and Schuster, 1991), *A Stranger's House* (Viking Press, 1988), and *The Man Who Owned Vermont* (Viking Press, 1987). A sixth novel, *My Story, My Song*, will be out in 2004. Lott also has authored three story collections—*An Evening on the Cusp of the Apocalypse* (Invisible Cities Press, planned for 2004), *How to Get Home* (John F. Blair, 1996),

Bret Lott

and *A Dream of Old Leaves* (Viking Press, 1989). He has written the memoir *Fathers, Sons and Brothers* (Harcourt Brace, 1997) and is co-editor of the anthology *A Year in Place: Essays, Stories and Poetry on Where We Are Now* (University of Utah Press, 2001). His stories and nonfiction have been published by most of the leading little magazines and journals, and he is also widely anthologized.

Lott's honors are extensive. His essays have been chosen as "Notable Essays" in *Best American Essays 1994, 1995, 1996,* and *2002*. "The Ironic Stance and the Law of Diminishing Returns" appeared in *Best Spiritual Writing, 2002*, and his "Toward Humility" was chosen for *Best Spiritual Writing, 2001* and as the lead essay in *Pushcart Prize Anthology XXV*. He is the recipient of the University of Massachusetts Chancellor's Medal (2000), the College of Charleston Distinguished Research Award (1995), a Bread Loaf Fellowship in Fiction (1991), three PEN/NEA Syndicated Fiction Project Awards (1993, 1991, and 1985), and other awards too numerous to

mention. His novel, *Jewel*, was an Oprah's Book Club Selection for February 1999. Lott's interviews with Patti Just are Programs Numbers 101 and 508 of *The Writers' Circle of South Carolina.*

Address: Department of English,
The College of Charleston,
Charleston, SC 29424; (843) 953-5664
Email: lottb@cofc.edu

Susan Ludvigson

Ludvigson, Susan (b. 1942). One of South Carolina's most accomplished contemporary poets, Ludvigson is professor of English and poet-in-residence at Winthrop University in Rock Hill. Born in Rice Lake, Wisconsin, she attended the University of Wisconsin (B.A.) and the University of North Carolina-Charlotte (M.A.). She did not begin writing seriously until she was thirty years old and attended poetry readings in Ann Arbor, Michigan; then in Charlotte in the early 1970s she became a member of a women writers group. Louisiana State University Press published *Northern Lights* in 1981 and has published six more volumes of her work since: *The Swimmer* (1983), *The Beautiful Noon of No Shadow* (1986), *To Find the Gold* (1990), *Everything Winged Must Be Dreaming* (1993), *Trinity* (1996), and *Sweet Confluence: New and Selected Poems* (2000). A new book, *Escaping the House of Certainty*, is scheduled in 2005. Ludvigson's poetry has also appeared in *The Atlantic Monthly, The Nation, Poetry, The Georgia Review, The Southern Review, The Virginia Quarterly Review*, and elsewhere.

Ludvigson believes with Karl Shapiro that "[w]hat makes a poet different from other people is a way of looking at the world," and her own work provides ample evidence of her personal poetic perspective. One group of poems is based upon the photographs and stories in *Wisconsin Death Trip*, another about imagined stories behind outrageous newspaper

headlines, others in response to paintings and to trips she has taken. She also writes personal poems based on dreams and relationships.

Ludvigson's work has been recognized by numerous awards. Among them are a Writer's Fulbright Fellowship to Yugoslavia; Fellowships from the Guggenheim Foundation, the Rockefeller Foundation, the National Endowment for the Arts, the Witter Bynner Foundation, the North Carolina Arts Council, and the South Carolina Arts Commission; and the Emily Clark Balch Award of the *The Virginia Quarterly Review*. Patti Just interviews Ludvigson in Program Number 207 of *The Writers' Circle of South Carolina.*

Address: Department of English,
Winthrop University, Rock Hill, SC 29733;
(864) 323-4565
Email: ludvigsons@winthrop.edu or
sludvigson@rhtc.net.

MacNicholas, John (1943). Carolina Distinguished Professor of English at the University of South Carolina since 1987, MacNicholas has long been a presence in regional and national theater. His produced plays include *Dumas* (Walnut Street Theatre, Philadelphia, 1987; Alabama Shakespeare Festival, 1993), *Déjà Vu* (Clarence Brown Theatre Company, Knoxville, 1989; The Barter Theatre, Virginia, 1994), *Booth* (USC, 1991), *Crossings* (Workshop Theatre, Columbia, 1981; UNC-Charlotte, 1982), *The Liar* (USC Summer

John MacNicholas

Rep., Columbia, 1993), and *The Christmas Fix* (Town Theatre, 1996). *The Moving of Lilla Barton* was produced by USC Summer Rep, 1989; Alabama Shakespeare Festival, 1995; The Barter Theatre, 1996; and Flat Rock Playhouse, North Carolina, 1997. It was translated into French and produced by Theatre Jean Duceppe in every region of the country. It was made into a film and televised

nationally on CBS in 2000. Among MacNicholas's awards are the Roger L. Stevens Award for Playwriting (John F. Kennedy Center for the Performing Arts, Washington, DC, 1995), Playwright of the Year (the Southeastern Theatre Association, 1982), and First Place in the Southeastern Theatre Association National Playwriting Competition (1981).
Address: Department of English,
University of South Carolina,
Columbia, SC 29208; (803) 777-2186
Email: jmmacnic@gwm.sc.edu

Madden, Ed (b. 1963). A native of Arkansas, Madden is a poet and professor in the M.F.A. program at the University of South Carolina. He received his Ph.D. from the University of Texas at Austin in 1994. His work includes the poetry collection *Prodigal*, and a textbook anthology of AIDS literature is in progress. He has co-edited (with Patricia Munhall) an anthology of poems, stories, and essays on masculinity and the male experience: *The Emergence of Man into the 21st Century* (Jones and Bartlett, 2002). His work has appeared in *College English, Solo, River City, Cold Mountain Review, James White Review, Christianity and Literature*, and other journals. Madden has poems forthcoming in *The Book of Irish American Poetry from the 18th Century to the Present* (edited by Daniel Tobin, Notre Dame). His work was also included in *Gents, Bad Boys, and Barbarians: New Gay Male Poetry* (edited by Rudy Kikel, Alyson, 1994), an anthology of the best new gay writers in the nation.
Address: Department of English,
University of South Carolina,
Columbia, SC 29208; (803) 777-2171
Email: emadden@sc.edu or
EdMaddenSC@aol.com

Maggiari, Massimo (b. 1960). A native of Genova, Italy, Maggiari received his *Laurea in lingue e letterature straniere* from the Magistero di Genova (1986), his M.A. from the University of Washington (1987), and his Ph.D. from the University of North Carolina at Chapel Hill (1992). He has taught at the University of Washington, at UNC-Chapel Hill, and at Clemson University; he is currently an assistant professor in the Division of Languages at the College of Charleston. In addition to his scholarly research in twentieth-century Italian poetry, Maggiari is engaged in a wide variety of activities promoting the culture and literature of Italy in the United

States. He has translated the work of Arturo Onofri and Leonardo Sinisgalli into English and is an accomplished poet in his own right, both in Italian and English. His books include *The Waters of Hermes/Le acque di Ermes* (Chapel Hill: Annali díItalianistica, 2000); *The Waters of Hermes II/Le acque di Hermes II* (La Spezia: Agorà, 2003); and *Terre Lontane/Lands Away* (Campanotto Editore, 1999). Rooted in both a strong sense of place and a personal symbolic vision, Maggiari's work has won the Poetry Award of the *Festival della poesia di Sanremo* and the Poetry Award *ó Italo Alighiero Chiusano*; he has also won grants from the National Italian American Foundation, the Olivetti Foundation, and the National Endowment for the Humanities Endowment Fund.
Address: Division of Languages,
College of Charleston, 66 George Street,
Charleston, SC 29424; (843) 953-5489;
Email: maggiarim@cofc.edu.

Marshall, J. Quitman. Columbia native Marshall is a freelance indexer with more than two hundred books indexed to his credit. He is also a respected poet with two books, *The Birth Gift* (Hale Press, 1986) and *14th Street* (Hale Press, 1989), and periodical appearances in *Black Warrior Review, The Laurel Review, New Virginia Review, Poetry Now, Southern Poetry Review* and elsewhere. Five of his poems also appeared in *45/96: The Ninety-Six Sampler of South Carolina Poetry*. He was selected for the 1996 Writers Exchange program of Poets & Writers, Inc., has been a member of the board of governors of the South Carolina Academy of Authors, and has served as the coordinator of the Sundown Poetry Series held each spring during the Spoleto Festival in Charleston.
Address: 1306 Woodrow Street,
Columbia, SC 29205; (803) 252-8950

Maxim, John R. (b. 1937). A native of New York City, Maxim attended Fordham University (B.A., 1958) and worked as a senior advertising executive specializing in international clients before deciding to try his hand at writing. His first novel, *Platforms* (Putnam, 1981), which he sold within six months of starting it, was not published until he was forty-four years old. Since then he has published eleven additional novels, including the Bannerman series, the international crime bestseller, *The Shadow Box* (Avon Books, 1996), and the espionage/terrorism thriller *Haven* (Avon Books, 1997). He also has published one nonfiction work: *Dark Star* (St.

Martin's, 1985). As he did to writing, Maxim came late in life to South Carolina and now resides on Hilton Head Island.
Website: www.geocities.com/john_r_maxim
Email: JohnMaxim@compuserve.com

Thomas McConnell

McConnell, Thomas (b. 1962). A 1999 addition to the English department at the University of South Carolina Spartanburg, McConnell received his B.A. *magna cum laude* from the University of the South (1984), and his M.A. and his Ph.D. from the University of Georgia (1990, 1995). His story collection, *Silence for Several Voices*, is forthcoming from Texas Tech University Press, and his stories have appeared in *Yemassee, Connecticut Review, Calabash, Orb Literary Magazine, Psychotic Education* and as chapters five and fifteen of the Hub City Writers Project serial novel, *In Morgan's Shadow*. He wrote a winning story in the 2002 South Carolina Fiction Contest. He is currently working on *End of Earth*, a novel.
Address: Department of English,
University of South Carolina Spartanburg,
800 University Way, Spartanburg, SC 29303;
(864) 503-5681
Email: tmcconnell@gw.uscs.edu

McCray, Carrie Allen (b. 1913). Although she is a native of Lynchburg, Virginia, and retired after a full career as a social worker and schoolteacher, McCray is today strongly identified as a South Carolina writer. She was a founder and board member of the SC Writers Workshop, and she has the additional distinction of being the first *Point* poet in Tom Johnson's distinguished series for the now-defunct news monthly. Chicory Blue Press issued her chapbook, *Piece of Time*, in 1993, and her memoir, *Freedom's Child: The Life of a Confederate General's Black Daughter*, was published to widespread acclaim by Algonquin

Books of Chapel Hill in 1998. McCray's poetry has appeared in *Ms.* magazine, *The River Styx*, *The South Carolina Collection*, *Cave Canem I*, *The Squaw Review*, and a number of anthologies. Still an active writer, McCray conducts writing workshops for young and beginning writers and enjoys encouraging others to find their own voices. She was the 2002 recipient of the Lucy Hampton Bostick Award. She has lived in Columbia since 1986. She is interviewed by Patti Just in Program Number 6 of the 2003 season of *The Writers' Circle of South Carolina*.
Address: 250 Crossbow Drive, #K-12, Columbia, SC 29212; (803) 749-3273

McMahan, Janna. Columbian McMahan became a full-time writer after working for eight years in public relations in the arts. She received a B.A. in journalism from the University of Kentucky and an M.A. from the University of South Carolina. Her first novel, *Undertow* (Writers Bloc Press, 2001), is about a former inmate at the Central Correctional Institute in Columbia, an ambitious university president, and questionable scientific research. McMahan's nonfiction appears frequently in *South Carolina Wildlife*, *Charleston*, *Skirt!*, and *South Carolina Homes & Gardens*.

Millican, Arthenia J. Bates (b. 1920). Born in Sumter, where she still lives, into a devoutly religious middle-class family, Millican graduated from Morris College (1941) and received her M.A. from Atlanta University (1948)—where she studied under Langston Hughes—and her Ph.D. from Louisiana State University (1972). She taught for many years at Norfolk State University and Southern University and toiled at her writing for years in relative obscurity until finally making her mark as an author with her fiction collection, *Seeds Beneath the Snow: Vignettes from the South* (Greenwich, 1969). The stories in this collection were praised for the realism of their mostly young characters and the authenticity of the narrator's voice. Her subsequent novel, *The Deity Nodded* (Harlo Press, 1973), found a more regional audience. More recently she has received recognition for her poetry, which has appeared in *Point* and elsewhere, and for her scholarly research into the life and works of the writer James Weldon Johnson.

Minus, Ed. Something of a legendary teacher on the Wofford campus in the 1970s, Minus is currently assistant professor of English at

Ed Minus

Raritan Valley Community College in New Jersey. His undergraduate degree is from Presbyterian College and his M.A. from Boston University. He is the author of *Kite: A Novel* (Viking, 1985) and poems and short fiction in a variety of journals and magazines.
Address: Department of English, Raritan Valley Community College, Route 28 and Lamington Road, North Branch, NJ 08876; (908) 526-1200
Email: eminus@raritanval.edu

Mary Alice Monroe

Monroe, Mary Alice. Isle of Palms resident Monroe earned a master's in Asian studies/education from Seton Hall University. After a subsequent move to Washington, DC, she was confined to bed during pregnancy and began to write her first novel, which was published in 1995. Today she is a best-selling author of eight novels, including *Skyward* (Mira Books, 2003) and *The Beach House* (Mira Books, 2002), both set in South Carolina; *The Four Seasons* (Mira Books, 2001); *The Book Club* (Mira Books, 1999); *Girl in the Mirror* (Mira Books, 1998); and *The Long Road Home* (Harper, 1995). Writing as Mary Alice Kruesi, she published two romantic fantasies, *One Summer's Night* (Avon, 2000) and *Second Star*

to the Right (Avon, 1999). *Girl in the Mirror* and *The Four Seasons* were finalists for the RITA Award.
Address: c/o MIRA, 225 Duncan Mill Road, Don Mills, Ontario, Canada M3B 3K9.
Phone: c/o her publicist Marjory Wentworth (843) 883-0237
Website: www.maryalicemonroe.com

Mulkey, Richard D. (b. 1963). Converse College English professor Mulkey is one of South Carolina's talented crop of younger poets. He received his B.A. in English/theater from Bluefield College (1986), his M.S. in English from Radford University (1987), and his M.F.A. from Wichita State University

Richard Mulkey

(1992). He is the author of the poetry collection *Before the Age of Reason* (Pecan Grove Press, St. Mary's University, 1998), and his poems are included in *Denver Quarterly*, *The Literary Review*, *Connecticut Review*, *Emrys Journal*, *The Hollins Critic*, *North Dakota Quarterly*, *The South Carolina Review*, and many other periodicals. He has been awarded a Hawthornden Fellowship to the Hawthornden International Retreat for Writers, Lasswade, Scotland (2001); the Charles Angoff Award from *The Literary Review* (2001); the T. Reese Marsh Award of the Academy of American Poets (1990); and a number of academic grants from various institutions. Mulkey coordinates the annual Converse Writers Series.
Address: Department of English, Converse College, Spartanburg, SC 29302; (864) 596-9099
Email: rick.mulkey@converse.edu

Mullis, Kary B. (b. 1944). Born in Lenoir, North Carolina, and reared in Columbia, Mullis is one of South Carolina's three recipients of the Nobel Prize (see also **Charles H. Townes**). He received his B.S. in chemical engineering

from Georgia Tech in 1964 and his Ph.D. in biochemistry from the University of California, Berkeley, in 1972. After additional postdoctoral study at the University of Kansas Medical School and elsewhere, Mullis developed the polymerase chain reaction, a process enabling scientists to produce many multiples of a DNA molecule in very short order. It was this work for Cetus Corporation that led to his 1993 Nobel Prize in Chemistry. He subsequently worked for Xytronyx, Inc., and as an independent consultant. A polymath and highly original thinker, Mullis enjoys photography, music, studying virtual intelligence, and surfing, among many other pursuits. He spends much of his time now writing, one of the products of which has been his engaging and occasionally outrageous memoir *Dancing Naked in the Mind Field* (Pantheon Books, 1998). He lives in Newport Beach and Anderson Valley, California.
Website: www.karymullis.com
Email: lectures@karymullis.com

Myers, Tamar (b. 1948). Born to American missionary parents in the Belgian Congo, Myers returned to the United States with her family in 1964 in the aftermath of the violence following the former colony's 1960 independence. She began submitting novels to publishers while still in college, but it was twenty-three years before one was accepted. Today she is the author of two long-running mystery series: the Pennsylvania Dutch Mystery Series, which features an Amish-Mennonite sleuth who runs a bed and breakfast in the mythical town of Hernia, and the Den of Antiquity Mystery Series, which highlights the adventures of Charlotte antique store owner Abigail Timberlake. Myers is a member of Pennwriters, Sisters in Crime, Novelists, Inc., and Mystery Writers of America. She serves on the Advisory Council of the South Carolina Writers Workshop and is chairperson of the Edgars committee, which in 2002 was chosen to select the Best First Novel. Myers is a resident of Mount Pleasant. She is interviewed by Patti Just in program Number 707 of T*he Writers' Circle of South Carolina*.
Address: 2506 Long Cove Ct.,
Mt. Pleasant, SC 29466; (843) 881-0418
Website: www.tamarmyers.com
Email: tamar@tamarmyers.com

Newall, Liz (b. 1948). The managing editor of *Clemson World* magazine, Newall grew up in "the tiny cotton town of Starr, SC" and currently lives in the Wild Hog community of

Liz Newall

Pendleton. Her stories and nonfiction have appeared in *Southern Magazine*, *Country Woman*, *Sandlapper*, *Emrys Journal*, *Black Bear Review*, *St. Andrews Review*, *The State*, and *The State Magazine*. Her 1994 novel, *Why Sarah Ran Away with the Veterinarian* (Permanent Press, Sag Harbor, NY), was praised by Lee Smith and ranked among the state's best fiction for the year by Bill Starr of *The State* newspaper; it has since been translated into German. Newall is a four-time winner of the South Carolina Fiction Project.
Address: Clemson World, Clemson University, Clemson, SC 29634; (864) 656-0737
Email: lnewall@clemson.edu

Nolan, Lucy A. Short-story and children's author Nolan has twice won the South Carolina Fiction Project competition. She is the author of three books: the picture books *Jack Quack* (Marshall Cavendish, 2001) and *The Lizard Man of Crabtree County* (Marshall Cavendish, 1999), and the juvenile novel *Secret at Summerhaven* (Atheneum, 1987), which tells the story of three cousins who accidentally film a drug sale. *The Lizard Man of Crabtree County* was featured in *Southern Living* and was nominated for a Nevada Young Reader's Award.

Palmer, Kate Salley (b. 1946). A native of Orangeburg, Palmer received a B.A. from Clemson University in 1968, then taught for two years before becoming an editorial cartoonist for the *Clemson-Seneca Messenger* (1973-74), *The Greenville News* (1975-1984), the *Greenville Piedmont* (1985-86), and the New America Syndicate (1980-88). Since 1989 she has been a children's book author/illustrator and freelance writer/cartoonist/artist.
Palmer's awards are extensive. She was the third woman to join the American Association of Editorial Cartoonists, the first full-time

editorial cartoonist in South Carolina, and the second nationally syndicated woman editorial cartoonist. She has won the 1981 Freedom Foundation's Principal Award, the George Washington Honor Medal, and her work has been featured in *The Best Editorial Cartoons of the Year* (1978-86), *The Art of Caricature*, and *Newsweek*'s special edition "100 Years in Cartoons."
Palmer is the author and illustrator of three books for children: *A Gracious Plenty* (Simon and Schuster, 1991), *The Pink House* (Warbranch Press, 1999), and *The Little Chairs* (Warbranch Press, 2000). She has also illustrated five books by other authors: *How Many Feet in the Bed* by Diane Johnston Hamm (Simon and Schuster, 1991), now in its sixth

Kate Salley Palmer

printing; *Octopus Hug* by Lawrence Pringle (Boyds Mills Press, 1993), currently in its fifth printing; *Night of the Five Aunties* by Mesa Somer (Albert Whitman Co., 1996); Upstairs by Judith Ross Enderle and Stephanie Gordon Tessler (Boyds Mill Press, 1998); and *Bear Hug* by Laurence Pringle (Boyds Mill Press, 2003). She has also illustrated more than twenty Reading Recovery books for Kaeden Corporation. Palmer makes frequent appearances before educational and civic audiences and has been featured on SCETV and SCERN. Her interview with Patti Just for *The Writers' Circle of South Carolina* is Program Number 802.
Address: P.O. Box 209,
Clemson, SC 29633; (864) 654-4503
Website: www.warbranchpress.com
Email: kspalmer@aol com.

Peterson, Jim (b. 1948). Poet and playwright Peterson was born in Augusta, Georgia, but soon moved to South Carolina and received his B.A., M.A., and Ph.D. from the University of South Carolina, where he studied under

James Dickey and George Garrett. The founding editor of *Kudzu*, he was later editor of *The Devil's Millhopper*. His poetry appears in *The Antioch Review, The Chariton Review, Cincinnati Poetry Review, The Georgia Review, Southern Poetry Review* and Poetry. He has published three books of poetry—*The Man Who Grew Silent* (Bench Press, 1989); *An Afternoon with K* (Holocene Press, 1996); and *The Owning Stone* (Red Hen Press, 2000), the winner of the 1999 Benjamin Saltman Award. He also has written two chapbooks, *Carvings on a Prayer Tree* (Holocene, 1994) and *Jim Peterson's Greatest Hits 1984-2000* (Pudding House, 2001). Peterson's play "The Shadow Adjuster" was selected for the New American Plays Festival of 1995, was published by Palmetto Play Service in 1998, and was

Jim Peterson

given full productions by Montana State University-Billings and Strawdog Theater in Chicago. *Ruby Cat and Mister Dog* was produced at Venture Theater in Billings and at Randoph-Macon Women's College in Lynchburg, Virginia. A novel, *Paper Crown*, is scheduled for publication by Red Hen in 2004. Peterson's awards include a poetry fellowship from the Virginia Arts Commission (2002-03), the Academy of American Poets Regional Award (1976), the USC Frank Durham Creative Writing Award (1977), and First Place in the Emrys Room of One's Own Poetry Competition (1987). He is currently coordinator of creative writing at Randolph-Macon Woman's College.
Address: 555 Elmwood Avenue,
Lynchburg, VA 24503
Email: jepete@aol.com

Pinckney, Roger (b. 1946). Born and raised in Beaufort County, Pinckney is a colorful and often crusty storyteller of the South Carolina Lowcountry. He graduated from the University of South Carolina and holds an M.F.A. in

Roger Pinckney

creative writing from the Iowa Writers' Workshop. An award-winning journalist, his essays and short stories appear regularly in national sporting magazines. He comes from a family with a long history in Beaufort County; he is the son of Roger Pinckney X, who served for thirty-six years as county coroner, built docks on Daufuskie Island, and strung the first electrical power line to the isolated island. His books of nonfiction include: *The Beaufort Chronicles* (1996), an architectural guidebook; *Blue Roots: African-Folk Magic of the Gullah People* (Llewellyn Publications, 1998), an illustrated look at the history, practice, and people of Gullah country; and *Right Side of the River: Romance, Rage and Wonder* (Wyrick, 2002), a memoir about his life on Daufuskie Island and his skirmishes with "plantation" developers. His novel, *Little Glory* (Wyrick, 2003), is about a boy growing up in World War II-era coastal South Carolina. Film rights have been optioned by Running Horse Productions. A second set of essays is due from Wyrick in 2004.
Address: Box 37, Daufuskie Island SC 29918; (843-686-5452)

Platt, Eugene (b. 1939). Charleston native Platt is perhaps South Carolina's most prolific contemporary poet, having published hundreds of poems in dozens of periodicals. He was educated at the University of South Carolina (B.A., 1964), Trinity College, Dublin (Diploma in Anglo-Irish literature, 1970), and Clarion University of Pennsylvania (M.A., 1973). After military service as a paratrooper and chaplain's assistant with the U.S. Army (1957-1960), he worked for a number of U.S. government agencies, retiring from the U.S. Department of Labor in 1989.

His books of poetry are *coffee and solace* (Commedia, 1970), *Six of One/Half Dozen of the Other* (with John Tomikel, Allegheny Press,

1971), *Allegheny Reveries* (Commedia Pub. Division, 1972), *An Original Sin* (Briarpatch Press, 1974), *South Carolina State Line* (J. Huguley, 1980), and *Summer Days with Daughter* (Hawkes Publishing, 1999). He has also written a story collection, *Bubba, Missy, and Me* (Tradd Street Press, 1992), which is excerpted from *Saint Andrew's Parish*, a novel-in-progress. Among the many periodicals in which Platt's work has appeared, the following are especially notable: *Arizona Highways, Bitteroot, Caryatid, Crazyhorse, Icarus, Kudzu, Poet Lore, Point, Sandlapper, The South Carolina Review*, and *Tar River Poetry*. Platt has won awards from the Poetry Society of South Carolina, the Virginia Center for the Fine Arts, the Charleston Area Arts Council, and other arts organizations. In 1994 he donated $2,000 from the sales of *Bubba, Missy, and Me* to Charleston's Interfaith Crisis Ministry. In 2002, he was appointed poet laureate of the Town of James Island. His wife, Mary, whom he has described as his "main muse," died in 2003. Address: 734 Gilmore Court, Charleston, SC 29412; (843) 795-9442

Marsha Poliakoff

Poliakoff, Marsha L. (b. 1932). Spartanburg resident and playwright Poliakoff earned her B.A. from the University of South Carolina Spartanburg and her M.A. in English with emphasis in creative writing from the University of South Carolina. Her play *Jacksey's Lawyer* was produced at the 1994 Baltimore Playwrights Festival and ran for a month at Spotlighters Theatre in Baltimore. It was also produced at the University of South Carolina Spartanburg. Her plays, short stories, and essays have won awards from Converse College, the National League of American Pen Women and the Hub City Writers Project. Currently Poliakoff is at work on *The Letters 18*, a World War II novel, and a history of Temple B'nai Israel, Spartanburg. She is past president of the Spartanburg Branch of the National League of American Pen Women and the Spartanburg Legal Auxiliary.

Address: 340 Lake Forest Drive, Spartanburg, SC 29307; (864) 579-0748

Padgett Powell

Powell, Padgett (b. 1952). A native of Gainesville, Florida, Powell lived in Florence as a boy, received his B.A. in chemistry from the College of Charleston (1975) and his M.A. in creative writing from the University of Houston (1982). He teaches English and creative writing at the University of Florida in Gainesville and reviews books for a number of literary journals and *The New York Times Book Review*. His first novel, *Edisto* (Farrar, Straus and Giroux, 1984), featured a character named Simons Manigault who, despite his patrician heritage, lived a decidedly un-Old South existence. The book was immediately recognized as the work of a creative and original mind and attracted widespread critical acclaim. It was followed by two more novels: *A Woman Named Drown* (Farrar, Straus and Giroux, 1987) and *Edisto Revisited* (Holt, 1996); and two short-story collections: *Typical* (Farrar, Straus and Giroux, 1991) and *Aliens of Affection* (Holt, 1998). Powell's nonfiction has appeared in periodical publications as varied as *Harper's, Southern Living, Gentlemen's Quarterly*, and *The New York Times Magazine*; and his short stories appear in *Esquire, Harper's, The New Yorker* and *Paris Review*. Among his awards and honors are an American Book Award nomination (1984), a Rome fellowship from the American Academy of Arts and Letters (1987), a Fulbright award (1989), a Pushcart Prize (1990), and an O. Henry Award (1995).

Address: Department of English, University of Florida, Box 117310, Gainesville, FL 32611; (352) 392-36650, ext. 236
Email: powell@english.ufl.edu

Rash, Ron (b. 1953). Rash burst upon the literary South Carolina scene with a handful of exciting books in the 1990s and the first decade of the twenty-first century, and has established a commanding presence among the first ranks of the state's authors. A native of Chester, Rash graduated from Gardner-Webb College and Clemson University. He taught at Tamassee-Salem High School in the late seventies and at Clemson University and the University of Georgia in the early eighties. He is currently serving as professor of Appalachian studies at Western Carolina University, and he has been a faculty member in the M.F.A. program at Queens University.

Rash's family has lived in the southern Appalachian mountains since the mid-1700s, and it is this region and its people that are the primary focus of his writing. *Eureka Mill* (Bench Press, 1998, and Hub City Writers Project, 2001) is an uncompromising collection of poetry about the unfulfilled

Ron Rash

promises, the tragedies, and the occasional triumphs of life in a textile mill village. *Among the Believers* (Iris Press, 2000) examines the lives and the beliefs of the people of the southern Appalachians. *The Night the New Jesus Fell to Earth and Other Stories from Cliffside, North Carolina* (Bench Press, 1994) contains some of the funniest writing to come out of the South in the last decade, but it is always humor with an undercurrent, an edge, an awareness of the seriousness of life that is always just beneath the surface. Rash's other books are *Raising the Dead* (Iris Press, 2002), his third collection of poetry, which begins and ends with the flooding of the Jocassee Valley; *Casualties* (Bench Press, 2000), a second story collection; and *One Foot in Eden* (2002), Rash's first novel, which won the 2002 Novello Literary Award. His second novel, *Saints at the River*, will be published by Henry

Holt in 2004.

Rash's awards outnumber his books. He won a 1990 Pushcart Prize "Special Mention" award and has been nominated twelve times for the Pushcart Prize. In addition, he is a four-time winner of the South Carolina Fiction Project, a three-time winner of the South Carolina Arts Commission Readers' Circuit award, and a two-time winner of the South Carolina Academy of Authors Poetry Prize. He was awarded the 1996 Sherwood Anderson Prize, a 1994 National Endowment for the Arts Poetry Fellowship, and the 1987 General Electric Younger Writing Award. His work has appeared in more than eighty-five journals and little magazines. If ever a writer burned with a creative fire, Ron Rash is that person. His interview with Patti Just is Program Number 708 of *The Writers' Circle of South Carolina*.

Address: 320 Princess Grace Avenue, Clemson, SC 29631; (864) 653-8791

Reynolds, Sheri (b. 1967). Born and reared on a small farm between Conway and Gallivants Ferry, Reynolds graduated from Davidson College and received her M.F.A. from Virginia Commonwealth University, where she studied with writer Lee Smith. Her first book, *Bitterroot Landing* (Putnam, 1994), set in an area not unlike rural Horry County, was widely praised and led to a contract for two subsequent novels. The first of these, *The Rapture of Canaan* (Putnam, 1996), became a bestseller after it was chosen as an Oprah's Book Club selection, and there are now more than a million copies of it in print. Reynolds's third novel, *A Gracious Plenty* (Harmony, 1997), features a protagonist who listens to the conversations of the dead in a small-town cemetery; it was written partly in response to the death of a friend. Reynolds is associate professor, holding the Ruth and Perry Morgan Chair of Southern Literature at Old Dominion University.

Address: Department of English, Old Dominion University, Hampton Boulevard, Norfolk, VA 23529; (757) 683-3991
Email: sreynold@odu.edu

Rhyne, Nancy (b. 1926). Few writers work with more enthusiasm for their subjects than North Carolina native Rhyne in her headlong rush to chronicle the legends, lore, and culture of the South Carolina Lowcountry. Rhyne, a resident of Myrtle Beach, became an author almost by accident: she took a writing workshop while laid up for three weeks recuperating from a snake bite. Since then she has dedicated more than thirty years of study to the preservation of the heritage of the Southeast coast and devotes extensive research to her books. She is also an indefatigable traveler and spends many days

Nancy Rhyne

each year addressing public audiences on the subjects of her books. One of the benefits of becoming a Nancy Rhyne fan, in fact, is the probability of meeting this gracious and gregarious author and her husband and traveling companion, Sid, somewhere in the course of her wanderings throughout the Palmetto State.

Among Rhyne's most popular titles are *Alice Flagg: The Ghost of the Hermitage: A Novel* (Pelican Publishing Co., 1990), *Chronicles of the South Carolina Sea Islands* (John F. Blair, 1998), *Coastal Ghosts* (Sandlapper Publishing, 1989), *Murder in the Carolinas* (John F. Blair, 1988), *Slave Ghost Stories: Tales of Hags, Hants, Ghosts, & Diamondback Rattlers* (Sandlapper Publishing, 2002), *The South Carolina Lizard Man* (Pelican Publishing Co., 1992), *Tales of the South Carolina Low Country* (John F. Blair, 1982); and *Touring the Coastal South Carolina Backroads* (John F. Blair, 1992). Her interview with Patti Just is Program Number 206 of *The Writers' Circle of South Carolina*.
Address: c/o Sandlapper Publishing,
P.O. Box 730, Orangeburg, SC 29116;
(800) 849-7263

Rice, Linda Lightsey (b. 1950). Knoxville, Tennessee, resident Rice grew up in the Elmwood Park neighborhood of Columbia and based her first novel, *Southern Exposure* (Doubleday, 1991), upon her experiences as a child with her grandmother in Fairfax. "There is a small town inside every one of us," she says, and small-town life is a touchstone of her fiction. A painting, voodoo, and a murder

also figure in the plot of *Southern Exposure*, which was nominated for a PEN Hemingway Award. Rice has completed a second novel, *This Half-Mad Dance*, and is currently working on a literary memoir, *The Magic Palm*. Her interview with Patti Just is program 108 of *The Writers' Circle of South Carolina*.

Rigney, James Oliver, Jr. (b. 1948). Better known to his fans as **Robert Jordan**, Rigney has a large and loyal following as an author of fantasy and science fiction. Rigney was born in Charleston and lives there today in a house built in 1797. After graduating from The Citadel, he served two tours of duty in Vietnam, where he received the Distinguished Flying Cross, the Bronze Star with "V," and two Vietnamese Crosses of Gallantry. He has been a writer since 1977. His "Wheel of Time" series includes ten titles: *The Eye of the World, The Great Hunt, The Dragon Reborn, The Shadow Rising, The Fires of Heaven, Lord of*

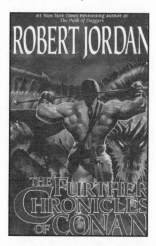

Chaos, A Crown of Swords, The Path of Daggers, Winter's Heart, and *Crossroads of Twilight*. He is also the author of seven "Conan Chronicles," including, among others, *Conan the Destroyer, Conan the Defender, Conan the Triumphant,* and *Conan the Magnificent*. Writing under the pen name **Reagan O'Neal**, Rigney has authored the "Fallon" series—*The Fallon Legacy, The Fallon Pride,* and *The Fallon Blood*—and, as **Jackson O'Reilly**, the Western series "Cheyenne Raiders." He contributes to *Library Journal* and other periodicals as **Chang Lung**.
Website: www.tor.com/sites/wheel_of_time

Ripley, Alexandra (b. 1934). A native of Charleston, Ripley attended Vassar College on a scholarship from the United Daughters of the Confederacy, a foreshadowing perhaps of the setting for much of her fiction. Acclaimed

as one of the most popular and successful of the nation's practitioners of historical fiction, Ripley is probably best known as the author of *Scarlett* (Warner Books, 1991), the authorized sequel to Margaret Mitchell's *Gone With the Wind*. By the time she wrote *Scarlett*, however, she had already had three bestsellers: *Charleston* (Doubleday, 1981), *On Leaving Charleston* (Doubleday, 1984), and *New Orleans Legacy* (MacMillan, 1987). She is also the author of *The Time Returns* (Doubleday, 1985), *From Fields of Gold,* and *A Love Divine*. Ripley lives in Charlottesville, Virginia.

Rod Rogers

Rogers, Rod (b. 1940). Mullins native Rogers left a career as vice president and general manager of a major distribution company in 1987 to pursue a new career as an historical novelist. *Blue-Gray Mist and a Black Dawn* (Writer's Showcase Press, 2000) deals with the lives of ordinary soldiers during the Civil War in 1864. Rogers says, "My novels give me the medium to communicate [the] ideas and express the real human emotions that drive our history." He is featured in Program Number 2 of the 2003 season of *The Writers' Circle of South Carolina*.
Address: c/o Levan C. Rogers,
1384 Southern Magnolia Lane,
Mount Pleasant, SC 29464; (843) 356-3155
Email: rculture@aol.com

Rosengarten, Dale (b. 1948). New York City native Rosengarten was educated at Radcliffe College (B.A., *summa cum laude*, 1969) and Harvard University (M.A., 1975; Ph.D., 1997). From 1984 through 2002 she served McKissick Museum at the University of South Carolina in a number of research, curatorial, and consulting capacities; since 1995 she has been historian and curator of the Jewish Heritage Collection at the College of Charleston. She has also been a consultant, curator, and grant writer for a variety of other institutions, including the San Francisco Airport Museum, the American Museum of Natural History, the National Endowment for the Arts, the Henry Ford Museum and Greenfield Village, the Avery Research Center for African-American History and Culture, Penn Center Inc., and the Charleston Museum. She was a co-founder and director of the McClellanville Arts Council from 1977 to 1984. Rosengarten has written important studies of South Carolina Lowcountry history and culture; among these are *Row Upon Row: Sea Grass Baskets of the South Carolina Lowcountry* (McKissick Museum, University of South Carolina, 1986), *Between the Tracks: The Heritage of Charleston's East Side Community* (Charleston Museum Leaflet No. 30, co-authored with Kimberly Grimes, Martha Zierden, and Elizabeth Alston, Charleston Museum, 1987), *The Proceedings of the Sweetgrass Conference* (edited with Gary Stanton, McKissick Museum, USC, 1989), and *A Portion of the People: Three Hundred Years of Southern Jewish Life* (co-edited with Theodore Rosengarten, USC Press in association with McKissick Museum, 2002).

Address: Dale Rosengarten, Curator, Jewish Heritage Collection, Special Collections, College of Charleston Library, College of Charleston, Charleston, SC 29424; (843) 953-8028 Email: rosengartend@cofc.edu

Rosengarten, Theodore (b. 1944). Although Rosengarten grew up in the suburbs of New York City and was educated at Amherst College (B.A.) and Harvard University (Ph.D.), he has now lived in McClellanville longer than he has lived anywhere else. He is another of South Carolina's gifted historians who can make the lessons of history come to life for a popular as well as an academic audience. Best known for *Tombee: Portrait of a Cotton Planter* (Morrow, 1986), which won the National Book Critics Circle Award, he is also the author of *All God's Dangers: The Life of Nate Shaw* (Knopf, 1994), which won the National Book Award. He has also co-edited *A Portion of the People: Three Hundred Years of Southern Jewish Life* (University of South Carolina Press in association with McKissick Museum, 2002). Rosengarten says that he knew he would become a writer "from age six or seven" and shortly after that, that he would write about race. Rosengarten was named a MacArthur Fellow in 1989. His interview with Patti Just is Program Number 102 of *The Writers' Circle of South Carolina.*

Address: Department of History, College of Charleston, 66 George Street, Charleston, SC 29424 Email: tedrsc@aol.com

Rubin, Louis D., Jr. (b. 1923). A native Charlestonian, Rubin began his collegiate education at the College of Charleston but left during his junior year when his family moved. He earned his A.B. in history from the University of Richmond (1946) and his M.A. in creative writing (1949) and Ph.D. in the aesthetics of literature (1954) from the Johns Hopkins University in Baltimore. He worked at a number of mid-Atlantic states newspapers and taught at Hollins College in Virginia (1957-1967) before taking a position in the English department of the University of North Carolina, which then became his home institution for the remainder of his professional life. Rubin's contributions have been noteworthy in a number of areas, including as a bibliographer, historian, and anthologist of Southern literature; literary critic; novelist (*The Golden Weather*, Atheneum, 1961; and *Surfaces of a Diamond*, Louisiana State University Press, 1981), memoirist (*Small Craft Advisory*, Atlantic Monthly Press, 1992); and founder of Algonquin Books of Chapel Hill, one of the leading publishers of contemporary Southern and Western authors of fiction. It may well be Rubin's legacy at Algonquin Books that turns out to be his most important contribution to the culture of the region. Working together with Shannon Ravenel, a former student of his at Hollins, Rubin shepherded through the press the novels of a group of contemporary writers whose works can stand shoulder to shoulder with any group from any region of the country. Among others, these have included Clyde Edgerton, Jill McCorkle, Kaye Gibbons, Larry Brown, Dori Sanders, and Josephine Humphreys. Rubin's interview with Patti Just is Program Number 212 of *The Writers' Circle of South Carolina*. Among other subjects, Just and Rubin discuss his childhood in downtown Charleston and the neighborhood of Adger's Wharf, "a place for grounding my imagination to reality." Rubin lives quietly in retirement. He was the second living inductee of the South Carolina Academy of Authors (1987).

Sanders, Dori (b. 1934). One of the closest things South Carolina has to a state treasure, Sanders hails proudly from Filbert, where in peach season she can still be found managing

Dori Sanders

her family's fruit stand. Educated at Roosevelt High School in Clover, she also attended community colleges in Prince George's County and Montgomery County, Maryland. In the late 1980s, Algonquin Books of Chapel Hill accepted her first novel, *Clover* (1990), the story of a young black girl suddenly forced to live with a white stepmother she barely knows when her father is killed in an automobile accident on his wedding day. The warm humanity of the novel and its engaging young narrator endeared the book to readers across the nation, and today it is one of the most beloved of all books by a South Carolina writer. Sanders followed *Clover* with *Her Own Place* (Algonquin Books, 1993), the story of Mae Lee Barnes, a strong black woman protagonist, and the family she sustains through the heart of the twentieth century, and *Dori Sanders' Country Cooking: Recipes and Stories from the Family Farm Stand* (Algonquin Books, 1995), which has itself become something of a classic. Dori Sanders was inducted into the South Carolina Academy of Authors in 2000. Her interviews with Patti Just constitute Programs Numbers 104 and 508 of *The Writers' Circle of South Carolina*.

Address: P.O. Box 818, Clover, SC 29710

Sawyer, Corinne Holt (b. 1924). Author of the popular Angela Benbow and Caledonia Wingate murder mysteries, Sawyer reports that she has been "a murder buff from the time I was a little kid." Born in Chisolm, Minnesota, she graduated from the University of Minnesota and earned a Ph.D. from the Birmingham University Shakespeare Institute. Her work experience includes television programming, commercials, and a stint as Clemson University's director of special projects, her position when she retired. Her primary characters, Angela Benbow and Caledonia Wingate, are modeled upon real people she met at her own parents' retirement village. Sawyer's novels belong to the gentle mystery genre of the "cozy," a type of mystery containing very little sex or violence and no bad language. Sawyer's books include *The Geezer Factory Murders* (Donald I. Fine Books, 1996), *Murder Has No Calories* (D.I. Fine, 1994); *Murder Olé* (Donald I. Fine, 1997), *The Peanut Butter Murders* (D.I. Fine, 1993), and *Ho-Ho Homicide* (Fawcett Books, 1996). Sawyer is interviewed by Patti Just in Program Number 306 and in *The Writers' Circle of South Carolina* segment for February 2, 1993.

Valerie Sayers

Sayers, Valerie (b. 1952). A native of Beaufort, Sayers has written a group of five novels set in the fictional town of Due East, South Carolina, which, she says, is "suspiciously like" her hometown. Sayers moved to New York City when she was seventeen and received her M.F.A. from Columbia University. Her novels include *Brain Fever* (Doubleday, 1996), *The Distance Between Us* (Doubleday, 1994), *Who Do You Love* (Doubleday, 1991), *How I Got Him Back, or, Under the Cold Moon's Shine* (Doubleday, 1989), and *Due East* (Doubleday, 1987). *Who Do You Love* and *Brain Fever* were *New York Times* "Notable Books of the Year." Sayers reviews books regularly for *The New York Times Book Review* and *The Washington Post Book World*. She has taught at New York University and Polytechnic University and currently teaches at Notre Dame. Her interview with Patti Just is Program Number 203 of *The Writers' Circle of South Carolina*.
Address: Department of English, University of Notre Dame, 356 O'Shaughnessy Hall, Notre Dame, IN 46556-5639; (574) 631-0485
Email: Sayers.1@nd.edu

Rosa Shand

Shand, Rosa (b. 1937). One of South Carolina's most admired fiction writers, Shand was reared in Columbia and has lived in Uganda, New York City, Oxford and London, England, and several Southern states. She received her B.A. from Randolph-Macon Woman's College (1959) and her M.A. (1981) and Ph.D. (1983) from the University of Texas at Austin. She has served as the Larrabee Professor Emerita of English at Converse College and is currently a visiting writer at Wofford College in Spartanburg. A six-time winner of the South Carolina Fiction Project, Shand has also won PEN Syndicated Fiction Project Awards and the Katherine Anne Porter Prize. She has been named an NEA Fellow, the Scherman Fellow at the MacDowell Colony, and a Dakin Fellow at Sewanee, and has held fellowships from Yaddo and the Virginia Center for the Creative Arts. She has been elected to membership in the Texas Institute of Letters. More than thirty of her stories have appeared in literary magazines across the nation. Her first novel, *The Gravity of Sunlight* (Soho, 2000), received the Jesse H. Jones Award for Best Fiction and the Steven Turner Award for Best First Fiction from the Texas Institute of Letters, the first time the same book has won both awards. *The New York Times* also named the novel a "Notable Book of the Year." Her three stories in *New Southern Harmonies: Four Emerging Fiction Writers* (Hub City Writers Project, 1998) were introduced by Josephine Humphreys, and the book was recognized with the Independent Publishers Award for best short fiction collection in 1998. Shand is interviewed by Patti Just in Program Number 311 of *The Writers' Circle of South Carolina*, where she observes that the short story "is the real poetry of prose writing."
Address: 189 Clifton Avenue, Spartanburg, SC 29302, (864) 582-2302
Email: rosashand@mindspring.com

Shelnutt, Eve (b. 1941). A native of Spartanburg, Shelnutt grew up in various cities on the east and west coasts as her parents, a broadcaster and a musician, moved often in pursuit of interesting work. She began taking writing classes at Wright State University in Dayton, Ohio, in the early 1960s, and her first story won the *Mademoiselle* Fiction Award. In the late sixties she divorced her first husband, began to write for local newspapers, and received her B.A. in English from the University of Cincinnati in 1972. The next year she won a Randall Jarrell fellowship and enrolled in the M.F.A. program at the University of North Carolina at Greensboro. At Greensboro she worked with Fred Chappell, a seminal influence, and she has held a number of academic appointments: assistant professor at Western Michigan University (1975-1980), teacher in the Warren Wilson M.F.A. Program (1980-81), associate professor at the University of Pittsburgh (1980-88), professor at Ohio University (1988-1994), and professor at the College of the Holy Cross, the position she holds today. Shelnutt began publishing soon after she began teaching. Especially praised for her stories, which are tightly unified and striking in the clarity of their often-poetic language, she has written a half-dozen collections of short fiction: *Sparrow 62* (Black Sparrow Press, 1977), *The Love Child* (Black Sparrow Press, 1979), *The Formal Voice* (Black Sparrow, 1982), *Descant* (Palaemon Press, 1982), *The Musician* (Black Sparrow, 1987), and *The Girl, Painted* (Carnegie Mellon University Press, 1996). One critic, in characterizing her fiction, remarks upon "its dense yet economical style, its reliance on images, and its daring in form and content."

Shelnutt has also published three well-received volumes of poetry—*Air and Salt* (Carnegie Mellon University Press, 1983), *First a Long Hesitation* (Carnegie Mellon, 1992), and *Recital in a Private Home* (Carnegie Mellon, 1988)—two popular texts on writing and the teaching of writing—*The Magic Pencil: Teaching Children Creative Writing* (Peachtree Publishers, 1988) and *The Writing Room: Keys to the Craft of Fiction & Poetry* (Longstreet Press, 1989)—and *My Poor Elephant: 27 Male Writers at Work* (Longstreet, 1992). She continues to publish in a wide range of little magazines and journals and is currently at work on a collection of novellas for Carnegie Mellon University Press and a creative writing text for undergraduates.
Address: Department of English, The College of the Holy Cross, P.O. Box 198A, Worcester, MA 01610; (508) 793-2759

George Singleton

Singleton, George (b. 1958). A native of Greenwood, Singleton was educated at Furman University and the University of North Carolina at Greensboro. One of the state's most accomplished writers of short fiction, Singleton has had his work published in *Playboy, The Atlantic Monthly, Harper's, The Georgia Review, Shenandoah, American Literary Review, Cimarron, Denver Quarterly, The South Carolina Review*, and elsewhere. He is the author of two story collections, *The Half-Mammals of Dixie* ("A Shannon Ravenel Book" for Algonquin Books, 2002) and *These People Are Us* (River City Press, 2001), and three of his stories are included in the Hub City Writers Project's award-winning *New Southern Harmonies: Four Emerging Fiction Writers* (1998). His stories have also appeared in the 1994, 1998, 1999, 2001, and 2002 editions of *New Stories from the South*, among other anthologies. A profile of Singleton on NPR called him "a raconteur of trends, counter-trends, obsessions and odd characters in his adopted state of South Carolina," but this characterization fails to account for the utter authenticity of the author's fictional creations and the voice with which he tells their stories. Singleton is an instructor at the South Carolina Governor's School for the Arts and Humanities. He is featured in Program Number 11 of the 2003 season of *The Writers' Circle of South Carolina*.

Address: SCGSAH, 15 University Street, Greenville, SC 29601; (864) 282-3777

Sparks, Nicholas Charles (b. 1965). Few authors have acquired as devoted a following as Sparks has since his first book, *The Notebook* (Warner Books), appeared in 1996. Sparks was born in Omaha, Nebraska, and lived in California and the Midwest before his family settled into Fair Oaks, California, when he was eight. He was the valedictorian of his high school class and attended the University of Notre Dame on a full track scholarship, graduating with a degree in Business Finance in 1985. He worked at a number of jobs in business before a collaboration with Olympian Billy Mills resulted in his first modestly successful book in 1990. After moving to North Carolina, he wrote *The Notebook* in six months in 1994. When it was published, it became a domestic and international bestseller, as have all of his subsequent books, which have been translated into more than thirty-five languages. *Message in a Bottle* (Warner Books, 1998) was made into a motion picture in 1999, as was *A Walk to Remember* (Warner Books, 1999) in 2001; a film version of *The Notebook* will also be released. Two other novels—A

Nicholas Sparks

Bend in the Road (Warner Books, 2001) and *Nights in Rodanthe* (Warner Books, 2002)—have been optioned to Hollywood as well, and *The Rescue* (Warner Books, 2000) is being adapted as a television series. Sparks and Harry Potter creator J.K. Rowling have the distinction of being the only contemporary novelists to have a novel spend more than a year on both *The New York Times* hardcover and paperback bestseller lists. At one time Sparks was a pharmaceutical sales rep in South Carolina; today he lives in North Carolina. Website: www.nicholassparks.com. (He may be reached via email at the site.)

Spillane, Mickey (b. 1918). One of America's most successful mystery novelists, Brooklyn native Spillane calls himself "a writer and not an author—I'm in business. A writer keeps writing every day." Likewise, he says, his readers are not fans; they're customers. This hard-nosed, pragmatic attitude to his craft developed early and is absolutely characteristic of the man and his work.

Spillane began writing in the 1930s, even-

Mickey Spillane

tually working on a variety of novels, short stories, books for children, comic books, and movie and television scripts. During World War II he recognized that paperbacks were the wave of the future. "When I wrote my first book," he reported to Patti Just, "I wrote it for the reprint. But to get it in the reprint, I had to get it in hardback." That first book sold ten thousand copies at $2.50 each. Since then, Spillane's books have sold more than 180 million copies in sixteen languages. At one time he was one of the five most translated authors in the world, the other four being Lenin, Trotsky, Gorky, and Jules Verne. Also, seven of the top ten American bestsellers between 1895 and 1965 were Spillane titles. Spillane's most well-known character is detective Mike Hammer, who, in addition to being the protagonist of six of Spillane's books, is also the hero of television and the movies. Hammer's prototype was Spillane's comic book hero Mike Danger. The writer also worked for the Captain America, Human Torch, and Submariner comic magazines.

Among Spillane's many popular novels are *I, the Jury* (New American Library, 1947), his first book, written in less than a month and, to date, an eight-million-plus seller; *The Big Kill* (New American Library, 1951); *The Death Dealers* (New American Library, 1966); *The Deep* (New American Library, 1962); *The Delta Factor* (New American Library, 1968); *The Last Cop Out* (Dutton, 1973); *Survival...Zero!* (Dutton, 1970); and *Tomorrow I Die* (Mysterious Press, 1984). He has also written award-winning books for children, including the Junior Literary Guild Award-winner *The Ship That Never Was* (Bantam Books, 1982). In 1995 he was named the Grand Master of the Mystery Writers of America. Today Spillane lives in Murrells Inlet and writes "whenever I need the money." His interview with Patti Just, Program Number 1006 of *The Writers' Circle of*

South Carolina, is a classic.
Address: c/o Postmaster, Murrells Inlet,
South Carolina 29576,
or c/o Signet Publicity, 375 Hudson Street,
New York, NY 10014.

Starkey, David. Poet and writing teacher Starkey, who taught at Francis Marion University in Florence in 1990-95, was also an instructor in the Governor's School Rural Outreach Program in 1991-95. In the fall of 1999 he was Fulbright Professor of English at the University of Oulu, Finland. He was an assistant professor, then tenured associate professor at North Central College in Naperville, Illinois, from 1995 to 2001. Currently he is a part-time instructor at Santa Barbara City College, a lecturer in the writing program of the University of California-Santa Barbara, and an associate faculty member in the M.F.A. in Creative Writing Program at Antioch University-Los Angeles. He holds a B.A. in English from the University of California, Davis (1984); an M.A. in English from the University of California, Los Angeles (1986); and an M.F.A. in creative writing-poetry from Louisiana State University (1990).

An accomplished poet, Starkey has published more than three hundred poems in journals including *The American Scholar, Beloit Poetry Journal, The Chattahoochee Review, Cimarron Review, Hollins Critic, Kansas Quarterly, Mid-American Review, Tar River Poetry, Wormwood Review, Writers' Forum,* and many others. His poetry, fiction, and essays on teaching writing are also widely anthologized. His book publications include *Open Mike Night at the Cabaret Voltaire* (Kings Estate Press, 1996); *Starkey's Book of States* (Boston Books, 1995); *Koan Americana* (Colonial Press, 1992); four poetry chapbooks; and, as author or editor, five books about the teaching of writing. He has also received a number of awards including two Fulbright Scholarships and four Pushcart Prize nominations.
Address: 1336 Camino Manadero,
Santa Barbara, CA 93111; (805) 729-2013
Email: starkey_d@hotmail.com

Starr, William W. (b. 1940). Atlanta native Starr exerted a profound influence upon literary South Carolina as book editor of Columbia's *The State* newspaper for more than thirty years. During that time he reviewed most of the books written by South Carolina authors, and he interviewed many of the writers. He is the author of *Southern Writers* (with

photographs by David G. Spielman, University of South Carolina Press, 1997) and the associate editor of the *South Carolina Encyclopedia,* forthcoming from USC Press. He has also written *A Guide to South Carolina Beaches* (USC Press, 2001), a model of graceful expository prose that reveals a genuine affection for the region. Starr is currently director of the Georgia Center for the Book in Atlanta.
Address: Georgia Center for the Book,
c/o DeKalb County Public Library,
215 Sycamore Street, Decatur, GA 30030;
(404) 370-8450
Email: starrw@dekalblibrary.org.

Steadman, Mark (b. 1930). A native of Statesboro, Georgia, Steadman was educated at Armstrong Junior College, Emory University (A.B., 1951), and Florida State University (M.A., 1956; Ph.D., 1963). He served in the United States Navy from 1951 to 1953, worked as an advertising copywriter for W.R.C. Smith Publishing Company in Atlanta from 1953 to 1955, and taught at Clemson University from 1957 to 1997, when he retired. He was also visiting associate professor of American literature at American University in Cairo in 1968-69 and a Fulbright lecturer in American literature at Leningrad State University in 1983. Steadman's so-called "gothic" collection of stories, *McAfee County: A Chronicle* (Holt, Rhinehart and Winston, 1971), modeled upon Sherwood Anderson's *Winesburg, Ohio,* was widely praised in the United States and also found appreciative audiences in France (1974) and Germany (1975). This collection, and Steadman's three subsequent novels—*A Lion's Share* (Holt, Rhinehart and Winston, 1975), *Angel Child* (Peachtree Publishers, 1987), and *Bang-Up Season* (Longstreet Press, 1990)— all exhibit a wry humor and sympathy for even the most troubled and afflicted characters that are rarely encountered in fiction. Steadman's short stories have appeared in *The Oconee Review, The Southern Review, The South Carolina Review, Red Clay Reader, Sandlapper,* and in the anthology 3 x 3 (Peachtree Publishers, 1985), in which they accompany the work of Shirley Ann Grau and Doris Betts. Steadman is interviewed in Program Number 309 of *The Writers' Circle of South Carolina.*
Address: 450 Pin du Lac Drive,
Central, SC 29630; (864) 639-6673
Email: steadms@bellsouth.net

Sully, Susan (b. 1962). Sully, a native of Alexandria, Virginia, graduated from Yale

University with a B.A. in art history (1984) and lectures frequently on regional architectural history and design at institutions such as the Smithsonian's National Building Museum, the Los Angeles County Art Museum, and the international auction firm Sotheby's. She also writes regularly for *Southern Accents, Coastal Living,* and *The New York Times,* and is the author of three influential books on style: *Charleston Style: Past and Present* (photos by John Blais, Rizzoli International, 1999), *Savannah Style: Mystery and Manners* (photos by Steven Brooke, Rizzoli International, 2001), and *The New Moroccan Style: The Art of Sensual Living* (Clarkson Potter, 2003). Her books have been featured in *House Beautiful, World of Interiors, Southern Accents, Ladies Home Journal, The Christopher Lowell Show,* and SCETV. Although Sully's writing is not belletristic in the conventional meaning of the term, her style is both literary and elegant, a good read in every sense of the word. She has also written a children's book, *Fish & Soup* (Rizzoli International, 1995), illustrated by her husband, the artist Thomas Sully, and the motivational *Late Bloomer's Guide to Success at Any Age* (Quill/A Division of Harper Collins, 2001).
Address: 73 Moultrie Street,
Charleston, SC 29403; (843) 723-2734
Email: susansully@mindspring.com

Tate, Eleanora (b. 1948). A native of New Jersey, Tate now lives in Myrtle Beach. Many of her books are based on her own childhood in Canton, Missouri, near the Mississippi River. She graduated from Drake University (1973) with a B.A. in journalism and worked as news editor for the *Iowa Bystander* and reporter for *The Des Moines Register* and *Tribune* before moving to Myrtle Beach, where she saw the need to write about contemporary African-American children dealing with their own lives. *The Secret of Gumbo Grove* (Dell Publishing, 1996) draws upon the history and legends of Myrtle Beach and Horry County. *Don't Split the Pole: Tales of Down-Home Folk Wisdom* (Delacorte Press, 1997) draws upon the author's experience as a storyteller. *A Blessing in Disguise* (Delacorte Press, 1995) and *Front Porch Stories: At the One-Room School* (Dell, 1993) both feature strong young female protagonists with interesting fathers. Tate has also written *African American Musicians* (John Wiley & Sons, 2000) and *Thank You, Dr. Martin Luther King, Jr.!* (F. Watts, 1990). *A Blessing in Disguise* was an American Bookseller "Pick of the Lists," and *The Secret of Gumbo Grove* won a Parents' Choice Gold Seal Award. Tate's stories have appeared in *American Girl*, *Scholastic Story Works*, and *Goldfinch*. She frequently speaks before educator and civic groups and is a past president of the National Association of Black Storytellers. Her interviews with Patti Just are Programs Numbers 109 and 704 in *The Writers' Circle of South Carolina*.

Address: Box 3581, Morehead City, NC, 28557

Susan Tekulve

Tekulve, Susan (b. 1967). A graduate of the M.F.A. program at Wichita State University (1992), Tekulve is an assistant professor of English at Converse College in Spartanburg. Her nonfiction and short stories have appeared in *Denver Quarterly*, *Beloit Fiction Journal*, *ACM*, *Indiana Review*, *Crab Orchard Review*, *The Literary Review*, and *Black Warrior Review*. She was the First Alternate for the 1999 South Carolina Fiction Fellowship and received a Bread Loaf Writers' Conference Scholarship. Her story collection *Rooms People Live In* was a finalist for the 2002 G.S. Charat Chandra Prize with BookMark Press. Tekulve is a regular contributor to *Book* magazine.

Address: Department of English, Converse College, Spartanburg, SC 29301; (864) 596-9186

Email: susan.tekulve@converse.edu

Teter, Betsy Wakefield (b. 1958). Godmother, guiding light, and executive director of the Hub City Writers Project, Teter was one of the four principals who founded the project in 1995. Seven years later she accepted the Governor's Elizabeth O'Neill Verner Award for outstanding contribution to the arts in South Carolina on behalf of Hub City and its board. A former business editor for the Spartanburg *Herald-Journal*, Teter and her colleagues recognized the high quality and

Betsy Teter

surprising quantity of writing being produced by Upstate writers and dedicated themselves to making that writing both more widely known and more widely accessible. She also realized that there were many little-known but important community stories that would be lost forever if some organization did not step in to foster their preservation. Hub City's resounding success and growing national reputation are testimony to the legitimacy of Teter's vision. The Hub City offices are on the fifth floor of the historic Montgomery Building in downtown Spartanburg. Teter is married to poet John Lane.

Address: Hub City Writers Project, P. O. Box 8421, Spartanburg, SC 29305; (864) 577-9349

Email: bteter@bellsouth.net

David Tillinghast

Tillinghast, David (b. 1936). A prolific and respected poet and short-story writer, Tillinghast received his B.A. from Louisiana Polytechnic Institute (1961), his M.A. from the University of Wisconsin (1963), and his Ph.D. from the University of South Carolina (1974). He has taught at Clemson University, where since 1975 he has been a full professor in the Department of English. He is the author

of *Women Hoping for Rain and Other Poems* (State Street Press, 1987) and the editor of *Boiler Room* (South Carolina Arts Commission, 1975) and *Ears Quickly* (South Carolina Arts Commission, 1976). His poems have appeared in *The South Carolina Review*, *Poet Lore*, *The Southern Review*, *Georgia Journal*, *Cross Timbers Review*, *The Southern Humanities Review*, and a number of anthologies. His fiction and nonfiction prose have been published in *The Virginia Quarterly Review*, *Texas Review*, *The Antigonish Review*, *St. Andrews Review*, and elsewhere. Tillinghast is a multiple winner of the South Carolina Fiction Project and the South Carolina Readers' Circuit. He has won the Frank Durham Memorial Award in Creative Writing from the University of South Carolina (1973), was runner-up for the Fanny Fae Wood Award of the Academy of American Poets (1973), and received first place and best-in-show awards from the Greenville Arts Festival (1984). He is a writer's writer.

Address: Department of English, Clemson University, Clemson, SC 29634-1503

Tindall, George Brown (b. 1921). Greenville native Tindall was educated at Furman University (A.B., 1942) and the University of North Carolina (M.A., 1948; Ph.D., 1951). After sojourns at Eastern Kentucky College (1950-51), the University of Mississippi (1951-52), the Women's College of the University of North Carolina, now UNC-Greensboro (1952-53), and Louisiana State University (1953-58), he taught at the University of North Carolina at Chapel Hill, where he became Kenan Professor of History, for thirty years. He is the winner of many major awards including a Guggenheim Fellowship (1957-58), the Charles S. Sydnor Award of the Southern Historical Association (1968), the Lillian E. Smith Award of the Southern Regional Council (1968), the Mayflower Cup of the North Carolina Society of Mayflower Descendants (1968), and an honorary D.Litt. from Furman University (1971). One of the deans of Southern history, he has written or edited six major studies of the region and its culture and contributed to almost another dozen. Among his most important works are *South Carolina Negroes* (University of South Carolina Press, 1952); *The Emergence of the New South, 1913-1945* (Louisiana State University Press, 1970); *The Disruption of the Solid South* (LSU Press, 1972); *The Persistent Tradition in New South Politics* (LSU Press, 1975); and, with David E. Shi, *America: A Narrative History*, now in its sixth edition (W.W. Norton and Company, 2003). His essays and reviews have appeared in most major historical journals.

Address: History Department, CB# 3195, University of North Carolina, Chapel Hill, NC 27599-3195; (919) 962-2115.

Townes, Charles H. (b. 1915). Greenville native Townes attended the public schools there and graduated from Furman University at age nineteen, *summa cum laude*, with a B.S. in Physics and a B.A. in Modern Languages. He subsequently received his M.A. in Physics from Duke University (1936) and his Ph.D. from California Institute of Technology (1939). His professional career included positions at Bell Telephone Laboratories (1933-1947), Columbia University (1948-1955), the Institute for Defense Analysis (1959-1961), Massachusetts Institute of Technology (1961-66), and the University of California at Berkeley (1967-current). In 1964 Townes received the Nobel Prize in Physics for his work on the maser/laser. He has written of his life and career in several autobiographical works: *How the Laser Happened: Adventures of a Scientist* (Oxford University Press, 1999), *A Life in Physics: Bell Telephone Laboratories and World War II, Columbia University and the Laser, MIT and Government Service, California and Research Astrophysics* (Regional Oral History Office, Bancroft Library, University of California, 1994), and *Making Waves* (American Institute of Physics, 1995).

Address: Physics Department, 301 Leconte Building, University of California, Berkeley, CA 94720-7300; (510) 642-1128 Email: cht@ssl.berkeley.edu

Trakas, Deno P. (b. 1952). Long-time Spartanburg resident Trakas was educated at Eckerd College (B.A., 1974), the University of Tulsa (M.A., 1976), and the University of South Carolina (Ph.D., 1981). His poetry and fiction have appeared in two dozen periodicals, including *Oxford American*, *Uwharrie Review*, *Tinderbox*, *The Crucible*, *Denver Quarterly*, *Kansas Quarterly*, *The Louisville Review*, and *Poetry Now*. He is the author of two poetry chapbooks, *The Shuffle of Wings* (Holocene Press, 1990) and *Human and Puny* (Holocene, 2001), and his work is featured in the Hub City Writers Project anthology *New Southern Harmonies: Four Emerging Fiction Writers* (1998). He is a four-time winner of the South Carolina Fiction Project and has also won the

Deno Trakas

South Carolina Fellowship in Fiction and the Academy of American Poets Award (University of South Carolina, 1978 and 1979). In 2001 he was a finalist in the James Jones Foundation First Novel Contest. *After Paris*, his first novel, is currently making the rounds with his agent, and a second novel, *Stone Boats*, is in progress. "Dust," Trakas's response to the 9/11 tragedy in New York, has been issued as a broadside poster illustrated by his sister Irene.

Address: Department of English, Wofford College, Spartanburg, SC 29303; (864) 597-4573 Email: trakasdp@wofford.edu

Tuttle, Jon (b. 1959). Playwright-in-residence and literary manager at the Trustus Theatre in Columbia, Tuttle is also professor of English at Francis Marion University in Florence. He has won numerous national and regional awards as a playwright, including fellowships from the South Carolina Arts Commission and the South Carolina Academy of Authors. His plays have received about fifty productions across the country, among which are the following: *The White Problem*—commissioned by the University of South Carolina and produced at the 2001 Piccolo Spoleto Festival after premiering in April 2001 at USC's Longstreet Theatre; *Drift*—winner of the 1998 South Carolina Playwrights' Festival Award, premiering at Trustus; *The Hammerstone*—winner of the 1994 SC Playwrights' Festival Award after premiering at Trustus and having since been produced in Los Angeles, Chicago, New York, and elsewhere, a finalist for three major awards; *Terminal Cafè*—produced by Workshop Theatre, Columbia, and theatres in Albuquerque and Los Angeles, receiving its Equity premiere at the Bailiwick Arts Center in Chicago; *Sonata for Armadillos*, produced a dozen times by

theaters across the nation; and *A Fish Story*—produced by theaters in New Mexico and South Carolina. Tuttle is Patti Just's interview subject in Program Number 605 of *The Writers' Circle of South Carolina*.

Address: Department of English, Francis Marion University, P.O. Box 100547, Florence, SC 29501; (843) 661-1521 Email: jtuttle@fmarion.edu

Wall, Kathryn R. (b. 1945). Hilton Head resident Wall's first published story was "The Sky Is Falling," which won *Hilton Head Monthly's* 1999 Summer Fiction contest. Her first novel, *In for a Penny* (Writers Club Press, 2000), the first Bay Tanner mystery, appeared a little over a year later. The second edition was released in 2002 by Coastal Villages Press. Tanner, the series' protagonist, is a widow still coming to grips with her loss, working out the personal mystery of her own identity at

Kathyrn Wall

the same time that she inadvertently becomes involved in a series of criminal cases. *And Not a Penny More* (Coastal Villages Press, 2002), the second novel in the series, is popular with fans of the first and received a favorable notice from *Midwest Book Review*. St. Martin's Press published the third mystery, *Perdition House*, in 2003, and has purchased the fourth Bay Tanner mystery.

Website: www.kathrynwall.com Email: kathy@pennynovels.com

Warlick, Ashley (b. 1972). Reared in Charlotte, Greenville resident Warlick was educated at Dickinson College in Pennsylvania (1994), where she began her first novel as an independent-study fiction assignment. It so impressed her professors and then editor Janet Silver at Houghton Mifflin that it was bought by the publisher before it was even completed. *The Distance from the Heart of Things* (Mariner

Ashley Warlick

Books, 1997) won the Houghton Mifflin Literary Fellowship Award, making her the youngest author ever to win the honor that she was to discover she shared with Robert Penn Warren and Philip Roth. Southern reviewers especially liked her book, and her second novel, *The Summer After June*, was published in 2000. Warlick's husband is a professor at Furman University.

Warmus, John. Chicago native Warmus has traveled extensively, including to Kenya and Costa Rica, and has lived in the Hilton Head/ Bluffton area for the last ten years. His novels all deal with unconventional subject matter: *The Suicide Club* (1stbooks Library, 1996) is about "what happens to a utopian town when some teenagers commit suicide"; *The Institut* (Barclay Books, 2001) is a surprisingly timely story of "priests that have gone astray and an Immaculate Conception;" and *Stations of the Cross* "deals with the Cathedral Underground where the Catholic Church helped Nazis escape the war." Warmus is also the author of the original screenplay *Adonis*, as well two other screenplays based on two of his earlier novellas, *The Grapplers* and *The Green Man*.

Clemmie Webber

Webber, Clemmie E. (b. 1913). Long active in education and civic affairs, Webber is a retired professor of science education at South Carolina State University in Orangeburg. The recipient of many honors for her work in these areas, Webber became an author with the publication of *My Treadwell Street Saga: From its Beginning to 1950* (Williams Associates, Orangeburg), an important anecdotal history of the black middle-class Treadwell Street neighborhood in Orangeburg.
Address: 492 Woodland Drive, Orangeburg, SC 29115; (803) 534-5753; or, c/o Williams Associates, P. O. Box 1894, Orangeburg, SC 29116; (803) 531-1662

Ceille Baird Welch

Welch, Ceille Baird (b. 1941). Hopkins resident Welch describes herself as "playwright, poet, songwriter, short-fiction writer, speaker, lecturer, teacher, and licensed professional counselor." She holds a B.A. in psychology and an M.Ed. in counseling from the University of South Carolina, and she received an honorary D.A. degree from Lander University in 1998 for her literary accomplishments. A five-time winner of the "New Voices" South Carolina Scriptwriters Competition, she has also been a winner of the South Carolina Fiction Project, the Savannah Playwrights Festival, and the New York Competition for Playwrights Over 50. Her fiction and nonfiction have appeared in *Inheritance: Selections from the South Carolina Fiction Project*, *Kaleidoscope: A Journal for Women*, and *Lander Magazine*. Her plays *On Wings Like a Paper Crane*, *A Rainbow of a Different Color*, and *Dayporch at East Jesus* have been performed in numerous productions in Georgia and South Carolina; *The Snake Handler* was winner of the New York Competition for Playwrights Over 50. She is also the author of the children's musical videos *The Very First Milo Moose Day Celebration*, which played on PBS

stations across the country, and *A Rainbow of a Different Color* and of the music CD *What'll I Do with My Dreams* (Traxside).
Address: 116 Tom's Creek Court, Hopkins, SC 29061; (803) 776-7764
Email: ryegatecc@aol.com

Marjory Wentworth

Wentworth, Marjory (b. 1958). Wentworth was born in Lynn, Massachusetts, and educated at Mount Holyoke College (B.A., 1980), Oxford University, and New York University (M.A.). Her poetry has been widely published in little magazines including *Appalachia*, *Beloit Poetry Journal*, and *Peregrine*, and she has twice been nominated for the Pushcart Poetry Prize. *Nightjars*, a chapbook, was published by Laurel Publishing in 1995; *What the Water Gives Me*, a collaboration including monotype prints by Mary Edna Fraser, was published by Booksurge in 2002. Wentworth teaches poetry in "Expressions and Healing," an arts and healing program for cancer patients and their families and creative writing at the Charleston County School of the Arts. She is also on the board of the Southern Literature Council of Charleston and has completed a manuscript about her work with cancer patients. Wentworth participated in the 1999 exhibition *A Celebration Of Barrier Islands: Restless Ribbons of Sand*, an exhibition featuring her work together with the Barrier Island batiks of artist Fraser and Dr. Orrin Pilkey's scientific text at the Duke University Museum of Art, and the National Science Foundation. In 2003 Governor Mark Sanford named her to succeed the late Bennie Lee Sinclair as poet laureate of South Carolina. Her collection *Noticing Eden* was published in fall 2003 by Hub City Writers Project.
Address: 1914 Middle Street, Sullivan's Island, SC 29482
Email: marjwpub@aol.com

Wilder, Effie Leland (b. 1909). A resident of the Presbyterian Home in Summerville, Wilder became a book author for the first time at age eighty-five with the publication of her novel about life in a retirement home, *Out to Pasture (But Not Over the Hill)* (Peachtree Publishers, 1995). Dan Harmon of *Sandlapper* magazine captures the appeal of this lovely collection of sketches exactly when he says that it is "captivating in its complete ordinariness"; it became a runaway hit. The success of Wilder's first book led to a second, *Over What Hill? Notes from the Pasture* (Peachtree, 1996); a third, *Older But Wilder: More Notes from the Pasture* (Peachtree, 1998); and then two more, *One More Time – Just for the Fun of It: Notes from FairAcres* (Peachtree, 1999) and *Oh, My Goodness: More Surprises from FairAcres* (Peachtree, 2001). Wilder is also the co-author of a book on Pawley's Island, *Pawley's Island ... A Living Legend: An Historical Sketch of The Blessed Isle and Its Environs* (with Charlotte Kaminski Prevost, State Printing Company, 1972). More information about Wilder and her books is available at www.peachtree-online.com, the Peachtree Publishers Website. In recognition of her philanthropic work, Wilder has been made a member the Order of the Palmetto (1994) and received the Converse College Distinguished Alumna Award (1982). She is featured in Program Number 702 of *The Writers' Circle of South Carolina*.

Williams, Susan Millar (b. 1956). Williams received her B.A. from Hendrix College, her M.A. from the University of Arkansas, and her Ph.D. from Louisiana State University. She is best known for her award-winning biography, *A Devil and a Good Woman, Too: The Lives of Julia Peterkin* (University of Georgia Press, 1997), recipient of the 1998 Julia Cherry Spruill Prize given by the Southern Association for Women Historians for the Best Work Published in Southern History. She won the South Carolina Arts Commission's Fiction Fellowship for 2001. She is also the editor of two McClellanville cookbooks and is at work on a novel set during the Charleston earthquake of 1886.

Address: English Department,
Trident Technical College, P.O. Box 118067, Charleston, SC 29423-8067; (843) 722-5538 or (843) 887-3890;
or P.O. Box 266, McClellanville, SC 29458
Email: susan.williams@ tridenttech.edu

Clyde Wilson

Wilson, Clyde (b. 1941). An historian widely praised for the style of his historical writing as well the meticulousness of his scholarship, Wilson received his B.A. (1963), M.A. (1964), and Ph.D. (1971) from the University of North Carolina. Since 1971 he has taught in the History department of the University of South Carolina, where he is currently professor and editor of the papers of John C. Calhoun. In addition to editing volumes 10-28 (1977-2003) of the *Calhoun Papers*, Wilson has also edited three volumes of the *Dictionary of Literary Biography* and the important anthology *Why the South Will Survive, By Fifteen Southerners* (University of Georgia Press, 1981). He is the author of *Carolina Cavalier: The Life and Mind of James Johnston Pettigrew* (University of Georgia, 1995) and *John C. Calhoun: A Bibliography* (Meckler, 1990).

Address: Department of History,
University of South Carolina,
Columbia, SC 29208; (803) 777-4580
Email: clyde-wilson@sc.edu

Youmans, Marly (b. 1953). A native of Aiken, Youmans grew up in Louisiana, where her father was completing his Ph.D. and her mother worked for the state library. She was educated at Hollins College, Brown University, and the University of North Carolina, and worked as a tenured professor at the State University of New York before becoming a full-time writer. She is the author of three novels: *Little Jordan* (David R. Godine, 1995), *Catherwood* (Farrar, Straus and Giroux, 1996), and *The Wolf Pit* (Harcourt Harvest Books, 2001); a fantasy novel for younger readers set in the mountains of Tennessee and the Carolinas, *The Curse of the Raven Mocker* (Farrar, Straus and Giroux Books for Young Readers, 2003); and a collection of poetry, *Claire* (forthcoming, Louisiana State University

Press, 2003). *Catherwood*, the story of a young English colonist lost with her infant in the woods of seventeenth-century New York state, is based upon a true story. *The Wolf Pit*, which intertwines the story of a young Confederate soldier in a prison camp with that of a mute young slave who manages to survive and even triumph over her victimization, won the 2001 Michael Shaara Award for excellence in Civil War Fiction. She currently lives in Cooperstown, New York.

Art Young

Young, Art (b. 1943). Not himself a writer of poetry or fiction, Young is included in *Literary South Carolina* because of his influence upon the teaching of writing in both the public schools and at universities throughout the country. His *Language Connections: Writing and Reading Across the Curriculum* (co-edited with Toby Fulwiler, NCTE, 1982) and *Writing Across the Disciplines: Research into Practice* (also co-edited with Fulwiler, Boynton/Cook, 1986) were followed by *Programs that Work: Models and Methods for Writing Across the Curriculum* (also with Fulwiler, Boynton/Cook, 1990) and *Programs and Practices: Writing Across the Secondary Curriculum* (co-edited with Pamela Farrell-Childers and Anne Ruggles Gere, Boynton/Cook, 1994). These four books, used widely in teacher-education programs and National Writing Project Summer Institutes across the United States, helped to revolutionize the teaching of writing and give students and their teachers greater confidence and increased competence as writers and as creators of imaginative literature. More recently Young's work has broadened to include the universe of electronic communication (*Electronic Communication Across the Curriculum*, NCTE, 1998) and the teaching of critical theory (*Critical Theory and the Teaching of Literature: Politics, Curriculum, Pedagogy—* co-edited with James F. Slevin—NCTE, 1996).

Young holds the Campbell Chair in technical communication and is professor of English and professor of engineering at Clemson University. In 2000 he was presented the state's highest award, the Order of the Palmetto, by Governor Jim Hodges.

Address: Department of English,
Clemson University,
Clemson, SC 29634-0523; (864) 656-3062
Email: apyoung@clemson.edu

Young, Tommy Scott (b. 1943). Blair native Young received his B.A. from California State University in Los Angeles, where he studied painting, sculpture, and theatre. He worked with Kathleen Freeman and Yaphet Kotto at the Watts Writers Workshop, toured with the Writers Workshop, and founded the Meat Theater in Los Angeles. In 1974 Young founded the Kitani Foundation, a community cultural arts organization in Columbia, and for the next decade promoted all of the arts, especially with and for groups of students and their teachers. The Kitani Foundation under Young's leadership won the Columbia Urban League's Community Service Award for Outstanding Service in the Field of Performing Arts and the Elizabeth O'Neill Verner Award of the South Carolina Arts Commission. Young is an accomplished author, storyteller, actor, director, and sculptor. He is the author of two books of poetry, much of it influenced by the rhythms of jazz—*Black Blues and Shiny Songs* (Red Clay Books, 1977) and *Crazy Wolf Sings a Crazy Wolf Song* (Red Clay Books, 1973)—and of books and recordings of *Tommy Scott Young Spins Magical Tales, Vols. I and II* (Raspberry Recordings). Young is also an active storyteller, having performed at the 1988 Sixth Annual National Black Storytelling Festival (Oakland, CA), the 1989 Seventh Annual National Black Storytelling Festival (Brooklyn, NY), and the 1991 Ninth Annual National Black Storytelling Festival. Young was Resident Storyteller for the Lincoln Center Institute in 1999 and 2000. He performs in radio and television broadcasts and has been an artist-in-residence for arts groups in South Carolina, North Carolina, and Georgia. Younger readers will appreciate that Young is the father of popular television actor Lee Thompson Young, star of the Disney Channel's *The Famous Jett Jackson* series.

Address: 244 Fifth Avenue, Suite 2478,
New York, NY 10001; (718) 622-8796
Email: tom.scot@verizon.net

In advance of a second printing, additions to this list will be posted at www.hubcity.org/litsc.htm

9
CHAPTER

Promoters, Publishers, and Purveyors of Literary South Carolina

The universe of South Carolina letters is a large and diverse one, as this volume amply demonstrates. Moreover, as important as the writers themselves are, they don't form the only constellation in these bright heavens, for without the publishers and the little magazines and a select group of others who shepherd them into print and otherwise promote their efforts, the authors could not reach their public. What follows is a brief directory of organizations, societies, and firms that take a special interest in literary South Carolina. Contact information is provided for those who would like to solicit current publishers' catalogs, to subscribe to the magazines, or to submit their own writing. Patronize as many of these good folks as possible; they deserve to stay in business.

Bench Press
2507 Brighton Lane, Beaufort, SC 29902; (843) 322-0532; slesin@islc.net
The Bench Press had its beginnings in Pennsylvania in 1985 when founder Warren Slesinger reprinted William Stafford's little-known memoir, *Down in My Heart*. At the time Slesinger worked as the eastern sales manager for the University of Chicago Press but "wanted to see what I could do on my own." The success of the Stafford book was followed in 1986 by *Stories We Listened To* by John Haines and in 1987 by *The Sisters: New and Selected Poems* by Josephine Jacobsen.

By 1987 Slesinger was working for the University of South Carolina Press as senior editor, but since the university was not

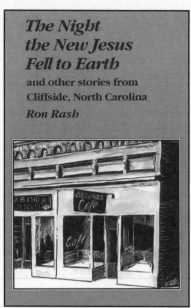

A Bench Press publication

publishing much original literature at the time, he "decided to publish poetry, fiction, and creative nonfiction of a regional nature." With support from the South Carolina Center for Teacher Recruitment, the Richland-Lexington Cultural Council, and the South Carolina Arts Commission, he was able to publish a small but important group of titles. These included *Hard Weather* by Roger Sauls (1987); *Rhythms, Reflections, and Lines on the Back of a Menu: Writing by South Carolina Teachers*, edited by Libby Bernardin and Linda Kirszenbaum (1988); *The Man Who Grew Silent* by Jim Peterson (1989); and three books by Ron Rash: *The Night the New Jesus Fell to Earth and Other Stories from Cliffside, North Carolina* (1994), *Eureka Mill* (1998), and *Casualties* (2000).

Slesinger has also edited and published two collections of essays by the editors of twenty literary magazines: *Spreading the Word: Editors on Poetry* (1990) and *The Whole Story: Editors on Fiction* (1995). Each of the editors explains the choice of a representative poem or story and describes the editorial process of selection. These well-received collections are used in creative writing courses across the country.

In addition to conducting the work of the press, Slesinger, who is now semi-retired, has taught part-time and solicited grant funding to supplement the press's income. He currently teaches at the University of South Carolina Beaufort. The Bench Press's books are distributed by Parnassus Book Distribution, 200 Academy Way, Columbia, SC 29206; (803) 782-7748 or (800) 782-7760.

Caught in the Creative Act

c/o Janette Turner Hospital, Department of English, University of South Carolina, Columbia SC 29208; www.cla.sc.edu/cica

Coordinated by writer-in-residence Janette Turner Hospital, this fall series in Columbia annually attracts as many as 500 students to hear "writers talk about their writing." The course, free and open to the public, is held at large venues such as the USC Law School Auditorium and the Koger Center, and meets two evenings per week for three months. The 2003 slate of visiting writers included Sue Monk Kidd, Derek Walcott, Joe Kinsella, Kelly Cherry, Jack Bass, and others. Dovetailed into this initiative is the USC Fall Festival of Authors, held in October each year.

Crazyhorse

Department of English, College of Charleston, 66 George Street, Charleston, SC 29424.

Crazyhorse, a biannual literary magazine produced at the College of Charleston and distributed nationally, publishes short fiction, poetry, and creative nonfiction "that engages in the work of honest communication." In considering submissions, its editors ask, "What's at stake in the writing?" and "What's reckoned with that's important for other people to read?" They seek "a mix of writing regardless of its form, genre, school, or politics" and are "especially on the lookout for writing that doesn't fit the categories."

This formula—or, rather, lack of one—has proven successful. Past issues have included work by established writers as varied as Gilbert Allen, Robert Bly, Linda Lee Harper, Susan Ludvigson, Mary Ruefle, and Gary Soto, as well as an interesting mix of younger talent. Editors include Bret Lott, Paul Allen, Carol Ann Davis, and Garrett Doherty. *Crazyhorse* has published for more than forty years, moving to Charleston from the University of Arkansas-Little Rock in 2001.

Each year *Crazyhorse* sponsors three competitions, each awarding a prize of $1,000: the *Crazyhorse* Fiction Prize, the *Crazyhorse* Nonfiction Prize, and the Lynda Hull Memorial Poetry Prize. The editors read year-round and welcome submissions of up to twenty-five pages of prose or three to five poems. Subscription rates are $15 for two issues.

The Devil's Millhopper/TDM Press

Dr. Stephen Gardner, Department of English, Box 26, University of South Carolina-Aiken, 471 University Parkway, Aiken, SC 29801-6309; (803) 641-3239; gardner@vm.sc.edu

TDM Press, founded in 1976 by Stephen Gardner, conducts an annual chapbook competition and the Kudzu Poetry Contest, and publishes one issue annually of *The Devil's Millhopper*, a magazine devoted to the presentation of the best in contemporary poetry. Poets published by the press include Susan Ludvigson, Ann Darr, Lynne H. deCourcy, Ricardo Pau-Llosa, Dorothy Barresi, and Richard Frost. Sample issues are available from the above address for $4, as are submission guidelines. Also see the current *Poet's Market* from Writer's Digest Books. TDM went on hiatus in 2003.

Emrys Foundation

P. O. Box 8813, Greenville, SC 29604; www.emrys.org

Founded in 1983, the Emrys Foundation (*Emrys* is Welsh for "child of light") "promotes excellence in the arts, especially literary, visual, and musical works by women and minorities." To meet that goal, the foundation sponsors a variety of musical competitions and concerts, art exhibitions, creative writing awards, poetry workshops, readings, and lectures. As a result, the Foundation is a powerful advocate for the arts in Greenville, and its competitions and publications have extended its influence far beyond the city limits of its home base.

Two of the Emrys Foundation's publication projects are primarily literary. The respected *Emrys Journal* is an annual spring anthology of previously unpublished poetry, short fiction, and essays submitted by authors from across the United States and abroad. It is supported in part by a grant from Dorothy Peace Ramsaur in memory of her father, Roger C. Peace; and by the Sarah Jane Tracy Hagy Emrys Intern Award presented by Mr. and Mrs. Dexter Hagy in memory of Mr. Hagy's mother. Writers' guidelines are available online as well as in the *Journal* itself, copies of which are widely available in South Carolina libraries. The Emrys Foundation also sponsors The Emrys Poetry Series, an annual chapbook begun in 1995 that has published collections by Jan Bailey, Marian Willard Blackwell, Becky Gould Gibson, Sue Lile Inman, Cynthia Sheperd Jaskwhich, and Keller Cushing Freeman.

Annual membership in the Emrys Foundation is $50, in return for which members receive the current issue of the *Emrys Journal*, full access to the online version of the journal, invitations to foundation events, discounts on workshop fees, and "inclusion in a lively community of women and men committed to encouraging and enjoying the natural creativity of their fellow citizens."

Holocene Press
P.O. Box 101, Wofford College, Spartanburg SC, 29303;
864-597-4518.

Founded in 1982 by poet John Lane, Holocene calls itself a "micropublisher," issuing "limited editions of poetry, broadsides, travel journals, novels, and intelligent prose." Recent titles include work by Jim Peterson, Janet Wondra, Deno Trakas, David Romtvedt, Stephen Sandy, and David Lehman. In 1996 Holocene gave birth to Spartanburg's Hub City Writers Project, issuing its first four titles. Holocene currently accepts manuscript submissions by invitation only. In recent years Holocene has published a series of short novels and memoirs by winners of Wofford College's Benjamin Wofford Prize, which annually selects a student manuscript to publish.

The Hub City Writers Project
Betsy Teter, executive director, P. O. Box 8421, Spartanburg,
SC 29305; (864) 577-9349; www.hubcity.org

In May 1995 a trio of writers in Spartanburg began to talk in a downtown coffee shop about how they could help preserve a sense of place in their rapidly changing Southern city. What their community needed, they said, was a literary identity. Modeling their organization after the Depression-era Federal Writers Project, they began to marshal the talents of writers across South Carolina to create a series of books characterized by a strong sense of place. They chose the name Hub City Writers Project because it both invoked Spartanburg's past as a nineteenth-century railroad center and challenged them to make their hometown a center for literary arts.

From its beginning, Hub City's emphasis has been place-based literature that encourages readers to form a deeper connection with their home territory. Over the years, Hub City has published in a variety of genres, including fiction, personal essay, poetry, non-fiction, biography, humor, nature writing, children's literature, and history. A 1998 title, *New Southern Harmonies: Four Emerging Fiction Writers* was named best book of short fiction in North America by *Independent Publisher* magazine.

Hub City was shepherded in its early days by Wofford College poet John Lane, journalists Betsy Teter and Gary Henderson, and photographer/graphic designer Mark Olencki; gradually the organization broadened its scope by publishing more than one hundred South Carolina writers, creating a fifteen-member board of directors, and attracting the financial support of hundreds of South Carolina residents and businesses. In May 2002 the writers project received the Governor's Elizabeth O'Neill Verner Award for outstanding contribution to the arts in South Carolina. In addition to its active publication program, Hub City sponsors the annual Hardegree Writing Awards for Spartanburg County residents in fiction, nonfiction, and poetry; hosts a monthly readers series called "Reading at the Depot"; and every summer the organization sponsors a creative writing conference, "Writing in Place," at Wofford College. Hub City is the publisher of *Literary South Carolina*.

Annual membership for students is $15 and others, $30, for which members receive discounts on books and workshops. For $100, members receive a copy of the year's lead title in hardback.

The Humanities Council
P.O. Box 5287, Columbia, SC 29250; (803) 771-2477;
www.schumanities.org

The South Carolina Humanities Council was founded in 1972 by "a group of men and women who came together with a desire to engage each other—and the rest of the state—in an appreciation of literature, history, culture and heritage."

The council, which is supported by the National Endowment for the Humanities, promotes a number of literary endeavors: the "Let's Talk About It" book discussion series and "Speakers Bureau" lectures, both of which are available free to non-profit groups. Grants by the Humanities Council support exhibitions, films, and various kinds of publications, a list of which is available from the council and which currently includes substantial support for the *South Carolina Encyclopedia* project, due to be completed by 2005. The council's newsletter appears three times a year and is available, without charge, on request. Membership in the council is available at a number of support levels, ranging from Student at $15 a year on up.

Kitemaug Press ("Small things are important.")
229 Mohawk Drive, Spartanburg, SC 29301; (864) 576-3338;
kitemaugpresswhq@msn.com

Frank Anderson, the owner, proprietor, editorial chairman, designer, compositor, binder, sales manager, and advertising director of the Kitemaug Press, is one of South Carolina's secret treasures. After a stint as a submariner in World War II and education into the mysteries and pitfalls of librarianship in Kansas, Anderson settled into a comfortable career as head librarian of the Sandor Teszler

Library at Wofford College in Spartanburg. In addition to attending to the duties of his profession at Wofford, however, Anderson managed to find time to pursue his two chief avocations: contributing to the literature and bibliography of the field of submarining and establishing one of the longest-lived and most creative miniature presses in America.

Anderson established the Kitemaug Press in 1965—*Kitemaug* is a Mohegan word meaning "the place of good fishing"—and soon acquired a small Kelsey press, type, and type forms from the estate of a librarian in Topeka, Kansas. Beginning with a whimsical collection of the sayings of "St. Arithmeticus" for children, the press has issued more than 100 books, mostly miniatures, three inches or less in their largest dimensions. Kitemaug's publications are usually issued in small editions of fifty to a hundred copies each, and the prices are modest, ranging from $7.50 to $50 depending upon the labor and the paper and binding materials.

Ninety-Six Press

c/o Dr. Gilbert Allen or Dr. William Rogers, Department of English, Furman University, 3300 Poinsett Highway, Greenville, SC 29613; (864) 294-3152 or (864) 294-3156; www.furman.edu/~wrogers/ 96Press/press.htm

The Ninety-Six Press is another of South Carolina's closely guarded secret treasures. Established at Furman in 1991, the name of the press is derived from the old name of the area around Greenville: the "Ninety-Six District." The present town of Ninety-Six also preserves the heritage of the earlier region.

In keeping with its name, Ninety-Six Press publishes books of poetry by South Carolina writers. In most cases, these are collections by a single author, but the 1994 collection *45/96: The Ninety-Six Sampler of South Carolina Poetry* featured work by forty-five different poets of various ethnic, racial, gender, and cultural backgrounds. Poets featured in *45/96* included the best-known names in contemporary Palmetto State versification: Gilbert and Paul Allen, Alice Cabaniss, Starkey Flythe, Grace Freeman, John Lane, Susan Ludvigson, Ron Rash, Bennie Lee Sinclair, David Tillinghast, and others. The National Endowment for the Arts, The South Carolina Arts Commission, Furman University, and the Emrys Foundation all supported *45/96*.

The Ninety-Six Press receives support from the Metropolitan Arts Council of Greenville, the Emrys Foundation, and Furman University. Ninety-Six Press currently selects manuscripts for publication by invitation only. Additional information is in the current *Poet's Market* from Writer's Digest Books.

Palanquin Press/Palanquin Poetry Series

Dr. Phebe Davidson, Department of English, University of South Carolina Aiken, 471 University Parkway, Aiken, SC 29801; phebed@aiken.sc.edu

Founded by Phebe Davidson in 1988 in Flanders, New Jersey, Palanquin originally published six broadsides a year and expanded to include a chapbook contest when the editor moved to the University of South Carolina Aiken. From 1994 through 2001 the press ran two chapbook contests and published six to twelve chapbooks per year as well as occasional full-length volumes. As of the 2002-2003 academic year, the press publishes by invitation only. Poets published by the press include Stuart Bartow, Gay Brewer, and Laura Lee Washburn. Additional information is available in the current *Poet's Market*.

The Poetry Society of South Carolina
P.O. Box 1090, Charleston, SC 29402.

Writing about the Poetry Society of South Carolina in *The Sewanee Review* ten years after the founding of the Society in 1920, poet Josephine Pinckney observed, "Charleston cannot claim that her population is interested in poetry to the same degree that it is interested in taxes, say, or grocers' bills, but relatively speaking the former owns a considerable and steady following." The statement is still true today more than seventy years later. The society conducts writers' workshops and a variety of competitions, publishes an annual chapbook and an annual anthology of prize-winning poems, conducts a local cooperative program with visual artists through the Gibbes Museum of Art, and keeps members informed of regional literary activities. It awards no fewer than twenty annual and spring contest prizes and sponsors the Sundown Poetry Series during the Piccolo Spoleto Festival.

One might expect such a display of vigor from the oldest state literary society in the nation, of course, but the beginnings of the society were inauspicious indeed. In late 1920 Hervey Allen, DuBose Heyward, and John Bennett were in the habit of meeting once a week to critique and encourage one another in their mutual literary ambitions. Bennett, the senior member, was the only published author. Heyward was a young insurance agent on the verge of prosperity. Allen was an equally young high school teacher at Porter Military Academy. In the midst of their weekly meeting Heyward had the impetuous idea to "start a poetry society here in South Carolina," and the rest, as they say, is history. The three composed an ad hoc mailing list from the Charleston telephone directory, mailed invitations, and cheerfully greeted some two hundred charter members to the inaugural meeting at the South Carolina Society Hall in October 1920.

Heyward was soon devoting more of his time to the society's work than to his own insurance and real estate promotions, first as secretary and then as editor of the first *Yearbook*. He and Allen also collaborated on a volume of poetry, *Carolina Chansons*, and co-edited a special Southern issue of Harriet Monroe's *Poetry*. A genuinely golden aura seemed to emanate from the Society and its good works. The group was compared to the Agrarians at Vanderbilt, and Charlestonians were privileged to hear some of the foremost poets of the era reading in their own city. These included Carl Sandburg, Harriet Monroe, Amy Lowell, Archibald Rutledge, James Stephens, Louis Untermeyer, Donald Davidson, John Crowe Ransom, Robert Frost, and others. The list is remarkable by any standards, and especially so for a city still recovering from the bitter aftertaste of Reconstruction. The society also encouraged its own. Local authors who found validation via the society's prizes included Pinckney herself together with Beatrice Ravenel, Henry Bellamann, and Drayton Mayrant (Katherine Drayton Mayrant Simons).

Very early on, the society met its goal of two hundred and fifty resident members, and it continues to have a vigorous membership of both writers and "aficionados of literature." Meetings now take place in a variety of venues, dress is a matter of personal taste, and readings and other events are open to the public.

Readers interested in membership in the Poetry Society of South Carolina should write to the treasurer, including a check for $25.

Sandlapper, The Magazine of South Carolina
P. O. Box 1108, Lexington, SC 29071; (803) 359-9954;
www.sandlapper.org

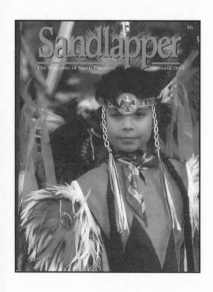

Having existed in several different incarnations over the last thirty-plus years—including monthly, bi-monthly, and semi-annually—in hard- and soft-cover formats, *Sandlapper* currently appears quarterly as a high-quality full-color magazine. Not strictly speaking a *literary* magazine at all, it is included here because it is quite simply the handiest and most entertaining of all sources of information about the Palmetto State.

Widely circulated in public schools and libraries, *Sandlapper* bills itself as "a magazine grandparents can read to their grandchildren." The assessment is a fair one: There are no articles on political, controversial, or scandalous topics. Its mission is to promote "the best of South Carolina," and it strives to fulfill this mission with taste, zest, and pride. A typical issue might include a profile of a popular musical group from the fifties, a pictorial feature on a little-known state park, a boosterish article on a newly revitalized small-town downtown, and recipes for Frogmore stew and cornpone. Regular features include restaurant tips ("Stop Where the Parking Lot's Full"), reports on inns and small hotels ("*Sandlapper* Slept Here"), a "Children's Challenge" puzzle page, book notices, and news of special events of interest to South Carolinians.

Always a good read, *Sandlapper* solicits articles that are "fresh" and "quirky," not run-of-the-mill stories about the fun of Myrtle Beach and the romance of Charleston. Its style is upbeat and no-nonsense, and it appeals to a wide range of readers. Forty percent of its articles are written by freelancers, the remainder by an experienced veteran staff. Its photography is always attractive and frequently spectacular. An additional appeal of the magazine is that it periodically offers special products, which recently have included a poster and *Carolina Cooks*, a cookbook that from personal experience I can vouch for as mouth-wateringly appealing and nearly failsafe.

Sandlapper is published by Sandlapper Society, Inc., a tax-exempt organization. Individual memberships, including a magazine subscription, are $25 a year; Patron memberships, which include ten gift memberships and listing on the "patrons page" and website, are $200 a year; a variety of Business Patron memberships, which include magazines that can be distributed to customers and patrons, are also available.

Sandlapper Publishing Co., Inc.
1281 Amelia Street, Orangeburg, SC 29115; (800) 849-7263;
agallman1@mindspring.com

Sandlapper Publishing Co., Inc. is an independent regional publisher specializing in nonfiction, history, travel, nature, culture, literature, cooking, and photography books about South Carolina. The company seeks to publish "inspiring and informative books that include an unusual angle or different approach" to providing readers with education about the state. Established in 1983, Sandlapper Publishing issues up to six new titles a year.

Among Sandlapper's perennial favorites are Nancy Rhyne's ghost stories, cookbooks and restaurant guides, a paddling guide to the state's rivers, and a biography of the late Senator Strom Thurmond. More recent titles include Nancy Rhyne's *Voices of Carolina Slave Children*, Robert Bass's *The Green Dragoon*, and *All 'Bout Charleston*, an ABC book by author Ruth Paterson Chappell and artist Dean Gray Wroth. Sandlapper catalogs are free and may be requested via telephone or at the Sandlapper Book Outlet at 1281 Amelia Street in Orangeburg.

South Carolina Academy of Authors
c/o Institute of Southern Studies, 107 Gambrell Hall,
University of South Carolina, Columbia SC 29208.

Founded in 1986 at Anderson College, the Academy identifies and honors South Carolina's outstanding writers in all genres, as well as encourages discovery and rediscovery of their works. Traditionally, the organization has inducted one living and two deceased writers each year; a total of forty-three had been inducted through 2003, including, William Gilmore Simms, Benjamin Elijah Mays, Elizabeth Boatwright Coker, Dori Sanders and Pat Conroy. Through an active fellowship program, it also promotes new talent by awarding grants to emerging writers. The Academy is governed by a board of directors, which meets quarterly in Columbia.

South Carolina Arts Commission
Sara June Goldstein, program director for Literary Arts; 1800
Gervais Street, Columbia, SC 29201; (803) 734-8694;

goldstsa@arts.state.sc.us; www.SouthCarolinaArts.com

The South Carolina Arts Commission, a state agency funded in part by the National Endowment for the Arts, was established in 1967 as an agency of state government to develop and implement a comprehensive program to advance the arts in South Carolina, and to assure their excellence. The commission directs its resources toward making the arts a part of the life of every South Carolinian.

The SCAC's primary source of funding is state tax dollars appropriated by the South Carolina General Assembly. Grants from the federal government through the NEA comprise the commission's secondary source of funding. Additional support for Arts Commission projects is provided by private foundations and community sponsors.

The Arts Commission provides fellowships for artists in many disciplines, including writers. Each year it selects a poet and a prose writer to receive fellowships of $5,000. In conjunction with *The* (Charleston) *Post & Courier* newspaper the state agency sponsors the South Carolina Fiction Project, an annual short story competition in which winning authors receive $500 each. The agency's director of literary arts is involved in many statewide collaborative activities that promote the literary arts and support the notion that writers are important resources to their communities and the state. In addition, the commission maintains a Roster of Approved Artists for its Arts in Education initiative and provides grants to schools to promote Arts in the Basic Curriculum. The Arts Commission makes annual and biennial grants to various arts organizations across the state, such as the South Carolina Writers Workshop, the South Carolina Young Writers Conference, and the Hub City Writers Project. Its Elizabeth O'Neill Verner Governor's Awards for the Arts, bestowed annually, constitute the highest honor the state gives in the arts to South Carolina organizations, businesses and individuals participating in the growth and advancement of the arts in South Carolina.

The South Carolina State Library
1430 Senate Street, P.O. Box 11469, Columbia SC 29211; 803-734-8658; www.state.sc.us/scsl

Originally known as the State Library Board, the South Carolina State Library has worked to develop and improve public library services across South Carolina since 1929. In 1969 it became the South Carolina State Library. It has responsibility for public library development, services for the blind and physically handicapped, and library service to state government agencies.

The State Library collaborates with the South Carolina Humanities Council on the "Let's Talk About It" book discussion series held in public libraries across the state. It serves as a major sponsor of the South Carolina Book Festival. The library provides support for early literacy and literature-related projects aimed at children and families in public libraries. It also administers a state aid program to public libraries that assists libraries in providing quality service to citizens by supporting activities such as purchasing books and other materials and providing adequate staffing. The State Library also provides statewide access to online research databases through the DISCUS program (www.scdiscus.org).

The State Library is funded by tax dollars appropriated through the South Carolina General Assembly. Funds from the federal Institute of Museum and Library Services also support statewide project and a grant program for public libraries seeking to develop new services.

The South Carolina Literary Arts Partnership

Vicki Parsons, Humanities Council; P.O. Box 5287, Columbia, SC 29250; vparsons@schumanities.org

This collaboration, which is a project of the Humanities Council, the SC Arts Commission, and the SC State Library, funds a literary arts program position, held by Vicki Parsons. Begun in 1999, the position expands the efforts of all three partners to develop and implement statewide programs in the literary arts for public libraries, arts councils, community organizations, writers, and for the general public of South Carolina. Activities include the planning and administering of book discussions, writing workshops, publishing industry lectures and presentations and directing the annual SC Book Festival (www.scbookfestival.org) held in February in Columbia. The festival, which is free, plays host to dozens of well-known authors for readings and panel discussions, as well as over a hundred booksellers and exhibitors.

The South Carolina Literary Tour

The Palmetto Book Alliance, (the Library of Congress Center for the Book in South Carolina), 1430 Senate Street, P.O. Box 11469, Columbia SC 29211; 803-734-8658; janec@leo.scsl.state.sc.us; www.scpalmettobookalliance.org

Also known as "the literary map," this reference tool features information on nearly two hundred writers in all forty-six counties. Published in 2002 by the Palmetto Book Alliance—which is co-sponsored by the S.C. State Library, and the University of South Carolina's School of Library and Information Science—the map is available at libraries and welcome centers across South Carolina. A committee headed by Tom Johnson worked more than two years to create the map, which is kept updated on the website listed above.

The South Carolina Review

Center for Electronic and Digital Publishing, 810 Strode Tower, Box 340522, Clemson, SC 29634-0522; (864) 656-5399; www.clemson.edu/caah/cedp/scrintro.htm

South Carolina's premier literary journal, *The South Carolina*

The South Carolina Review

Volume 35, Number 1 (Fall 2002)

Review, since 1968 has published fiction, poetry, interviews, unpublished letters and manuscripts, essays, and reviews from well-known and aspiring scholars and writers. Among these have been such important names as Cleanth Brooks, Donald Davidson, Donald Hall, Garrison Keillor, Joyce Carol Oates, Flannery O'Connor, Kurt Vonnegut, Thomas Wolfe, and Virginia Woolf. South Carolina writers featured in the pages of the Review include James Dickey, Josephine Humphreys, Ron Rash, Bennie Lee Sinclair, George Singleton, Mark Steadman, and many others, some of them veteran and popular professionals, others at the beginnings of their careers.

Established at Furman University, *The South Carolina Review* moved to Clemson University in 1973, where it is produced at the Center for Electronic and Digital Publishing. Current editors continue to share the *Review*'s original vision, explained in 1983 by Richard J. Calhoun, one of the founders and currently editor emeritus, as follows: "We publish essays on contemporary literature and creative works by American writers; but we are nowhere limited to these interests. ... When we want to declare a special issue, we can. The little magazine may never discover a Pound, an Eliot or a Hemingway, but ... we have published early writers who have gone on to the larger magazines and yet not quite forgotten us. As long as we get good manuscripts from good young writers, we shall continue to play this role." Past special issues of *The South Carolina Review* have celebrated Virginia Woolf, Robert Frost, Mary Gordon, Walker Percy, and James Dickey.

Subscriptions to *The South Carolina Review* are $15 per year or $23 for two years for individuals, $20 and $28 for institutions. Checks should be made payable to Clemson University. Additional information may be found in the *Poet's Market* from Writer's Digest Books.

South Carolina Writers Workshop
P.O. Box 7104, Columbia, SC 29202; (843) 884-7631; www.scwriters.com; Barbie Perkins-Cooper, SCWW Membership, barbiepc@bellsouth.net, (803) 407-9482; Peggy Cwiakala, Editor, "The Quill," qeditor@bellsouth.net

Founded in 1990 as "a literary arts organization serving both new and established writers throughout the state," the South Carolina Writers Workshop "offers a supportive environment for people to become better writers." This support takes a variety of forms, including readings and critiques at chapter meetings across the state, the bi-monthly newsletter *The Quill*, two free seminars a year, and *Catfish Stew*, an annual anthology of members' work (formerly known as *Horizons*). Chapter meetings are held in libraries, bookstores, and other public places and are open to the public.

The SCWW Advisory Council is a veritable Who's Who of the literary arts in South Carolina: Idella Bodie, Gene Fehler, Starkey Flythe, Sara June Goldstein, Gwen Hunter, Wanda Jewell, John Lane,

Bob Mayer, Tamar Myers, Marjorie Reynolds, Dori Sanders, Barbara Taylor, Terry Ward Tucker, Jon Tuttle, Ashley Warlick, and emeritus members Carrie McCray and Max Steele. Partial support of SCWW activities is provided by a grant from the South Carolina Arts Commission, which receives support from the National Endowment for the Arts. Membership is $50 per year for individuals, $75 for families; an application form may be downloaded at the SCWW website.

The Southern Literature Council of Charleston
P.O. Box 21436, Charleston, SC 29412; 347-451-6455;
www.southernlit.org

Incorporated in 2002 and supported by some of the biggest names in southern literature, the SLCC offers two-to-four week residencies for emerging southern writers at a historic house on Sullivan's Island. The residencies are open to writers who are natives or residents of South Carolina, North Carolina, Georgia, Florida, Alabama, Mississippi, Louisiana, Arkansas, Tennessee, Virginia, or Kentucky. Writers from elsewhere may qualify if their current work is about or set in the American South. Applications are accepted in fiction, non-fiction, poetry, and drama. Three to four writers are accepted at a time with special consideration accorded those writers "whose work may be unrecognized because of their race, sexual orientation or economic circumstances." The SLCC also intends to create a writers' conference in 2005. The organizer is Delacey Skinner, a communications consultant for non-profits; its board of directors and advisors include such notables as Lee Smith, Josephine Humphreys, Pat Conroy, and Shannon Ravenel, co-founder of Algonquin Books.

University of South Carolina Poetry Initiative
c/o Kwame Dawes, Department of English, University of South
Carolina, Columbia SC 29208; (803) 777-2230;
wwwpoetryinitiativesc.com

Unveiled in the fall of 2003, the ambitious USC Poetry Initiative is the brainchild of Jamaican poet Kwame Dawes. Although still in its infancy, the initiative establishes a statewide center for the promotion, celebration, and production of poetry at USC. Among its plans are a statewide poetry book contest, a nationwide poetry chapbook contest, a summer poetry camp for high school students, and various public workshops.

University of South Carolina Press
Business Office: 718 Devine Street, Columbia, SC 29208; (803)
777-1774. Administrative Offices: 937 Assembly Street, Carolina
Plaza, 8th Floor, Columbia, SC 29208; (803) 777-5245.

The University of South Carolina Press shares the university's central mission: to advance knowledge and enrich the state's cultural heritage. Established in 1944, it is one of the oldest publishing houses in the South and among the largest in the Southeast. With more than fourteen hundred books published, the press is important in enhancing the scholarly reputation and worldwide visibility of the University of South Carolina. The press publishes in a variety of disciplines, including history (African-American, American, Civil War, maritime, Southern, and women's), contemporary literature, regional studies, religious studies, rhetoric, and social work. The press has about six hundred titles in print and publishes approximately forty-five new books annually, including the papers of John C. Calhoun and Henry Laurens.

While the USC Press no longer publishes new original literature, a number of its series are primarily or partially literary in their emphases. These include the *Works of William Gilmore Simms*, *African American Studies* (including DuBose Heyward's *Mamba's Daughters* and *When I Can Read My Title Clear: Literacy, Slavery, and Religion in the Antebellum South*), *Fishing & Hunting* (including modern selections from Havilah Babcock and Archibald Rutledge), *Folklore* (including John Bennett's *The Doctor to the Dead* and a number of ghost story collections gathered by Nancy Rhyne), *Women's Diaries and Letters of the South*, and a group of important titles on Southern and Palmetto State art and folk art published in conjunction with the McKissick Museums of the University.

To date Dr. Walter Edgar's *South Carolina: A History* is the press's bestseller, with more than 37,000 copies in print and over 32,000 sold. Other popular titles include artist Jonathan Green's *Gullah Images*, issued in an initial print run of 10,000 copies and twice reprinted since, and James Cothran's *Gardens of Historic Charleston*, reprinted several times after a first printing of 5,000.

USC Press issues seasonal catalogs of books, and it sponsors an annual sale at the press's warehouse. In addition, the USC Press exhibit at the annual South Carolina Book Festival in Columbia is one of the most popular features of the event.

The Writers' Circle of South Carolina
Patti Just, host; Bruce Mayer, producer/director; WRJA-TV, 18 North Harvin Street, Sumter, SC 29150; (803) 773-5546.

Having begun production in 1991, *The Writers' Circle of South Carolina* is the South Carolina Educational Television network's highly successful series of profiles of Palmetto State writers. As *Literary South Carolina* was going to press, the *Writers' Circle* had featured over one hundred thirty different writers in a series of thirty-minute interviews conducted by host Patti Just. One hundred and nine programs in the series are available to South Carolina teachers through the Instructional Television network, and most are also available on loan on videocassettes via the ETV Endowment of South Carolina, 401 East Kennedy Street, Spartanburg, SC 29302; phone (864) 591-0046.

Just, host/interviewer for the program since its inception, is quick to deny that she has favorites. "Everybody has put their best foot forward," she says, adding that the show's staff goes out of its way to ensure that the writers are comfortable during each taping. "If they're happy, they're going to give you a good interview," she explains.

Just's enthusiasm for her job and her subjects is obvious to even the most casual viewer. She reads each author's books and does considerable research in preparation for each session. She sees herself "as a facilitator for the authors, to give them a platform," and the authors clearly appreciate her approach. They all seem at ease chatting with her, and the general tone of the show is neighborly and inviting.

In the beginning, no one connected with *The Writers' Circle* envisioned its longevity. Just believed "that there would probably be half a dozen people, never dreaming that we would go so long with the show." Early on, however, she found that "one writer would say, 'Well, do you know so-and-so?'" and this casual remark would lead her to another and then another and so on. Now, she complains, one of her biggest problems is "not being able to do everybody" for lack of time.

Still, the list of her guests is a virtual directory of the current crop of South Carolina authors, an index of the condition of literary South Carolina. Moreover each author appears in his or her most characteristic persona in these interviews. Dori Sanders radiates what Just calls the "inner joy that she shares with everybody," and the late Bennie Lee Sinclair embodied "a piece of heaven" through the revelation of her gentle spirit. Some do turn out to be surprises, but pleasant ones. Mickey Spillane, for example, often irascible in interviews, was "an absolute delight," and Louis Rubin, another writer with a reputation for being crotchety, Just found to be "a pleasure" as he sat talking with her, a sort of guardian spirit of Charleston Harbor. Other subjects have been Bret Lott, the first writer interviewed for the program; Marquetta Goodwine, the Queen of the Gullah/Geechee Nation; columnist James J. Kilpatrick; poet James Dickey; science fiction author Orson Scott Card; and scholar/children's author Dianne Johnson.

The Writers' Circle of South Carolina is broadcast at 5:30 p.m. on Friday afternoons; local SCETV station schedules contain additional information. Besides Just and producer/director Mayer, a graduate of the Ringling School of Art in Sarasota who has been with SCETV since 1977, the show is produced with technical support by Allen Tapp, Will Anderson, Tommy Burgess, Eleanore Vaughan, Kimberly Combs, and production assistant Jenny Gamble. Their combined efforts have paid dividends besides a large and devoted audience: In 1993 the show won both the Governor's Award for Promoting Literary Talent in South Carolina and a Georgi for Excellence in Promoting the Written Word.

Wyrick & Company

1-A Pinckney Street, Charleston, SC 29401-2626; (843) 722-0881; wyrickco@bellsouth.net

A small, independent publisher, Wyrick & Company Publishers issues four to eight titles a year, both fiction and nonfiction. The company was founded in 1986, but neither its relative youth nor its relatively short backlist should give the impression that it is nonselective. To the contrary, its authors include some of the more original of the current crop of Sandlapper scribes, from Max Childers, one of the funniest writers alive, to Virginia Mixson Geraty, who has worked hard to preserve and foster a better understanding of the Gullah language. Wyrick & Company's titles also include Richard Lederer's books about the use and misuse of the English language, Harlan Greene and James Hutchisson's *Literary Charleston*, visitors' guides to Savannah and Myrtle Beach, popular works about food in Atlanta and Charleston, Roger Pinckney's Daufuskie Island books, and local-interest books such as *Thomas Elfe: Cabinet Maker* and *Baking with Brother Boniface*.

Wyrick and Company's sales and distribution are handled by the Independent Publishers Group, whose catalogs are available online at www.ipgbook.com or at 814 North Franklin Street, Chicago, IL 60610.

Yemassee

Department of English, University of South Carolina, Columbia, SC 29208; www.cla.sc.edu/ENGL/yemassee/index.htm.

The literary journal of the University of South Carolina, *Yemassee* bears the distinction of having been edited and written by graduate students at the university from its inception in 1993. As might be expected from an English department that has boasted James Dickey, William Price Fox, and Janette Turner Hospital as writers-in-residence, the result has been felicitous. During its first seven years *Yemassee* published Dickey, Robert Coover, William Price Fox, Susan Ludvigson, Scott Ely, Tom Absher, Vivien Shipley, Phillip Lee Williams, Ellen Wehle, and Thomas David Lisk. It also actively seeks quality fiction and poetry by emerging and new writers.

Supported by an initial donation from English department alumnus Joseph Capalbo, *Yemassee* is funded by subscriptions and contributions from patrons. Student subscriptions are $6 per year, individual subscriptions are $15, and donor categories range from Sponsor at $25 to Distinguished Sponsor at $100 to $500. Well worth a perusal, *Yemassee* is more than just one more, dry academic journal.

Bibliography

The following bibliography is intended to be comprehensive, not exhaustive, although for some authors it will prove to be the latter. Non-literary publications of authors whose primary field of endeavor was something other than belles-lettres—for example, Mitchell King and James L. Petigru—are omitted unless they contain unusual historical value or otherwise intrinsic merit. Likewise, although many pamphlet publications are included herein because of their literary or intrinsic interest, many others are omitted. In rendering titles, I have capitalized words according to modern practice rather than as they appear on their respective title pages. When the cities Columbia, Charleston, and Spartanburg are cited in entries, it is understood that these names refer to the locations in South Carolina unless otherwise indicated.

In compiling this list, I have obviously been unable to examine individual copies of each title cited. When possible, I have done so, and/or I have cross-checked bibliographies against one another and/or against the online catalogues of the University of South Carolina Libraries, the Charleston County Public Library, and—on a few occasions—the South Carolina Historical Society and the Library of Congress. I am frankly amazed at the indefatigable skill and energy of librarians everywhere, and I encourage readers desiring more information than I have provided here to consult a public or university librarian in their communities.

There will inevitably be errors in any compilation such as this, but I am confident that they will be relatively few. In any event, there is no comparable bibliography anywhere of literature by and for South Carolinians. I only ask that readers who notice errors and omissions will make these known to me so that I may correct them in the future.

General Sources

Aiken, David. *Fire in the Cradle: Charleston's Literary Heritage*. Charleston: Charleston Press, 1999.

Ayers, Edward L., and Bradley C. Mittendorf (Eds.). *The Oxford Book of the American South: Testimony, Memory, and Fiction*. New York and Oxford: Oxford University Press, 1997.

Bain, Robert, Joseph M. Flora, and Louis D. Rubin, Jr. (Eds.). *Southern Writers: A Biographical Dictionary*. Baton Rouge and London: Louisiana State University Press, 1979.

Bradbury, John M. *Renaissance in the South: A Critical History of the Literature, 1920-1960*. Chapel Hill: The University of North Carolina Press, 1963.

Edgar, Walter. *South Carolina: A History*. Columbia: University of South Carolina Press, 1998.

Jones, Lewis. *South Carolina: One of the Fifty States*. Orangeburg: Sandlapper Publishing, Inc., 1985.

Manly, Louise. *Southern Literature From 1579—1895: A Comprehensive Review, With Copious Extracts and Criticisms For the General Use of Schools and the General Reader Containing an Appendix with a Full List of Southern Authors*. Richmond: B.F. Johnson Publishing Company, 1907.

Matuz, Roger (Ed.). *Contemporary Southern Writers*. Detroit and London: St. James Press/An Imprint of Gale, 1999.

Parks, Edd Winfield (Ed.). *Southern Poets: Representative Selections, With Introduction, Bibliography, and Notes*. New York: American Book Company, 1936.

Rubin, Louis D., Jr. (Ed.). *A Bibliographical Guide to the Study of Southern Literature*. Baton Rouge: Louisiana State University Press, 1969.

------. *The Edge of the Swamp: A Study in the Literature and Society of the Old South*. Baton Rouge: Louisiana State University Press, 1989.

------ et al., eds. *The History of Southern Literature*. Baton Rouge and London: Louisiana State University Press, 1985.

Sherman, Joan R., ed. *African-American Poetry of the Nineteenth Century: An Anthology*. Urbana and Chicago: University of Illinois Press, 1992.

South Carolina: A Guide to the Palmetto State. Compiled by Workers of the Writers' Program of the Work Projects Administration in the State of South Carolina. American Guide Series. Sponsored by Burnet R. Maybank, Governor of South Carolina. New York: Oxford University Press, 1941.

Tindall, George Brown. *The Emergence of the New South 1913-1945. Volume X of A History of the South*. Edited by Wendell Holmes Stephenson and E. Merton Coulter. Baton Rouge: Louisiana

State University Press and the Littlefield Fund for Southern History of the University of Texas, 1967.

Trent, W.P. (Ed.). *Southern Writers: Selections in Prose and Verse*. New York: The Macmillan Company; London: Macmillan & Co., Ltd., 1905.

Wallace. David Duncan. *South Carolina: A Short History 1520-1948*. Columbia: University of South Carolina Press, 1951.

Young, Thomas Daniel, Floyd C. Watkins, and Richmond Croom Beatty (Eds.). *The Literature of the South*. Revised Edition. Glenview, IL: Scott, Foresman and Company, 1968.

Anthologies, Histories, and Studies of South Carolina Literature

Calhoun, Richard James, and John Caldwell Guilds (Eds.). *A Tricentennial Anthology of South Carolina Literature 1670—1970*. Columbia: University of South Carolina Press for the South Carolina Tricentennial Commission, 1971.

Durham, Frank. "South Carolina's Poetry Society." South Atlantic Quarterly, LII (1953), 277-285.

Epps, Edwin C. South Carolina Literature: *A Reading List for Students, Educators, and Laymen*. Revised Edition. Spartanburg, SC: Woodspurge Books, 1989.

From the Green Horseshoe: Poems by James Dickey's Students. Introduction by James Dickey. Columbia: University of South Carolina Press, 1987.

Gould, Scott, and Rosa Shand, George Singleton, Deno Trakas. *New Southern Harmonies: Four Emerging Fiction Writers*. Spartanburg: Holocene Press for the Hub City Writers Project, 1998.

Hungerpiller, J.C. (Ed.). *South Carolina Literature with Biographical Notes and Critical Comments*. Columbia: Press of the R.L. Bryan Company, 1931.

Johnson, Thomas L. (Ed.). *You, Year: New Poems by POINT Poets*. [Columbia:] Harbinger Publications, 1996. Anthology of poems by 34 contemporary poets whose work appeared in the "365 Degrees" poetry page of POINT from 1993 to 1996.

Jones, Katharine M., and Mary Verner Schlaefer (Eds.). *South Carolina in the Short Story*. Columbia: University of South Carolina Press, 1952.

Martin, Floride Milner. *A Chronological Survey of South Carolina Literature*. No place: No publisher, no date. Privately printed ca. 1977.

McMurtrie, Douglas C. *A Bibliography of South Carolina Imprints 1731-1740*. Charleston: Privately Printed, 1933. Reprint of McMurtrie's article in the July 1933 issue of The South Carolina Historical and Genealogical Magazine.

Mishoe, Billy, and Ronald G. Midkiff (Eds.). *Patches of Carolina Sun: An Anthology of New Voices*. Columbia: American Literary Associates, Inc., 1973.

Mott, Sara L. *Southern Literary Scenes, Part One*. Illustrated by Tom Savory. Columbia: The R.L. Bryan Company, 1977. Driving tours to southern sites with significant literary associations.

------. *Southern Literary Scenes*. Part Two. Illustrated by Tom Savory. Columbia: Kohn Printing, Inc., 1980. Literary tours to three states not included in Part One.

Pinckney, Josephine. "Charleston's Poetry Society." Sewanee Review, XXXVIII (1930), 50-56.

The South Carolina Review. Edited by Richard C. Calhoun. Clemson: Clemson University. Published biannually.

South Carolina Writers Directory: A Compendium of Literary Artists, Presenters, Magazines, Publishers, and Organizations—With a Listing of Libraries, Arts Councils, and Funding Sources. Columbia: South Carolina Arts Commission, 1993.

Spears, Beverly (Ed.) *A Literary Map of South Carolina*. 2nd edition. Florence, SC: Francis Marion University Press, 1994.

Swanson, Gayle R., and William B. Thesing (Eds.). *Conversations with South Carolina Poets*. With a Foreword by James Dickey. Winston-Salem, NC: John F. Blair, Publisher, 1986.

Wauchope, George Armstrong. *The Writers of South Carolina: With a Critical Introduction, Biographical Sketches, and Selections in Prose and Verse*. Columbia: The State Co., Publishers, 1910.

Beginnings: The Colonial and Early National Periods
Allston, Washington. *Lectures on Art, and Poems*. Ed. Richard Henry Dana, Jr. New York: Baker and Scribner, 1850.

------. *Monaldi: A Tale*. Boston: Charles C. Little and James Brown, 1841.

——————. *The Sylphs of the Seasons, with Other Poems*. London: W. Pople; Boston: Cummings and Hilliard, 1813.

Bartram, William. *Travels through North and South Carolina, Georgia, East & West Florida, the Cherokee country, the extensive territories of the Muscogulges, or Creek confederacy, and the country of the Choctaws; containing an account of the soil and natural productions of those regions, together with observations on the manners of the Indians*. Philadelphia: Printed by James & Johnson, 1791; ed. Francis Harper. New Haven: Yale University Press, 1958.

Drayton, John. *Letters Written during a Tour through the Northern and Eastern States of America*. Charleston: Harrison and Bowen, 1794.

——————. *Memoirs of the American Revolution from Its Commencement to the Year 1776, Inclusive*. 2 vols. Charleston: A.E. Miller, 1821.

——————. *A View of South Carolina as Respects Her Natural and Civil Concerns*. Charleston: W. P. Young, 1802.

Hilton, William. *A Relation of a Discovery lately made on the Coast of Florida*. London: Printed for J.C. by Simon Miller, 1664.

Ladd, Joseph Brown. *The Poems of Arouet*. Charleston: Bowen and Markland, 1786.

Laurens, Henry. *The Papers of*. Ed. Philip M. Hamer, George Rogers, and David Chesnutt. 10 vols. Columbia: University of South Carolina Press, 1968-1985.

Lawson, John. *A New Voyage to Carolina*. London, 1709; ed. Hugh Talmadge Lefler. Chapel Hill: University of North Carolina Press, 1967.

Moultrie, William. *Memoirs of the American Revolution so far as It Relates to the States of North and South Carolina and Georgia*. New York: Printed by David Longworth for the Author, 1802.

Nairne, Thomas. *A Letter from South Carolina, Giving an Account of the Soil, Air, Products, Trade, Government, Laws, Religion, People, Military Strength, Etc. of That Province*. London: A Baldwin, 1710.

Pinckney, Eliza Lucas. *Journal and Letters*. Ed. Harriett Pinckney Holbrook. Wormsloe, GA, 1850.

——————. *Letterbook*. Ed. Elise Pinckney with Marvin R. Zahniser. Chapel Hill: University of North Carolina Press, 1972.

Pringle, Robert. *The Letterbook of Robert Pringle 1737-1745*. Ed. Walter B. Edgar. 2 vols. Columbia: University of South Carolina Press, 1972.

Ramsay, David. *History of the Revolution in South-Carolina from a British Province to an Independent State*. 2 vols. Trenton, NJ: Isaac Collins, 1785.

——————. *The History of South Carolina, from Its Settlement in 1670, to the Year 1808*. 2 vols. Charleston: David Longworth, 1809.

The South-Carolina Gazette. Weekly newspaper begun by Thomas Whitmarsh, Charleston, South Carolina, running from issue no. 1 (8 January 1832), with some occasional interruptions, through mid-December 1775.

Wells, Louisa Susannah. *The Journal of a Voyage from Charleston, South Carolina to London Undertaken During the American Revolution*. New York: New York Historical Society, 1906.

Wilkinson, Eliza. *Letters...During the Invasion and Possession of Charleston, S.C., by the British in the Revolutionary War*. Ed. Caroline Howard Gilman. New York: Samuel Colman, 1839.

Woodmason, Charles. *The Carolina Backcountry on the eve of the Revolution; the Journal and other writings of Charles Woodmason, Anglican itinerant*. Ed. Richard James Hooker. Chapel Hill, Published for the Institute of Early American History and Culture at Williamsburg, Va., by the University of North Carolina Press, 1953.

The Antebellum Period

Calhoun, John C. *A Disquisition on Government and a Discourse on the Constitution and Government of the United States*. Charleston: Walker & James, 1851;

——————. *The Works of*. Edited by Richard K. Crallé. 6 vols. New York: D. Appleton & Co., 1883;

——————. *The Papers of*. Edited by Robert E. Lee Meriwether, W. Edwin Hemphill, and Clyde N. Wilson. 23 vols. Columbia: University of South Carolina Press, 1959-1997.

Cooper, Thomas. *Lectures on the Elements of Political Economy*. Columbia: Doyle and Sweeney, 1826.

——————. *Letters on the Slave Trade*. Manchester: C. Wheeler, 1787. A pamphlet..

Crafts, William. *A Selection in Prose and Poetry, from

the Miscellaneous Writings of the Late William Crafts. Charleston: C.C. Sebring & J.S. Bruges, 1828.

------. Sullivan's Island, the Raciad, and Other Poems. Charleston: T.B. Stephens, 1820

Elliott, Stephen. A sketch of the botany of South-Carolina and Georgia. 2 vols. Charleston, S.C.: J.R. Schenck, 1821-1824.

Elliott, William. Carolina Sports by Land and Water: Including Incidents of Devil-Fishing. Charleston: Burges and James, 1846.

------. Fiesco, a Tragedy. New York, Printed for the author, by Trehern & Williamson, 1850.

------. The Letters of Agricola. Greenville, S. C.: Office of the Southern patriot, 1852.

Gilman, Caroline Howard. The Little Wreath of Stories and Poems for Children. New York: C. S. Francis & Co., 1846.

------. "Letters of a Confederate Mother: Charleston in the Sixties." In Atlantic Monthly 137: 4 (April 1926), 503-515.

------. Love's Progress. New York: Harper & Brothers, 1840.

------. Oracles for Youth: A Home Pastime. New York: G.P. Putnam & Co., 1852.

------. Oracles from the Poets: A Fanciful Diversion for the Drawing Room. New York & London: Wiley and Putnam, 1844.

------. Recollections of a Housekeeper. New-York: Harper & Brothers, 1834.

------. Recollections of a Southern Matron. New York: Harper, 1838.

------. Recollections of a Southern Matron and a New England Bride. Rev. ed. Philadelphia, J. E. Potter, [1867].

------. The RoseBud, or, Youth's Gazette. Charleston, S.C.: Printed by J. S. Burges for the editor, Mrs. C. Gilman, 1832-1833.

------. Southern Rose Bud. Charleston, S.C.: Printed for the editor, Mrs. C. Gilman by James S. Burges, 1833-1835.

------. Stories and Poems by Mother and Daughter. Boston: Lee & Shepard, 1872.

------. Tales and Ballads. Boston: W. Crosby &

Company, 1839.

Grayson, William John. The Hireling and the Slave. Charleston: J. Russell, 1854.

------. The Hireling and the Slave, Chicora, and Other Poems. Charleston: McCarter, 1856.

------. James Louis Petigru: A Biographical Sketch. New York: Harpers, 1866.

------. Letter to His Excellency Whitemarsh B. Seabrook, on the Dissolution of the Union. Charleston: A.E. Miller, 1850.

------. The Letters of Curtius. Charleston: A.E. Miller, 1851.

------. Selected Poems. Ed. Mrs. William H. Armstrong. New York and Washington: Neale, 1907.

------. The Union, Past and Future: How It Works and How to Save It. Charleston: A.E. Miller, 1850.

Hammond, James Henry. "Slavery in the Light of Ethnology." In Cotton Is King, and Pro-Slavery Arguments. E.N. Elliott . Augusta: Pritchard, Abbot, & Loomis, 1860.

Horton, Thomas Bruce. Moses Waddel: Nineteenth-century South Carolina Educator. Thesis (Ed. D.)—University of South Carolina, 1992.

King, Susan Petigru. An Actress in High Life: An Episode in Winter Quarters. New York: Derby & Jackson, 1860.

------. Busy Moments of an Idle Woman. New York: D. Appleton & Co., 1854.

------. Gerald Gray's Wife and Lily: a Novel. Durham: Duke University Press, 1993

------. Lily, a Novel. New York: Harper, 1855.

------. Sylvia's World and Crimes Which the Law Does Not Reach. New York: Derby & Jackson, 1859.

Lee, Mary Elizabeth. The Poetical Remains of the Late Mary Elizabeth Lee. Charleston: Walker & Richards, 1851.

------. Social Evenings; or, Historical Tales for Youth. Boston: Marsh, Capen, Lyon, and Webb, 1840.

Legaré, Hugh Swinton. Writings. Ed. Mary S. Legaré. 2 vols. Charleston: Burges and James, 1845-6.

Longstreet, Augustus Baldwin. Georgia Scenes. New York: Harper & Bros., 1835.

Moise, Penina. *Fancy's Sketch Book*. Charleston: J.S. Burges, 1833

------. *Secular and Religious Works of Penina Moise, with a Brief Sketch of Her Life*. Charleston: N. G. Duffy, printer, 1911.

Waddel, Moses. See above: Horton, Thomas Bruce.

William Gilmore Simms and the Charleston School

Bruns, John Dickson. *Address to the White League of New Orleans*. New Orleans: A.W. Hyatt, 1875.

------. *Life: Its Relations, Animal and Mental: An Inaugural Dissertation*. Charleston: Walker, Evans, & Co., 1857.

Chesnut, Mary Boykin Miller. *A Diary from Dixie, as Written by Mary Boykin Chesnut, Wife of James Chesnut, Jr., United States Senator from South Carolina, 1859-1861, and Afterward Aide to Jefferson Davis and a Brigadier General in the Confederate Army*. Ed. Isabella D. Martin and Myrta Lockett Avary. New York: D. Appleton, 1905.

------. *A Diary from Dixie*. Ed. Ben Ames Williams. Boston: Houghton Mifflin Co., 1949.

------. *Mary Chesnut's Civil War*. Ed. C. Vann Woodward. New Haven and London: Yale University Press, 1981.

Dickson, Samuel Henry. *Address Delivered at the Opening of the New Edifice of the Charleston Apprentices' Library Society on the Evening of the 13th January, 1841*. Charleston: W. Riley, 1841.

------. *Address of Dr. S.H. Dickson, Delivered at the Inauguration of the Public School, Fourth of July, 1856*. Charleston: Walker, Evans & Co., Stationers and Printers, 1856.

------. *Remarks on Certain Topics Connected with the General Subject of Slavery*. Charleston: Observer Office Press, 1845.

------. *Writings*. 3 vols. [1857.]

------. Note: The Dickson bibliography runs to another twenty or so titles, many of them pamphlets or printings of addresses delivered before various societies. Most of these are medical in nature and have therefore been omitted from this listing.

Gildersleeve, Basil L. *Correspondence: Selections*. Baltimore: Johns Hopkins University Press, 1987.

------. *The Creed of the Old South, 1865-1915*. Baltimore: The Johns Hopkins Press, 1915; rpt. New York: Arno Press, 1979.

------. *Essays and Studies, Educational and Literary*. Baltimore: N. Murray, 1890.

------. *Essays: Selections*. Atlanta: Scholars Press, 1992.

------. *Gildersleeve's Latin Grammar*. 3rd ed., revised and enlarged. New York and Boston: University Publishing Company, 1894.

------. *Hellas and Hesperia: or, The Vitality of Greek Studies in America*. University of Virginia, Barbour-Page Foundation lecture series. New York: H. Holt and Company, 1909.

------. *Latin Composition*. New York and Boston: University Publishing Company, 1899; 2nd ed., 1904.

------. *A Latin Grammar*. New York: University Publishing Company, 1881.

------. *A Latin Primer; Introductory to Gildersleeve's Latin Series*. New York: University Publishing Company, 1875.

------. *Syntax of Classical Greek from Homer to Demosthenes*. 2 vols. New York: American Book Co., 1900-1911; rpt. In 1 vol., Groningen: Bouma, 1980.

Hayne, Paul Hamilton. *Avolio: A Legend of the Island of Cos*. Boston: Ticknor & Fields, 1860.

------. *The Correspondence of Bayard Taylor and Paul Hamilton Hayne*. Ed. Charles Duffy. Baton Rouge: Louisiana State University Press, 1945.

------. *Legends and Lyrics*. Philadelphia: Lippincott, 1872.

------. *Lives of Robert Young Hayne and Hugh Swinton Legaré*. Charleston: Walker, Evans & Cogswell, 1878.

------. *The Mountain of the Lovers*. New York: E. J. Hale, 1875

------. *Paul Hamilton Hayne as a Man of Letters: Selected Correspondence*. Ed. Rayburn S. Moore. Baton Rouge: Louisiana State University Press, 1980.

------. *Poems*. Boston: Ticknor & Fields, 1855.

------. *Poems*. Complete edition. Boston: D. Lothrop,

1882.

------. Sonnets, and Other Poems. Charleston: Harper & Calvo, 1857.

[------.] Moore, Rayburn S. "Paul Hamilton Hayne." In Myerson, pp. 144-147.

[------.] Moore, Rayburn S. Paul Hamilton Hayne. New York: Twayne, 1972.

[------.] Parks, Edd Winfield. Henry Timrod. New York: Twayne, 1964.

[------.] Westcott, Warren. "Paul Hamilton Hayne." In Spears, pp. 20-27.

King, Mitchell. Address Delivered in the First Presbyterian Church, Before the St. Andrew's Society of the City of Charleston, on Their Centennial Anniversary, the 30th of November, 1829, at Their Request, by Mitchell King, Esq. a Member of the Society and Published by Them. Charleston: J. S. Burges, 1829.

------. A Discourse on the Qualifications and Duties of an Historian; Delivered Before the Georgia Historical Society, on the Occasion of Its Fourth Anniversary, on Monday, 13th February, 1843. Savannah: The Society, 1843.

------. The History and Culture of the Olive: The Anniversary Address of the State Agricultural Society of South Carolina, Delivered in the Hall of the House of Representatives, November 26th, 1846. Columbia: State Agricultural Society, 1846.

Miles, William Porcher. Admission of Kansas. [Washington]: Printed at the Congressional Office, [1858].

------. American Literature and Charleston Society. Charleston: Walker and James, 1853.

------. Human Duty: An Address Delivered Before Society of Cadets of the Virginia Military Institute, July 2, 1871. Richmond. Whig Job Office, 1872.

------. Physician, Heal Thyself: How to Educate Our Young Doctors Address to the Graduated Class of the South Carolina Medical College at Charleston, March 1st, 1882. N.p., [1882].

------. Republican Government Not Everywhere and Always the Best; and Liberty Not the Birthright of Mankind. Charleston: Walker & James, 1852.

------. Some Views on Sugar. N.p., [1894].

------. True Education: How to Make Education "The Cheap Defence of a Nation." Columbia: Presbyterian Publishing House, 1882.

------. Universal Education: How to Purify the Ballot Box. Address Before the Winyaw Indigo Society, on their 128th Anniversary at Georgetown, S.C., May 15th, 1882. Charleston: The News and Courier Book Presses, 1882.

------. Women "Nobly Planned." How to Educate Our Girls. An Address Delivered ... Before the Young Ladies of the Yorkville Female College. N.p.: n.p., n.d.

Petigru, James L. Argument of James L. Petigru, Esq. : Delivered Before the Court of Appeals, at Charleston, on the Constitutionality of an Act of the Legislattre [sic], Passed 19th December, 1833, Entitled An Act to Provide for the Military Organization of This State. Charleston: J.S. Burges, 1834.

------. Life, letters and speeches of James Louis Petigru, the Union man of South Carolina. Washington, DC: W.H. Lowdermilk & Co., 1920.

------. Oration: Delivered Before the Charleston Library Society, at Its First Centennial Anniversary, June 13th, 1848. Charleston: J.B. Nixon, 1848.

------. Oration Delivered on the Third Anniversary of the South Carolina Historical Society, at Hibernian Hall, in Charleston, on Thursday evening, May 27, 1858. Charleston: Walker, Evans, & Co., 1858.

Simms, William Gilmore. As Good as a Comedy and Paddy McGann. Ed. James B. Meriwether. Columbia; University of South Carolina Press, 1972.

------. Atalantis. New York: J. & J. Harper, 1832.

------. Beauchampe. 2 vols. Philadelphia: Lea & Blanchard, 1842; London: N. Bruce, 1842.

------. Border Beagles. 2 vols. Philadelphia: Carey & Hart, 1840.

------. The Cassique of Kiawah. New York: Redfield, 1859.

------. The Charleston Book. [Ed.]. Charleston: Samuel Hart, 1845.

------. Confession. 2 vols. Philadelphia: Lea & Blanchard, 1841; London: J. Cunningham, 1841.

------. Count Julian. Baltimore: William Taylor, 1845; London: Bruce & Wyld, 1846.

------. *The Damsel of Darien*. 2 vols. Philadelphia: Lea & Blanchard, 1839; London: N. Bruce, 1843.

------. *Eutaw*. New York: Redfield, 1856.

------. *The Forayers*. New York: Redfield, 1855.

------. *The Geography of South Carolina*. Charleston: Babcock, 1843.

------. *Guy Rivers*. 2 vols. New York: Harper, 1834; London: J. Clemens, 1841.

------. *The History of South Carolina*. Charleston: S. Babcock, 1840.

------. *Joscelyn: A Tale of the Revolution*. Ed. Keen Butterworth. Columbia: University of South Carolina Press, 1975.

------. *Katharine Walton*. Philadelphia: A. Hart, 1851.

------. *The Kinsmen* [later retitled *The Scout*]. 2 vols. Philadelphia: Lea & Blanchard, 1841; London: John Cunningham, 1841.

------. *The Life of Captain John Smith*. New York: Geo. F. Cooledge, 1846.

------. *The Life of Chevalier Bayard*. New York: Harper, 1847.

------. *The Life of Francis Marion*. New York: Henry G. Langley, 1844.

------. *Lyrical and Other Poems*. Charleston: Ellis & Neufville, 1827.

------. *Martin Faber*. New York: J. & J. Harper, 1833; London: J. Clements, 1839.

------. *Mellichampe*. 2 vols. New York: Harper, 1836.

------. *The Partisan*. 2 vols. New York: Harper, 1835.

------. *Pelayo*. 2 vols. New York: Harper, 1838.

------. *Poems Descriptive, Dramatic, Legendary and Contemplative*. 2 vols. New York: Redfield, 1853.

------. *Richard Hurdis*. 2 vols. Philadelphia: Carey & Hart, 1838.

------. *Sack and Destruction of the City of Columbia, S.C.* Columbia: Daily Phoenix, 1865.

------. *Simms's Poems*. Charleston: Russell & Jones, 1860.

------. *South Carolina in the Revolutionary War*. Charleston: Walker & James, 1853.

------. *Southward Ho!* New York: Redfield, 1854.

------. *Stories and Tales*. Ed. John Caldwell Guilds. Columbia: University of South Carolina Press, 1974.

------. *The Sword and the Distaff*. [Later retitled *Woodcraft*.] Charleston: Walker, Richards, 1852.

------. *Vasconselos*. New York: Redfield, 1853.

------. *Views and Reviews*. First and Second Series. New York: Wiley & Putnam, 1846; London: Wiley & Putnam, 1846.

------. *Voltmeier or the Mountain Men*. Ed. James B. Meriwether. Columbia; University of South Carolina Press, 1969.

------. *War Poetry of the South*. [Ed.] New York: Richardson, 1866.

------. *The Wigwam and the Cabin*. First and Second Series. New York: Wiley & Putnam, 1845; London: Wiley & Putnam, 1846.

------. *The Yemassee*. 2 vols. New York: Harper, 1835; London: N. Bruce, 1842.

Timrod, Henry. *The Collected Poems of Henry Timrod*. Ed. Edd Winfield Parks and Aileen Wells Parks. Athens: University of Georgia Press, 1965.

------. *The Essays of Henry Timrod*. Ed. Edd Winfield Parks. Athens: University of Georgia Press, 1942.

------. *Poems*. Boston: Ticknor & Fields, 1859.

------. *The Poems of Henry Timrod*. Ed. Paul Hamilton Hayne. New York: E.J. Hale, 1873.

------. *Poems of Henry Timrod*. Memorial Edition. Boston: Houghton, Mifflin, 1899.

------. *The Uncollected Poems of Henry Timrod*. Ed. With an Introduction by Guy A. Cardwell, Jr. Athens: The University of Georgia Press, 1942.

Early African-American Writing from South Carolina

Fordham, Mary Weston. *Magnolia Leaves: Poems*. Charleston: Walker, Evans & Cogswell Co., 1897.

Payne, Daniel Alexander. *History of the African Methodist Episcopal Church*. Philadelphia: Book Concern of the A.M.E. Church, 1922; rpt. New York: Johnson Reprint, 1968; New York: Arno

Press, 1969.

------. *The Pleasures and Other Miscellaneous Poems*. Baltimore: Sherwood & CO., 1850.

------. *Recollections of Seventy Years*. 1888; rpt. New York: Arno Press, 1968.

------. *Sermons and Addresses, 1853-1891*. New York: Arno Press, 1972.

Rowe, George Clinton. *Our Heroes: Patriotic Poems on Men, Women and Sayings of the Negro Race*. Charleston: Walker, Evans & Cogswell Co., Printers, 1890.

------. *Thoughts in Verse: A Volume of Poems*. Charleston: Kahrs, Stolze & Welch, Printers, 1887.

Stroyer, Jacob. *My Life in the South*. Salem: Salem Observer Book and Job Print, 1885.

The Postwar Malaise

Allston, Joseph Blyth. *The Battle of Lake Erie*. Charleston: Walker, Evans & Cogswell Co., 1897.

------. Sumter. N.p.: N.p., [1874]. Verses "published in memory of those who fell in the defense of their country."

Davidson, James Wood. *The Correspondent*. New York: D. Appleton, 1886.

Davidson, James Wood. *The Florida of To-day: A Guide for Tourists and Settlers*. New York: D. Appleton, [1888?].

------. *The Living Writers of the South*. New York: Carleton, 1869.

------. *The Poetry of the Future*. New York: J.B. Alden, 1888.

------. *School History of South Carolina*. Columbia: Duffie & Chapman, [1869]; rev. ed., [1894].

Davis, Robert Means. *Art Work Scenes in South Carolina*. 12 vols. in 1. Chicago: W. H. Parrish Publishing Co., 1895.

Dickson, Samuel Henry. See above under William Gilmore Simms and the Charleston School.

Gregg, Alexander. *A Few Historic Records of the Church in the Diocese of Texas, During the Rebellion. Together with a Correspondence Between the Right Rev. Alexander Gregg ... and the Rev. Charles Gillette ...* New York: J.A. Gray & Green, Printers, 1865.

------. *History of the Old Cheraws; Containing an Account of the Aborigines of the Pedee, the First White Settlements, Their Subsequent Progress, Civil Changes, the Struggle of the Revolution, and Growth of the Country Afterward...*New York: Richardson and Company, 1867; Columbia: The State Co., 1905; rpt. Spartanburg: The Reprint Co., 1965, 1975; Greenville: Southern Historical Press, 1991.

Gwyn, Laura. *Miscellaneous Poems*. Greenville: G.E. Elford, Printer, 1860.

------. *Wanita: A Novel*. Charleston: Walker, Evans & Cogswell, 1880.

La Borde, Maximilian. *History of the South Carolina College*. Columbia: P. B. Glass, 1859; 2nd ed., Charleston: Walker, Evans & Cogswell, 1874.

------. *An Introduction to Physiology*. Designed for the Use of Students, and of the General Reader. New York: R.B. Collins; Charleston: McCarter, 1855.

------. *Story of Lethea and Verona*. Columbia: Printed at the Southern Guardian Office, 1860.

Lieber, Francis (Note: Many of Lieber's works went through several editions, and there are many pamphlet and ephemeral publications in the Lieber bibliography. What follows is of necessity only a sampling of the more important titles).

------. *The Character of the Gentleman*. Philadelphia: J. B. Lippincott & Co., 1864.

------. *On Civil Liberty and Self-government*. 2 vols. Philadelphia: J.B. Lippincott, 1853; enlarged edition in 1 vol., 1859.

------. *Essays on Property and Labour as Connected with Natural Law and the Constitution of Society*. New York: Harper & Brothers, 1841.

------. *Legal and Political Hermeneutics*. Boston: C.C. Little and J. Brown, 1839; rpt. Buffalo: W.S. Hein, 1970.

------. *Manual of Political Ethics*. 2 vols. Boston: C.C. Little and J. Brown,, Francis. 1838-1839.

------. *The Miscellaneous Writings of*. 2 vols. Philadelphia: J.B. Lippincott, 1881.

------. *The Stranger in America: Comprising Sketches of the Manners, Society, and National Peculiarities of the United States, in a Series of Letters to a Friend in Europe*. 2 vols. London: R. Bentley, 1835.

------. *The West, A Metrical Epistle*. New York: Putnam, 1848.

Logan, John Henry. *A History of the Upper Country of South Carolina, from the Earliest Periods to the Close of the War of Independence*. Charleston: S.G. Courtenay & Co.; Columbia: P.B. Glass, 1859.

------. *History of the Upper Country of South Carolina Vol. II : Biographical & Historical Extracts from the Unpublished Manuscript of Volume II*. Atlanta, GA: Kimsey's Book Shop, 1910; rpt. Easley, SC: Southern Historical Press, 1980.

McCord, Louisa Susannah Cheves. *Caius Gracchus: A Tragedy in Five Acts*. New York: H. Kernot, 1851.

------. Louisa S. McCord: *Poems, Drama, Biography, Letters*. Publications of the Southern Text Society. Charlottesville, VA: University Press of Virginia, 1996.

------. Louisa S. McCord: *Selected Writings*. Publications of the Southern Text Society. Charlottesville, VA: University Press of Virginia, 1997.

------. Louisa S. McCord: *Political and Social Essays*. Publications of the Southern Text Society. Charlottesville, VA: University Press of Virginia, 1995.

------. *My Dreams*. Philadelphia: Carey and Hart, 1848.

McCrady, Edward. *Charleston and Its Exposition*. N.p., [1902].

------. *The History of South Carolina in the Revolution, 1775-1780*. New York: The Macmillan Company; London: Macmillan & Co., Ltd., 1901.

------. *The History of South Carolina in the revolution, 1780-1783*. New York: the Macmillan Co.; London: Macmillan & Co., Ltd., 1902.

------. *The History of South Carolina Under the Proprietary Government, 1670-1719*. New York: The Macmillan Company; London: Macmillan & Co., Ltd., 1897.

------. *The History of South Carolina Under the Royal Government, 1719-1776*. New York: The Macmillan Company; London: Macmillan & Co., Ltd., [1889].

McKinley, Carlyle. *An Appeal to Pharaoh: The Negro Problem, and Its Radical Solution*. New York: Fords, Howard & Hulbert, 1889.

------. *The August Cyclone. A Descriptive Narrative of the Memorable Storm of 1885. Some Mention of the Destruction of Property in and Around Charleston—The Character of the Disturbance Explained, and Its Progress Traced from Its Origin in the West Indies to Its Disappearance in the North Atlantic Ocean*. Charleston: The News and Courier Book Presses, 1886.

------. *A Descriptive Narrative of the Earthquake of August 31, 1886 : Prepared Expressly for the City Year Book, 1886*. Charleston: Walker, Evans & Cogswell Co., 1887.

------. *Selections from the Poems of Carlyle McKinley*. Columbia: The State Co., 1904.

Poyas, Catharine Gendron. *The Huguenot Daughters, and other poems*. Charleston: J. Russell, 1849.

------. *Year of Grief, and Other Poems*. Charleston: Walker, Evans & Cogswell, 1869.

Requier, Augustus Julian. *The Old Sanctuary: A Romance of the Ashley*. Boston: Redding & Company, 1846.

------. *Poems*. Philadelphia: Lippincott, 1860.

Sass, George Herbert. *The Heart's Quest: A Book of Verses*. New York: G.P. Putnam, 1904.

Simmons, William Hayne. *American Sketches*. London: J. Miller, 1827.

------. *Notices of East Florida*. Bicentennial Floridiana Facsimile Series. Gainesville: University of Florida Press, 1973.

------. *Onea: An Indian Tale*. Charleston: T.B. Stephens, Printer, 1820.

Trescot, William Henry. *The Diplomacy of the Revolution: An Historical Study*. New York: D. Appleton & Co., 1852.

------. *The Diplomatic History of the Administrations of Washington and Adams, 1789-1801*. Boston: Little, Brown and Company, 1857.

The Twentieth Century Part One

Allen, Hervey. *Action at Aquila*. New York: Farrar & Rinehart, 1938.

------. *Anthony Adverse*. New York: Farrar and Rinehart, Inc., 1933.

------. *Bedford Village*. New York: Farrar & Rinehart Inc., 1944.

------. *The Blindman: A Ballad of Nogent L'Artaud*. New Haven: Yale University Press, 1921.

------. *The Bride of Huitzil: An Aztec Legend*. New York: James F. Drake, Inc., 1922.

------. *Carolina Chansons: Legends of the Low Country*. With DuBose Heyward. New York: The Macmillan Company, 1922.

------. *The City in the Dawn*. New York: Rinehart, 1950.

------. *DuBose Heyward: A Critical and Biographical Sketch, Including Contemporary Estimates of His Work*. New York: G.H. Doran Co., n.d.

------. *Earth Moods: And Other Poems*. New York and London: Harper & Brothers, 1925.

------. *The Forest and the Fort*. New York: Farrar & Rinehart, Inc., 1943.

------. *Israfel: The Life and Times of Edgar Allan Poe*. 2 vols. New York: George H. Doran, 1926.

------. *It Was Like This: Two Stories of the Great War*. New York: Farrar & Rinehart, Inc., 1940.

------. *New Legends: Poems*. New York: Farrar & Rinehart, Inc., 1929.

------. *Sarah Simon: Character Atlantean*. Garden City, NY: Doubleday, Doran, 1929.

------. *Songs for Annette*. One of a limited edition of 100 copies. New York: William Edwin Rudge, 1929.

------. *Toward the Flame*. New York: George H. Doran Company, 1926.

------. *Toward the Morning*. New York: Rinehart, 1948.

------. *Wampum and Old Gold*. Yale Series of Younger Poets. New Haven: Yale University Press, 1921.

Bennett, John. *Barnaby Lee*. New York: The Century Co., 1902.

------. *Blue Jacket, War Chief of the Shawnees, and His Part in Ohio's History*. Chillicothe, OH: Ross County Historical Society Press, 1943.

------. *The Doctor to the Dead: Grotesque Legends & Folk Tales of Old Charleston*. New York: Rinehart & Company, Inc., 1946; Columbia: University of South Carolina Press, 1995.

------. *Madame Margot: A Grotesque Legend of Old Charleston. The Bat Series*. New York: The Century Co., 1921; Columbia: University of South Carolina Press, 1951.

------. *Master Skylark: A Story of Shakespeare's Time*. New York: The Century Co., 1897.

------. *Master Skylark: A Dramatization of the Book by John Bennett, Prepared for the Use of Elementary Schools in New York City*. New York: The Century Co., 1914.

------. *The Pigtail of Ah Lee Ben Loo, With Seventeen Other Laughable Tales & 200 Comical Silhouettes*. New York and London: Longmans, Green & Co., 1928.

------. *The Treasure of Peyre Gaillard; Being an Account of the Recovery, on a South Carolina Plantation, of a Treasure, Which Had Remained Buried and Lost in a Vast Swamp for Over a Hundred Years*. New York: The Century Co., 1906.

Heyward, DuBose. *Ankle: A Play in Three Acts*. New York: Farrar & Rinehart, 1931.

------. *Carolina Chansons: Legends of the Low Country*. [With Hervey Allen.] New York: The Macmillan Company, 1922.

------. *Brass Ankle*. New York: George H. Doran Company, 1926.

------. *The Country Bunny and the Little Gold Shoes, As Told to Jenifer*. Boston and New York: Houghton Mifflin Company, 1939.

------. *Fort Sumter*. With Herbert Ravenel Sass. New York: Farrar & Rinehart, 1938.

------. *The Half Pint Flask*. New York: Farrar & Rinehart, 1929.

------. *Jasbo Brown and Selected Poems*. New York: Farrar & Rinehart, 1931.

------. *Lost Morning*. New York: Farrar & Rinehart, 1936.

------. *Mamba's Daughters: A Novel of Charleston*. Garden City: Doubleday, Doran and Company, 1929.

------. *Mamba's Daughters: A Play*. With Dorothy Heyward. New York: Farrar & Rinehart, 1939.

------. *Peter Ashley*. New York: Farrar & Rinehart, 1932.

------. *Porgy*. New York: George H. Doran Co., 1925.

------. *Porgy: A Play in Four Acts*. With Dorothy Heyward. New York: Doubleday, Page & Company for the Theatre Guild, 1927.

------. *Porgy and Bess: An Opera in Three Acts*. With George and Ira Gershwin. New York: Random House, 1935.

------. *Star Spangled Virgin*. New York: Farrar & Rinehart, 1939.

------. *Skylines and Horizons*. New York: The Macmillan Company, 1924.

Pinckney, Josephine. *Great Mischief*. New York: Viking Press, 1948.

------. *Hilton Head*. New York: Farrar & Rinehard, Inc., 1941.

------. *My Son and Foe*. New York: Viking Press, 1952.

------. *Sea-Drinking Cities: Poems*. New York and London: Harper & Brothers, 1927.

------. *Splendid in Ashes: A Novel*. New York: Viking Press, 1958.

------. *Three O'Clock Dinner*. New York: The Viking Press, 1945; rpt., Southern Classics Series, Columbia: University of South Carolina Press, 2001.

Ravenel, Beatrice Witte. *The Arrow of Lightning*. New York: H. Vinal, 1926.

------. *The Yemassee Lands: Poems of Beatrice Ravenel*. Selected and edited, with an Introduction by Louis D. Rubin, Jr. Chapel Hill: University of North Carolina Press, 1969.

Sass, Herbert Ravenel. *Adventures in Green Places*. New York: Minton, Balch and Company, 1926.

------. *Charleston Grows: An Economic, Social and Cultural Portrait of an Old Community in the New South*. Charleston: Carolina Art Association, 1949.

------. *Emperor Brims*. New York: Doubleday, Doran, 1941.

------. *Fort Sumter*. With DuBose Heyward. New York and Toronto: Farrar & Rinehart, Incorporated, 1938.

------. *Gray Eagle*. New York: Minton, Balch and Company, 1927.

------. *Hear Me, My Chiefs*. New York: W. Morrow & Company, 1940.

------. *Look Back to Glory*. Indianapolis: The Bobbs-Merrill Company, 1933.

------. *On the Wings of a Bird*. Garden City, NY: Doubleday, Doran & Company, 1929.

------. *Outspoken: 150 Years of the News and Courier*. Columbia: University of South Carolina Press, 1953.

------. *The Story of the South Carolina Low Country*. 3 vols. West Columbia, SC: J.F. Hyer, 1956.

------. *War Drums*. Garden City, NY: Doubleday, Doran & Company, Inc., 1928.

------. *The Way of the Wild*. New York: Minton, Balch & Company, 1925.

The Twentieth Century Part Two

Adams, Edward C.L. *Congaree Sketches: Scenes from Negro Life in the Swamps of the Congaree and Tales by Tad and Scip of Heaven and Hell with Other Miscellany*. Chapel Hill: University of North Carolina Press, 1927.

------. *Nigger to Nigger*. New York and London: C. Scribner, 1928.

------. *Potee's Gal: A Drama of Negro Life Near the Big Congaree Swamps*. Columbia: The State Co., 1929.

------. *Tales of the Congaree*. Edited with an Introduction by Robert G. O'Meally. Chapel Hill: University of North Carolina Press, 1987.

Bellamann, Henry. *Crescendo*. New York: Harcourt, Brace, & Company 1928.

------. *Cups of Illusion*. Boston and New York: Houghton Mifflin Company, 1923.

------. *Floods of Spring*. New York: Simon and Schuster, 1942.

------. *The Gray Man Walks*. Garden City: Pub. For the Crime Club, Inc., by Doubleday, Doran & Company, Inc., 1936.

------. *Kings Row*. New York: Simon and Schuster, 1940.

------. *A Music Teacher's Notebook*. New York: New York Poetry Book Shop, 1920.

------. (with Katherine Jones Bellamann). *Parris Mitchell of King's Row*. New York: Simon and Schuster, 1948. Published posthumously.

------. *Petenera's Daughter*. New York: Harcourt, Brace, and Company, 1926.

------. *The Richest Woman in Town*. New York and London: The Century Co., 1932.

------. *The Upward Pass*. Boston and New York: Houghton Mifflin Company, 1928.

------. *Victoria Grandolet*. New York: Simon and Schuster, 1943.

Gonzales, Ambrose Elliott. *The Black Border: Gullah Stories of the Carolina Coast*. Columbia: The State Company, 1922.

------. *The Captain: Stories of the Black Border*. Columbia: The State Company, 1924.

------. *Laguerre: A Gascon of the Black Border*. Columbia: The State Company, 1924.

------. *Rumbling of the Chariot Wheels: Doings and Misdoings in the Barefooted Period of a Boy's Life on a Southern Plantation*. Columbia: The State Co., 1918. [10-page pamphlet]

------. *With Aesop Along the Black Border*. Columbia: The State Company, 1924.

Peterkin, Julia Mood. *Black April*. Indianapolis: Bobbs-Merrill, 1927;rpt. Athens: University of Georgia Press, 1998.

------. *Bright Skin*. Indianapolis: Bobbs-Merrill, 1932.

------. *Collected Short Stories*. Ed. Frank Durham. Columbia: University of South Carolina Press, 1970.

------. *Green Thursday: Stories*. New York: Knopf, 1924.

------. *A Plantation Christmas*. Boston: Houghton Mifflin Company, 1934.

------. *Roll, Jordan, Roll*. New York: Robert O. Ballou, 1933.

------. *Scarlet Sister Mary*. Indianapolis: Bobbs-Merrill, 1928; rpt. with Foreword

by A.J. Verdelle, Athens and London: University of Georgia Press, 1998.

Rutledge, Archibald. *America's Greatest Game Bird: Archibald Rutledge's Turkey Hunting Tales*. Columbia: University of South Carolina Press, 1994.

------. *The Angel Standing; or, Faith Alone Gives Poise*. New York: Fleming H. Revell, 1948.

------. *The Ballad of the Howling Hound and Other Poems*. Richmond: Dietz, 1965.

------. *The Banners of the Coast*. Columbia: Presses of the State Co., 1908.

------. *Beauty in the Heart*. Westwood, NJ: F.H. Revell Co., 1953.

------. *The Beauty of the Night*. New York and London: Fleming H. Revell Company, 1947.

------. *Bolio and Other Dogs*. New York: Frederick A. Stokes Company, 1930.

------. *Bright Angel and Other Poems*. Columbia: R.L. Bryan Co., 1955.

------. *Brimming Tide and Other Poems*. Westwood, NJ: F.H. Revell Co., 1954.

------. *Children of Swamp and Wood*. Garden City, NY: Doubleday, Page & Company, 1927.

------. *Christ Is God*. New York: Fleming H. Revell Company, 1941.

------. *Collected Poems*. Columbia: The State Co., 1925.

------. *Days Off in Dixie*. Garden City, NY: Doubleday, Page & Company, 1924.

------. *Deep River: The Complete Poems of Archibald Rutledge*. Columbia: R.L. Bryan Co., 1960.

------. *The Everlasting Light, and Other Poems*. Athens: University of Georgia Press, 1949.

------. *Fireworks in the Peafield Corner: A Treasury of the Best of the Sage of Hampton Plantation and the First Poet Laureate of South Carolina*. Clinton, NJ: Amwell, 1986.

------. *The Flower of Hope*. New York and Chicago: Fleming H. Revell Company, 1930.

------. *From the Hills to the Sea: Fact and Legend of the Carolinas*. Indianapolis: Bobbs-Merrill, 1958.

------. *God's Children*. Indianapolis: The Bobbs-Merrill Company, 1947.

------. *The Heart Has Its Daybreak*. Verse craft series. Emory University, Georgia: Banner Press, 1950.

------. *Heart of the South*. Columbia: The State Company, 1924.

------. *The Heart's Citadel and Other Poems*. Richmond: Dietz, Press, 1953.

------. *The Heart's Quest*. N.p.: N.p., n.d.

------. *Home by the River*. Indianapolis and New York: The Bobbs-Merrill Company, 1941.

------. *How Wild Was My Village*. Illus. D.P. McGuire. Columbia: Wing Publications, 1969.

------. *Hunter's Choice*. New York: A.S. Barnes and Company, 1946.

------. *Hunting & Home in the Southern Heartland: The Best of Archibald Rutledge*. Columbia: University of South Carolina Press, 1992.

------. *Hunting the Southlands*. Clinton, NJ: Amwell Press, 1986.

------. *I Hear America Singing*. Columbia: R.L. Bryan Co., 1970.

------. *It Will Be Daybreak Soon*. New York: Fleming H. Revell Company, 1938.

------. *Life's Extras*. New York and Chicago: Fleming H. Revell Company, 1928.

------. *Lincoln: A Southern View*. Chapel Hill, NC: Leonidas Polk Chapter, United Daughters of the Confederacy, [1925].

------. *Love's Meaning*. New York and London: Fleming H. Revell Company, 1943.

------. *A Monarch of the Sky*. Little Classics of the South. South Carolina. New York:

Purdy Press, 1926. Bound with *Two Gullah Tales: The Turkey Hunter* and *At the Cross Roads Store* by Ambrose E. Gonzales.

------. *My Colonel and His Lady*. Indianapolis: Bobbs-Merrill, 1937.

------. *New Poems*. N.p.: N.p., 1915.

------. *Old Plantation Days*. New York: Frederick A. Stokes Company, 1921.

------. *Peace in the Heart*. Garden City, NY: Doubleday, Doran & Company, 1930.

------. *Plantation Game Trails*. Boston and New York: Houghton Mifflin Company, 1921.

------. *Poems in Honor of South Carolina Tricentennial*. Columbia: R.L. Bryan Co., 1970.

------. *Rain on the Marsh*. Columbia: Bostick & Thornley, Inc., 1940.

------. *Santee Paradise*. Indianapolis: Bobbs-Merrill Co., 1956.

------. *Songs from a Valley*. Chambersburg, PA: Public Opinion Print, 1919.

------. *The Sonnets of Archibald Rutledge*. N.p.: N.p., 1938.

------. *South of Richmond*. Chambersburg, PA: J.R. Kerr & Bro., 1923.

------. *Strayed Shots and Frayed Lines: Being Classics of American Sporting Humor*. Clinton, NJ: Amwell Press, 1982. Also contains pieces by John E. Howard and Havilah Babcock.

------. *Tales of Whitetails: Archibald Rutledge's Great Deer Hunting Stories*. Ed. James A. Casada. Columbia: University of South Carolina Press, 1992.

------. *Those Were the Days*. Richmond: Dietz Press, 1955.

------. *Tom and I on the Old Plantation*. New York: Frederick A. Stokes Company, 1918.

------. *Under the Pines and Other Poems*. Winchester, VA: Eddy Press Corp., 1906.

------. *Veiled Eros*. New York: H. Harrison,

1933.

Rutledge, Archibald. *Voices of the Long Ago: Bible Stories Retold*. Columbia: R.L. Bryan Co., 1973.

------. *When Boys Go Off to School*. New York: Fleming H. Revell Company, 1935.

------. *Wild Life of the South*. Philadelphia: J.B. Lippincott Company, 1935.

------. *The Wild Turkey Book: An Anthology*. Clinton, NJ: Amwell Press, 1981. Also contains pieces by J. Wayne Fears and Havilah Babcock.

------. *A Wildwood Tale: A Drama of the Open*. New York: Revell, 1950.

------. *Willie Was a Lady*. Columbia: Wing Publications, 1966.

------. *The Woods and Wild Things I Remember*. Columbia: R.L. Bryan Co., 1970.

------. *The World Around Hampton*. New York: Bobbs-Merrill, 1960.

The Twentieth Century Part Three

Allan, Glenn. *Boysi Himself*. New York: Curl, 1946.

------. *Little Sorrowful*. New York: S. Curl, 1946.

------. *Old Manoa: A Novel*. New York and London: D. Appleton and Company, 1932.

Ashmore, Harry S. *Arkansas: A Bicentennial History. The States and Nation Series*. New York: Norton, 1978.

------. *Challenge '65: The Emerging World of the American Negro*. Winston-Salem: Wake Forest College, 1965.

------. *Civil Rights and Wrongs: A Memoir of Race and Politics, 1944-1996*. Columbia: University of South Carolina Press, 1997.

------. *Civil Rights and Wrongs: A Memoir of Race and Politics 1944-1994*. New York: Pantheon Books, 1994.

------. *An Epitaph for Dixie*. New York: Norton, 1958.

------. *Fear in the Air: Broadcasting and the First Amendment: The Anatomy of a Constitutional Crisis*. New York: W.W. Norton, 1973.

------. *Hearts and Minds: The Anatomy of Racism from Roosevelt to Reagan*. New York: McGraw- Hill, 1982.

------. *Hearts and Minds: A Personal Chronicle of Race in America*. Cabin John, MD: Seven Locks Press, 1988.

------. *The Man in the Middle*. Columbia, MO: University of Missouri Press, 1966.

------. *Mission to Hanoi: A Chronicle of Double-Dealing in High Places, A Special Report from the Center for the Study of Democratic institutions*. New York: Putnam, 1968.

------. *The Negro and the Schools*. Chapel Hill: University of North Carolina Press, 1954.

------. *The Other Side of Jordan*. New York: Norton, 1960.

------. *Unseasonable Truths: The Life of Robert Maynard Hutchins*. Boston: Little, Brown, 1989.

Babcock, Havilah. *According to Hoyle: A Glossary of Idiomatic and Colloquial Usage*. Columbia: The State Company, 1928.

------. *The Best of Babcock*. New York: Holt, Rinehart and Winston, 1974.

------. *The Education of Pretty Boy*. New York: Holt, 1960.

------. *Hunting the Southlands*. Clinton, NJ: Amwell Press, 1986.

------. *I Don't Want to Shoot an Elephant*. New York: Holt, 1958.

------. *I Want a Word: A Word Manual and Exercise Book*. Columbia: Ashley Printing Co., 1944.

------. *Jaybirds Go to Hell on Friday and Other Stories*. New York: Holt, Rinehart and Winston, 1964.

------. *My Health Is Better in November*. 3 vols. Louisville, KY: American Printing

House for the Blind, 1949.

------. *My Health Is Better in November: Thirty-Five Stories of Hunting and Fishing in the South*. New York: Holt, Rinehart and Winston, 1947.

------. *Tales of Quails 'N Such*. New York: Greenberg, 1951.

Ball, William Watts. *The State That Forgot: South Carolina's Surrender to Democracy*. Indianapolis: The Bobbs-Merrill Company, 1932.

Blue, Kate Lily. *The Hand of Fate: A Romance of the Navy*. Chicago: C.H. Kerr and Company, 1895.

------. *History of Marion County, South Carolina and the Background of Her Present and Future Development: A Radio Address at WBT, Charlotte, N.C., November 24, 1933*. South Carolina Economic Association Series, no. 9. N.p., 1933.

Bonner, Paul Hyde. *Aged in the Woods: Stories and Sketches of Fishing and Shooting*. New York: Scribner, 1958.

------. *Amanda*. New York: Scribner, 1957.

------. *Ambassador Extraordinary*. New York: Scribner, 1962.

------. *The Art of Llewellyn Jones*. New York: C. Scribner's Sons, 1959.

------. *Excelsior!* New York: C. Scribner's Sons, 1955.

------. *The Glorious Mornings: Stories of Shooting and Fishing*. New York: Scribner, 1954.

------. *Hotel Talleyrand: A Novel*. New York: Scribner, 1953.

------. *S.P.Q.R.: A Romance*. New York: Scribner, 1952.

------. *With Both Eyes Open*. New York: Scribner, 1956.

Brawley, Benjamin Griffith. *The Best Stories of Paul Laurence Dunbar*. New York: Dodd, Mead, 1938.

------. *Doctor Dillard of the Jeanes Fund*. New York: Fleming H. Revell Company, 1930.

------. *Early Black American Writers: Selections with Biographical and Critical Introductions*. New York: Dover, 1992.

------. *History of Morehouse College, Written on the Authority of the Board of Trustees*. Atlanta, GA: Morehouse College, 1917.

------. *Negro Builders and Heroes*. Chapel Hill: University of North Carolina Press, 1937.

------. *The Negro in Literature and Art in the United States*. New York: Duffield, 1919.

------ (Ed.). *New Era Declamations*. Sewanee, TN: The University Press, 1918.

------. *A New Survey of English Literature*. New York: Alfred A. Knopf, 1925.

------. *A Short History of the American Negro*. New York: The Macmillan Co., 1913.

------. *A Short History of the English Drama*. New York: Harcourt, Brace & Co., 1921.

------. *A Social History of the American Negro*. New York: The Macmillan Co., 1921.

Bristow, Gwen. *Calico Palace*. New York: Crowell, 1970.

------. *Celia Garth*. New York: Crowell, 1959.

------. *Deep Summer*. New York: Grossett & Dunlap. 1937.

------. *Golden Dreams*. New York: Lippincott & Crowell, 1980.

------ with Bruce Manning. *The Gutenberg Murders*. New York: The Mystery League, Inc., 1931.

------. *Gwen Bristow: A Self-Portrait*. New York: Crowell, 1941?

------. *Handsome Road*. New York: Crowell, 1938.

------ and Bruce Manning. *The Invisible Host*. New York: The Mystery League, Inc., 1930.

------. *Jubilee Trail*. New York: Crowell, 1950.

------ with Bruce Manning. *The Mardi Gras Murders*. New York: Mystery League, 1932.

------. *This Side of Glory*. New York: T.Y. Crowell, 1940.

------. *Tomorrow Is Forever*. New York: Crowell, 1943.

------ with Bruce Manning. *Two and Two Make Twenty-two*. New York: Mystery League, 1932.

Cash, Wilbur Joseph. *The Mind of the South*. New York: Knopf, 1941.

Cassels, Louis. *A Bad Investment*. New York: Pyramid Books, 1974.

------. *Christian Primer*. Garden City, NY: Doubleday, 1964.

------. *Coontail Lagoon: A Celebration of Life*. Philadelphia: Westminster Press, 1974.

------. *A Faith for Skeptics*. New York: New Family Library, 1972.

------. *A Feast for a Time of Fasting: Meditations for Lent*. Nashville: Abingdon Press, 1973.

------. *Forbid Them Not*. Independence, MO: Independence Press, 1973.

------. *Haircuts and Holiness: Discussion Starters for Religious Encounter Groups*. Nashville: Abingdon Press, 1972.

------. *The Negro in Revolt: What Now?* New York: United Press International, 1967.

------. *Preludes to Prayer: 365 Daily Meditations*. Nashville: Abingdon Press, 1974.

------. *The Real Jesus: How He Lived and What He Taught*. Garden City, NY: Doubleday, 1968.

------. *The Reality of God*. Garden City, NY: Doubleday and Company, 1971.

------. *This Fellow Jesus*. Anderson, IN: Warner Press, 1973.

------. *The Unexpected Exodus*. Aiken, SC: Sand Hill Press, 1971.

------. *What's the Difference? A Comparison of the Faiths Men Live By*. Garden City, NY: Doubleday, 1965.

Childress, Alice (Ed.). *Black Scenes*. Garden City: Zenith Books, 1971.

------. *A Hero Ain't Nothin' but a Sandwich*. New York: Coward, McCann, & Geoghegan, 1973.

------. *Let's Hear It for the Queen*. New York: Coward, McCann, & Geoghegan, 1976.

------. *Like One of the Family: Conversations from a Domestic's Life*. Brooklyn, NY: Independence Publishers, 1956.

------. *Mojo and String: Two Plays*. New York: Dramatists Play Service, 1971.

------. *Rainbow Jordan*. New York: Coward, McCann & Geoghegan, 1981.

------. *A Short Walk*. New York: Coward, McCann, & Geoghegan, 1979.

------. *Those Other People*. New York: Putnam, 1989.

------. *Troubles in Mind*. In Black Theatre. Ed. Lindsay Patterson. New York: New American Library, 1971.

------. *Wedding Band: A Love/Hate Story in Black and White*. New York: French, 1973.

------. *When the Rattlesnake Sounds: A Play*. New York: Coward, McCann, & Geoghegan, 1975.

------. *Wine in the Wilderness: A Comedy-Drama*. New York: Dramatists Play Service, 1969.

Christopher, Matt. *Baseball Flyhawk*. Boston: Little, Brown, 1963.

------. *Baseball Pals*. Boston: Little, Brown 1956.

------. *The Basket Counts*. Boston: Little, Brown, 1968.

------. *Basketball Sparkplug*. Boston: Little, Brown, 1957.

------. *Break for the Basket*. Boston: Little, Brown, 1960.

------. *Catch That Pass!* Boston: Little, Brown, 1969.

------. *The Catcher with a Glass Arm*. Boston: Little, Brown, 1964.

------. *Challenge at Second Base*. Boston: Little, Brown, 1962.

------. *The Counterfeit Tackle*. Boston: Little, Brown, 1965.

------. *Crackerjack Halfback*. Boston: Little, Brown, 1962.

------. *Desperate Search*. Boston: Little, Brown, 1973.

------. *Devil Pony*. Boston: Little, Brown, 1977.

------. *The Diamond Champs*. Boston: Little, Brown, 1977.

------. *Dirt Bike Racer*. Boston: Little, Brown, 1979.

------. *Dirt Bike Runaway*. Boston: Little, Brown, 1983.

------. *The Dog That Called the Signals*. Boston: Little, Brown, 1982.

------. *The Dog That Pitched a No-Hitter*. Boston: Little, Brown, 1988.

------. *The Dog That Stole Football Plays*. Boston: Little, Brown, 1979.

------. *Drag Strip Racer*. Boston: Little, Brown, 1982.

------. *Earthquake*. Boston: Little, Brown, 1975.

------. *Face-Off*. Boston: Little, Brown, 1972.

------. *Favor for a Ghost*. Westminster, 1983.

------. *Football Fugitive*. Boston: Little, Brown, 1976.

------. *The Fox Steals Home*. Boston: Little, Brown, 1978.

------. *Front Court Hex*. Boston: Little, Brown, 1974.

------. *Glue Fingers*. Boston: Little, Brown, 1975.

------. *The Great Quarterback Switch*. Boston: Little, Brown, 1984.

------. *Hard Drive to Short*. Boston: Little, Brown, 1969.

------. *The Hit-Away Kid*. Boston: Little, Brown, 1988.

------. *The Hockey Machine*. Boston: Little, Brown, 1986.

------. *Ice Magic*. Boston: Little, Brown, 1973.

------. *Jackrabbit Goalie*. Boston: Little, Brown, 1978.

------. *Jinx Glove*. Boston: Little, Brown, 1974.

------. *Johnny Long Legs*. Boston: Little, Brown, 1970.

------. *Johnny No Hit*. Boston: Little, Brown, 1977.

------. *The Kid Who Only Hit Homers*. Boston: Little, Brown, 1972.

------. *Little Lefty*. Boston: Little, Brown, 1959.

------. *Long Shot for Paul*. Boston: Little, Brown, 19626.

------. *Long Stretch at First Base*. Boston: Little, Brown, 1960.

------. *Look for the Body*. Phoenix Press, 1952.

------. *Look Who's Playing First Base*. Boston: Little, Brown, 1971.

------. *The Lucky Baseball Bat*. Boston: Little, Brown, 1954.

------. *Lucky Seven*. Boston: Little, Brown, 1970.

------. *Miracle at the Plate*. Boston: Little, Brown, 1967.

------. *Mystery Coach*. Boston: Little, Brown, 1973.

------ (as Fredric Martin). *Mystery at Monkey Run*. Boston: Little, Brown,

1966.

—————— (as Fredric Martin). *Mystery on Crabapple Hill*. Boston: Little, Brown, 1965.

—————— (as Fredric Martin). *Mystery Under Fugitive House*. Boston: little, Brown, 1968.

——————. *No Arm in Left Field*. Boston: Little Brown, 1974.

——————. *The Pigeon with a Tennis Elbow*. Boston, Little, Brown, 1975.

——————. *Power Play*. Boston: Little, Brown, 1976.

——————. *Red Hot Hightops*. Boston: Little, Brown, 1987.

——————. *The Reluctant Pitcher*. Boston: Little, Brown, 1966.

——————. *The Return of the Headless Horseman*. Westminster, 1982.

——————. *Return of the Home Run Kid*. Boston: Little, Brown, 1992.

——————. *Run, Billy, Run*. Boston: Little, Brown, 1980.

——————. *Shadow Over Back Court*. New York: Frederick Watts, 1959.

——————. *Shortstop from Tokyo*. Boston: Little, Brown, 1970.

——————. *Sink It, Rusty*. Boston: Little. Brown, 1963.

——————. *Skateboard Tough*. Boston: Little, Brown, 1991.

——————. *Slide, Danny Slide*. Steck, 1958.

——————. *Soccer Halfback*. Boston: Little, Brown, 1978.

——————. *The Spy on Third Base*. Boston: Little, Brown, 1988.

——————. *Stranded*. Boston: Little, Brown, 1974.

——————. *The Submarine Pitch*. Boston: Little, Brown, 1976.

——————. *Supercharged Infield*. Boston: Little,

Brown, 1985.

——————. *Tackle Without a Team*. Boston: Little, Brown, 1989.

——————. *Takedown*. Boston: Little, Brown, 1990.

——————. *Tall Man in the Pivot*. Boston: Little, Brown, 1961.

——————. *The Team That Couldn't Lose*. Boston: Little, Brown, 1967.

——————. *The Team That Stopped Moving*. Boston: Little, Brown, 1975.

——————. *Tight End*. Boston: Little, Brown, 1981.

——————. *Touchdown for Tommy*. Little, Brown, 1959.

——————. *Tough to Tackle*. Boston: Little, Brown, 1971.

——————. *The Twenty-One Mile Swim*. Boston: Little, Brown, 1979.

——————. *Two Hot to Handle*. Boston: Little, Brown, 1965.

——————. *Two Strikes on Johnny*. Boston: Little, Brown, 1958.

——————. *Wild Pitch*. Boston: Little, Brown, 1980.

——————. *Wingman on Ice*. Boston: Little, Brown, 1964.

——————. *Wing T. Fullback*. New York: Frederick Watts, 1960.

——————. *The Year Mom Won the Pennant*. Boston: Little, Brown, 1968.

Cohen, Octavus Roy. *Assorted Chocolates*. New York: Dodd, Mead, 1922.

——————. *The Backstage Mystery*. New York: D. Appleton, 1930.

——————. *Bigger and Blacker*. Boston: Little, Brown and Company, 1925.

——————. *Borrasca*. New York: Macmillan, 1953.

——————. *A Bullet for My Love: A Novel*. New York: Macmillan, 1950.

------. *Cameos*. New York: D. Appleton and Company, 1931.

------. *Carbon Copies*. New York and London: D. Appleton and Company, 1932.

------. *Child of Evil*. New York: D. Appleton-Century Company, 1936.

------. *Come Seven*. New York: Dodd, Mead and Company, 1920.

------. *The Corpse That Walked*. New York: Fawcett Publications, 1942.

------. *The Crimson Alibi*. New York: Grosset & Dunlap, 1919.

------. *Danger in Paradise*. New York: Popular Library, 1944.

------. *Dangerous Lady*. New York: Popular Library, 1946.

------. *Dark Days and Black Knights*. New York: Dodd, Mead and Co., 1923.

------. *Detours*. Boston: Little, Brown, and Company, 1927.

------. *Don't Ever Love Me: A Novel*. New York: Macmillan, 1947.

------. *East of Broadway*. New York: D. Appleton-Century Company, Inc., 1938.

------. *Epic Peters, Pullman Porter*. New York: D. Appleton, 1930.

------. *Florian Slappey*. New York: D. Appleton-Century, 1938.

------. *Florian Slappey Goes Abroad*. Boston: Little, Brown, and Company, 1928.

------. *The Golden Hussy (Borrasca)*. New York: Fawcett Publications, 1956.

------. *Gray Dusk*. New York: Dodd, Mead, 1920.

------. *The Intruder*. New York: Graphic Books, 1956.

------. *The Iron Chalice*. Boston: Little, Brown, 1925.

------. *Jim Hanvey, Detective*. New York: Grosset & Dunlap, 1923.

------. *Kid Tinsel*. New York: Appleton-Century, 1941.

------. *Lady in Armor*. New York and London: Appleton-Century, 1941.

------. *The Light Shines Through*. Boston: Little, Brown, 1928.

------. *Lilies of the Alley*. New York: D. Appleton, 1931.

------. *Lost Lady*. New York: Fawcett Publications, 1951.

------. *Love Can Be Dangerous: A Novel*. New York: Macmillan, 1955.

------. *Love Has No Alibi*. New York: Popular Library, 1945.

------. *Midnight*. New York: Dodd, Mead, 1922.

------. *More Beautiful than Murder*. New York: Macmillan Co., 1948.

------. *My Love Wears Black: A Novel*. New York: Macmillan, 1947.

------. *The Other Woman*. New York: Macaulay Company, 1917.

------. *The Outer Gate*. Boston: Little, Brown, 1927.

------. *Polished Ebony*. New York: Dodd, Mead, 1919.

------. *Romance in Crimson*. New York: D. Appleton-Century, 1940.

------. *Romance in the First Degree*. New York: Macmillan, 1943.

------. *Scarlet Woman*. New York: D. Appleton-Century, 1934.

------. *Scrambled Yeggs*. New York and London: D. Appleton-Century Company, Incorporated, 1934.

------. *Six Seconds of Darkness*. New York: Dodd, Mead, 1921.

------. *Sound of Revelry*. New York: Macmillan, 1943.

------. *Spring Tide*. New York and London: D. Appleton and Company, 1928.

------. *Star of Earth*. New York: D. Appleton, 1932.

------. *Strange Honeymoon*. New York: D. Appleton-Century, 1939.

------. *Sunclouds*. New York: Dodd, Mead, 1924.

------. *The Townsend Murder Mystery*. New York and London: Appleton-Century, Incorporated, 1933.

------. *Transient Lady*. New York: Appleton-Century, 1934.

------. *The Valley of Olympus*. New York: D. Appleton, 1929.

------. *With Benefit of Clergy*. New York: D. Appleton-Century, 1935.

Coker, Elizabeth Boatwright. *The Bees: A Story of a Family*. New York: Dutton, 1968.

------. *La Belle: A Novel Based on the Life of the Notorious Southern Belle, Marie Boozer*. New York: Dutton, 1959.

------. *The Big Drum*. New York: Dutton, 1957.

------. *Blood Red Roses: A Romantic Novel of Hilton Head Island, South Carolina, During the War Between the States*. New York: Dutton, 1977.

Coker, Elizabeth Boatwright. *Daughter of Strangers*. New York: Dutton, 1950.

------. *The Day of the Peacock*. New York: Dutton, 1952.

------. *The Grasshopper King: A Story of Two Confederate Exiles in Mexico During the Reign of Maximilian and Carlota*. New York: Dutton, 1981.

------. *India Allan*. New York: Dutton, 1953.

------. *Lady Rich: A Novel of Penelope Devereux at the Court of Queen Elizabeth*. New York: Dutton, 1953.

Dabbs, James McBride. *Civil Rights in Recent Southern Fiction*. Atlanta: Southern Regional Council, 1969.

------. *Haunted by God*. Richmond, VA: John Knox Press, 1972.

------. *Pee Dee Panorama Revisited*. Greenville: Published for the Pee Dee Heritage Center by A Press, 1984.

------. *The Road Home*. Philadelphia: Christian Education Press, 1960.

------. *The Southern Heritage*. New York: Knopf, 1958.

------. *Who Speaks for the South?* New York: Funk & Wagnalls, 1964.

Daniels, Jonathan Worth. *The Devil's Backbone: The Story of the Natchez Trace*. New York: McGraw-Hill, 1962.

------. *The End of Innocence*. Philadelphia: Lippincott, 1954.

------. *The Forest Is the Future*. New York: International Paper Company, 1957.

------. *Frontier on the Potomac*. New York: The Macmillan Company, 1946.

------. *The Gentlemanly Serpent and Other Columns from a Newspaperman in Paradise: From the Pages of the Hilton Head Island Packet, 1970-1973*. Columbia: University of South Carolina Press, 1974.

------. *The Man of Independence*. Philadelphia: J.B. Lippincott Company, 1950.

------. *Mosby: Gray Ghost of the Confederacy*. Philadelphia: Lippincott, 1959.

------. *Ordeal of Ambition: Jefferson, Hamilton, Burr*. Garden City, NY: Doubleday, 1970.

------. *Prince of Carpetbaggers*. Philadelphia: J.B. Lippincott Company, 1958.

------. *The Randolphs of Virginia*. Garden City, NY: Doubleday, 1972.

------. *A Southerner Discovers New England*. New York: Macmillan, 1940.

------. *A Southerner Discovers the South*. New York: The Macmillan Company, 1938.

——————. *Tar Heels: A Portrait of North Carolina*. New York: Dodd, Mead, 1941.

——————. *The Time Between the Wars: Armistice to Pearl Harbor*. Garden City, NY: Doubleday, 1966.

——————. *Washington Quadrille: The Dance Beside the Documents*. Garden City, NY: Doubleday, 1968.

——————. *White House Witness, 1942-1945*. Garden City, NY: Doubleday, 1975.

DuBose. *Louise Jones. Enigma: The Career of Blondelle Malone in Art and Society, 1879-1951, As Told in Her Letters and Diaries*. Columbia: University of South Carolina Press, 1963.

——————. *A History of Columbus, Georgia, 1828-1928*. Columbus, GA: The Historical Publishing Co., 1929.

——————. *South Carolina Lives: The Palmetto Who's Who, A Reference Edition Recording the Biographies of Contemporary Leaders in South Carolina, with Special Emphasis on Their Achievements in Making It One of America's Greatest States*. Hopkinsville, KY: Historical Record Association, 1963.

Durham, Francis Marion. *DuBose Heyward: The Man Who Wrote Porgy*. Columbia: University of South Carolina Press, 1954.

——————. *DuBose Heyward's Use of Folklore in His Negro Fiction*. The Citadel Monograph Series, no. 2. Charleston: The Citadel, 1961.

——————. *Elmer Rice. Twayne's United States Authors Series, no. 167*. New York: Twayne Publishers, 1970.

——————. *Fire of the Lord: A Play of Religious Fanatics*. New York: S. French, 1937.

——————. *Government in Greater Cleveland*. Cleveland, OH: H. Allen, 1963.

——————. *The Merrill Studies in Cane*. Columbus, OH: Merrill, 1971.

——————. *My Late Espoused Saint: A Comedy Drama*. Evanston, IL: Row, Peterson & Company, 1942.

——————. *Sounding Brass: A Comedy in One Act*. In One Act Play Magazine, 4.5 (Sept.-Oct. 1941): 349-380.

——————. *Time for Everything: A Comedy in One Act*. Evanston, IL: Row, Peterson & Company, 1943.

Few, Mary Dodgen. *Azilie of Bordeaux: A Novel*. Greenwood, SC: Carolina Editions, 1973.

——————. *Carolina Jewel: A Novel*. Anderson, SC: Hallux, 1970.

——————. *Under the White Boar*. Atlanta: Droke House/Hallux, 1971.

Ford, Nick Aaron. *Best Short Stories by Afro-American Writers, 1925-1950*. Boston: Meador Publishing Co., 1950.

——————. *Black Insights: Significant Literature by Black Americans, 1760 to the Present*. Waltham, MA: Xerox College Publishing, 1971.

——————. *Black Studies: Threat or Challenge*. Kennikat Press National University Publications. Series in American Studies. Port Washington, NY: Kennikat Press, 1973.

——————. *The Contemporary Negro Novel: A Study in Race Relations*. Boston: Meador Publishing Company, 1936.

—————— (Comp.). *Extending Horizons: Selected Readings for Cultural Enrichment*. New York: Random House, 1969.

——————. *Language in Uniform: A Reader on Propaganda*. New York: Odyssey Press, 1967.

——————. *Seeking a Newer World: Memoirs of a Black American Teacher*. Great Neck, NY: Todd & Honeywell, 1983.

——————. *Songs from the Dark*. Boston: Meador Publishing Co., 1940.

Freeman, Grace Beacham. *Children Are Poetry*. New Orleans: Tulane University Press, 1951.

——————. *Midnight to Dawn*. Laurinburg, NC: St. Andrews Press, 1981.

——————. *No Costumes or Masks*. Red Clay Reader, vol. 10, no. 2. Charlotte, NC: Red Clay Books, 1975.

——. *Remembering a Gentle Father.* Laurinburg, NC: St. Andrews College Press, 1996.

——. *Stars and the Land.* Rock Hill, SC: John's Press, 1983.

——. *This Woman Called Mother.* Laurinburg, NC: St. Andrews Press, 1992.

Graydon, Nell S. *The Amazing Marriage of Marie Eustis & Josef Hofmann.* Columbia: University of South Carolina Press, 1965.

——. *Another Jezebel.* Columbia: R.L. Bryan Co., 1958.

——. *Edisto Island, South Carolina: A Brief Illustrated History and Comprehensive Map of the Island.* Columbia: R.L. Bryan, 1955.

——. *Eliza of Wapoo: A Tale of Indigo.* Columbia: R.L. Bryan Co., 1967.

——. *From My House to Your House.* Greenwood, SC: Drinkard Printing Company, 1968.

——. *South Carolina Ghost Tales.* Beaufort, SC: Beaufort Book Shop, 1969.

——. *Tales of Beaufort.* Beaufort, SC: Beaufort Book Shop, 1963.

——. *Tales of Columbia.* Columbia: R.L. Bryan Co., 1964.

——. *Tales of Edisto.* Columbia: R.L. Bryan Co., 1955.

——. *South Carolina Gardens.* Beaufort, SC: Beaufort Book Co., 1973.

Hartley, Lodwick Charles, comp. *Katherine Anne Porter: A Critical Symposium.* Athens: University of Georgia Press, 1969.

——. *Laurence Sterne in the Twentieth Century: An Essay and a Bibliography of Sternean Studies, 1900-1965.* Chapel Hill, NC: University of North Carolina Press, 1966.

——. *Laurence Sterne, 1965-1977: An Annotated Bibliography with an Introductory Essay-Review of the Scholarship.* Boston: G.K. Hall, 1978.

——. *Plum Tree Lane.* Lexington, SC: Sandlapper Store, 1978.

——. *This Is Lorence: A Narrative of the Reverend Laurence Sterne.* Chapel Hill, NC: University of North Carolina Press, 1943.

——. *William Cowper, Humanitarian.* Chapel Hill, NC: University of North Carolina Press, 1938.

——. *William Cowper: The Continuing Revaluation: An Essay and a Bibliography Of Cowperian Studies from 1895 to 1960.* Chapel Hill, NC: University of North Carolina Press, 1960.

Haselden, Kyle. *Changing Man: The Threat and the Promise.* Garden City, NY: Doubleday, 1968.

——. *Death of a Myth: New Locus for Spanish American Faith.* New York: Friendship Press, 1964.

——. *Mandate for White Christians.* Richmond: John Knox Press, 1966.

——. *Morality and the Mass Media.* Nashville: Broadman Press, 1968.

——. *The Racial Problem in Christian Perspective.* New York: Harper, 1959.

——. *What's Ahead for the Churches: A Report.* New York: Sheed and Ward, 1964.

Heyward, Dorothy Hartzell Kuhns. *Love in a Cupboard: A Comedy in One Act.* New York: S. French; London: S. French, Ltd., 1926.

——. *Mamba's Daughters: A Play.* New York and Toronto: Farrar & Rinehart, 1939.

——. *Porgy: A Play in Four Acts.* Garden City, NY: Published for the Theatre Guild by Doubleday, Page & Company, 1927.

——. *The Pulitzer Prize Murders.* New York: Farrar & Rinehart Incorporated, 1932.

——. *Three-a-Day.* New York and London: The Century Co., 1930.

Holman, Clarence Hugh (comp.). *The American Novel Through Henry James. Goldentree Bibliographies.* New York: Appleton-Century-Crofts, 1966.

------. *Another Man's Poison*. New York: New American Library, 1949.

------. *A Handbook to Literature: Based on the Original Edition by William Flint Thrall and Addison Hibbard*. 4th ed. Indianapolis: Bobbs-Merrill Education Pub., 1980.

------. *The Immoderate Past: The Southern Writer and History*. Lamar Lectures (Wesleyan College), 1976. Athens: University of Georgia Press, 1977.

------. John P. Marquand. *University of Minnesota Pamphlets on American Writers, no. 46*. Minneapolis: University of Minnesota Press, 1965.

------. *The Loneliness at the Core: Studies in Thomas Wolfe*. Baton Rouge: Louisiana State University Press, 1975.

------. *The Roots of Southern Writing: Essays on the Literature of the American South*. Athens: University of Georgia Press, 1972.

------. *Slay the Murderer: A Sheriff Macready Detective Story*. New York: New American Library, 1948.

------. Thomas Wolfe. *University of Minnesota Pamphlets on American Writers, no. 6*. Minneapolis: University of Minnesota Press, 1960.

------. *Three Modes of Modern Southern Fiction: Ellen Glasgow, William Faulkner, Thomas Wolfe. Lamar Memorial Lectures, no. 9*. Athens: University of Georgia Press, 1966.

------. *Up This Crooked Way: A Sheriff Macready Detective Story*. London and New York: W. Foulsham, 1951.

------. *Windows on the World: Essays on American Social Fiction*. Knoxville: University of Tennessee Press, 1978.

------. *The World of Thomas Wolfe*. A Scribner Research Anthology. New York: Scribner, 1962.

------ and Louis Decimus Rubin. *Southern Literary Study: Problems and Possibilities*. Chapel Hill: University of North Carolina Press, 1975.

------ (ed.). *The Short Novels of Thomas Wolfe*. New York: Charles Scribner's Sons, 1961.

------ (ed.), and Sue Fields Ross (ed). *The Letters of Thomas Wolfe to His Mother*. Chapel Hill: University of North Carolina Press, 1968.

Hyer, Helen von Kolnitz. *Danger Never Sleeps*. Columbia: Wing Publications, 1970.

------. *Hurricane Harbor*. Boston: Marshall Jones Company, 1927.

------. *The Magnificent Squeak*. New York: Saalfield Publishing Company, 1902.

------. *On Shiny Wings*. Boston: Marshall Jones Co., 1926.

------. *Santee Songs*. Columbia: The State Co., 1923.

------. *Stories by Seasons*. Boston: Marshall Jones Company, 1930.

------. *What the Wind Forgets: A Woman's Heart Remembers*. Lexington, SC: Sandlapper Store, 1975.

------. *Wine Dark Sea*. Boston: Marshall Jones Co., 1930.

Jacobs, Thornwell. *Drums of Doomsday*. New York: Dutton, 1942.

------. *Islands of the Blest, and Other Poems*. Oglethorpe, GA: Oglethorpe University Press, 1928.

------. *The Law of the White Circle*. Nashville: Taylor-Trotwood, 1908.

------. *The Life of William Plumer Jacobs*. New York: Fleming H. Revell Company, 1918.

------. *The Midnight Mummer, and Other Poems*. Atlanta: Redbrook Co., 1911.

------. *My People*. Clinton, SC: N.p., 1954.

------ (writing as "Lonnie Loyle"). *Neath the Shadow of His Wing*. Clinton, SC: Thornwell Orphanage Press, 1900.

------. *The New Science and the Old Religion*. Oglethorpe, GA: Oglethorpe University Press, 1927.

------. *Not Knowing Whither He Went*. Oglethorpe, GA: Oglethorpe University press, 1933.

------. *The Oglethorpe Story*. Oglethorpe University Bulletin, Vol. 1, no. 8 (July 1916).

------. *Red Lanterns on St. Michael's*. New York: E.P. Dutton & CO., Inc., 1940.

------. *Sinful Sadday, Son of a Cotton Mill: A Story of a Little Orphan Boy Who Lived to Triumph*. Nashville: Smith & Lamar, 1907.

------. *Step Down, Dr. Jacobs: The Autobiography of an Autocrat*. Atlanta: The Westminster Publishers, 1945.

------. *When for the Truth*. Charleston: Walker, Evans, and Cogswell, 1950.

------ (ed.), assisted by Mary Brent Whiteside and James Edward Routh. *The Oglethorpe Book of Georgia Verse*. Oglethorpe, GA: Oglethorpe University Press, 1930.

Johnson, Barbara Ferry. *Delta Blood*. New York: Avon, 1977.

------. *Echoes from the Hills*. New York: Avon, 1982.

------. *The Heirs of Love*. New York: Avon, 1980.

------. *Homeward Winds the River*. New York: Avon, 1979.

------. *Lionors*. New York: Avon, 1975.

------. *Tara's Song*. New York: Avon, 1978.

Lattimore, Eleanor Frances. *Adam's Key*. New York: Morrow, 1976.

------. *Bayou Boy*. New York: W. Morrow and Company, 1946.

------. *Beachcomber Boy*. New York: W. Morrow, 1960.

------. *Bells for a Chinese Donkey*. New York: Morrow, 1951.

------. *Bird Song*. New York: Morrow, 1968.

------. *The Bittern's Nest*. New York: Morrow, 1962.

------. *The Bus Trip*. New York: W. Morrow, 1965.

------. *The Chinese Daughter*. New York: Morrow, 1960.

------. *Christopher and His Turtle*. New York: Morrow, 1950.

------. *The Clever Cat*. New York: Harcourt, Brace and Company, 1936.

------. *Cousin Melinda*. New York: Morrow, 1961.

------. *Davy of the Everglades*. New York: W. Morrow, 1949.

------. *Deborah's White Winter*. New York: W. Morrow, 1949.

------. *Diana in the China Shop*. New York: Morrow, 1955.

------. *Fair Bay*. New York: Morrow, 1958.

------. *Felicia*. New York: Morrow, 1964.

------. *The Fig Tree*. New York: Morrow, 1951.

------. *First Grade*. New York: Harcourt, Brace and Company, 1944.

------. *Holly in the Snow*. New York: Morrow, 1954.

------. *Indigo Hill*. New York: Morrow, 1950.

------. *Janetta's Magnet*. New York: Morrow, 1963.

------. *Jasper*. New York: Morrow, 1953.

------. *Jeremy's Isle*. New York: W. Morrow, 1947.

------. *Jeremy and the Pusa*. New York: Harcourt, Brace and Company, 1932.

------. *The Journey of Ching Lai*. New York: Morrow, 1957.

------. *Junior, A Colored Boy of Charleston*. New York: Harcourt, Brace and Company, 1938.

------. *Laurie and Company*. New York: Morrow, 1962.

------. *Little Pear and His Friends*. New York: Harcourt, Brace, 1934.

------. *Little Pear and the Rabbits*. New York: Morrow, 1956.

------. *Little Pear: The Story of a Little Chinese Boy*. New York: Harcourt, Brace, 1931.

------. *The Little Tumbler*. New York: Morrow, 1963.

------. *Lively Victoria*. New York: Morrow, 1952.

------. *The Mexican Bird*. New York: Morrow, 1965.

------. *Molly in the Middle*. New York: Morrow, 1956.

------. *The Monkey of Crofton*. New York: Morrow, 1957.

------. *Peachblossom*. New York: Harcourt, Brace and Company, 1943.

------. *Proudfoot's Way*. New York: Morrow, 1978.

------. *The Questions of Lifu: A Story of China*. New York: Harcourt, Brace and Company, 1942.

------. *The Search for Christina*. New York: W. Morrow, 1966.

------. *The Seven Crows*. New York: Harcourt, Brace, 1933.

------. *Storm on the Island*. New York: Harcourt, Brace, 1942.

------. *The Story of Lee Ling*. New York: Harcourt, Brace and Company, 1940.

------. *The Three Firecrackers*. New York: W. Morrow, 1970.

------. *Three Little Chinese Girls*. New York: W. Morrow, 1948.

------. *The Two Helens*. New York: Morrow, 1967.

------. *Willow Tree Village*. New York: Morrow, 1955.

------. *The Wonderful Glass House*. New York: Morrow, 1961.

------. *Wu, The Gatekeeper's Son*. New York: Morrow, 1953.

------. *The Youngest Artist*. New York: Morrow, 1959.

Lewisohn, Ludwig. *Adam: A Dramatic History in a Prologue, Seven Scenes, and an Epilogue*. New York and London: Harper & Brothers, 1929.

------. *Aesop and Hyssop: Being Fables Adapted and Original with the Morals Carefully Formulated*. Chicago: Open Court Publishing Co., 1912.

------. *An Altar in the Fields: A Novel*. New York and London: Harper & Brothers, 1934.

------. *The American Jew: Character and Destiny*. New York: Farrar, Straus, 1950.

------. *Among the Nations: Three Tales and a Play About Jews*. Philadelphia: The Jewish Publication Society of America, 1948.

------. *Anniversary*. New York: Farrar, Straus, 1946.

------. *Breathe Upon These*. Indianapolis and New York: The Bobbs-Merrill Company, 1944.

------. *The Broken Snare*. New York: B.W. Dodge, 1908.

------. *The Case of Mr. Crump*. Paris: E.W. Titus, 1926.

------. *Cities and Men*. New York and London: Harper & Brothers, 1927.

------ (ed.). *Creative America*. New York and London: Harper & Brothers, 1933.

------. *The Creative Life*. New York: Boni and Liveright, 1924.

------. *The Defeated*. London: T. Butterworth, Limited, 1927.

------. *Don Juan*. New York: Boni and Liveright, 1923.

------. *The Drama and the Stage*. Freeport, NY: Books for Libraries Press, 1969.

------. *The Eternal Road: A Drama in Four*

Parts. New York: Viking Press, 1936.

------. *Expression in America*. New York and London: Harper & Brothers, 1932.

------. *Gegen den Strom: Eine Amerikanische Chronik*. Frankfurt am Main: Frankfurter Societts-druckerei G.m.b.H., 1924.

------. *German Style: An Introduction to the Study of German Prose*. New York: H. Holt and Company, 1910.

------. *Goat Alley: A Tragedy of Negro Life*. Cincinnati: Stewart Kidd Company, 1922.

------. *The Golden Vase*. New York and London: Harper & Brothers, 1931.

------. *In a Summer Season: A Novel*. New York: Farrar, Straus, 1955.

------. *The Island Within*. New York: Harper, 1928.

------. *Israel*. New York: Boni & Liveright, 1925.

------. *A Jew Speaks: An Anthology from Ludwig Lewisohn*. New York and London: Harper & Brothers, 1931.

------. *Jewish Short Stories*. New York: Behrman House, 1945.

. ------. *The Last Days of Shylock*. New York and London: Harper & Brothers, 1931.

------. *The Magic Word: Studies in the Nature of Poetry*. New York: Farrar and Straus, 1950.

------. *The Memories of Stephen Escott*. London: Thornton Butterworth, 1930.

------. *Mid-Channel: An American Chronicle*. New York and London: Harper & Brothers, 1929.

------ (ed.). *A Modern Book of Criticism*. New York: Boni & Liveright, 1919.

------. *The Modern Drama: An Essay in Interpretation*. New York: B.W. Huebsch, 1915.

------. *The Permanent Horizon: A New Search for Old Truths*. New York and London: Harper & Brothers, 1934.

------. *The Poets of Modern France*. New York: B.W. Huebsch, 1918.

------. *Renegade*. Philadelphia: Jewish Publication Society of America, 1942.

------. *Roman Summer*. New York and London: Harper & Brothers, 1927.

------. *The Romantic: A Contemporary Legend*. Paris: E.W. Titus, 1931.

------. *Stephen Escott*. New York and London: Harper & Brothers, 1930.

------. *The Story of American Literature*. New York: The Modern Library, 1939.

------. *This People*. New York and London: Harper & Brothers, 1933.

------. *Trumpet of Jubilee*. New York: Harper & Brothers, 1937.

------. *The Tyranny of Sex: The Case of Mr. Crump*. New York: New American Library, 1947.

------. *Upstream: An American Chronicle*. New York: Boni and Liveright, 1922.

------. *The Vehement Flame: The Story of Stephen Escott*. New York: Farrar, Straus, 1948.

------. *What Is This Jewish Heritage?* New York: B'nai B'rith Hillel Foundations, 1954.

Macomber, Daria. *A Clearing in the Fog*. New York: World Pub. Co., 1970.

------. *Hunter, Hunter Get Your Gun*. London: Hodder and Stoughton, 1966.

------. *Return to Octavia*. New York: New American Library, 1967.

Mayer, Orlando Benedict. *The Dutch Fork*. Ed. James E. Kibler. Columbia: Dutch Fork Press, 1982.

------. *John Punterick: A Novel of Life in the Old Dutch Fork*. Ed. James E. Kibler. Spartanburg: The Reprint Co., 1981.

------ and John A. Chapman. *Mallodoce, the Briton: His Wanderings from Druidism to Christianity*. Richmond: E. Waddey Co., 1891.

Mays, Benjamin Elijah. *Born to Rebel: An*

Autobiography. New York: Scribner, 1971.

------. *Disturbed About Man*. Richmond: John Knox Press, 1969.

------. *The Negro's Church*. New York: Russell & Russell, 1969.

------. *The Negro's God as Reflected in His Literature*. New York: Atheneum, 1968.

------. *Seeking to Be Christian in Race Relations*. New York: Friendship Press, 1946.

McCants, Elliott Crayton. *History, Stories, and Legends of South Carolina*. Dallas: Southern Publishing Co., 1927.

------. *In the Red Hills: A Story of the Carolina Country*. New York: Doubleday, Page, 1904.

------. *Ninety Six*. New York: Thomas Y. Crowell, 1930.

------. *One of the Grayjackets*. Columbia: The State Co., 1908.

------. *White Oak Farm*. New York and London: Longmans, Green, 1928.

McGhee, Zach. *The Dark Corner*. New York: The Grafton Press, 1908.

------. *A Study in the Play Life of Some South Carolina Children*. N.p., 1900.

------ and Hazel Lewis Scaife. *Life at the Citadel : A Sketch Book Containing a Collection of Verse, Comic Essays, Parodies, Humorous Delinquent Reports, and Amusing Incidents, Illustrative of the Life of a Cadet at the South Carolina Military Academy. Compiled and edited by Cadets McGhee and Scaife...* Charleston: Walker, Evans & Cogswell, 1891.

McKinley, Carlyle. *An Appeal to Pharaoh: The Negro Problem, and Its Radical Solution*. New York: Fords, Howard & Hulbert, 1889.

------. *The August Cyclone: A descriptive Narrative of the Memorable Storm of 1885*. Charleston: The News and Courier Book Presses, 1886.

------. *A Descriptive Narrative of the Earthquake of August 31, 1886: Prepared Expressly for the City Year Book, 1886*. Charleston: Walker. Evans & Cogswell Co., Printers, 1887.

------. *Selections from the Poems of Carlyle McKinley*. Columbia: The State Co., 1904.

------. *1863-73: "After Ten Years."* Walhalla: Keowee Courier Presses, 1902.

Miller, Kelly. *An Appeal to Conscience*. New York: Arno Press, 1969.

------. *As to the Leopard's Spots: An Open Letter to Thomas Dixon, Jr.* Washington, DC: K. Miller, 1905.

------. *From Servitude to Service: Being the Old South Lectures on the History and Work of Southern Institutions for the Education of the Negro*. Boston: American Unitarian Association, 1905.

------. *Kelly Miller's History of the World War for Human Rights: An Intensely Human and Brilliant Account of the World War, and Why and for What Purpose America and the Allies Are Fighting, and the Important Part Taken by the Negro, Including the Horrors and Wonders of Modern Warfare, the New and Strange Devices, Etc.* N.p.: Jenkins, Keller, 1919.

------. *Out of the House of Bondage*. 1914; rpt. New York: Arno Press, 1969.

------. *Race Adjustment: Essays on the Negro in America*. New York: The Neale Publishing Company, 1908.

Molloy, Robert. *An Afternoon in March*. Garden City, NY: Doubleday, 1958.

------. *The Best of Intentions*. Philadelphia: J.B. Lippincott Co., 1949.

------. *Charleston: A Gracious Heritage*. New York: D. Appleton-Century Co., 1947.

------. *A Multitude of Sins*. Garden City, NY: Doubleday, 1953.

------. *The Other Side of the Hill*. Garden City, NY: Doubleday, 1962.

------. *Pound Foolish*. Philadelphia: J.B. Lippincott, 1950.

------. *Pride's Way*. New York: Macmillan, 1945.

------. *The Reunion*. Garden City, NY:

Doubleday, 1959.

------. *Uneasy Spring*. New York: The Macmillan Company, 1946.

Murray, Chalmers Swinton. *Here Comes Joe Mungin: A Novel*. New York: Putnam, 1942.

------. *This Our Land: The Story of the Agricultural Society of South Carolina*. Charleston: Carolina Art Association, 1949.

Nelson, Annie Greene. *After the Storm: A Novel*. Columbia: Hampton Publishing Company, 1942.

------. *The Dawn Appears*. Columbia: Hampton Publishing Company, 1944.

------. *Don't Walk on My Dreams*. Columbia: Privately printed, 1961.

Oemler, Marie Conway. *...Flower of Thorn*. New York and London: The Century Co., 1931.

------. *His Wife-in-Law*. New York and London: The Century Co., 1925.

------. *The Holy Lover*. New York: Boni & Liveright, 1927.

------. *Johnny Reb: A Story of South Carolina*. New York and London: The Century Co., 1929.

------. *The Purple Heights*. New York: The Century Co., 1920.

------. *Sheaves: A Comedy of Manners*. New York and London: The Century Co., 1928.

------. *Shepherds*. New York & London: The Century Co., 1926.

------. *Slippy McGee: Sometimes Known as the Butterfly Man*. New York: The Century Co., 1917.

------. *Two Shall Be Born*. New York: The Century Co., 1922.

------. *A Woman Named Smith*. New York: The Century Co., 1919.

Ottolengui, Rodrigues. *An Artist in Crime*. New York: G.P. Putnam, 1892.

------. *A Conflict of Evidence*. New York: G.P. Putnam's Sons, 1893.

------. *The Crime of the Century*. New York: G.P. Putnam's Sons, 1896.

------. *Final Proof; or, The Value of Evidence*. New York and London: G.P. Putnam's Sons, 1898.

------. *Methods of Filling Teeth: An Exposition of Practical Methods Which Will Enable the Student and Practitioner of Dentistry Successfully to Prepare and Fill All Cavities in Human Teeth*. Philadelphia: White Dental Mfg. Co., 1898.

------. *A Modern Wizard*. New York: G.P. Putnam's Sons, 1894.

------. *Table Talks on Dentistry*. Brooklyn, NY: Dental Items of Interest Publishing Co., Incorporated, 1928.

Rice, John Andrew. *I Came Out of the Eighteenth Century*. London: Harper & Brothers, 1942.

------. *Local Color*. New York: Dell, 1955.

------. *Black Moon*. New York: Harcourt, Brace, 1933.

------. *Cities of Fear and Other Adventure Stories*. Charleston: Warren Ripley, 1990.

------. *Devil Drums*. New York: Brewer & Warren, Inc., 1930.

------. *Dust and Sun*. New York: Payson & Clarke Ltd., 1929.

------. *Gold Is Where You Find It*. New York: Grosset & Dunlap, 1936.

------. *Mississippi Belle*. New York and London: D. Appleton-Century Company, Incorporated, 1942.

------. *Murder Walks Alone*. New York: J. Messner, Inc., 1935.

Ripley, Katharine Ball. *Crowded House*. Garden City, NY: Doubleday, Doran & Company, 1936.

------. *Sand Dollars*. New York: Harcourt, Brace and Company, 1933.

------. *Sand in My Shoes*. New York: Brewer, Warren & Putnam, 1931.

Robertson, Ben. *I Saw England*. New York: Grosset & Dunlap, 1940.

------. *Red Hills and Cotton: An Upcountry Memory*. New York: Knopf, 1942.

------. *Travelers' Rest*. Clemson: The Cottonfield Publishers, 1938.

Robinson, Patricia Colbert. *The Burning Tide*. [S.l.: s.n.], 1979. Play produced at the Dock Street Theatre in 1961, 1965, and 1971.

------. *A Clearing in the Fog*. New York: World Pub. Co., 1970.

------. *Love and Death in Charleston*. New York: Avalon Books, 1998.

------. *The Secrets of Farand Isle*. New York: Avalon Books, 1996.

------. *Something to Hide*. New York: St. Martin's Press, 1990.

------. *A Trick of Light*. New York: St. Martin's Press, 1994.

------ and Katherine Drayton Mayrant Simons. *Held in Splendor: A Charleston Cavalcade*. [Charleston, SC?]: The authors, n.d.

Simmons, Dawn Langley. *Dawn: A Charleston Legend*. Charleston: Wyrick, 1994.

------. *Dear Vagabonds: The Story of Roy and Brownie Adams*. New York: Tara Books, 1964.

------ (as Gordon Langley Hall). *Golden Boats from Burma*. Philadelphia: Macrae Smith Co., 1961.

------ (as Gordon Langley Hall). *Lady Bird and Her Daughters*. Philadelphia: M. Smith Co., 1967.

------. *Margaret Rutherford: A Blithe Spirit*. New York: McGraw-Hill, 1983.

------.*Me Papoose Sitter*. New York: Crowell, 1955.

------. *Mr. Jefferson's Ladies*. Boston: Beacon Press, 1966.

------ (as Gordon Langley Hall). *Osceola*. New York: Holt, Rinehart and Winston, 1964.

------. *A Rose for Mrs. Lincoln: A Biography of Mary Todd Lincoln*. Boston: Beacon Press, 1970.

------ (as Gordon Langley Hall). *The Sawdust Trail: The Story of American Evangelism*. Philadelphia: Macrae Smith Co., 1964.

------. *She-Crab Soup*. Westminster, MD: Acme Press, 1993.

------. *The Two Lives of Baby Doc*. Philadelphia: Macrae Smith Co., 1962.

------ (as Gordon Langley Hall). *Vinnie Ream: The Story of the Girl Who Sculptured Lincoln*. New York: Holt, Rinehart and Winston, 1963.

Simons, Katharine Drayton Mayrant. *Always a River*. New York: Appleton-Century-Crofts, 1956.

------. *Courage Is Not Given*. New York: Appleton-Century-Crofts, 1952.

------. *First the Blade*. New York: Appleton-Century-Crofts, 1950.

------. *Lamp in Jerusalem*. New York: Appleton-Century-Crofts, 1957.

------. *The Land Beyond the Tempest*. New York: Coward-McCann, 1960.

------. *The Patteran*. Columbia: The State Company, 1925.

------. *The Running Thread*. New York: Appleton-Century-Crofts, 1949.

------. *Shadow Songs*. Charleston: Presses of J.J. Furlong Charleston Printing House, 1912.

------. *Stories of Charleston Harbor*. Columbia: The State Company, 1930.

------. *A Sword from Galway*. New York: Appleton-Century-Crofts, 1948.

------. *White Horse Leaping*. Columbia: University of South Carolina Press, 1951.

Sinclair, Bennie Lee. *The Arrowhead Scholar*. Cleveland, SC: Wildernesse Books, 1978.

------. *The Endangered: New and Selected Poems*. Greenville, SC: Ninety-Six Press,

1992.

------. *Little Chicago Suite*. Cleveland, SC: Wildernesse Books, 1978.

------. *The Lynching*. New York: Walker and Co., 1992.

------. *Taproots: A Study in Cultural Exploration*. Columbia: South Carolina Arts Commission, 1975.

Spears, Monroe Kirklyndorf. *American Ambitions: Selected Essays on Literary and Cultural Themes*. Baltimore: Johns Hopkins University Press, 1987.

------. *Dionysus and the City: Modernism in Twentieth-Century Poetry*. New York: Oxford University Press, 1970.

------. *Hart Crane: Minnesota Pamphlets on American Writers, no. 47*. Minneapolis: University of Minnesota Press, 1965.

------. *One Writer's Reality*. Columbia, MO: University of Missouri Press, 1996.

------. *The Poetry of W.H. Auden: The Disenchanted Island*. New York: Oxford University Press, 1963.

------. *Space Against Time in Modern Poetry*. Monographs in Literary Criticism, no. 2. Fort Worth: Texas Christian University Press, 1972.

------ (ed.). *Auden: A Collection of Critical Essays*. Twentieth Century Views. Englewood Cliffs, NJ: Prentice-Hall, 1964.

------ (ed.). *The Literary Works of Matthew Prior*. 2 vols. Oxford: Clarendon Press, 1959.

Springs, Elliott White. *Above the Bright Blue Sky: More About the War Birds*. Garden City, NY: Doubleday, Doran & Company, 1928.

------. *Clothes make the Man*. New York: J.J. Little & Ives Co., 1949.

------. *Contact: A Romance of the Air*. London: Hamilton, 1930.

------. *In the Cool of the Evening*. New York: Sears Publishing Co., 1929.

------. *Leave Me With a Smile*. Garden City,

NY: Doubleday, Doran & Company, 1928.

------. *Nocturne Militaire*. New York: George H. Doran Company, 1927.

------. *Pent Up on a Penthouse*. New York: E. Springs, 1931.

------. *The Rise and Fall of Carol Banks*. Garden City, NY: Doubleday, Doran, 1931.

------ (ed.). *War Birds*. By John MacGavock Grider. New York: George H. Doran Company, 1926.

Sprunt, Alexander, Jr. *Carolina Low Country Impressions*. New York: Devin-Adair, 1964.

------. *Dwellers of the Silences*. New York: Dodd, Mead, 1931.

------. *Florida Bird Life*. New York: Coward-McCann, 1954.

------. *Gamebirds: A Guide to North American Species and Their Habitats*. New York: Golden Press, 1961.

------. *North American Birds of Prey*. New York: Harper and Brothers, 1955.

------. *Second Supplement to Arthur T. Wayne's Birds of South Carolina*. Charleston: Charleston Museum, 1931.

------. *South Carolina Bird Life*. Columbia: University of South Carolina Press, 1949.

Steele, Max. *Debby*. New York: Harper, 1950.

------. *The Goblins Must Go Barefoot*. New York: Harper & Row, 1966.

------. *The Hat of My Mother: Stories*. Chapel Hill, NC: Algonquin Books; Dallas, TX: Taylor Publishing Co., 1988.

------. *Seasonal Jobs on Land and Sea*. New York: Harper Colophon Books, 1979.

------. *Where She Brushed Her Hair, and Other Stories*. New York: Harper & Row, 1968.

Stoney, Samuel Gaillard, Jr. *Black Genesis: A Chronicle*. New York: The Macmillan Company, 1930.

------. *Charleston: Azaleas and Old Bricks*. Photographs by Bayard Morgan Wootten.

Boston: Houghton Mifflin Company, 1939.

------. *Plantations of the Carolina Low Country*. Charleston: The Carolina Art Association, 1938.

------. *Po' Buckra*. New York: The Macmillan Company, 1930.

------. *South Carolina: Appraising a Culture. An Address*. Florence, SC: W.J. Stricklin, 1970.

------. *The Story of South Carolina's Senior Bank: The Bank of Charleston, Mother of the South Carolina National Bank of Charleston*. Columbia: R.L. Bryan, 1955.

------. *This Is Charleston: A Survey of the Architectural Heritage of a Unique American City*. Charleston: The Carolina Art Association, 1944.

Talbert, Robert Beveridge. *Good Moanin'*. Detroit: Free Press, 1984.

Thompson, Dorothy Perry. *Fly with the Puffin*. Greenville, SC: Ninety-Six Press, 1995.

------. *Hurrying the Spirit: Following Zora*. Aiken, SC: Palanquin Press, 2002.

------. *Out of the Rough: Women's Poems of Survival and Celebration*. Charlotte: Novello Festival Press, 2001.

------. *Priest in Aqua Boa*. Greenville, SC: Ninety-Six Press, 2001.

Woolsey, Gamel. *The Last Leaf Falls*. North Walsham: Warren House Press, 1978.

------. *The Letters of Gamel Woolsey to Llewelyn Powys, 1930-1939*. North Walsham: Warren House Press, 1983.

------. *Malaga Burning: An American Woman's Eyewitness Account of the Spanish Civil War*. Introduction by Zalin Grant. Reston, Virginia, and Paris: Pythia Press, 1998.

------. *Middle Earth: Poems*. New York: Simon and Schuster, Inc., 1932.

------. *The Search for Demeter*. Norfolk: Warren House Press, 1980.

------. *Twenty Eight Sonnets*. North Walsham: Warren House Press, 1977.

------. *The Weight of Human Hours*. North Walsham: Warren House Press, 1980.

Workman, William D., Jr. *The Bishop from Barnwell: The Political Life and Times of Senator Edgar A. Brown*. Columbia: R.L. Bryan Co., 1963.

------. *The Case for the South*. New York: Devin-Adair Co., 1960.

------ (ed.). *The Settling of South Carolina: The Tricentennial Editions*. 4 vols. Columbia: The State, 1969.

------ (ed.). *The South Carolina Digest: A Governmental Survey*. Columbia: Columbia Newspapers, 1978.

------ (ed.). *South Carolina in Revolution: The Bicentennial Editions*. Columbia: The State, 1976.

------ *The Case for the South*. New York: Devin-Adair Co., 1960.

------ *Charles E. Daniel: His Philosophy and Legacy*. Columbia: R.L. Bryan Co., 1981.

Wright, Louis Booker. *American Literature: An Anthology with Critical Introductions*. New York: Washington Square Press, 1966.

------. *The American Tradition: National Characteristics, Past and Present*. New York: F.S. Crofts & Co., 1943.

------. *The Atlantic Frontier: Colonial American Civilization, 1607-1763*. New York: Alfred A. Knopf, 1947.

------. *Barefoot in Arcadia: Memories of a More Innocent Era*. Columbia: University of South Carolina Press, 1974.

------. *The Cultural Life of the American Colonies, 1607-1763*. New York: Harper, 1957.

------. *The Elizabethans' America*. Cambridge: Harvard University Press, 1965.

------. *The First Gentlemen of Virginia: Intellectual Qualities of the Early Colonial Ruling Class*. San Marino, CA: The Huntington Library,   1940.

------. *The Folger Guide to Shakespeare*. New

York: Washington Square Press, 1969.

------. *The Great American Gentleman, William Byrd of Westover in Virginia: His Secret Diary for the Years 1709-1712*. New York: Capricorn Books, 1963.

------. *Middle-Class Culture in Elizabethan England*. Chapel Hill: University of North Carolina Press, 1935.

------. *Of Books and Men*. Columbia: University of South Carolina Press, 1976.

------. *Shakespeare for Everyman*. New York: Washington Square Press, 1964.

Post-World War II New Directions

Conroy, Pat. *Beach Music*. New York: Nan A. Talese/An Imprint of Doubleday, 1995.

------. *The Boo*. Verona, VA: McClure, 1970.

------. *The Great Santini*. Boston: Houghton Mifflin, 1976.

------. *The Lords of Discipline*. Boston: Houghton Mifflin, 1980.

------. *My Losing Season*. Nan A. Talese/An Imprint of Doubleday, 2002.

------. *The Prince of Tides*. Boston: Houghton Mifflin, 1986.

------. *The Water Is Wide*. Boston: Houghton Mifflin, 1972.

Davenport, Guy. *Apples and Pears and Other Stories*. San Francisco: North Point, 1984.

------. *August*. Tuscaloosa, AL: The Close-Grip Press, 1986.

------. *Belinda's World Tour*. New York: Dim Gray Bar Press, 1991.

------. *The Bicycle Rider*. New York: Red Ozier, 1985.

------. *The Cardiff Team: Ten Stories*. New York: New Directions, 1996.

------. *Cities on Hills: A Study of XXX of Ezra Pound's Cantos*. Ann Arbor: UMI Research, 1983.

------. *Da Vinci's Bicycle: Ten Stories*. Baltimore: Johns Hopkins University Press, 1979.

------. *The Drummer of the Eleventh North*

Devonshire Fusiliers. San Francisco: North Point, 1990.

------. *Eclogues: Eight Stories*. San Francisco: North Point, 1981.

------. *Every Force Evolves a Form: Twenty Essays*. San Francisco: North Point, 1987.

------. *Flowers and Leaves: Poema vel Sonata, Carmina Autumni Primaequae Veris Transformationum*. Highlands, NC: Williams, 1966.

------. *The Geography of the Imagination: Forty Essays*. San Francisco: North Point, 1981.

------. *Goldfinch Thistle Star*. New York: Red Ozier Press, 1983.

------. *The Hunter Gracchus and Other Papers on Literature and Art*. Washington, DC: Counterpoint, 1996.

------. *Jonah*. New York: Nadja, 1986.

------. *The Jules Verne Steam Balloon: Nine Stories*. San Francisco: North Point, 1987.

------. *The Lark*. New York: Dim Gray Bar Press, 1993.

------. *A Table of Green Fields: Ten Stories*. New York: New Directions, 1993.

------. *Tatlin!* New York: Scribners, 1974.

------. *Thasos and Ohio: Poems and Translations, 1950-1980*. Manchester, UK: Carcanet, 1985; San Francisco: North Point, 1986.

------. *Trois Caprices*. Louisville, KY: Pace Trust, 1981.

------. *12 Stories*. Washington, DC: Counterpoint, 1997.

   In addition to the titles listed above, Davenport is also the author of nearly a dozen translations from the Greek, an equal number of books of literary and art criticism, an edition of his own drawings and paintings, and study guides to the Iliad and the Odyssey; he is also an illustrator.

Dickey, James. *Alnilam*. Garden City: Doubleday, 1987.

------. *Babel to Byzantium: Poets and Poetry Now*. New York: Farrar, Straus, and Giroux, 1968.

------. *Bronwen, the Traw, and the Shape-Shifter: A*

Poem in Four Parts. Illus. Richard Jesse Watson. San Diego: Bruccoli Clark/Harcourt Brace Jovanovich, 1986.

------. *Buckdancer's Choice: Poems*. Middletown, CT: Wesleyan University Press, 1965.

------. *Deliverance*. Boston: Houghton Mifflin, 1970.

------. *Drowning with Others*. Middletown, CT: Wesleyan University Press, 1962.

------. *The Eagle's Mile*. Hanover & London: The University Press of New England (for Wesleyan University Press, 1990.

------. *The Early Motion: Drowning with Others and Helmets*. Middletown, CT: Wesleyan University Press, 1981.

------. *The Enemy from Eden*. Northridge, CA: Lord John Press, 1978.

------. *The Eye-Beaters, Blood, Victory, Madness, Buckhead and Mercy*. Garden City: Doubleday, 1970.

------. *Falling, May Day Sermon, and Other Poems*. Middletown, CT: Wesleyan University Press, 1981.

------. *False Youth/Four Seasons*. Dallas: Pressworks Publishing, 1983.

------. *Four Poems*. Privately printed, 1979.

------. *God's Images: The Bible: A New Vision*. Illus. Marvin Hayes. Birmingham: Oxmoor House, 1977.

------. *Head-Deep in Strange Sounds*. N.p.: Palaemon Press, 1979.

------. *Helmets*. Middletown, CT: Wesleyan University Press, 1964.

------. *In Pursuit of the Grey Soul*. Columbia & Bloomfield Hills: Bruccoli Clark, 1978.

------. *Intermissions: Poems & Photographs*. [Poems by Dickey, photography by Sharon Anglin Kuhne.] Foreword by Betty Adcock. Penland, NC: Visualternatives, 1983.

------. *Jericho: The South Beheld*. Illus. Hubert Shuptrine. Birmingham: Oxmoor House, 1974.

------. *Metaphor as Pure Adventure*. Washington, DC: Library of Congress, 1968.

------. *Night Hurdling: Poems, Essays, Conversations, Commencements, and Afterwords*. Columbia and Bloomfield Hills: Bruccoli Clark, 1983.

------. *Poems 1957—1967*. Middletown, CT: Wesleyan University Press, 1967.

------ et al. *Poets of Today VII*. New York: Charles Scribner's Sons, 1960.

------. *Puella*. Garden City: Doubleday, 1982

------. *Scion*. Illustrations by Timothy Engelland. Deerfield, MA The Deerfield Press; Dublin: The Gallery Press, 1980.

------. *Self-Interviews*. Recorded and edited by Barbara and James Reiss. New York: Doubleday, 1970.

------. *Sorties: Journals and New Essays*. Garden City: Doubleday, 1971.

------. *Spinning the Crystal Ball: Some Guesses at the Future of American Poetry*. Washington: Library of Congress, 1967.

------. *The Starry Place Between the Antlers: Why I Live in South Carolina*. Bloomfield Hills & Columbia: Bruccoli Clark, 1981.

------. *The Strength of Fields*. Bloomfield Hills, Michigan, and Columbia, South Carolina: Bruccoli Clark, 1977; Garden City, NY: Doubleday, 1979.

------. *Striking In: The Early Notebooks of James Dickey*. Edited by Gordon Van Ness. Columbia, MO: University of Missouri Press, 1996.

------. *The Suspect in Poetry*. Madison, MN: The Sixties Press, 1964.

------. *Tucky the Hunter*. Illus. Marie Angel. New York: Crown Publishers, Inc., 1978.

------. *Two Poems of the Air*. Portland, OR: Centicort Press, 1964.

------. *Veteran Birth: The Gadfly Poems 1947-1949*. Illus. Robert Dance. N.p.: Palaemon Press Limited, 1978.

------. *Wayfarer: A Voice from the Southern Mountains*. Photographs by William A. Bake. Birmingham: Oxmoor House, 1988.

------. *The Water-Bug's Mittens: Ezra Pound: What We Can Use*. Bloomfield Hills, MI, and Columbia, SC: Bruccoli Clark, 1980.

------. *The Whole Motion: Collected Poems 1945-1992*. Hanover, NH, and London: Wesleyan University Press, 1992.

------. *To the White Sea*. Boston & New York: Houghton Mifflin Co., 1993.

------. *The Zodiac*. Garden City, NY: Doubleday, 1976.

Fox, William Price, Jr. *Chitlin' Strut and Other Madrigals*. Atlanta: Peachtree Press, 1983.

------. *Dixiana Moon*. New York: Viking, 1981.

------. *Dr. Golf*. Philadelphia: Lippincott, 1963.

------. *Golfing in the Carolinas*. Winston-Salem: John F. Blair, 1990.

------. *How 'Bout Them Gamecocks!* Columbia: University of South Carolina Press, 1985.

------. *Lunatic Wind: Surviving the Storm of the Century*. Chapel Hill: Algonquin Books of Chapel Hill, 1992.

------. *Moonshine Light, Moonshine Bright*. Philadelphia: Lippincott, 1967.

------. *Ruby* ed. Philadelphia: Lippincott, 1971.

------. *South Carolina: Off the Beaten Path*. Old Saybrook, CT: Globe Pequot Press, 1996.

------. *Southern Fried*. New York: Gold Medal Books, 1962.

------. *Southern Fried Plus Six*. Philadelphia: Lippincott, 1968.

In addition to the above titles, Bill Fox has also written screenplays for The Beverly Hillbillies (CBS Television, 1964-1965); Southern Fried (1967), Off We Go (1968); Cold Turkey (1968), and Fast Nerves (1969).

Jakes, John. *The Asylum World*. New York: Paperback Library, 1969.

------. *The Best of John Jakes*. Ed. Martin H. Greenberg and Joseph D. Olander. New York: DAW, 1977.

------. *The Best Western Stories of John Jakes*. Ed. Martin H. Greenberg and Bill Pronzini. Athens, OH: Ohio University Press, 1991.

------. *Black in Time*. New York: Paperback Library, 1970.

------. *Brak the Barbarian*. New York: Avon, 1968.

------. *Brak the Barbarian Versus the Sorceress*. New York: Paperback Library, 1969.

------. *Brak Versus the Mark of the Demons*. New York: Paperback Library, 1969.

------. *Brak: When the Idols Walked*. New York: Pocket Books, 1978.

------. *California Gold*. New York: random House, 1989.

------. *Conquest of the Planet of the Apes*. New York: Award, 1974.

------. *The Devil Has Four Faces*. New York: Bouregy, 1958.

------. *Fortunes of Brak*. New York: Dell, 1980.

------. *G.I. Girls*. Derby, CT: Monarch, 1963.

------. *The Hybrid*. New York: Paperback Library, 1969.

------. *The Impostor*. New York: Bouregy, 1959.

------. *Johnny Havoc*. New York: Belmont, 1960.

------. *Johnny Havoc and the Doll Who Had "It."* New York: Belmont, 1963.

------. *Johnny Havoc Meets Zelda*. New York: Belmont, 1962.

------. *The Kent Family Chronicles: The Bastard* (New York: Pyramid, 1974); *The Rebels* (New York: Pyramid, 1975); *The Seekers* (New York: Pyramid, 1975); *The Furies* (New York: Pyramid, 1976); *The Titans* (New York: Pyramid, 1976); *The Warriors* (New York: Pyramid, 1977); *The Lawless* (New York: Jove, 1978); *The Americans* (New York: Jove, 1980).

------. *The Last Magicians*. New York: Signet, 1969.

------. *Making It Big*. New York: Belmont, 1968.

------. *Mask of Chaos*. New York: Ace, 1970.

------. *Master of the Dark Gate*. New York: Lancer, 1970.

------. *My Name in Atlantis...*New York: DAW, 1972.

------. *Monte Cristo #99*. New York: Curtis, 1970.

------. *A Night for Treason*. New York: Bouregy, 1956.

------. *North and South Trilogy: North and South* (New York: Harcourt Brace, 1982); *Love and War* (New York: Harcourt Brace, 1984); *Heaven and*

Hell (New York: Harcourt Brace, 1987).

------. *On Wheels*. New York: Warner, 1973.

------. *The Planet Wizard*. New York: Ace, 1969.

------. *Secrets of Stardeep*. Philadelphia: Westminster Press, 1969.

------. *Six-Gun Planet*. New York: Paperback Library, 1970.

------. *The Texans Ride North*. Philadelphia: Winston, 1952.

------. *Time Gate*. Philadelphia: Westminster Press, 1972.

------. *Tonight We Steal the Stars*. New York: Ace, 1969.

------. *Wear a Fast Gun*. New York: Arcadia House, 1956.

------. *When the Star Kings Die*. New York: Ace, 1967.

------. *Witch of the Dark Gate*. New York: Lancer, 1972.

------ writing as William Ard: *Make Mine Mavis* (Derby, CT: Monarch, 1961); *And So to Bed* (Derby, CT: Monarch, 1962); *Give Me This Woman* (Derby, CT: Monarch, 1962).

------ writing as Alan Payne: *This'll Slay You* (New York: Ace, 1958); *Murder, He Says* (New York: Ace, 1958).

------ writing as Jay Scotland: *The Seventh Man* (New York: Bouregy, 1958); *I, Barbarian* (New York: Avon, 1959); *Strike the Black Flag* (New York: Ace, 1961); *Sir Scoundrel* (New York: Ace, 1962); *Veils of Salome* (New York: Avon, 1962); *Arena* (New York: Ace, 1963); *Traitors' Legion* (New York: Ace, 1963).

------ as Playwright: *Dracula, Baby* (Chicago: Dramatic Publishing Company, 1970); *Wind in the Willows* (Elgin, IL: Performance Publishing, 1972); *A Spell of Evil* (Chicago: Dramatic Publishing Company, 1972); *Violence* (Elgin, IL: Performance Publishing, 1972); *Stranger with Roses* (Chicago: Dramatic Publishing Company, 1972); *For I Am a Jealous People* (Elgin, IL: Performance Publishing, 1972); *Gaslight Girl* (Chicago, Dramatic Publishing Company, 1973); *Pardon Me, Is This Planet Taken?* (Chicago: Dramatic Publishing Company, 1973); *Doctor! Doctor!* (New York: McAfee Music, 1973); *Shepherd Song* (New York: McAfee Music, 1974).

------ as Author of Nonfiction: *Tiros: Weather Eye in Space* (New York: Messner, 1966); *Famous Firsts in Sports* (New York: Putnam, 1967); *Great War Correspondents* (New York: Putnam, 1968); *Great Women Reporters* (New York: Putnam, 1969); *The Bastard Photo Story* (New York: Jove, 1980); *Susanna at the Alamo: A True Story* (New York: Harcourt Brace, 1986).

------ with Gil Kane: *Excalibur!* (New York: Dell, 1980).

Rees, Ennis. *Brer Rabbit and His Tricks*. Illus. Edward Gorey. New York: Young Scott Books, 1967.

------. *Fables from Aesop*. Illus. J.J. Grandville. New York and London: Oxford University Press, 1966.

------. *Fast Freddie Frog and Other Tongue-Twister Rhymes*. Illus. John O'Brien. Honesdale, PA: Caroline House, 1993.

------. *Gillygaloos and Gollywhoppers: Tall Tales About Mythical Monsters*. Illus. Quentin Blake. London and New York: Abelard-Schuman, Ltd., 1969.

------. *Lions and Lobsters and Foxes and Frogs: Fables from Aesop*. Illus. Edward Gorey. Reading, MA: Young Scott Books, 1971.

------. *The Little Greek Alphabet Book*. Illus. George Salter. Englewood Cliffs, NJ: Prentice-Hall, 1968.

------. *More of Brer Rabbit's Tricks*. Illus. Edward Gorey. New York: Young Scott Books, 1968.

------. *Pick-a-Riddle*. New York: Scholastic Book Services, 1964.

------. *Poems*. Columbia: University of South Carolina Press, 1964.

------. *Potato Talk*. Illus. Stanley Mack. New York: Pantheon, 1969.

------. *Pun Fun*. Illus. Quentin Blake. London and New York: Abelard-Schuman, 1965.

------. *Riddles, Riddles Everywhere*. Illus. Quentin Blake. London and New York: Abelard-Schuman, 1964.

------. *Selected Poems*. Columbia: University of South Carolina Press, 1973.

------. *Short Tall Tales to Tell: Selected from Tiny Tall Tales*. New York: Scholastic Book Services, 1967.

------. *The Song of Paul Bunyan and Tony Beaver*. Illus. Robert Osborn. New York: Pantheon Books,

1964.

------. *Teeny Tiny Duck and the Pretty Money*. Illus.
Paul Freeman. Englewood Cliffs, NJ: Prentice-
Hall, 1967.

------. *Tiny Tall Tales*. London and New York:
Abelard-Schuman, 1967.

------. *The Tragedies of George Chapman:
Renaissance Ethics in Action*. Cambridge: Harvard
University Press, 1954.

------. *Windwagon Smith*. Illus. Peter Plasencia.
Englewood Cliffs: Prentice-Hall, 1966.

------ (Trans.). *The Iliad of Homer*. New York:
Random House, 1963.

------ (Trans.). *The Odyssey of Homer*. New York:
Random House, 1960.

In addition to the titles listed above, Ennis Rees
has also recorded two volumes of selections from
The Iliad and The Odyssey, a selection from his
Fables from Aesop, and two collections of folk
tales.

Index

The Hub City Writers Project is a non-profit organization whose mission is to foster a sense of community through the literary arts. We do this by publishing books from and about community; encouraging, mentoring, and advancing the careers of writers; and seeking to make Spartanburg a center for the literary arts.

Our metaphor of organization purposely looks backward to the nineteenth century when Spartanburg was known as the "hub city," a place where railroads converged and departed.

At the beginning of the twenty-first century, Spartanburg has become a literary hub of South Carolina with an active and nationally celebrated core group of poets, fiction writers, and essayists. We celebrate these writers—and the ones not yet discovered—as one of our community's greatest assets. William R. Ferris, former director of the Center for the Study of Southern Cultures, says of the emerging South, "Our culture is our greatest resource. We can shape an economic base…And it won't be an investment that will disappear."

— 📖 —

Hub City Anthology • John Lane & Betsy Teter, editors
Hub City Music Makers • Peter Cooper
Hub City Christmas • John Lane & Betsy Wakefield Teter, editors
New Southern Harmonies • Rosa Shand, Scott Gould, Deno Trakas, George Singleton
The Best of Radio Free Bubba • Meg Barnhouse, Pat Jobe, Kim Taylor, Gary Phillips
Family Trees: The Peach Culture of the Piedmont • Mike Corbin
Seeing Spartanburg: A History in Images • Philip Racine
The Seasons of Harold Hatcher • Mike Hembree
The Lawson's Fork: Headwaters to Confluence • David Taylor, Gary Henderson
Hub City Anthology 2 • Betsy Wakefield Teter, editor
Inheritance • Janette Turner Hospital, editor
In Morgan's Shadow • A Hub City Murder Mystery
Eureka Mill • Ron Rash
The Place I Live • The Children of Spartanburg County
Textile Town • The Hub City Writers Project
Come to the Cow Pens! • Christine Swager
Noble Trees • The Hub City Writers Project
Noticing Eden • Majory Wentworth